CRIMINAL   CONSULTING

www.detectivemikeproctor.com

Antidote for a Stalker

Our newest guide designed to promote
a better understanding of the ever-evolving
menace of stalking

Mike Proctor
Detective, Retired • 2013

D1501727

ISBN-10: 147745313x
ISBN-13: 9781477453131
Library of Congress Control Number: 2012908611
CreateSpace Independent Publishing Platform
North Charleston, South Carolina.

Additional Reviews

"Mike Proctor, a former homicide detective and one of the world's
foremost specialists on both the subject of stalking as well as investigative procedures for addressing stalking cases provides an invaluable insight into the subject in his latest book, *Antidote for a Stalker*.
Having used his previous book, *How to Stop a Stalker*, for several
years as required reading in my Family Violence classes; I found that
his first book opened the eyes of students to the world of stalking that
was transpiring around them, and thus educated them to the dangers
that this type of crime presented to its victims. *Antidote For a Stalker*
greatly expands on the information presented in Proctor's first book,
adding new and valuable data. It should be required reading for students who plan on entering into careers in law enforcement, child
protective services, victim services, family protective services, and
psychology. Proctor utilizes case studies that assist the lay person in
better understanding topics presented throughout the text. The book
assists readers in learning how to develop the tools necessary to classify and threat assess stalkers, as well as what it takes to formulate an
investigative plan of attack designed to successfully prosecute and
neutralize each variety of stalker. Law enforcement field supervisors
and detectives, along with all professionals who work with stalking
victims, should both read the book and have a copy readily available
as a reference guide for when they encounter any stalking situation."

**Raymond Teske, Jr. PhD, Criminal Justice Department, Sam
Houston State University, Huntsville, Texas. (*Dr. Teske, who is
also a sworn police officer, is heavily involved in victim advocacy
as well as being an expert in the study of death penalty cases.*)**

"Det. Proctor describes both the similarities and the differences among U.S. and international laws. He explains how the growing plague of stalking is impacting victims worldwide. He utilizes examples and case studies to enhance his message. This book is an asset to everyone—from the layperson, victim advocate, those in criminal justice, educators, as well as those in my profession—brilliant!"

Casey Comstock, PhD, LMHC, Roger Williams University (psychology adjunct), Clinic Director (outpatient behavioral health clinic). (Besides being an administrator and teaching, Dr. Comstock has also provided court ordered counseling and evaluations of stalkers.)

"The author, a retired California police detective who now lectures and consults with law-enforcement agencies, aims to present practical information about stalking and how to avoid it. He discusses various states' and countries' stalking laws as well as 19 different "stalking behaviors" to watch out for. He draws on his investigative background to illustrate his points with specific case histories and categorizes various kinds of stalkers, including the stranger stalker, in which "the victim/target is hounded by an unknown entity." Proctor also offers an entire chapter of advice for people who are currently being stalked. Proctor provides a precise table of contents and an index so that readers can quickly locate relevant material. **A valuable source of facts and guidance on avoiding a frightening crime.**"

Kirkus Reviews, Kirkus Indie, Kirkus Media, Indie@kirkusreviews.com

Contents

Acknowledgements

This book is dedicated to all the hard working victim advocates involved in formulating change in the world concerning both domestic violence and stalking. These people are continually striving to promote stronger legislation, better education, and the development of more and improved programs for those afflicted with this criminal burden. Without these people and the organizations they represent, I fear not much would get done.

Along this same path, I would hope that those that read this text would look to joining the ranks of these advocates. The more voices raised in the hope of change, the greater likelihood that very thing will come to be.

Introduction

This is my second book on the stalking phenomenon. The first—*How to Stop a Stalker*—was published in 2003, and it is still out there doing what it was designed to do: assist the victims of stalking as well as educate those that are tasked with bringing these predators to justice. So why write another book? You've heard the phrase, "time changes all." The same holds true for stalking. With every passing year, consultants like me, who are charged with teaching and training people about the stalking phenomenon, learn more about stalking and its mechanics. Therefore it is time to share what I have learned with those that still may need help.

Stalking is a radical criminal issue that is rearing its ugly head throughout the world in ever-growing numbers. It is not just in the United States. Every day I hear from victims from a variety of countries, including Germany, the United Kingdom, Australia, Japan, India, Turkey, and elsewhere throughout the world. In 2010, I received a request to lecture in Norway due to the growing concerns regarding stalkers in Scandinavian countries. The truth is, wherever there are groups of people, there will be some form of stalking.

This new text discusses what stalking is, the types of stalkers, their behaviors or behaviours—if you are British, how stalkers prosecute their particular brand of stalking—It also includes new information on cyberstalking and cyberbullying, which as you will see we believe are forms of stalking. I have broken stalking behavior down into further subsets that I feel will assist the reader better understand the form of stalking they may have or currently be experiencing. I will discuss the growing campus threat as well as how to protect oneself if you become a stalking victim. I will also present portions of a protocol designed to best case manage a stalking investigation, thus allowing those charged with going after the stalker additional tools designed to better bring him or her to justice. As always there are many case examples to better illustrate the points made throughout the book.

Before you get started, I feel it is extremely beneficial for you to become acquainted with my background. The following are some of the questions you should ask yourself before you put down your hard-earned money and start to peruse the pages of this book. Why should you even read this book? Are the author and the information he will present worthy of your time? One should always ponder the question: who the heck is this guy/author anyway?

Here is my background. Prior to getting involved in police work, I was a teacher and a coach, primarily baseball. I graduated from Long Beach State (now California State University at Long Beach). I obtained a lifetime standard secondary teaching credential along with a Bachelor of Arts in Geography. That's right. Not all cops have degrees in criminal justice. I also received a minor in safety education with teachable minors in business and physical education. By the way, the minor in safety education allowed me to instruct kids in driver's education. I strongly believe that is the primary reason my hair turned white so early in my life. After teaching for about a year, I began my thirty-three year career in law enforcement with the Westminster Police Department. The Westminster Police Department is a midsized law enforcement agency located in central Orange County, California.

During those thirty-plus years on the job, I held many posts, which included that of chief's administrative aide, where I wrote programs for the department. This included developing a school resource officer program so that I could teach an introduction to police science class at the two high schools in the city. I then became a Field Training Officer, a Crime Specifics Unit detective—a division that works major felons—a burglary detective, and finally a robbery, homicide, and predator crimes detective, where I stayed for the last thirteen years of my career. At the time I was a police detective in the city, Westminster was a fast-moving town with a high level of gang violence in the Hispanic, white, and Asian, primarily Vietnamese, communities. The city is known for having Little Saigon within its borders.

While involved in robbery/homicide, I began investigating stalkers. In fact, I ended up working the first stalking case in the county. It was arguably only the second in the nation just after the anti-stalking law had been implemented in the State of California. Due to the fact, that no one had prosecuted a stalking case in the county none of the prosecutors had any idea how to take one on. It took us three months of pleading and pushing to get the case finally filed by the Orange County district attorney's Special Prosecutions Unit.

My partner and I knew just from investigating this initial case that stalking was a unique animal, and it had to be approached differently than other types of crimes we were dealing with. For this reason I developed what we believe to be the first stalking protocol designed to deal with not only this stalker, but those we would encounter in the future. The stalker in this particular situation had been terrorizing the victim for nine years before she got Detective Terry Selinske and I involved. The suspect was successfully prosecuted and profiled on *America's Most Wanted*, where I appeared as one of the consultants on a stalking special hosted by John Walsh. I arrested this stalker on three separate occasions, helped develop other cases against him in other jurisdictions, and eventually testified in Alabama in the penalty phase of his murder trial. (He and an accomplice were convicted for strapping a Tuscaloosa city employee to a chair and beating him to death.)

Since that first case, I have written articles and book(s) on stalking and stalking investigation. I have taught at various venues throughout the United States and most recently in another country. I was one of the consultants on the first stalking training video and workbook put together by California's Peace Officer Standards and Training (POST). I have consulted on and helped develop various states' anti-stalking programs as well as assisted in helping change those states' anti-stalking legislation. In 2003 I was presented with the Defender of Justice Award from a member of the California legislature for my continuing work in the field of stalking. In early 2009 I and others in my field assisted the University of Southern California in developing an anti-stalking and threat assessment protocol.

Author hard at work doing a remote radio broadcast for Liverpool Radio from his house in the mountains.

This was not only for their campuses but other campuses as well via a Department of Justice grant they had obtained. I have consulted throughout the world and continue to be quoted in the national and international press. I have consulted for magazines such as *Cosmopolitan, The Economist,* and others. I regularly do radio (both in the United States and abroad) along with television interviews. I have appeared on *20/20*, CNN, *Nancy Grace*, Fox, *Maury Povich*—in his earlier years—Japanese and Korean specials on stalking, *Unsolved Mysteries*, as indicated *America's Most Wanted*, and a one-hour segment on stalking for *E! Hollywood*. I also assisted a production crew for Atlas Media in developing a stalking special for Investigation Discovery (Discovery Channel's ID) entitled "Stalked: Someone's Watching." These episodes began airing in January of 2011. I also conduct online training from time to time for the Office for Victims of Crime (OVC) out of Washington, DC, for which I am a consultant, and in January of 2013 I was "spotlighted" by that organization for the work I am involved with. I recently assisted victim advocates attempting to get a stalking law implemented in Scotland, (which they did), and as previously indicated currently working with Norway in the hopes of having their advocates push through a viable stalking law. I am also a consultant for the National Stalking Training Academy, which was recently initiated in the United Kingdom via the Home Secretary's Office. These are just some of the venues where I am able to get the word out about stalking.

For a more detailed report on my background, you can always go to my website, www.DetectiveMikeProctor.com. On that website I have an e-mail address to contact me. I am pretty good about answering those that query my site. If I can help you, I will. Keep in mind, one of the things I will probably advise you to do is contact your local law enforcement professionals to try and get them involved. I am <u>not</u> a PI (private investigator), so even though I am contacted by attorneys and the like, I do not work on cases unless invited in by law enforcement or, on rare occasions, specific victim advocate groups. I also rarely testify as an expert in court; not that I am not qualified, but I did enough of that as a homicide detective.

Now, I do not have letters behind my name. So if you are looking for that kind of "expert," you will be disappointed. I have probably investigated and/or consulted on well over three hundred stalking cases. As I tell my clients/students, you will not need a dictionary or a medical degree to understand what I am saying. Those who asked me to write my first book were well aware I was going to give them practical information in an easy-to-understand format. One of my colleagues summed it up by saying, "Hey, Mike, we want you to write this book because we all know you are pretty simple, and anything you write will probably be the same." I really wasn't too sure that was a compliment, but I wrote the first book anyway. I have been told by many who have read my book and articles that they feel I am talking directly to them. They say I am not just spouting a bunch of information that may or may not help them.

These people included college professors who used and continue to use my book in their classrooms. They tell me, they like the fact that their students "get it" after they have reviewed the text.

Once again, if you are looking for someone that has developed cases, arrested, helped prosecute, testified against, and sat across from a variety of stalkers as well as worked with their victims, then I am your man. If you are searching for an academic who may have conducted clinical research on the topic of stalking, or researched the material available on this subject putting it down on paper, I am not that person.

I want to be clear. There are researchers out there that are brilliant in this field, like the following PhDs: Lorraine Sheridan, Rosemary Purcell, J. Reid Meloy, Kris Mohandie as well as others that have attained goals I could never reach. They work hard to gather the proper statistics on stalking and develop better ways to threat assess stalkers. (More of these researchers' names will be expressed throughout the pages of this book. If interested in furthering your background on stalking, please review their work.) This type of research is not only valuable but essential. One of the primary reasons for my appreciation of their academic/scientific findings is because their work tends to validate those of us who work stalkers and other predators on a basic gut and street level. I applaud their work, but frankly when it comes to dealing with the actual stalker, those researchers I would consider "the really good ones"—those that actually conduct valid research studies — are few and far between. In my opinion, there appears to be a growing number that are out there espousing their "expertise," when in fact they truly have very little. Discerning between the legitimate and illegitimate researcher is up to you. I once attended a lecture where the presenter gave a complete overview on the dynamics of stalking. He had a PhD in communications, and he had never been involved in a stalking case, of any kind, but did comment that he had reviewed the existing material.

That would be like those of us that investigate stalkers getting up in front of a group of mental health professionals and saying we had reviewed narcissistic personality disorder and would be advising on the best way to treat individuals with that malady. I would expect those professionals in the class to roll their eyes or get up and leave the presentation.

I like to begin my lectures with—there are a couple of rules one needs to know before we get started. First, stalking is not an exact science; second, I do not know everything there is to know about the phenomenon of stalking. That is true; I learn something new on a regular basis. Also, in my humble opinion, the word "expert" is thrown around much too freely these days. Therefore I would not classify myself as an expert. I am only one that has dealt with stalkers and their behaviors for the past twenty or so years. That probably makes me just a little more knowledgeable than the average person on the street. I once had a highly respected theologian— a true expert in his field—tell me that the definition of an expert was someone no one knew who came to teach from out of town.

Another rule is I will not *always* give the exact Internet address where you can find more information on what I have written. Instead I will tell you what phrase or sentence to type into a standard search engine to get you the information. I have found that if you don't put in the exact Internet address, it always comes up with something to the effect of can't locate this address or URL. I don't know about you, but I don't have the time to try to figure out what comma, period, or letter I left out of the address request. I find just putting in the search phrase and letting the computer do what it is capable of doing works a whole lot better for this dummy non-computer whiz. Also I have found these addresses change over time because someone on the site adds some bit of information and then puts it back onto the Net with a different address. That is why copy editors tell us "authors" that if the address works at the time the book is printed, don't sweat it down the road if it doesn't key up when someone does a search.

Because the majority of stalkers are in fact male, oftentimes I will refer to the stalker in that gender. Even though women do stalk, and I have arrested my share; as well as consulted on several cases concerning women, it just makes the writing a little easier.

There are a few other things I would like to clear up concerning the rest of this book. One, I will not use most of the true names of the victims and/or the stalkers presented as examples. I really see no need, except in a few situations. Second, I have been using "I" throughout the introduction because it just flows better. I really don't like saying, "I did this" and "I did that" on a regular basis. "We" and "our" just suits me better, when laying down the prose in the rest of this text so that is what I will be using as much as I can. I had one person comment on my writing style saying my last book could have been "great" if I would have stopped writing in the third person. Obviously I am not Shakespeare or someone that would even classify himself as a "real" writer. All I really care about is that the reader understands what I say and is helped by what I write. I am not trying to win a literary contest. One thing I have learned over the years—at the completion of this book, I will have turned sixty-something—is you just can't please everyone. Oh, by the way, there may be *cop humor* throughout some of the pages of this text. It goes with the territory.

From time to time, throughout this text you will see a little icon I have developed indicating it is time for you and me to sit down and discuss some topic as if we were sitting together in front of a fire. As previously discussed, I have been told I write like I talk, and it seems as if I am talking to whoever is scrolling—if you have a digital copy, or reading if you have a hardcopy— through the pages of whatever I write. I prefer that style and hope you do too.

The primary reason I wrote this book is not to make money but to assist law enforcement, stalking victim advocates, educators, and those who are currently being stalked. If you read my last book, thanks, but keep in mind you might find some initial repetition with different examples in a small portion of this text. Why? Because anyone who hasn't read the other book has to establish the same foundation you did to better understand the entire stalking phenomenon. We promise there will be enough new information to keep you both interested and much better informed.

Finally, as always, if you are a stalker reading this book, you should be able to recognize that is what you are. Therefore, you need to try to get some help and stop your stalking behaviors. Of course, I know from past experience that probably will not happen, but I have to make this plea anyway. **Also, I want anyone who believes he or she is being stalked to contact their local law enforcement professionals and get them up to speed on what is happening in your particular stalking scenario.**

Chapter 1
Stalking History and Stalking Definitions

The History of Stalking

Before we can get into the rest of the information covered in this book, a foundation needs to be built. One cannot put the proverbial cart before the horse. Stalking has been with us probably as long as human history has been recorded. It is definitely not a new phenomenon.

Because we are now in the computer age, I will use Webster's Online Dictionary as a resource. According to good old Webster, stalking is defined as: "to pursue quarry or prey stealthily." Now we know where the word stalking has its roots, but the framers of the legislation that made stalking a crime could have easily called it pursuit or the crime of pursuit. Pursuit is what we often are talking about when we discuss the crime of stalking. In the case of criminal stalking, this **pursuit would obviously be defined as unwanted**. One of the most often asked questions directed to us when either teaching or being interviewed is when does a person really know he or she is being stalked? Of course, the answer could be broken down into individual segments for discussion, but the easiest response is always when the **pursuit becomes uncomfortable and/or unwanted by the person being pursued**.

In fact, for stalking to be considered a crime, it does not have to be stealthy at all, as indicated in Webster's definition. Many times the pursuit of the stalker's target is right in one's face and out in the open. A lot of times, when you interview a stalker, he will tell you, "Detective, I don't have any idea what you are talking about. All I was trying to do was get her to go out with me," or, "Detective, I was merely trying to get her to get back with me." In stalker's minds, they may actually want you to believe what they are doing is lawful and harmless pursuit when, for the most part, they know exactly what they are doing is wrong as well as criminal in nature. As we will discuss in another chapter, unfortunately, this type of pursuit is viewed as perfectly acceptable behavior in certain cultures.

So how did stalking become a criminal offense in the state of California and thus the world? On July 18, 1989, Robert John Bardo, a nineteen-year-old Tucson, Arizonian, contacted a young, attractive star named Rebecca Schaeffer from the sitcom *My Sister Sam* at the front door of her Los Angeles apartment. Bardo, who was obsessed with Schaeffer and other young Hollywood celebrities, had obtained Schaeffer's address by hiring a private investigator. According to published reports, he was angry at Schaeffer for having an onscreen romance in a movie with another actor. Bardo had traveled to CBS Studios on at least two other occasions prior to finally contacting Schaeffer at her residence. Both times he was turned away by studio security. (Remember, this was before any kind of threat assessment teams were in place.) When Bardo knocked on Schaeffer's apartment door, she opened it. He pulled out a Magnum revolver and shot her once in the chest, resulting in a fatal wound. Bardo was later taken into custody in Arizona, confessed to the crime, and was prosecuted by Los Angeles County District Attorney Marcia Clark, who was later became one of the lead prosecutors on the O. J. Simpson case. Bardo was eventually sentenced to life without the possibility of parole (LWOP). Interviews with Bardo indicated he felt he had a relationship with Schaeffer and that she talked to him via the television. Bardo also related that he got the idea to find Schaeffer via a private investigator by watching news blurbs concerning Theresa Saldana's stalker, who stabbed Saldana numerous times in 1982 in the street in front of her residence. (Saldana, another Hollywood celebrity, is now a stalking victim advocate.) As a direct result of Rebecca Schaeffer's death and the excellent legislative push from Saldana, private investigators and others can no longer obtain driver's license information due to the Driver's Privacy Protection Act enacted in 1994 by the United States Congress (18 U.S.C. 2721-2725)[1]. This act was amended on June 1, 2000 to require the express consent of the person whose driver's and other personal information is being requested before it can be released. *Of course it seems with the advent of recent Internet search websites, some of what that act' was trying to protect, laws like these seem to have been diminished in their effectiveness.)*

Many feel it was Schaeffer and Saldana's stories that caused a public outcry and forced some type of legislation to be enacted. No doubt these two incidents were pivotal and greatly enhanced that need. There were other more pressing reasons, however, why then-State Senator Ed Royce, from the Orange County city of Fullerton, and his legislative co-developer, Judge John Watson, (then an Orange County Municipal Court Judge, who actually penned much of the initial statutes' language) brought forth the bill in January of 1990, which later became California's stalking law, Penal Code 646.9. Judge Watson and Royce were also keenly aware of a series of Orange County murders, which stemmed from domestic violence relationships in which stalking behavior had transpired prior to the victims' deaths. At the time these women were murdered, there were restraining orders in place, but law enforcement advised that additional, more stringent laws were necessary in order to stop these types of murders. Thus the California stalking law was born.

We should also mention that Congressman Royce, along with Judge Watson's able assistance, was also responsible for presenting and helping pass the Interstate Stalking Punishment and Prevention Act in 1996. (This may also be referred to as the federal interstate anti-stalking act/law.) Those of us in law enforcement are grateful for these types of laws getting placed on the books.

Definitions of Stalking

Since California's law was enacted, the rest of the country soon followed suit. Now all fifty states, including the District of Columbia, along with three United States protectorates, Guam, Puerto Rico, and the United States Virgin Islands, have some type of anti-stalking legislation on the books. (To research each of the fifty stalking laws in the United States, go to the stalking resource center of the National Center for Victims of Crime.) Each state's articulation of its laws and the accompanying penalties is different, but once you begin to read through them, you will see that many closely mirror California's initial law. The federal government has also developed a model stalking law. This was set up as a guideline for other states, and in some cases it was utilized by other countries when developing their stalking legislation. (We will be discussing other countries' stalking laws a little further on in the book.) Due to the fact that many of the stalking laws in the United States as well as a few abroad resemble verbiage in California's stalking law we like to use California's Penal Code Section 646.9 as an example of what we believe a well-conceived stalking law should contain. The definition below was obtained from the stalking resource center of the National Center for Victims of Crime.

Stalking

Cal Pen Code § 646.9. Stalking. (2008)

(a) Any person who willfully, maliciously, and repeatedly follows or willfully and maliciously harasses another person and who makes a credible threat with the intent to place that person in reasonable fear for his or her safety, or the safety of his or her immediate family is guilty of the crime of stalking, punishable by imprisonment in a county jail for not more than one year, or by a fine of not more than one thousand dollars ($1,000), or by both that fine and imprisonment, or by imprisonment in the state prison.

(b) Any person who violates subdivision (a) when there is a temporary restraining order, injunction, or any other court order in effect prohibiting the behavior described in subdivision (a) against the same party, shall be punished by imprisonment in the state prison for two, three, or four years.

(c) (1) Every person who, after having been convicted of a felony under Section

273.5, 273.6, or 422, commits a violation of subdivision (a) shall be punished by imprisonment in a county jail for not more than one year, or by a fine of not more than one thousand dollars ($1,000), or by both that fine and imprisonment, or by imprisonment in the state prison for two, three, or five years.

(2) Every person who, after having been convicted of a felony under subdivision (a), commits a violation of this section shall be punished by imprisonment in the state prison for two, three, or five years.

(d) In addition to the penalties provided in this section, the sentencing court may order a person convicted of a felony under this section to register as a sex offender pursuant to Section 290.006.

(e) For the purposes of this section, "harasses" means engages in a knowing and willful course of conduct directed at a specific person that seriously alarms, annoys, torments, or terrorizes the person, and that serves no legitimate purpose.

(f) For the purposes of this section, "course of conduct" means two or more acts occurring over a period of time, however short, evidencing a continuity of purpose. Constitutionally protected activity is not included within the meaning of "course of conduct."

(g) For the purposes of this section, "credible threat" means a verbal or written threat, including that performed through the use of an electronic communication device, or a threat implied by a pattern of conduct or a combination of verbal, written, or electronically communicated statements and conduct, made with the intent to place the person that is the target of the threat in reasonable fear for his or her safety or the safety of his or her family, and made with the apparent ability to carry out the threat so as to cause the person who is the target of the threat to reasonably fear for his or her safety or the safety of his or her family. It is not necessary to prove that the defendant had the intent to actually carry out the threat. The present incarceration of a person making the threat shall not be a bar to prosecution under this section. Constitutionally protected activity is not included within the meaning of "credible threat."

(h) For purposes of this section, the term "electronic communication device" includes, but is not limited to, telephones, cellular phones, computers, video recorders, fax machines, or pagers. "Electronic communication" has the same meaning as the term defined in Subsection 12 of Section 2510 of Title 18 of the United States Code.

(i) This section shall not apply to conduct that occurs during labor picketing.

(j) If probation is granted, or the execution or imposition of a sentence is suspended, for any person convicted under this section, it shall be a condition of probation that the person participate in counseling, as designated by the court. However, the court, upon a showing of good cause, may find that the counseling requirement shall not be imposed.

(k) (1) The sentencing court also shall consider issuing an order restraining the defendant from any contact with the victim, that may be valid for up to 10 years, as determined by the court. It is the intent of the Legislature that the length of any restraining order be based upon the seriousness of the facts before the court, the probability of future violations, and the safety of the victim and his or her immediate family.

(2) This protective order may be issued by the court whether the defendant is sentenced to state prison, county jail, or if imposition of sentence is suspended and the defendant is placed on probation.

(l) For purposes of this section, "immediate family" means any spouse, parent, child, any person related by consanguinity or affinity within the second degree, or any other person who regularly resides in the household, or who, within the prior six months, regularly resided in the household.

(m) The court shall consider whether the defendant would benefit from treatment pursuant to Section 2684. If it is determined to be appropriate, the court shall recommend that the Department of Corrections and Rehabilitation make a certification as provided in Section 2684. Upon the certification, the defendant shall be evaluated and transferred to the appropriate hospital for treatment pursuant to Section 2684.[2]

With this example of a criminal definition of stalking (in the form of California's penal code), we need to advise you that each state may have enhancements for things such as having a restraining order present when the stalking takes place, age of the victim, or whether a weapon was used in the commission of the stalking, electronic stalking, GPS stalking, etc. That is why it is so important to become familiar with your state or country's definition of stalking and any subsections present in their various penal or criminal codes. Just like California's law, many states' stalking legislation has evolved over the years and probably will continue to do so. Due to our work abroad, we are finding that some countries' stalking legislation is also evolving.

If you don't have a computer, go to the library, and either obtain a copy of the penal code or use the public computer to access it. Don't guess. Get informed. The following is an example of the important of self-education regarding stalking. We were recently contacted by a web victim. (From this point on, we will refer to all web victims as W/Vs.) When we are contacted on our website, we only get one side of the story because we neither travel to the victim's location nor actively work his or her case unless local law enforcement invites us in. If that happens, we are then privy to both sides.

The W/V said she had been stalked by her neighbor for a prolonged length of time. The W/V described the type of stalking behavior taking place between her and her neighbor. The W/V said the law enforcement officer told her that her complaint did not fall under first-degree stalking. She was disheartened and felt there was nothing left to do. Upon inspection of that state's stalking law, we found it had a first-degree stalking statute, which had certain requirements that her complaint did not fulfill. However, this same state had a second-degree stalking section, which fit what she had been describing. We advised her to review those sections, re-contact her local law enforcement professionals, and ask them to look into this section as a way of eliminating her problem.

Sometimes it is just a matter of better communication that will get the stalking victim through his or her encounter with the police. In regard to stalking, it has been our experience that the victim has to become his or her own advocate concerning their case. *In chapter four, "I Am Being Stalked. What Do I Do?" we will explain how best to help your cause and, indirectly, the law enforcement agencies you are dealing with.*

I am not saying law enforcement was reluctant to get involved in this case, but unfortunately we have found that this does occasionally occur. As illustrated through other examples in this book, we have worked cases where victims obtained less than stellar service from their local law enforcement groups. We would of course hope that was because those individuals that were contacted lacked the requisite training to assist the victim asking for help. Sometimes an officer's response to stalking is dependent upon how those above him or her perceive a variety of crimes, not just stalking. Therefore we are not above telling some of our stalking victims, whether W/V or not, to look higher than just the local level. We may encourage certain victims to make contact at the county, state, or, in some cases, federal level. As you will soon see, we work for the victims. It's not the other way around.

Back to our stalking definitions, let's break down the parts of the stalking definition we have chosen to use. Any person who **willfully** (consciously knowing), **maliciously** (wishing to injure or conduct a wrongful act against another), and **repeatedly** (more than once)—keep in mind each state has a specific definition of how many times repeatedly is—in California it is two or more times) follows or willfully and maliciously **harasses** (in California harasses is defined as engaging in a knowing and willful course of conduct directed at a specific person that seriously alarms, annoys, torments, or terrorizes the person and that serves no legitimate purpose) another person with the intent to place that person in reasonable fear for his or her safety or the safety of his or her immediate family is guilty of the crime of stalking.

In the state of Oklahoma's stalking law, 21 Okl. St. 1173, harassment is defined under section F, subsection 1 "Harasses means a pattern or course of conduct directed toward another individual that includes, but is not limited to, repeated or continuing unconsented conduct, that would cause a reasonable person to suffer emotional distress, and that actually causes emotional distress to the victim. Harassment shall include harassing or obscene phone calls."[3]

"Course of conduct" and "credible threat" are germane to almost all stalking statutes in the United States and many other jurisdictions outside the United States. Here are some state's definitions of "course of conduct" as called out in their stalking statutes:

Section (f) of California Penal Code 646.9 describes "course of "conduct" as, "meaning two or more acts occurring over a period of time, however short, evidencing a continuity of purpose." Other states such as Michigan define "course of conduct" in 750.411h, section (1), subsection (a), as "a pattern of conduct composed of a series of 2 or more separate noncontinuous acts evidencing a continuity of purpose." As you can see, these definitions are very similar. There are, however, differences, as evidenced in the state of Delaware's definition. "Course of conduct" is described in Del Code 1312, section (e), subsection (1), as, "3 or more separate incidents, including but not limited to, acts in which the person directly, indirectly, or through third parties, by any action, method, device, or means, follows monitors, observes, surveys, threatens, or communicates to or about another, or interferes with, jeopardizes, damages, or disrupts another's daily activities, property, employment, business, career, education, or medical care."[4] Delaware's section is more specific and calls out third-party activity. In many states, threats can be transmitted by third parties. For example, Johnny tells Bob he is planning on killing Mary. Bob calls Mary and tells her what Johnny has told him. In most instances, even if Johnny told Bob in confidence, Johnny has transmitted a viable threat to Mary. In Delaware's definition they also account for third parties assisting the primary suspect in his course of conduct by transmitting threats, assisting in surveillance, etc. *We have investigated cases in which third parties were utilized by the stalker to damage a victim's property as well as to conduct surveillance.*

We are starting to see more countries beginning to use similar verbiage to stalking codes generated in the United States in their stalking laws. For example, in Scotland's new Criminal Justice and Licensing Act, under section 39, Offense of Stalking law, "course of conduct" is called out and specifically defined. The conduct must transpire on at least two occasions.[5]

Now onto "credible threat". In California's Penal Code section 646.9 (g), "credible threat" is defined as a verbal or written threat, including that performed through the use of an electronic communication device, or a threat implied by a pattern of conduct or a combination of verbal, written, or electronically communicated statements and conduct, made with the intent to place the person that is the target of the threat in reasonable fear for his or her safety or his or her family, and made with the apparent ability to carry out the threat so as to cause the person who is the target of the threat to reasonably fear for his or her safety or the safety of his or her family. **It is not necessary to prove that the defendant had the intent to actually carry out the threat.**[6] In California, as in many other states, making a credible threat while incarcerated does not stop that individual from being prosecuted under the stalking law. Of course electronic communication devices run the gamut—cell phones, fax machines, computers, video recorders, pagers, etc.

Missouri also has a credible threat requirement under (565.225.R.S.Mo). The definition is similar to California's in that it is the communication of a threat to instill reasonable fear for the victim's safety and the safety of "household members," but it goes one step further and adds "domestic animals or livestock." to things that can be covered under the credible threat definition.[7]

In California, the credible threat does not have to be one of bodily injury or death, but can be behavior that is so bizarre as to cause the victim to suffer emotional trauma, distress, or fear. Montana is another state that has in its definition the language of "A person commits the offense of stalking if the person purposely or knowingly causes another person substantial emotional distress or reasonable apprehension of bodily injury or death by repeatedly..." (Mont. Code Anno., 45-5-220).[8] In Tennessee's stalking statute, they define "emotional distress" as "significant mental suffering or distress that may, but does not necessarily, require medical or other professional treatment or counseling."[9] (Tenn. Code Ann. 39-17-315) As you traverse the pages of this book, you will encounter descriptions of the suffering that besets the victims of stalking.

Emotional distress does not appear to be called out in all states. Under Texas Penal Code 42.072, it is considered felony stalking if under subsection (1) the defendant (he is referred to as "actor") "the actor knows or reasonably believes the other person [victim] will regard as threatening: (A) bodily injury or death for the other person; (B) bodily injury or death of a member of the other person's [victim's] family or household or for an individual with whom the other person [victim] has a dating relationship; or (C) that an offense will be committed against the other person [victim's] property; (2) causes the other person, a member of the other person's family or household, or an individual with whom the other person has a dating relationship to be placed in fear of bodily injury or death or fear that an offense will be committed against the other person's property; and (3) would cause a reasonable person to fear; (A) bodily injury or death for himself or herself; (B) bodily injury or death for a member of the person's [victim's] family or household or for an individual with whom the person has a dating relationship; or (C) that an offense will be committed against the person's property.")[10] It appears that in Texas a victim must express fear from bodily injury or death, or that their property will be damaged for there to be a violation of stalking.

The crime of stalking in Texas we just defined is a felony in the third degree. If the stalker has been convicted previously for stalking, then the crime is charged as a felony in the second degree. Texas Penal Code Section 42.07 Harassment, which starts out with, "A person commits an offense if, with intent to harass, annoy, alarm, abuse, torment, or embarrass another," and goes on to describe in what situations. Texas' course of conduct under this harassment section expresses or covers behavior that is oftentimes part and parcel of stalking in other states' statutes. Therefore, when looking for a crime that fits what may be happening to you; review all your state's or country's criminal codes in regard to harassment as well as stalking.

Most stalking statutes have some type of reasonable person doctrine or stipulation implied or attached. In other words, would a man or woman on the street consider the behavior threatening, rude, annoying, and/or bizarre?

Before we go any further past credible threat, we should differentiate the difference between a credible threat and a **direct threat**. We would define a direct threat is one that is made to the victim so that he or she knows in no uncertain terms he or she is actually being threatened. If Tweety said to Monty, "I am going to blow your head off with this shotgun," that would definitely be a direct threat. There is no question in anyone's mind about Tweety's meaning. To reiterate, a **credible threat** is one that either by comments made or actions displayed to the victim by the suspect causes that victim to experience fear of bodily injury and/or emotional distress. It usually has to fit into what we refer to as the reasonable person standard. Again, read your particular state's stalking law to see how a credible threat is defined.

Some states, such as Alaska, go even further when defining "family member." Alaska Statutes, Section 11.41.270 —Stalking in the second degree—defines a family member as, "spouse, child, grandchild, parent, grandparent, sibling, uncle, aunt, nephew, or niece of the victim, whether related by blood, marriage, or adoption."[11] The statute further adds—a person who lives, or has previously lived, in a spousal relationship with the victim, or a person who lives in the same household as the victim, or has been in a dating, courtship, or engagement relationship with the victim.

We should note, some states require that the course of conduct takes place within a sixty-day period. Once again, we cannot impress upon you to arm yourself with knowledge, check your statutes.

In states like Louisiana, Nebraska, Delaware, and others, penalties as well as whether or not the crime of stalking will be classified in a certain fashion (felony versus misdemeanor, length of time in jail) can be influenced by the age of the person being stalked.

In states such as Vermont, there is both a straight stalking section and an aggravated stalking section. In the statute 13 V.S.A. 1063, aggravated stalking is defined as when, "A person commits the crime of aggravated stalking if the person intentionally stalks another person, and: such conduct violates a court order that prohibits stalking and is in effect at the time of the offense; or has been previously convicted of an offense an element of which involves an act of violence against the same person; or the person being stalked is under the age of 16 years; or had a deadly weapon, in their possession while engaged in the act of stalking."[12] Aggravated stalking has a greater prison term and fine. New Mexico also has an aggravated stalking section under New Mexico Statute Annotated 30-3A-3.1 with similar requirements. Even though other states may not refer to these types of embellishments as aggravated, they have similar requirements that add a greater penalty and fine upon conviction just the same.

We would like every state to have a statute that made the first-time offense of stalking a felony or at least a wobbler, meaning the case could be prosecuted as either a felony or a misdemeanor at the prosecutor's discretion. Sadly that is not the case. In states like Kansas Statute Annotated 21-3438, if a subject is arrested and convicted on his or her first stalking offense and no restraining order was in place at the time of arrest, then upon conviction it is a misdemeanor. Maryland Criminal Law Code Annotated 3-802 also states that first-offense stalking is a misdemeanor.

California initiated Civil Code, 1708.7—a stalking tort, 1993—which allowed victims to sue their stalkers for damages. We consulted on what is believed to be the first such action ever brought on a stalking case in the mid-1990s. More states, including Kentucky, Michigan, Nebraska, Oregon, Rhode Island, South Dakota, Tennessee, Texas, Virginia, Washington, and Wyoming, have enacted this type of legislation. Further on in the book we will discuss this topic again and talk about some of those states in greater detail.[13]

The Model Stalking Code

The National Institute of Justice first developed the Model Stalking Code in 1993. It was designed to provide other states or, in some cases, other countries with a set of guidelines to both evaluate and develop their stalking statutes. In 2007 the National Center for Victims of Crime, of which I am a current member, is a great resource for stalking and other victim information; took on the job of revising this model. This was largely because of the changes in stalking behavior seen by researchers and those like us that continue to investigate and deal with stalkers. These changes included the types of tools stalkers have begun to utilize, to perpetrate their crimes. This would include the advent of cyberstalking, GPS use, etc. After going over many of the committee's findings (who, by the way, did an outstanding job), we see much of what we and others who investigate stalkers have learned or experienced over the years being addressed. As I reviewed who was on the committee, I noted that some people who were around when I first began teaching for the California District Attorneys Association (CDAA) were still heavily involved in developing stalking educational treatments. Under one of the sections on page twenty-one of the report, the committee lists examples of stalking behaviors state laws, and in our opinion any legislative body developing a stalking legislation should be concerned with. (All of which we have dealt with and most of which we will cover throughout our discussions in the rest of this book.) Here is their list of nineteen items:

- Violating protection orders

- Using the legal system to harass a victim ("litigation abuse") by continuously filing motions for contempt or modifications or by filing retaliatory protection order applications or criminal charges against victims

- Harassing a victim through visitation or custody arrangements
- Stalking the victim in the workplace
- Using surveillance in person, through technology, or through third parties
- Engaging in obsessive or controlling behaviors
- Targeting third parties (e.g., a victim's family member, friend, or child) to scare victim
- Committing burglary or trespassing or moving items in a victim's home
- Killing animals (We have had stalkers not only kill but hold animals as hostage as a bargaining chip.)
- Using cultural context to stalk or scare a victim, such as immigration-related threats
- Attempting to harm self in the victim's presence
- Sending flowers, cards, or e-mail messages to a victim's home or workplace
- Contacting a victim's employer or forcing a victim to take time off from work
- Using humiliating or degrading tactics such as posting pictures of a victim on the Internet or disseminating embarrassing or inaccurate information about the victim
- Following a victim without the victim's knowledge with the intent of sexually assaulting her
- Assaulting a victim
- Using children to harass or monitor a victim
- Impersonating a victim through technology or other means[14]

Federal Stalking Laws in the United States

We should take this opportunity to discuss the laws that affect interstate stalking. This is one of the longer anti-stalking definitions we have seen. Perhaps it is because it is a government thing, unknown. Title 18 USCS § 2261A reads, "Whoever (1) travels in interstate or foreign commerce or within the special maritime and territorial jurisdiction of the United States, or enters or leaves Indian country, with the intent to kill, injure, harass, or place under surveillance with intent to kill, injure, harass, or intimidate another person, and in the course of, or as a result of, such travel places that person in reasonable fear of the death of, or serious bodily injury to, or causes substantial emotional distress to that person, a member of the immediate family (as defined in section 115 [18 USCS § 115]) of that person, or the spouse or intimate partner of that person; or (2) with the intent- (A) to kill, injure, harass, or place under surveillance with the intent to kill, injure, harass, or intimidate, or cause substantial emotional distress to a person in another State or tribal jurisdiction or within the special maritime and territorial jurisdiction of the United States; or (B) to place a person in another State or Tribal jurisdiction, or within the special maritime and territorial jurisdiction of the United States, in reasonable fear of the death of, or serious bodily injury to- (i) that person; (ii) a member of the immediate family (as defined in section 115 [18 USCS § 115]) of that person; or (iii) a spouse or intimate partner of that person; uses the mail, any interactive computer service, or any facility of interstate or foreign commerce to engage in a course of conduct that causes substantial emotional distress to that person or places that person in reasonable fear of the death of, or serious bodily injury to, any of the persons described in classes (i) through (iii) of subparagraph (B); shall be punished as provided in section 2261(b) of this title [18 USCS § 2261(b)]."[15]

We do like that the federal law has some serious penalties upon conviction, which includes twenty years for permanent disfigurement or life-threatening bodily injury and life if the victim is killed. (We are for the death penalty, so we would like to see that as one of the punishments for taking the life of another.) The federal penalty when no one is killed or injured and where no dangerous weapon is used can be up to five years. Since we have been investigating and consulting on various cases, it has been our *personal* experience that it is rare that the Federal Bureau of Investigation (FBI) actually gets involved with stalking cases. Remember, we said it is rare. (As to their reasoning, that probably depends on a case to case evaluation process. Remember, we are not here to judge, only to report what our experience has been.) They do occasionally engage. It is, however, oftentimes on high-profile cases such as the Peeping Tom that followed a female sportscaster from state to state and photographed her while she was changing clothes in various hotel rooms. The stalker rented a room next to the victim's and cut peepholes where a micro camera was placed. He then posted his video on the Internet.

What is important are victims of interstate stalking getting the assistance they need. Unfortunately if the stalking takes place in a state where stalking is a misdemeanor, the law enforcement agency working the case has to push for the Feds (in this case, the FBI) to get involved if the crime fits the federal stalking statue. When and if they decide to take the case, their prosecution should be handled in Federal Court; where their rules of law apply. Why? If the state where the victim lives can only file misdemeanor charges, that jurisdiction will not usually issue an extraditable arrest warrant and place it in the National Crime Information Center (NCIC) computer database. Any agency that places a warrant in that system should be telling which ever outside agency that takes the suspect into custody that they will respond within the required number of days to collect said suspect. This would include obtaining a Governor's warrant, if the suspect refuses to waive extradition. There are, of course, exceptions to that rule, but they are few and far between. When we profiled one of our stalkers on *America's Most Wanted*, we only had a misdemeanor warrant for his arrest, but the district attorney who handled extraditions in Orange County issued the warrant via NCIC due to the violent nature of this particular stalker. (For additional federal sections that may assist concerning stalking go to endnote sixteen).[16]

As an example of how a case can be filed in a state and prosecuted without the FBI, let us describe an Orange County case on which I consulted. A supervising district attorney for the Orange County District Attorney's Office called me at home. He advised that he had received a case from a law enforcement agency, who had initially filed the case as a rude and annoying phone call submission (misdemeanor). The district attorney, who had read my book and attended one of my training seminars, reviewed the case, and said he, felt there was much more going on than just some annoying phone calls. When we train, we advise law enforcement to always look further than the obvious. We especially advise those we teach to investigate further on calls such as vandalism, threatening phone calls, trespassing, peeping, etc. Oftentimes, especially when dealing with an intimate partner or instances of domestic violence, a little bit of digging reveals a stalker lurking in the background.

When I learned the facts of the crime, I completely agreed. A middle-aged, successful female executive had a brief dating relationship with a computer specialist she met at a conference in man's home state (a southern state about two thousand miles from Orange County). The woman found the man to be very manipulative and controlling almost from their first date, so she broke off their relationship. The subject was not only a computer specialist. He was some type of guru who had a fairly high-level security clearance that allowed him to work and consult on sensitive government and private contracts. Once she broke off the relationship, he began making threatening phone calls and sending her equally disturbing e-mails. The communication became extremely direct and violent when she threatened to go to the police and file charges. (Our boy knew a conviction would eliminate his security clearances and thus his lucrative contracts.)

The woman was able to tape-record some of his threats, which described finding her in a pool of her own blood and having a hole put into her head. The district attorney wanted to know if there was any way of getting a stalking case filed on the out-of-state stalker. We got the impression the district attorney was not receiving a great deal of help from the department that had submitted the initial crime report. Also the federal authorities were either not contacted or unwilling to assist in the investigation. We did not get into that aspect of the process with him. It has been our experience that it really doesn't make any difference as to what you are eventually going to do, especially if you able to develop a strategy that doesn't rely on an outside agency.

The district attorney agreed with our evaluation, that we had enough evidence to charge both stalking and criminal threats with what was presented in the tape recordings and e-mails. (In California, criminal threats, 422 of the Penal Code, is a part-one felony crime that upon conviction can add years to the suspect's sentence.) I told him to have one of his investigators (in California, as well as many other states, the District Attorney's Office has its own investigators) contact the victim and tell her to keep all records of incoming e-mails and calls as well as continue to tape-record any calls from the suspect. Then he should file the felony stalking and criminal threats case in Orange County, obtain an extradition warrant, and have a team of investigators go to the stalker's state with the warrant. From there the investigators could contact the city's local law enforcement, go before the magistrate, and get a search warrant for the stalker's house and all his computers. (The woman had gone to the stalker's house on one occasion, and she had seen a room that housed at least five separate computers the stalker used for his profession. The stalker also had a set of monitors in which he was able to view several areas surrounding his home.)

Once the investigators had the arrest and search warrant, they were to make entry, arrest the stalker, and confiscate all his computers and any other recording or digital devices. They were either to bring them back with them or have a forensics team, if available in that jurisdiction, search all devices for evidence of stalking via electronic transmission or Internet submissions. These could be used later as evidence in the case. We provided the district attorney with a copy of what to search for on the warrant, as well as how to articulate it in the body of said search warrant. We also included a warning concerning this particular suspect.

From what the woman told authorities about the layout of this stalker's computer room, it sounded like what we refer to as a "nest." The computers are oftentimes set up along one cabinet or table. Many times they are interconnected electronically via a hub system. Because this individual was somewhat paranoid as well as sophisticated, we felt he probably had some type of auto erase system built into his little nest. We advised the district attorney about what systems this stalker's nest might contain so he could forward that information to his investigators. We will not describe any of the devices in this book, but when contacted, by law enforcement will be more than happy to discuss these units and how to disable them. (After all, we don't want to educate potential stalkers about what we know. We try not to make what we write a stalkers training guide.) The district attorney said he never would have thought about any of our advice and thanked us for our assistance. The case was later adjudicated. (The exact outcome is unknown. The consult was completed, and we moved on.)

Keep in mind that what we advised the district attorney to do was expensive. You have to pay for your investigators to go to another jurisdiction and stay for however long it takes to complete the investigation. This could mean, especially on an extradition case, having to appear before that state's magistrate and coordinate with their law enforcement entities, which can take several days. With budgets being stretched to their limits, many times these types of cases unless a violent assault had also transpired as part of the crime, may not be adjudicated the way the District Attorney's Office would like.

The only other thing a district attorney could have done was file the case and put a warrant into the system. This would only allow the suspect to be arrested within a closer proximity to the state issuing the warrant. (It would be within driving distance but not flying distance.) We know this may sound petty, but most everything in this world is predicated on money. If you don't have the funds, then some things go by the wayside. We may not like it, but it is a fact.

We still have a female stalker in our system that was convicted of felony stalking but fled California to Hawaii prior to sentencing. A felony warrant was issued, but the district attorney would not permit it to be entered into a database that would allow her to be arrested and extradited. The district attorney commented, "She is now Hawaii's problem."

Since California's anti-stalking law came to fruition, more and more countries have become aware of their stalking problems. In this section, we will be giving you examples of some other countries' stalking laws. While going over those laws, we will also provide some statistics about the number and percentages of people stalked both in the United States and elsewhere. This may help better illustrate why not only the United States but many other countries feel these types of laws are necessary. Keep in mind that with any number of people surveyed and/or populations involved in the study, outcomes may get skewed.

Stalking Numbers In The United States

The first study, "Stalking in America: Findings from the National Violence Against Women Survey," was published by the United States Department of Justice's National Institute of Justice in 1998. Authored by Patricia Tjaden, PhD and Nancy Thoennes, it estimated that about 1,006,970 women and around 370,992 men are stalked annually in the United States. Even though the study was very well done, those of us actively working stalker cases felt those estimates were way too low.

In January of 2009, the Bureau of Justice Statistics issued a special report, "Stalking Victimization in the United States." This report came out with the most recent findings from a study initially conducted in 2006. Katrina Baum, PhD, Shannan Catalano, PhD, Michael Rand, and Kristina Rose authored the study, and it estimated a total of 5,857,030 persons were either being stalked or harassed annually in the United States.[17] Per their calculations, 3,424,100 persons (men and women) were stalked, and 2,432,930 persons (men and women) were harassed. The study explained that those being harassed experienced similar behavior to those being stalked. The primary difference was that those classified as stalking victims exhibited fear when harassed, and those categorized as harassed did not. So now they are telling us that almost 3.5 million people are being stalked annually in the United States, but we still don't feel that figure is high enough. (Again, we are not criticizing the study. These studies are well done and go a long way to helping all involved get a better handle on the stalking issue. We just feel the numbers are even higher. Obviously, this is just a gut feeling, and it is not backed by any scientific fact.)

The study also had the following overall observations:

- "During a 12-month period an estimated 14 in every 1,000 persons age 18 or older were victims of stalking.

- About half (46%) of stalking victims experienced at least one unwanted contact per week, and 11% of victims said they had been stalked for 5 years or more.

- The risk of stalking victimization was highest for individuals who were divorced or separated—34 per 1,000 individuals.

- Women were at greater risk than men for stalking victimization; however, women and men were equally likely to experience harassment.

- Male (37%) and female (41%) stalking victimizations were equally likely to be reported to the police.

- Approximately 1 in 4 stalking victims reported some form of cyberstalking such as e-mail (83%) or instant messaging (35%).

- 46% of stalking victims felt fear of not knowing what would happen next.

- Nearly 3 in 4 stalking victims knew their offender in some capacity.

- More than half of stalking victims lost 5 or more days from work.[18]

Prior to getting into some specifics concerning the anti-stalking laws from countries throughout the world, let's talk a little bit about stalking in the European Union (EU). The EU is a group of twenty-seven member countries: Austria, Belgium, Bulgaria, Cypress, Czech Republic, Denmark, Estonia, Finland, France, Germany, Greece, Hungary, Ireland, Italy, Latvia, Lithuania, Luxembourg, Malta, the Netherlands, Poland, Portugal, Romania, Slovakia, Slovenia, Spain, Sweden, and the United Kingdom. Croatia, the Republic of Macedonia, Turkey, Montenegro, and Serbia have currently placed their requests for membership. So why the need for a geography lesson? It's not just because I have a BA in that particular subject. It's to remind our readers, hopefully many from some of these countries that we are aware of the rest of the world and their issues concerning stalking. It is not just a problem dealt with in the good old USA. (There will be several footnotes in this part of chapter one. Why? We do not work for or reside in the countries discussed; therefore we need help trying to get the most valid information possible. Out of the twenty-seven countries in the EU, Austria, Belgium, Denmark, Germany, Italy, Ireland, Malta, the Netherlands, the United Kingdom, Scotland, and Sweden have specific stalking laws. (For more information on stalking in the EU, refer to the endnote.)[19] Please note Ireland addresses stalking under the harassment section of the Non-Fatal Offenses Against the Person Act of 1997.[20]

We have recently been contacted by those involved in threat assessment and helping stem the tide of stalking in a country outside the EU, Norway. They have requested we provide information about the growing stalking problem in their beautiful country. According to an Associated Press article from October 5, 2009, the United Nations listed Norway as number one in quality of life. As we have explained, stalking can take place anywhere, even in a country the United Nations deemed as having the highest quality of life in the world.

In early April of 2010, I had the opportunity to conduct a two-day seminar in Oslo, Norway, for Ronin Consulting Group. (Ronin Consulting, Larvik, Norway: www.ronin.no.) Ronin is a consulting and threat assessment group that provides close protection for certain Norwegian political party members, along with company CEOs and other executives, as just some of their tasks. They also volunteer to assist specific woman in their country's domestic violence shelters who may be at risk. The lecture was a culmination of several weeks of sending information to Ronin Associates International, domestic violence advocates, and certain members of their government. The information concerned assisting in the development of a stalking law, which they are still working to attain. While I was in Norway, Sweden passed a new anti-stalking law, so it appeared more and more Scandinavian countries were feeling the need to put laws in place. (At the writing of this book, we were not able to obtain a copy of Sweden's new law. According to our sources, it has not yet been made available to those outside their law enforcement community.)

Not long after the wife and I returned home from Norway, we flew to Michigan so that I could teach for the Michigan District Attorney's Association. While there, I received a text from Ronin's business manager stating that, probably due to the legislators and victim advocacy groups in their country, stalking was once again in the news. They hoped this would jump-start the way forward for a stalking law to be put in place. That is always good news.

Author teaching in Norway.

Whenever you teach in another country, you should always approach it as a learning experience as well as a training forum. We learned a great deal about how domestic violence and stalking was treated within Norway. We also found the people we taught to be extremely caring and professional individuals. Many of the Ronin Group were either former or current military personnel, and many were in the elite special forces network. They all wanted an implemented stalking law so they could better assist the victims of the crime. One of the things we found quite interesting was that some of the women at risk for violence are assigned a GPS locating device. This can be activated, allowing law enforcement to respond and assist them. They are still trying to get a similar GPS tag placed on those on probation for violent domestic crimes.

Examples of Stalking Laws Throughout Portions of the World

Under this heading we will be discussing stalking laws in some of the EU countries, Canada, The United Kingdom, as well as Japan and Australia. Several EU countries, as of the writing of this book, do not have actual stalking laws, but they do have harassment laws, many of which encompass some type of stalking behavior. That being said, as indicated, we are going to examine several EU countries' stalking laws to compare similarities with the United States. Because Canada borders the United States, we thought we should talk about their law before we get into the EU community. (Please note, we recently located a site to help the reader research many countries' stalking laws or lack thereof. Go to the stalking risk profile site www.StalkingRiskProfile.com. You will be able to look up a variety of stalking information beyond just countries' laws. (When we found the site it was still in development, but it promises upon completion to be a very helpful stalking resource.)

Canada

The Canadians have been actively involved with stalking issues since about 1993. Their legislation covering stalking behavior is known as criminal harassment and is defined in the Canadian Criminal Code Section 264.

264(1) states, "No person shall, without lawful authority and knowing that another person is harassed or recklessly as to whether the other is harassed, engage in conduct referred to in subsection (2) that causes that other person reasonably, in all circumstances, to fear for their safety or the safety of anyone known to them.

Subsection (2) Prohibited Conduct- "The conduct mentioned in subsection (1) consists of

(a) repeatedly following from place to place the other person or anyone known to them;

(b) repeatedly communicating with, either directly or indirectly, the other person or person or anyone known to them;

(c) besetting or watching the dwelling-house, or place where the other person, or anyone known to them, resides, works, carries on a business or happens to be; or

(d) engaging in threatening conduct directed at another person or any member of their family."

Punishment can be up to ten years upon conviction. (Information obtained from the Canadian Legal Information Institute.)[21]

The United Kingdom

Over the years, the United Kingdom has experienced a significant number of stalking cases. I continue to be contacted on my website by victims from that region asking for help. Most victims don't feel their stalkers are getting enough incarceration time. They also don't feel they are getting the protection they should from the existing law.

This type of complaint is common from victims who contact us from a wide variety of countries including the United States. Obviously there are stalkers who get more prison time or more severe law enforcement intervention than others. We are just advising what type of comments we are getting. Victims don't usually contact us when everything is going great in their lives.

When I first contacted the researchers who were developing statistics for the 1998 British Crime Survey, they advised that about 2.9 percent of adults ages sixteen to fifty-nine experienced stalking behavior. They also estimated about 0.88 million had been stalked during the course of the year being researched. Researchers went on to estimate about 0.55 million victims claimed fear or experienced a violent incident related to stalking.

The British Crime Survey published in March of 2004 indicated that about 8 percent of women and 6 percent of men surveyed complained of stalking during the time of the study. The study indicated that worked out to 1.2 million women and 900,000 men being stalked. (The Home Office Research Study 276, "Domestic Violence, sexual assault and stalking: British Crime Survey," was conducted by Sylvia Walby and Jonathan Allen)[22] The 2009/2010 British Crime Survey indicated that 1 in 20 women had been stalked at the time of the survey, and 1 in 5 women would be stalked in their lifetime.[23]

A March 2011 Home Office publication entitled "Call to End Violence Against Women and Girls: Equality Impact Assessment" found that since the age of sixteen, 19 percent of women had experienced stalking. It also stated that since age sixteen, 9 percent of males had experienced stalking as well.[24]

The United Kingdom has the Protection from Harassment Act of 1997. This law primarily deals with problems in England, Wales, and Northern Ireland. According to the law enforcement officers we contacted, the law was initially developed to stem the tide of stalking in the United Kingdom, but it also reaches out and covers a much wider range of harassment behavior. (We should advise you that the Brits have had groups who deal with what they refer to as "bullying" in their communities for many years; even prior to this act coming to light. Louise Burfitt-Dons is the founder of one of Britain's leading anti-bullying groups, Act Against Bullying. Burfitt-Dons reviewed our last book and said in part, the book, "contains a wealth of practical advice for those who find themselves in the unfortunate position of falling prey to a stalker." We hope this new book will do the same for you. We will be discussing bullying later on in the book. In certain scenarios bullying incorporates elements of stalking.

The Protection from Harassment Act allows for both civil and criminal penalties. According to Hamish Brown, retired inspector of the New Scotland Yard and whose expertise will be discussed in the next few pages, "civil penalties are hardly ever used, the strength of the law is with the criminal side." He went on to explain that there are two primary sections dealing with punishment, 2 and 4. "Section 2, (which carries a maximum sentence of 6 months imprisonment and which is easily the most used) covers harassment." "There is no definition of harassment, but it can include 'alarm' or 'distress'." "The beauty here is the acts themselves might not be a specific offense (such as following, standing outside property, leaving presents, etc.), but it is the totality of the behavior that counts if it causes harassment, alarm, or distress."

Hamish goes on to explain Section 4, "(which is far more serious and carries a maximum of 5 years imprisonment, but is not used as much) covers fear of violence." "Note, this is about a 'fear' and not a specific threat." "Examples of this can be leaving a wreath on a front door, digging a grave in someone's yard, sending sympathy cards about their death, etc."

Hamish indicated that when anyone is convicted of these offenses, or even in some situations where the court acquits an individual, the court is "open" (can so order) after sentencing "(custodial or not)" to issue a restraining order. The magistrate can specify whatever he or she deems necessary as to the regulations of the order. According to Hamish, "the restraining order can only be obtained after a prosecution is brought and the case is complete. He also stated that, as of September of 2009, restraining orders issued by the court can now apply to "all offenses not just stalking." Hamish said he sees these orders being issued in assault cases "(mostly covered by the Offences Against Person Act, 1861), and damage to property (Criminal Damage Act 1971)." He also agreed, that restraining orders are only pieces of paper unless upheld by the court and violations are prosecuted vigorously.

If you live in the United Kingdom, we thought you should be aware of the following terms. Prohibition of harassment is defined as: "(1) A person must not pursue a course of conduct—(a) which amounts to harassment of another, and (b) which he knows or ought to know amounts to harassment of the other."[25] Or the offense of putting people in fear of violence...which is defined as "(1) A person whose course of conduct causes another to fear, on at least two occasions, that violence will be used against him is guilty of an offense if he knows or ought to know that his course of conduct will cause the other so to fear on each of those occasions."[26] The law goes on to use what we refer to once again as the reasonable man doctrine, as well as gives instances where the behavior is described as lawful business. Under the section concerning penalties for a restraining order violation, punishment can be a fine, a prison term, or a combination if authorized by the court. Again, if you live in the United Kingdom and feel you are being stalked, review your law and contact the local law enforcement.

During the course of writing this book, I had the pleasure of communicated with members of the British Association of Chief Police Officers (ACPO) involved in developing programs to better deal with stalkers in their country. We exchanged information concerning protocols. They were

The United Kingdom does appear to be rapidly moving in the direction of developing stronger and more specific anti-stalking legislation, as well as programs to assist those that are the victims of stalking and domestic violence. Along those lines, there is a great deal of study being done in regard to cyberstalking. In November of 2011, the Home Office (London) issued a stalking consultation review of the 1997 Harassment Act. In March of 2012, Prime Minister David Cameron formally announced the government's intention to criminalize stalking. Due to the urging of victim advocate groups, there is a campaign formulated to get the UK's citizenry up to speed on the issue of stalking. This was evidenced by the creation of the first National Stalking Awareness Day that took place on April 18, 2012, which was well-received by the British public. So it appears that positive changes are a foot.

truly concerned about the issue and working towards better training for their members.

The Republic of Ireland has its own harassment law (Section 10 of the 1997 Non-Fatal Offences Against the Person Act). Under Section 10, "(1) Any person who, without lawful authority or reasonable excuse, by any means including by use of the telephone, harasses another by persistently following, watching, pestering, besetting or communicating with him or her, shall be guilty of an offense. "(2) For the purposes of this section harasses another where (a) he or she, by his or her acts intentional or recklessly, seriously interferes with the other's peace and privacy or causes alarm, distress or harm to the other, and (b) his or her acts are such that a reasonable person would realize that the acts would seriously interfere with the other's peace and privacy or cause alarm, distress or harm to the other."[27]

As of 2009 Scotland did not have a stalking law per se. They do have a harassment law listed under 1997 Chapter 40, which appears to be from the same chapter that houses of the Protection from Harassment Act of 1997. The law has both civil and criminal penalties. The criminal penalties stem from violating Section 234A non-harassment orders. Under that section the word harassment is defined as in the Protection from Harassment Act of 1997. That states, "(1) Every individual has a right to be free from harassment and, accordingly, a person must not pursue a course of conduct which amounts to harassment of another and—(a) is intended to amount to harassment of that person; or (b) occurs in circumstances where it would appear to a reasonable person that it would amount to harassment of that person."[28] Once again, the reasonable person doctrine appears. (Read on and see how the law in Scotland was changed in 2010.)

During the course of writing this section of the book, I was once again in contact with an associate who is one of the best-known stalking experts in the United Kingdom, one Hamish Brown

MBE. Brown was New Scotland Yard's leading expert on stalking, and retired to private consulting in 2004. He has received various honors, including the prestigious member of the Order of the British Empire (MBE). This honor of chivalry is given by the Queen and was first established in 1917 by King George V. Hamish and I met while attending the annual Association of Threat Assessment Professional (ATAP) conference[29] held at the Disneyland Hotel in Anaheim once a year. We are both members of this body that allows one to compare notes with a variety of national and international professionals in the threat assessment and stalking field.

Hamish, as do we continually consults with organizations involved in victim advocacy. I asked him about any changes in his country's laws or updates I might need to be aware of. Hamish said my UK readers might be interested in looking at the "Offences Against the Person Act of 1861 and the Criminal Damage Act of 1971," as other sections when reviewing what stalkers could also be charged with. I also asked Hamish if the Yard had any group specializing in threat assessment. He advised I look into the Metropolitan Police Department's Fixated Threat Assessment Centre (FTAC). If interested in gathering more information on this unit, go to your favorite search site and type in "Fixated Threat Assessment Centre."

He went on to say that he had recently been busy working with radio and media trying to get the word out on stalking. Earlier in the year, he did Dublin radio. (I had been on the Radio City's *Peter Price* show in Liverpool in June of 2009 pushing the same message.) Brown had also been working with advocacy groups trying to strengthen Scotland's harassment law by adopting some anti-stalking legislation. He mentioned a group who was working towards that same goal. It included Ann Moulds—a stalking victim herself—who was involved in the Action Scotland Against Stalking Campaign. (For more information, see Network for Surviving Stalking at www.NSS.org.net/Scotland and/or Action Against Stalking at www.ScotlandAgainstStalking.com.) *You will find from examples of stalking that have transpired that there are those that take the bull by the horns. These victims turn their disgust and rage into positive outlets, as did Ann, and push for better stalking laws and victim protection from this insidious crime. The stalker that pursued Moulds had no idea what he was about to unleash.*

Ann Mould's stalking experience. When I first began communicating with Ann, she was working with legislators and the heads of law enforcement in Scotland to get a strong anti-stalking law implemented. Ann got involved in her advocacy role because she was stalked by a stranger for over two and a half years. She has allowed us to share her story with you. We think you will find it extremely compelling.

According to Moulds, her stalker remained unnamed for two years. In February of 2004, she received a "filthy" (sexually explicit), unsolicited Valentine's Day card. That "escalated" into one of the most terrifying experiences of her life and according to Ann described by the media as, "one of the worst stalking incidences recorded in Scotland."

Moulds advised that in August of 2004, she began receiving very disturbing, sexually deviant photographs of a man lying atop a bed wearing women's underwear and stockings with his genitals exposed. The subject, who she could not recognize, was also expressing some type of ligature bondage ritual. This included an extremely graphic list of things he would do to her using a variety of sexual devices. Her stalker also talked about his sexual orientation and usage of rubberized as well as leather garments. These lists read like a how-to for graphic bondage sex procedures. It showed that Moulds' stalker had a very vivid fantasy life. (We obtained a copy of all of these photos along with the pages of lists sent by the stalker, but due to their very graphic nature, we have decided not to display any of the photos or the contents of the lists. We will leave these images up to your imaginations.) We can easily understand Ann's disgust and degree of intimidation. He had also written provocative comments on the photos. He then began sending her letters that detailed his sexual fantasies in much greater detail, that one day he would be able to make all his outlandish desires a reality.

Her stalker began making phone calls at night and staying silent on the other end. Ann began getting presents of women's undergarments and other clothing items dropped on her doorstep. The stalker would then comment about wanting to or having worn her clothes. This was another fantasy.

Ann explained her initial contact with local law enforcement was frustrating at best. She complained that no one in the police department seemed trained or to understand what was going on. Whenever she called to make a report, she would get a new responding officer, and would then have to reiterate her entire problem over again. (This is why we strongly suggest stalking cases be investigated either by a specialized unit or a detective that is well-trained in how to case manage a stalker. We will discuss this in the chapter dealing with how best to handle a stalking investigation.) Ann said the stalker's letters increased in frequency, as did their "sadomasochistically violent" content. She became increasingly afraid, especially when the stalker began describing the location(s) he would be acting out his fantasies upon her.

Moulds slowly lost contact with her friends and associates and became more and more reclusive. She lived behind locked doors and drawn curtains. She was "terrified" her pursuer was lurking outside her home. She became emotionally drained, lost weight, and started losing her hair. (These are oftentimes very common maladies for stalking victims.) Ann was a self-employed podiatric practitioner (one who deals with maladies of the feet and ankles) as well as a trained therapist, and as would be expected, her practice began to suffer from the overwhelming stressors placed upon her by her stalker. Moulds finally confided in a relative who was a high-ranking officer with the Metropolitan Police Service. Local law enforcement was again engaged but with little or no result.

(This is why we are continually training law enforcement concerning how to deal with the stalking phenomenon. Those jurisdictions not exposed to stalker training are less likely to understand or pursue an active investigation. Once they are up to speed, they tend to do a much better job.)

Even though the stalker was not damaging Ann's property, he was slowly destroying her bit by bit through his continued threatening and scary behavior. The stalker escalated his behavior. Finally he made a mistake by sending her a text message with a "slogan" that outed him. She knew exactly who it was by that message. Her stalker was a casual friend who had assisted her on tasks around her home. He was known to be a very "respectable" person whom she believed she could trust. (As you will see, that many "stranger stalkers" are actually known to their victims.) In fact, Ann had once called him for advice after receiving a very disturbing letter from her then-unknown stalker. The letter talked about a horrific sexual bondage fantasy that the stalker wanted to perform on her. At the time, the "friend" consoled her and said that whoever was doing this to her was indeed "very sick, crazy, and extremely dangerous." How very prophetic. The associate-turned-stalker then told her to call him if she felt frightened, and he would be right over. He would sleep on her couch and protect her. He then exclaimed, **"You are safe with me." He even suggested that Ann could sleep in his spare bedroom if she needed a "break" from all the stress and harassment.**

This individual was later contacted by the police as a process of their investigation, and according to Ann a DNA sample was taken from him. Yet he still continued to stalk her. Once he had been identified as her stalker, local police searched his home and found a "shrine." This is something a stalker may set up with photos, writings, and other things such as trophies—personal items the stalker has taken from his or her target. These assist the stalker in his obsession with the victim. Police also found women's lingerie, shoes, skirts, stockings, garters, and panties. They even located photos and other letters ready to be sent to Ann. Her stalker pleaded not guilty in court, and soon after the phone calls began anew.

Ann then began finding that broken pieces of garden slab were being moved around her home at night. Whenever she put it back in place, she would later find it moved back into the same position she had found it. Ann finally turned to Women's Aid, who then contacted the senior procurator fiscal. Finally something was done, but due to the risk evaluation by the magistrate and the lack of stringent stalking laws, the stalker never went to jail. He got "3 years sex offenders," (we believe that is similar to being a sex registrant but for only three years), "3 years probation, and 260 hours of community service." He was also served with a five-year non-harassment order.

The sad truth is that Ann was still so traumatized she moved away from her home of over thirty years, leaving her friends and business behind. To add insult to injury, Ann and her daughter had been the victims of a violent home invasion robbery just years before, and they were finally starting to get some closure when her stalker, who knew of her previous grief, began his transgressions. Ann advised she is now in the process of suing her stalker.

I sent Ann several copies of my previous book along with other information on stalking and stalking investigation, which she disseminated to both law enforcement as well as legislators in her country. At that time we wished her luck getting a stalking law in place.

During the course of writing this book, Ann was able to have several meetings with legislators in her country concerning the stalking issue. She advised that it looked very promising that an actual stalking law will soon be on the books in her country. We tip our hat to people like Ann and other victim advocates. Their tireless efforts can and often do bring about change.

As we were about to send this book off to our agents for first review, Ann contacted me and said that all their hard work had paid off. Scotland now has its own anti-stalking law. She also explained that her organization, Action Scotland Against Stalking, had won the prestigious "Campaign of the Year" at the Scottish Charity Awards in Edinburgh in June of 2010. Ann and her confederates continue to push for extensive stalking law enforcement training throughout her country.*

Ann advised me that she is currently working with Hamish Brown and others to develop a more extensive approach to working stalking cases throughout the United Kingdom via consults with that country's Home Office. She was recently interviewed with Nazir Afzal (director of prosecution services) on a YouTube segment (www.YouTube.com/SurvivingStalking). Googling Ann Moulds reveals a great deal of information on her crusade to make stalking a priority not only in Scotland but the rest of the EU.

Another tool The United Kingdom has recently developed to help combat the issue of stalking is the new National Stalking Training Academy, which is backed by the Home Secretary's Office. Ann Moulds, Hamish Brown, Nazir Afzal, and many other very distinguished educators, consultants, and magistrates are on staff. They even let the likes of me be a member of the prestigious academy consulting group. For more on this program, go to: http://www. CSPAcademy.ac.uk/NationalStalkingTrainingAcademy-Our People.htm.

The following is the crux of the new law which Ann and others worked so hard for. This criminal offense and others can be found by Googling "Criminal Justice and Licensing (Scotland) Act 2010."

---

* In June of 2011, Ann Moulds launched the Scottish National Stalking Group. This group is tasked with pushing for legislative changes in many issues concerning stalking in the United Kingdom. See more about Ann Moulds in the Appendix on Victim Advocates.

Under Section 39 states, "**Offence of stalking**

(1) A person ("A") commits an offence, to be known as the offence of stalking, where A stalks another person ("B").

(2) For the purposes of subsection (1), A stalks B where—

(a) A engages in a course of conduct,

(b) subsection (3) or (4) applies, and

(c) A's course of conduct causes B to suffer fear or alarm.

(3) This subsection applies where A engages in the course of conduct with the intention of causing B to suffer fear or alarm.

(4) This subsection applies where A knows, or ought in all the circumstances to have known, that engaging in the course of conduct would likely to cause B to suffer fear or alarm.

(5) It is a defense for a person charged with an offence under this section to show that the course of conduct—

(a) was authorized by virtue of any enactment or rule of law.

(b) was engaged in for the purpose of preventing or detecting a crime, or

(c) was, in the particular circumstances, reasonable.

(6) In this section—

"conduct" means—

(a) following B or any other person,

(b) contacting, or attempting to contact, B or any other person by any means,

(c) publishing any statement or other material—

(i) relating or purporting to relate to B or to any other person,

(ii) purporting to originate from B or from any other person,

(d) monitoring the use by B or by any other person of the internet, email or any other form of electronic communication,

(e) entering any premises,

(f) loitering in any place (whether public or private),

(g) interfering with any property in the possession of B or any other person,

(h) giving anything B or to any other person or leaving anything where it may be found, given to or brought to the attention of B or any other person,

(i) watching or spying on B or any other person,

(j) acting in any other way that a reasonable person would expect would cause B to suffer fear or alarm, and "course of conduct" involves conduct on at least two occasions.

(7) A person convicted of the offence of stalking is liable—

    (a) on conviction on indictment, to imprisonment for a term not exceeding 5 years, or to a fine, or to both,

    (b) on summary conviction, to imprisonment for a term not exceeding 12 months, or to a fine not exceeding the statutory maximum, or to both.

We included Scotland's entire stalking law into this text for two reasons. First, it is quite an accomplishment for an advocate group such as Moulds' to get such an extensive law placed on the books. This is especially true since Scotland's only existing law was that of harassment, and it contained no criminal resolution or penalties. Secondly, we feel that there is a movement stirring among the EU countries without stalking laws. The Scottish law, therefore, may well become a template for those countries to develop their own stalking legislation.

We should also note that under this new act, Scotland also produced Section 38, Threatening or Abusive Behaviour, which allows for criminal penalties for behaviors similar to stalking. We would liken this particular section to California's Criminal Threats Section 422 of the penal code.

Special Note: Just prior to sending this book off to the publisher, we were once again contacted by Ann Moulds who had been keeping us abreast of hers and her colleagues, such as Alexis Bowater—chief executive for The Network for Surviving Stalking—progress in pressing on with stalking legislation and awareness not only in the United Kingdom, but elsewhere in Europe. She

Due to the fact that we feel this new stalking legislation in the United Kingdom is so important, and should help so many more victims in that country, we have included the definition of 2A in Appendix E of this book.

advised that due to a huge push to educate the public on the issues of stalking by advocacy groups such as hers and others in the United Kingdom., new stalking legislation was passed amending The Protection From Harassment Act with a specific section on stalking. This section which can be found in the Protection of Freedoms Act of 2012, under section 111-Offences in relation to stalking—*states* (1) After section 2 of the Protection from Harassment Act 1997 (offense of harassment) insert—2A Offense of stalking—extensively calls out exactly what the crime of stalking will be. (When we reviewed the new legislation, we could see that it dramatically and specifically re-defines the criminal definition of stalking, and in our opinion puts a great deal more teeth into the law.) According to Moulds, this new section will go into effect for England and Wales on November 25, 2012.* Moulds also advised that bail in cases of domestic abuse and stalking will also go under legislative review. She advised that on April 7, 2011, The Council of Europe Convention on preventing and combating violence against women and domestic violence, also addressed the issue of stalking under Article 34 of the convention's agenda. (Refer to: http://conventions.coe.int/Treaty/EN/Treaties/Html/210.htm)

Germany

Germany's stalking law—Section 238 of their penal code—has only been on the books since 2007. Therefore, not too much in the way of victim research appears to be currently available. There is one study generated by the Central Institute of Mental Health of the University of Heidelberg near Mannheim. Christine Kuehner, PhD and Peter Gass, MD conducted the study, "Lifetime Prevalence and Impact of Stalking in a European Population." The study took place in a midsized German city. The 679 participants, 400 women and 279 men, responded. The results showed 12 percent of the people—68 women and 10 men—had been stalked. Additional interpellation of the respondents indi-

---

* For further on this go to The Protection of Freedoms Act 2012 under the section on stalking, http://www.legislation.gov.uk/ukpga/2012/9/section/111/enacted

cated a "significant" effect of victimization on the group's psychological well-being. The researchers' conclusion was that there was a "high lifetime prevalence of stalking" that caused a variety of psychological situations within the community.[30]

Section 238 of Germany's penal code states, "(1) Whosoever unlawfully stalks a person by:

1. seeking his proximity,

2. trying to establish contact with him by means of telecommunication or other means of communication or through third persons,

3. abusing his personal data for the purpose of ordering goods or services for him or causing third persons to make contact with him,

4. threatening him or a person close to him with loss of life or limb, damage to health or deprivation of freedom, or

5. committing similar acts, and thereby seriously infringes his lifestyle shall be liable to imprisonment of not more than three years or a fine.

The law goes on to state, "the penalty shall be three months to five years if the offender places the victim, a relative of or another person close to the victim in danger of death or serious injury." The law states if the stalker's actions cause death to the victim, a relative or another person close to the victim, the penalty can be from one to ten years.[31]

Los Angeles Assistant District Attorney Rhonda Saunders traveled to Germany in late 2004 to attend a stalking symposium in the city of Kassel. She was asked to assist representatives from the

German government who were in the process of developing their anti-stalking legislation. I am a consultant for OVC Office for Victims of Crime out of Washington, DC, and I also work with fellow members of the National Center for Victims of Crime (NCVC). Both hard working organizations have been sending representatives to certain factions in Germany to assist with stalking training. So as one can see, we in the States are finding ourselves more and more involved in training our brothers abroad and are enjoying every minute of it.

Early on in the development stages of this book, I was able to contact Josefine Stomper, minister for the German Ministry of Family, Seniors, Women, and Children, concerning stalking in her country. She advised that Germany was very interested in assisting the victims of stalking. She was kind enough to provide a copy of the Federal Republic of Germany's 2008 crime statistics. There were 11,401 reported stalking cases in the country in 2007 and 29,273 in 2008. (Remember, they just initiated this law in 2007.) The study also indicated their clearance rate was 88.4 percent in 2007 and 88.1 percent in 2008.[32] The 2009 report showed 28,536 persons reported the crime of stalking that year.[33] The 2010 report showed a decline in the number of reported stalking incidents, which totaled 26,848. [34]

Concerning the German stalking law, it is unclear why this particular definition uses the masculine gender to describe the victim, especially since the majority of stalking victims are female. Just as an aside, Rhonda Saunders, several other consultants, and I were slated to teach in Bremen, Germany, at the World Stalking Conference in 2008, but due to circumstances beyond the presenters' control, the Conference was postponed. This would have been an excellent platform in which to present training as well as learn from others representing other nations in attendance. Hopefully this conference will be resurrected. Anytime I can get to that beautiful country is always a bonus.

Italy

In April of 2009, the Parliament of Italy passed (or "converted," as they say) their first anti-stalking law via legislative bill Law No. 38/2009. Article 612 *bis* of the Italian Code of Criminal Procedure is their anti-stalking law. It states, "anyone who repeatedly and by means threatens or harass somebody, so as to cause her a serious psychological discomfort or to determine a justified fear for her personal safety or that of a close person or to relevantly affect her way of living, is punished—provided criminal action is brought by the victim—with detention for a period varying from six months to four years."[35] The evaluation of this section also states that if the victim is murdered as a result of the stalking, the stalker can get as much as life in prison.

We have recently been contacted by a member of the Italian Carabinieri (the Italian National Military Police) who is conducting extensive research on stalking for his agency. He requested training materials including our stalking protocol. Hopefully we were able to assist.

Austria

On July 01, 2006, Austria amended its Criminal Procedures Code and added Section 107a—Persistent Pursuit (Stalking) into the code. It states that certain illegal conduct that is repeated over an extended period and affects the victim's life unacceptably is a basis for stalking. Under Austrian law, stalking is defined as "deliberate, malicious and repeated persecution and harassment of a person that threatens a person's safety."[36] The acts perpetrated by the stalker must cause the victim to "feel fear, anxiety or panic." Examples of behavior that may constitute stalking include "psychological terror often over many years, repeated unwanted advances, repeated text messages to the mobile phone, hanging out near the victim, writing letters, calling at night, sending gifts, chasing after the victim, standing in front of the door of the victim's home, lying in wait for the victim, persecuting the victim in a car, etc."[37]

According to the Federal Chancellery of Austria's site, some of the prohibited behaviors of stalking include:

- "trying to be close to the victim (e.g. following by car, waylaying at home or in the workplace)

- contacting by telecommunication or any other means of communication or via third parties (e.g. frequent letters, emails or text messages)

- ordering goods or services for the victim by using the latter's personal data (e.g. clothes from a mail-order company)

- inducing third parties to contact the victim by using the latter's personal data (e.g. placing contact ads on behalf of the victim)"[38]

This last point is referred to as stalking by proxy, which is discussed in this book.

Belgium

Belgium's law, Penal Code Section 442 bis, referred to as belaging (harassing), was adopted first in 1998 and then amended in 2002 and 2003. The law basically states, Belaging is ""He, who has belaged (harassed) a person, while he knew or should have known that due to his behaviour he would severely disturb this person's peace, will be punished..." The behavior can occur once or more than once. "The term belaging can refer to a single act as well as to a pattern of different behaviours." These behaviors are described as anxiety, fear, expectations of violence, and malicious intent.[39]

For additional information and a look at how several stalking victims in Belgium and other areas of the Netherlands felt about stalking and law enforcement's response, go to a 2011 study entitled "Identifying the Needs of Stalking Victims and the Responsiveness of the Criminal Justice System: A Qualitative Study in Belgium and the Netherlands." The study was conducted by Suzan van der Aa and Anne Groenen, PhD and can be found at http://www.tandfonline.com/doi/abs/10.1080/15564886.2011.534006#preview.

Denmark

Section 265 of Denmark's criminal code has been in existence since 1930, although it did not address stalking by name. It was amended in 1965 and 2004. This criminal code states, "Any person who violates the peace of some other person by intruding on him, pursuing him with letters or inconveniencing him in any other similar way, despite warnings by the police, shall be liable to a fine or to imprisonment for any term not exceeding 2 years. A warning under this provision shall be valid for 5 years." Under this section, "'violating peace of some other person' may imply threatening, dishonouring, intruding, but it may also imply continuous unwanted attention, e.g. frequently sending unwanted flowers." According to the publication, these types of harassing behaviors must take place over a period of time. Once is *not normally* sufficient.[40]

The Netherlands

The Netherlands's stalking law, 285b of the Dutch Penal Code, was approved on July 12, 2000. The crime has also been referred to as belaging. The law defines stalking as "He, who unlawfully repeatedly, willfully intrudes upon a person's privacy with the intent to force that person to do something or to instigate fear in that person will be punished as guilty of belaging."[41]

As one can see, not all laws concerning stalking or stalking-type behavior are as specific or direct as others. This is especially true of those laws as compared to the ones in the United States. That being said, if it gets the job done, then it is a good thing.

That does it for our look at the stalking laws within the EU. Both Australia and Japan have had reported stalking issues for several years. Therefore, we thought it wise to look at some of their legislation on this topic. If nothing else, it gives us another glance through the world's stalking legislation looking glass.

Australia

A December of 2000 Australian Institute of Criminology study by The Australian Bureau of Statistics…showed that 2.4 percent of women aged over 18 years had been stalked by a man in the last 12 months, and 15 percent have been stalked by a man at least once in their lifetime." They stated that women were more likely to be stalked than be a victim of robbery or sexual assault.* A 2005 Australian Bureau of Statistics study, which was reissued August 21, 2006, stated that "in the 12 months prior to the survey 28% (31,000) of men and 31% (61,000) of women" that experienced some form of stalking were age eighteen to twenty-four. This was compared to "11% (12,500) men and 8.8% (17,200) of women aged 55 years or older."** The study offers other statistical data on stalking for those Australian readers or others who are interested.

In another section of the Australian Bureau of Statistics report, their research indicated that about one in ten men (9 percent) and one in five women (19 percent) had been stalked in his or her lifetime.[42] We contacted the Australian Domestic and Family Vio-

---

* For additional information go to http://www.AIC.gov.au/. Also try Googling "Stalking Risk Profile," which lists current websites for Australian stalking laws under their section entitled International Legislation. Please note, we try to offer the reader a variety of ways to get to some of our topics. We are sure, however, that most of you are much better at using a search engine than we are.
** *Refer to study*, Australian Bureau of Statistics 2005 Personal Safety Study *(Reissue)* http://www.abs.gov.au/ausstats/abs@.nsf/mf/4906.0/

lence Clearinghouse, but they advised there does not appear to be any more recent stalking informational studies that give this type of specific information.

There are eight states in Australia: Australian Capital Territory (ACT), New South Wales (NSW), Victoria (VIC), Tasmania (TAS), South Australia (SA), Western Australia (WA), Queensland (QLD), and Northern Territory (NT). Each state has its own version of an anti-stalking law. For our purposes, we will discuss the Australian Capital Territory law and then Victoria's law.

Australian Capital Territory, Crimes Act 1900 s34A states, (1) "A person shall not stalk another person with intent to cause—(a) apprehension or fear of harm, in the person stalked or someone else; or (b) to cause harm to the person stalked or someone else; or (c) to harass the person stalked."

(2) For this section, a person stalks someone else (the stalked person) if, on at least 2 occasions, the person does 1 or more of the following:

(a) follows or approaches the stalked person;

(b) loiters near, watches, approaches or enters a place where the stalked person resides, works or visits;

(c) keeps the stalked person under surveillance;

(d) interferes with property in the possession of the stalked person;

(e) gives or sends offensive material to the stalked person or leaves offensive material where it is likely to be found by, given to or brought to the attention of stalked person;

(f) telephones, sends electronic messages to or otherwise contacts the stalked person;

(g) sends electronic messages about the stalked person to anybody else.

(h) makes electronic messages about the stalked person available to anybody else;

(i) acts covertly in a way that could reasonably be expected to arouse apprehension or fear in the stalked person.

(j) engages in conduct amounting to intimidation, harassment or molestation of the stalked person."[43]

This Australian code has different penalties for different offenses such as stalking the victim when a court order is in place or using a deadly (or "offensive") weapon while stalking. Various states in Australia also have different sets of prison sentences. They are not all alike.

Rosemary Purcell, Michele Pathe, and Paul E. Mullen (all tireless researchers) conducted a 2006 study on 3,700 adult men and women in Victoria Australia. The study indicated that about 23 percent of those polled had experienced some type of stalking behavior in their lifetimes. (Younger adults, more than older ones, were more likely to report being the victims of stalking.) Most of the harassment was classified as unwanted phone calls, intrusive approaches, and following. About 29 percent experienced threats, and about 18 percent were physically assaulted as a result of the stalking. About 69 percent sought help when stalked.[44]

When I contacted Rosemary Purcell, PhD to discuss some of her more recent work (on juvenile stalkers), she informed me she thought the Victoria law was interesting, as it had one of the longer sentences for stalking—ten years. Rosemary forwarded a copy of the law to me.

In Victoria, stalking is listed under Section 21A of their penal code.

(1) "A person must not stalk another person. Penalty: Level 5 imprisonment (10 years maximum).

(2) A person (the offender) stalks another person (the victim) if the offender engages in a course of conduct which includes any of the following—

(a) following the victim or any other person;

(b) contacting the victim or any other person by post, telephone, fax, text message, e-mail or other electronic communication or by any other means whatsoever;

(ba) publishing on the Internet by an e-mail or other electronic communication to any person or other material—

(i) relating to the victim or any other person; or

(ii) purporting to relate to, or to originate from, the victim or any other person;

(bb) causing an unauthorized computer function (within the meaning of Subdivision (6) of Division 3) in a computer owned or used by the victim or any other person;

(bc) tracing the victim's or any other person's use of the Internet or of e-mail or other electronic communications;

(c) entering or loitering outside or near the victim's or any other person's place of residence or of business or any other place frequented by the victim or the other person;

(d) interfering with property in the victim's or any other person's possession (whether or not the offender has an interest in the property);

(da) making threats to the victim;

(db) using abusive or offensive words to or in the presence of the victim;

(dc) performing abusive or offensive acts in the presence of the victim;

(dd) directing abusive or offensive acts towards the victim;

(e) giving offensive material to the victim or any other person or leaving it where it will be found by, given to or brought to the attention of the victim or the other person;

(f) keeping the victim or any other person under surveillance;

(g) acting in any other way that could reasonably be expected—

(i) to cause physical or mental harm to the victim, including self-harm; or

(ii) to arouse apprehension or fear in the victim for his or her own safety or that of any other person—with the intention of causing physical or mental harm to the victim, including self-harm, or of arousing apprehension or fear in the victim for his or her own safety or that of any other person."[45]

For those readers interested in finding out more about the Australian stalking laws and the different types of restraining or protection orders, which they may refer to as apprehended violation orders (AVOs) or apprehended domestic violence orders (ADVOs), go online to Caslon Analytics at http://www.Caslon.com.au/StalkingNote2.htm.

As an aside, I consulted for a person preparing a possible piece for a fashion magazine in July of 2010 called *Grazia* (trust me, they didn't get in touch with me because I am a fashionista). Apparently the magazine has publishing roots in many areas, including Australia. The proposed article was to be on celebrity stalking, which is a topic we will touch on throughout this book. This type of stalking is something many countries experience. When we were done with the consult, the author of the pending article was very surprised to find out that celebrity stalking was such a small percentage of the overall stalking issue. As we explained to the author, we love the opportunity to spread the word about stalking through all venues, and we appreciated their interest in helping their readership.

Japan

In Japan, stalking appears to be a growing issue. Their stalking law was enacted November 24, 2000, and some say it was a direct result of a twenty-one-year-old female university student being stalked by her boyfriend. He reportedly hired some "hit men" to kill her, which they did in October of 1999.[46] This incident caused a major media uproar in the country, and it fueled the making of at least one made-for-television murder docudrama. Many in Japan complain that their stalking law, which is listed under the "petty offenses" section of their criminal code, does not go far enough in handling the problems experienced with the crime. We are told by victim advocates that we instruct as well as those that we encounter who have or continue to either visit or reside part-time in that country; that oftentimes stalking goes unreported for a variety of reasons. It could be due to a lack of education, a belief that law enforcement will not actively get involved, or due to the frailty of the law actually cannot do a great deal concerning the crime of stalking, or like a number of communities Asian or otherwise we have been involved with, pursuit, even unwanted pursuit, is still something that is tolerated at least to a certain degree.

It appears that under the Japanese law the stalker may be placed in jail for one year and be susceptible to a monetary fine, which may be adjusted depending on the degree of the offense. The first offense can cost the perpetrator up to 500,000 yen (about 6,000 US dollars or about 4,000 Euros), and six months in jail. Because we could not obtain a translated copy of the Japanese stalking law, we obtained an online copy in Japanese and ran it through Google translate.[47] From that, it looks as though the stalker must be warned by law enforcement. If he or she continues, the case is sent to a Public Safety Commission for review. The law does appear to discuss the types of intimidation required to qualify as stalking.

We also located a PDF file developed by Japan's National Police Agency Office for Crime Victims that summarized the eight acts that could be perpetrated by a stalker:

1. Stalking, lingering, or following

2. Telling the victim he or she is being watched

3. Demanding to meet and spend (time) with the victim

4. Rough talk and rowdy behavior

5. Silent phone calls

6. Sending rubbish and other unpleasant items to the victim

7. Slander

8. Preying on the victim's sense of sexual decency

That same presentation continued to define stalking as "Stalking means one of several acts through which the offender turns his or her resentment against the victim who refuses to accept the offender's love or favor."

To get more information concerning the requirements for stalking in Japan, in English, go www.npa. go.jp/english/police. Then go to the Crime Victims PDF file open, and scroll down until you locate the stalking information.

Thomasina Larkin wrote an interesting article concerning stalking in Japan in 2007. The article also discusses statistics about stalking in Japan.*

From all the information we have received from those that work with domestic violence issues in Japan, many women still feel more attention needs to be drawn to their plight. According to some we talked to, there may also be a great amount of stigma attached to the victim and victim's family members concerning these problems. Therefore, many women resist reporting these crimes to the police. As advanced by one of the comparative criminology studies we found, oftentimes victims move back to the security of their families.[48] In the last two training sessions we have conducted for victim advocate groups in Orange County, we have been contacted by Japanese American women. They advised the reason for taking my class as well as others couched in the area of domestic violence was so they could go back to Japan and work with advocates there. They said that there was a growing need for this type of victim advocate interaction in Japan. Our research does indicate there is a greater trend by law enforcement to diminish sexual assault, the crime of groping, along with others.

We hope that the Japanese government is beginning to look at stalking as a much more serious crime. We have not had the

---

* For review of this article, "Reported stalking cases likely just tip of iceberg," go to http://search.japantimes.co.jp/cgi-bin/fl20070417zg.html

opportunity to visit that vibrant country so we cannot comment on how things are progressing there.

There are many cultures where stalking is prevalent, underreported, and/or poorly investigated—if at all. In some cases it is not even considered a crime. Incidentally many (though not all) of these countries have terrible human rights reputations. This reputation extends especially to their outlook on women and the issue of pursuit. We will revisit these issues when we discuss the cultural aspects surrounding stalking.

Prior to exiting this chapter, we would like to emphasize the importance of grassroots advocacy groups that are and have been busy making their countries' legislatives bodies take notice. One such group we have been in communication with over several months in the past is an organization headed up by Joannah Bodden Small, a prominent attorney residing in the Cayman Islands. Joannah was involved with the Young BPW Sexual Harassment and Stalking task force. The task force, which was disbanded in 2009, was formed "with the aim of investigating, assessing and providing the necessary legislative recommendations as they related to the protection of victims of sexual harassment and stalking in the Cayman Islands."[49]

Although Bodden Small is quick to point out that neither she nor her organization can claim any direct responsibility for recent laws being placed on the books, from where we stand, their efforts did in point of fact cause their legislators to take a closer look at the problems associated with sexual assault and stalking. In 2010 a new law, the Protection from Domestic Violence Law, was set in place, which addressed stalking in greater detail than it had in the past. Even though the law does not encompass all that Joannah and her group would like to see, it is a step in the right direction. Again, we are proud of groups such as these and people such as Ann Moulds, Judie Dilday, Bridget Fitzpatrick and others we have dealt with throughout our career.* They are the foot soldiers in the fight to develop better stalking laws. Without them, the job just would not get done.

While on the subject of the types of victim advocates we encounter, we would like to take this opportunity to discuss two from the law enforcement side of the fence. Yes, cops can be advocates too. The first would be one Saratoga Springs Utah Detective/Corporal named Bruce Champagne. ** We met the second individual of mention while teaching a couple of stalking training seminars stressing victimology and campus stalking he had scheduled for us at Sam Houston University in October of 2012. At the time, this was a culmination of a five state teaching tour. Professor Raymond Teske Jr., PhD, is a long-time instructor within the prestigious Sam Houston University College of Criminology as well as being a sworn police officer with many years on the job. ***

Note: If you are interested in gathering more information concerning stalking legislation throughout the world, a fairly new website that we like is a good resource, *Stalking Risk Profile, https:// www.stalkingriskprofile.com/what-is-stalking/stalking-legislation/ international-legislation.* We have also listed it under Appendix D.

---

* Bridget, a police services officer for the Omaha Police Department, was one of the persons leading the charge in a successful move to change the Nebraska stalking law. She is a tireless worker for stalking victims' rights, and is someone we have had the pleasure of working with over the years.

** After spending months on two stranger stalking cases that we were able to assist him with, Bruce decided that his state, which had not been formally introduced to any stalker training via POST (Peace Officer Standards and Training) needed to get up to speed to better assist the growing number of stalking victims in Utah. Therefore he pushed and was able to get the first recognized eight hour POST training session on stalking in the state.

*** When you Google Dr. Teske, you will find an extensive and decorated academic background. He has been with Sam Houston University since 1973. He has been very active in developing victim programs on a variety of programs, his work on assisting the victims of murdered children is especially worth noting. Being an officer allows him to assist many agencies throughout the state with a variety of investigations. One site is http://www.cjcenter.org/directory/?mode=view&item=236 to find out more on him. However we find Googling his name is easier.

Chapter One's Summary

- The First Stalking Law was passed in California in 1990.
- We have chosen to define stalking in general as a person who willfully, maliciously, and repeatedly follows, harasses another person and who makes a credible threat with the intent to place that person in reasonable fear for his or her safety or the safety of his or her immediate family.
- The victim must exhibit fear or emotional trauma or distress.
- Stalking is a course of conduct crime.
- Stalking is a worldwide problem with many countries outside the United States either currently having or in the process of enacting their own form of stalking legislation.
- Grassroot advocacy groups are key to getting better stalking legislation developed throughout the world.

Chapter 2
Types of Stalkers

Before we discuss any of the topics in this chapter, simple percentages need to be addressed. Many people believe stalking mostly happens to the famous or those in the media. Like we have previously indicated, it just ain't so. Only a small percentage of stalking is media-related. The vast majority of stalking is domestic violence or intimate partner stalking, and we estimate it is around a whopping 80 percent of the stalking cases. The rest can be construed as falling under what we and others have referred to as stranger and/or acquaintance stalking. These are general categories, and they can be broken down into a multitude of other stalking typologies. We refer to these as stalking subsets.

Our General Overall View of Stalkers

Since the early to late nineties, research and discussion about stalking has been growing fairly rapidly. From our perspective, this is, of course, a good thing. Prior to getting into more specifics about disorders and other issues associated with stalking, we would like to give you a basic overview concerning our experience with stalkers up to this point. We are not going to get into stalker methodology or the tools used to stalk, in this chapter, but a slight overview feels appropriate here. There are no absolutes, but we have found many of the stalkers we have either encountered or consulted on to be:

- *Fairly intelligent.* This does not mean they are all book smart. Many are street-smart. Some have a great deal of intelligence. Of course, they are not smart enough not to commit the crime of stalking, but that is just one person's opinion. We have consulted on cases where members of the court, physicians, and even law enforcement officers have been stalkers. To reiterate, stalkers can and do come from all walks of life.

- *Single-minded.* When a stalker goes after a target, they do it with fervor. It is not a lackadaisical approach. Most spend inordinate amounts of time planning, surveilling, and most often pursuing their target. That is why many times we find that these individuals are often under-employed or live in some type of parasitical relationship, such as with a relative, someone that has befriended them, etc. We had one stalker that went to churches and obtained food, clothing, and aid. He would then find unsuspecting women from that particular church, most always older than him, and move in with them. He then controlled and manipulated their lives. He took their money, made these individuals drive him from one location to another, used their phone incessantly, and did not allow his "hosts" to be in touch with their friends and relatives. In our extensive investigation into his background, we also uncovered male victims, which he used to beat and control through intimidation. Thus sucking the life out them as well.

  While lecturing at a two day seminar at a law enforcement training center in Nebraska in 2012, I was contacted by a detective who had just heard me discussing stalker's parasitical ways. He told me that he just had recently investigated a case where a stalker, who was in construction, would sit inside various coffee houses within the detective's community, and strike up conversations with women he deemed to be single or divorced middle-aged successful business people. He would then get them to hire him to do some work on their home. While working on their residences, he was able to worm his way into their lives. Eventually he moved in with them and then began his parasitical ways. Once they had enough of him, and kicked him out, he began stalking them almost into submission; oftentimes extracting money from them with the caveat that he would leave them alone. According to the detective, the stalker was extremely adept at what he was doing, and obtained a good deal of money from these women prior to being taken into custody.

- *Prone to isolating victim(s).* Many stalkers, especially those in the intimate partner and/or domestic violence category, will try to isolate their targets from family members, friends, or associates. This control tactic stops the victim from gaining the requisite aid she or he needs to break away from the stalker.

- *Troubled within relationships.* Stalkers seem not to relate to others well. Many would be considered loners. Of course, there are stalkers who fit into society. As previously indicated, a stalker can be a judge, police officer, teacher, medical professional, etc. That being said, if you dig deeper into their lives, many of these characteristics are present but well-masked. We were recently made aware of a police officer that was a domestic violence stalker (DV) that not only assaulted his estranged spouse but utilized the state's computer network to run thousands of record checks on women he was interested in, as well as men that had or were in the process of dating his wife. These searches also included celebrities he was enamored with. He was, of course, fired and prosecuted. For those that knew this particular individual, they were in disbelief when his crimes were made public.

- *Manipulative of children.* We will discuss this in greater detail when we talk about the tools and methods used by stalkers, but if children are involved, they often are used as conduits for information. Also a variety of abuse can and does take place.

- *Oftentimes suffering from low self-esteem.* We see this trait exemplified oftentimes in bully's as well as a stalkers. This behavior is commonly present in DV stalkers. The stalker feels inadequate and must take out his frustrations on his spouse or significant other in a variety of ways. This includes everything from belittling that person to physical violence. This frustration can also be visited on his victim's children.

- *Controlling.* It's human nature to want to control our lives to some degree. The stalker, however, wants to control or, in some cases, possess what he or she cannot. Many do not have the requisite skills necessary to logically control not only their lives but the lives of others. For whatever reason they cannot direct and so must dominate. In celebrity stalking cases, the stalker often wants a relationship with the victim but has neither access nor the interpersonal skills to attain that goal. Many bring duct tape, knives, or other weapons on their stalking journeys. This way, if contact does play out, they will be ready to control their targets or, if necessary, fend off those that would deter them from their purpose. Yes, there are other mental issues at play, but control is still a big issue for them. In some form or another, control has been a huge part of all stalking cases we have consulted on or investigated.

- *Prone to reoffend.* Many stalkers either reoffend with the same target, or if some type of intervention transpires, move to another target. Once again, this is not true of all stalkers, but according to a study done on stalking recidivism by Dr. Barry Rosenfeld of Fordham University, about "49% of the offenders reoffended during the follow-up period, 80% of whom reoffended during the first year."[50] He went on to say that the strongest indicator that the stalker would reoffend was the presence of a "Cluster B" personality disorder such as being "antisocial, borderline, and/or narcissistic." Dr. Rosenfeld also noted abuse of drugs made the stalker a greater candidate to reoffend. He indicated that the stalker having a "delusional disorder (e.g., erotomania) was associated with a *lower* risk of offender (sic)."[51] His observations may be true in many scenarios, but we have found it always depends on a variety of factors that need to be threat assessed prior to making that kind of determination. Later we will discuss our fears concerning Erotomanic type delusional disorders.*

- *Willing to travel.* Not all—but enough do for us to note—stalkers will travel to stalk their victims. We have investigated cases where stalkers travel from state to state to pursue their victims. One stalker followed his estranged wife to London from California. A female stalker began stalking her male target in Eastern Europe, moved throughout several other countries, and into the United States. One of our investigators developed a case against a stalker that followed a major female sports figure from country to country. The stalker sent her nude photos of himself and attempted to force his way into her dressing room. He was finally arrested by the FBI and later imprisoned.

In regard to having multiple targets (being a serial stalker), we will give just one example of a stalker we investigated for several years. Working this stalker allowed us to come in contact with a number of his victims. It was uncanny how much they looked alike. Even though their ages were somewhat different, they were all auburn-haired, well-endowed, dark-eyed females. One of the victims was unfortunate enough to have married this stalker. This victim owned her own business. They had met at church. She was a long-time member, and he had just come into contact with the congregation. Unfortunately we do run across stalking that springs forth from a church environment. We will discuss the reasons later on in the book. Once he began stalking and threatening to kill her, she immediately divorced him and obtained a restraining order. She had a hard time believing he had stalked others and that she—a

---

* Another article to review is a paper presented at a 2009 conference by R. B. Harmon, "Anti-stalking Legislation, Recidivism and the Mentally Disordered Stalker" at http://www.AllAcademic.com/meta/p373200_index.html.

hard-nosed, professional woman—had been taken in by such a con man. We believe the stalker talked about his genesis victim (see definition in this chapter) to her, and she contacted that particular woman, who then called us. We asked this business woman to stop by the police department. We took her down to our briefing room and showed her a segment on *America's Most Wanted*. John Walsh had profiled her stalker now ex-husband on that show, and she was seeing it for the first time on our large screen display. Think about it. You are sitting in a darkened training/briefing room of a police department. It is designed to house over one hundred cops, and you are silently watching everything you never wanted to know about the guy you had been married to, and you had no clue. The poor woman left in a daze. We vowed to help her with the current stalking investigation, which was then playing out in an entirely different county. We had the district attorney that handled our particular stalking case contact the prosecuting attorney in this woman's jurisdiction hoping to get a strict felony charging order on the stalker. Unfortunately, the other attorney was not up to speed on stalking, and ended up filing lessor charges. Tragically, this happens far too much of the time.

Just as an aside, our stalker had been profiled on this episode of *America's Most Wanted* which was also billed as a special on the problems that stalkers can present in our society. One of the other cases profiled on that program was the first actual stalking case ever prosecuted under the new California law. Thus it was basically the first in the world, (ours became the second). The crime involved an attractive female in her twenties that lived in an upscale portion of Los Angeles. Her bodybuilder boyfriend experienced what cops refer as "roid" rage. This is when someone who takes steroids to enhance muscle mass has problems controlling the violent side of his or her temperament. In fact the drugs can be a catalyst to acting out violently. The boyfriend was arrested and convicted for felony stalking, (this particular stalker's arrest took place in 1991).

Interestingly enough, in 2004 we began getting calls from victims who had become neighbors of this same subject, because he was now stalking them. In fact, I was subpoenaed to testify as an expert on the case by the Northern California District Attorney's Office that was prosecuting same. I didn't end up going, though, because the defendant pled guilty to several charges stemming from his stalking behavior in that jurisdiction. The successful prosecution in this case can be primarily attributed to all the work the victims did on the case.

This all started after the stalking victims obtained a copy of our first book and followed the segment pertaining to what they should do if they were being stalked. Even though we walked them through some of the details, they did their homework and pushed their case through. Unfortunately, as we will discuss in later chapters, if you are a stalking victim, you may have to be your own advocate. So you see, like we have indicated, most stalkers have multiple targets and apparently just don't learn their lesson. By the way, we have never had a stalker go after more than one target at a time. This stalker, who at the time, was then in his early 40s, was living off and with his wealthy mother at the time he prosecuted his campaign of stalking against the victims that had contacted us.

- *Substance abusers.* Many, though not all, stalkers we encounter have drug problems. They either self-medicate or have an addiction. The ones that use drugs such as methamphetamine, alcohol, crystal meth, and cocaine concern us the most. These types of drugs are often a catalyst for violence. Of course, alcohol has been known for years to exacerbate negative behavior in those leaning towards violence.

  If you are around a person that does "meth" (methamphetamine) or speed, you will see them crash after not sleeping for prolonged periods. They are easily angered, can be extremely violent, and are, at times, incoherent. If they have used the drug for prolonged periods, they may begin showing tooth loss, kidney, liver, or other organ problems, rashes that they scratch to the point of infection, and exhibit a jaundice appearance. We have chased, fought, tasered, and shot these clowns. They often have to be restrained once contacted. Mental health professionals have developed a name for individuals with a chronic methamphetamine habit. They refer to it as "methamphetamine psychosis." Studies on these abusers reveal they have auditory, visual, and tactile hallucinations. Anyone that deals with these knuckleheads has seen them exhibit these maladies. Meth, especially crystal meth (a higher quality of the drug primarily manufactured in drug labs in Mexico) tends to give its user a prolonged high.

Before we get into our typologies of stalkers, you should know that a great deal of research has been done by a variety of folks that are eminent in their specific fields. Their studies are published in various books and journals. That being said, our purpose is to keep it simple. I wasn't encouraged to write these books because I am an academic, but because I was one of those guys that investigated the stalker and put their butts in jail; thus eliminating the threat. Therefore, from time to time, we may refer to one of these specialist's findings, but we are not going to get deeply involved in any of their specific works. The information is out there for anyone who wishes to immerse oneself into the more academic side of stalking. We encourage you to look up published findings by experts (all PhDs) such as J. Reid Meloy, Kris Mohandie, Rosemary Purcell, Michele Pathe, Paul E. Mullen, and Lorraine Sheridan, just to name a few. I have communicated with many of these individuals, some more than others. It is my opinion that these people are both dedicated to their craft as well as to assisting those in need.

There are a variety of published typologies on stalkers. John Lane Jr., MPA and Dr. Michael Zona introduced one if not the first sets of typologies. John Lane Jr. was a lieutenant in charge of the Los Angeles Police Department's Threat Management Unit (TMU). Lane is currently a vice president at Control Risks, an international crisis and resilience consulting firm. Once immersed in the world of threat assessment, Lane saw the need to develop an organization solely designed to assist and teach those involved in stalking issues as well as all those requiring a threat assessment approach as a solution to a variety of issues facing both law enforcement and those managing threats in the workplace. Thus the Association of Threat Assessment Professionals (ATAP) was born. Dr. Zona was a forensic psychiatrist consulting with the TMU. I first met John when we consulted on a stalking special for *America's Most Wanted*. I encountered Mike Zona when we—John and others like Rhonda Saunders—a Los Angeles County Deputy District Attorney and author, who has done a great deal to help change California's stalking law for the better—were working on California's Peace Officer Standards and Training (POST) video and workbook back in 1996.

We feel it cogent to discuss these next four typologies because as indicated they were one of the first, and commonly used by law enforcement for years. Since they were published, a great deal more research has gone into the field of stalker typologies. As is usually the case, more investigation has broadened the adjectival base. In other words, there are a lot more typologies floating around out there.

Dr. Zona's typology consisted of four separate categories. The first category *Simple Obsessional*. "These are cases wherein the victim and the suspect (perpetrator) have some prior knowledge of one another."[52] Many of these stalking cases stemmed from domestic violence or dating relationships, but according to them not all. The next category is *Love Obsessional*. Zona states, "These cases are characterized by the absence of an existing relationship between the perpetrator and the victim."[53] They described this type of stalker as one that tends to go after the media personality. They also advised that an average person can also be the target of this type of stalker. The third category is the *Erotomanic stalker*. Zona says this is when, "The suspect delusionally believes that he/she is loved by the victim."[54] We see this type of stalking transpiring in both the celebrity and non-media related cases. We will discuss later a recent celebrity stalking case in which a young Olympic skater was stalked by an individual who believed he and the skater had a relationship prior to him coming to Los Angeles and trying to kidnap her.

We consulted on what we would classify as an Erotomanic stalking that transpired in a wealthy community. The wealthy, male was relentless in his following and eventual prolonged harassment.

One of the interesting things we have seen both in this case and others we have consulted on similar to this scenario was a situation in which the woman was in an upscale men's store looking at a complete outfit on display. It included a coat, shirt, pants, and shoes. She thought it would look good on her husband, but in this case as in others, she never mentioned her viewing to anyone. Shortly after she had been in the store; the stalker showed up at her front doorstep wearing the exact same outfit she had been admiring.

We have also seen this in other stalking cases in which the target would wear a specific outfit one day and the next be confronted by their stalker wearing the same type of outfit. Obviously, this goes to the continual surveillance aspect of this crime.

Please note this type of reported behavior may fall on deaf ears if the law enforcement entity is not up to speed on this variety of stalker. Regrettably many agencies are not. This creates a great deal of frustration for the victim.

The last part of the typology is *False Victimization Syndrome*. Zona and Lane said that with this syndrome, "Cases develop when an individual constructs an elaborate scenario to falsely support the position that he or she is being stalked."[55] We as did Zona and Lane have found many of the individuals who claim to have been stalked are women, who are trying to restore broken relationships. Some will even damage themselves and claim to have been attacked. We thought we would share a couple of other False Victim scenarios that don't portray a "victim" trying to re-kindle a relationship, that we have encountered you might find interesting.

In 2004, my detective lieutenant called me into his office. He said, "You know, Duck, my nickname, because I was known a crap magnet, and crap rolls down a duck's back. They even nicknamed my partner, Terry Selinske, the damage control officer (DCO).* "That book of yours and being on the tube is creating problems." Of course, the lieutenant was kidding (kind of). He had received a crime report from an individual claiming he was being stalked and had his car damaged in the parking lot of the city's larger malls. The middle-aged man, who lived in a neighboring town, told the uniformed patrol officer taking the crime report to make sure Detective Proctor investigated this crime. He told the officer he had seen me on television and read my book. Keep in mind that writing a self-help book on any subject can be a two-edged sword. Thankfully my other book and hopefully this one will help many people, but the information can tend to fuel delusional individuals as well. I have received phone calls from people upset with me for writing articles and books because their mentally ill loved ones read them and begin quoting them chapter and verse. One individual said that if I were there, she would take the book and shove it...well, you get the picture. I try to explain to them, I just write, "em", I can't control who reads them. We understand it can be very difficult to deal with a person who lives in an alternative world. My wife would be the first to say I fit into that category. Just so there is no misunderstanding, I am not domesticated; I am institutionalized, and my wife is the warden.

---

* These two detectives nicknamed the Duck and the DCO had a very unusual way of handling crime. They even had a book written about them called, of all things, *The Duck and the DCO* by Damion Kane. This is just something the publisher thought the reader might find interesting.

When we read the police report, we had a pretty good idea of what we were dealing with. We contacted the agency where this man lived. They said they had had a few calls for service at that man's residence but nothing out of the ordinary. To debunk this case, we had to go to the man's house. When we got to his middle-class condo, we found pretty much what we expected. The front door of the residence did not have any door handles or locks. They had been removed. Foam covered the front sidelight (side door windows). When we went into his house, the back of his front door had a self-fashioned Rube Goldberg* type locking assembly that he had fabricated himself. The man was an accomplished artist. Much of his work hung on his walls. He claimed he was continually surveilled and stalked and that people were listening to him through his walls. He also claimed he found tracking devices in his car and other pieces of furniture in his house.

We really knew what was happening when we walked into his bedroom and saw aluminum foil covering his windows and portions of the walls. It was then that we asked him what kind of radiation he was trying to protect himself from and what planet he believed sent these "rays?" We then learned he was a ufologist (person who studies and believes in UFOs). He had a website and felt he was being visited. We eventually determined he was being harassed by the neighborhood kids because of his odd behavior. We slowed that down, and I got permission to call his psychiatrist. It just so happened we knew him, not because we went to him, but through dealings we had with him concerning his other patients. When we explained the situation and sent the psychiatrist copies of the photos we had taken. He commented that the man had never been delusional while at his office. He said he would change—you guessed it—his medication the next time he came in. (By the way,

---

* Ruben Garrett Lucius Goldberg was an American cartoonist, sculptor, engineer, and inventor. He would draw incredible machines designed to do simple tasks in an unusual way. Many people copy his designs and build the machines for contests and fun.

when you see people wearing aluminum foil underneath their clothing, please don't have them contact me.)

If you are an investigator charged with working stalking, and you get someone expressing some of the things this poor man did, you still need to look into the case. He or she may be suffering at the hands of another. You may be able to assist like we did.

The second group of people we frequently deal with are those that believe they are being electronically tracked for a variety of reasons. We are not talking about victims that are truly tracked by GPS (another topic we will discuss) but those like the following.

A potential W/V contacted me on my website. Initially her story of being stalked and raped seemed credible. She said she had been stalked for a period of weeks, and just recently had been kidnapped, sexually assaulted, and dumped off. She told us where she lived and the jurisdiction that would handle her case. The next day she contacted us and said she was now being manipulated sexually by her stalker(s). When we inquired as to how that was taking place, she said the stalker(s) had implanted a tracking/stimulus device in her "anus." When activated it caused her to have a sexual response, which somehow she could hear her stalkers comment on. That was when we asked this distraught woman when she had last been arrested for what we refer to in California as a "5150" of the welfare and institutions code. (This is a seventy-two hour commitment for a mental health evaluation.) She said she had recently been released from that commitment. We asked her to seek mental health assistance again.

After doing one radio broadcast, we received a great deal of contact from listeners who believed they were being electronically monitored/stalked by devices implanted in various portions of their bodies. So there are more than just a few people who feel this way. Perhaps, someday in the future, we will all get some type of chip inserted in our arms to allow us to make purchases or even be tracked in case of an emergency. Animals can get such an implant in case they are lost, but we are not aware of any such technology being used on humans. However, we are told the technology could be available in the not-too-distant future.*

Intimate partner violence is defined by the Center for Disease Control and Prevention (CDC) as "physical, sexual, or psychological harm by a current or former partner or spouse. This type of violence can occur among heterosexual or same-sex couples and does not require sexual intimacy."[56] The CDC further defines intimate partner abuse as occurring between two people in a close relationship.)[57] We will be using "intimate partner" as a classifier throughout this book. In most intimate partner relationships we have investigated, sex is transpiring or has transpired, but for this definition there does not have to be a sexual relationship.

Our Primary Stalking Typologies

The following categories are what we refer to as our primary typologies.

The Domestic Violence Stalker (DV)

Domestic violence, which we will refer to as DV or domestic violence stalking (DVS), accounts for the largest groups of stalkers. Domestic violence used to describe violence between a married couple or those cohabiting as married. Domestic violence now includes those in a dating relationship. These can all be referred to as intimate partner scenarios. Some prefer the term intimate partner because as we have said stalking is a world event, and some countries may not refer to certain situations as domestic violence

---

* For further information on false victimization, go to the 2000 article "Stalking: False Claims of Victimization" in the *British Journal of Psychiatry* by M. Path, P. E. Mullen, and R. Purcell. There is also Kris Mohandie, Chris Hatcher, and Douglas Raymond's work, "False Victimization Syndrome in Stalking." This can be found in chapter twelve of *The Psychology of Stalking: Clinical and Forensic Perspectives.*, ed.J.Reid Meloy (San Diego, Calif.: Academic Press, 1998.)

scenarios. I guess we are old-fashioned, so we will stick with DV as one of our stalking typologies. Because my last book was used as a supplementary college text (as hopefully this one will); students should refer to the stalking victim in a domestic violence situation as the victim of an intimate partner crime.

Due to the fact, that most of the victims of stalking are women. A word you will often hear bandied about when talking about violence against women is "femicide." This word first came into English literature about 1801 from England. It means the killing of women. A study compiled by Judith McFarlane, RN, DrPH, FAAN, and others found the frequency of stalking in intimate partner situations where the female was murdered was about 76 percent. Females in the study who were the victims of attempted murder were stalked prior to the event about 85 percent of the time.[58] We have always believed these types of statistics to be very telling.

Throughout the book you will come across this icon whenever we want to discuss a point in a more relaxed fashion. We want to talk to you about why we will not be outlining many media stalking cases. Media stalking is a very small portion of the number of stalking cases worldwide, but they seem to get the greatest attention. This is obviously because of the media personalities being stalked, which would include political figures. By no means should these types of cases have the greatest impact. Even though we don't want to minimize the trauma a celebrity might experience when stalked; in our opinion, stalking takes a greater toll on the average person than those cases that are spread throughout the pages of the tabloids and other media venues. Do we have a problem with the attention media personalities get? Not at all, our outlook is the more attention brought to bear on the issues of stalking the better for everyone, no matter how the word gets out there.

We do occasionally consult for media, television, and print, but we don't normally get involved in the actual handling of these cases. Media personalities have cadres of personnel trying to insulate them from unwanted exposure. This includes specialized security teams who are paid either by the studio or the celebrity to protect them and their families. They usually have publicists and attorneys. These entities act as another layer of protection from unwanted media and other associated exposure. The average person, unless wealthy, has none of these. Wherever the crime of stalking takes place, the investigation is handled by that jurisdiction's law enforcement entity. For example, the recent stalking of Sandra Bullock and now ex-husband Jesse James was handled by the Orange County Sheriff's Department. We were queried on the case, and sent the department a copy of our stalking protocol, but we had nothing more to do with the case. We suggested the sheriffs obtain a search warrant and conduct a search of the stalker's residence. We also suggested doing a background check—including a civil check— and an in-depth threat assessment to ascertain what type of stalker they were dealing with and what her violence quotient would be. In the case of Ms. Bullock's female stalker, we advised the Sheriff's Department to find out if the stalker was trying to protect Bullock because she felt James was not good enough for her or if she was actually enamored with Bullock. Some cities such as Los Angeles, San Diego, Anaheim, New York City, and the city I was a cop in, Westminster,

In regard to media or high profile person's cases, we will get involved, but normally do not on a regular basis because we find that there is too much insulation. In other words we usually like dealing directly with the victim for a variety of reasons. We are also used to having our victims do what we suggest because we have their best interest at heart.

We understand that celebrities oftentimes feel put upon or used by those that try and make contact. However to us, they are another victim that needs intervention. We are perfectly happy leaving their fame up to them.

have specialized details that specifically work stalking and other threats. Of course, LAPD's Threat Management Unit (TMU) handles a lot more celebrity stalking cases than most. The Los Angeles Sheriff's Department also uses a team approach to work these types of cases.

As for being famous, it is not all it is cracked up to be, especially for those of us who could not care less about fame. Recently my mail center called me to pick up my new band saw. I am an amateur wood worker. It used to be one of the things that kept me sane when I worked tons of hours generated by homicides and other violent crimes. When I arrived to pick up the saw, I saw the package truck still parked in front of the mail center's reception area. I asked where my three hundred-pound saw was. The clerk behind the counter said, "Mike, it is still in the truck, and the guy can't seem to get it out." I looked at this poor little Hispanic male hanging on the back of the big rig's trailer struggling with the locking mechanism. I approached and asked what was up. He told me he couldn't get the lock open and would have to go back to the depot to get it removed. I looked at the lock, went back to my truck, got my tools, returned, and fixed his lock. I then asked how he planned on getting this heavy tool out of the truck box without a lift gate. During my time as a cop, I broke my back in two places, had L-5-S-1 fusion surgery, broke both feet, replaced both knees, was run over twice, was rear-ended three times, and had a bunch of other injuries we don't need to get into. So there was no way I was lifting that saw out of the truck, especially when I paid extra for a lift to be on the delivery truck.

The little guy said, "Man, there is no way I can lift this either." I told him to stand by. I drove my 4x4 under the back of his trailer, and I told him to push the saw into the bed. As I was waiting, the guy kept staring at me. He then said, "Hey, ain't you on television?" I have seen you before." "You were just on something." "I watch all of that stuff." When I explained that, yes, I had just been on an E! Hollywood special and I do some television, he then said, "Hey man, I can't read your name on the receipt. Can you give me a card or write down your website?" It had already been over forty minutes since I came to get my tool. All I wanted was my saw. I said, "If you push the saw into my truck, I will give you my website." He obliged, and we were both on our way. So when people ask me if I would ever want to be famous, the answer is, "HELL NO." That being said, I wouldn't mind getting paid like a celebrity.

Obviously when it comes to domestic violence or DV stalking, we have many examples to choose from, but we want to take care of two scenarios with one example. As such, our first example is a DV stalking and a case involving a celebrity. As previously indicated in general we don't see a need to identify victims and or stalkers so we will not use dates, times, or true names. The victim, who has given us permission to discuss her case, in general, has asked us not to for a variety of reasons.

While still working as a homicide detective for the City of Westminster, I was contacted by a female who had also become aware of me via my book, articles, and television appearances. She not live in our city, or our county.

Due to the fact that that the victim had not been able to get the assistance she needed from the law enforcement entity where she currently resided, and because of my expertise, she asked our department to get involved with her case. Once apprised of her situation, I contacted my detective lieutenant who in turn contacted our chief of police for permission to get involved. The chief agreed

For those of you not familiar with Orange County, California, it encompasses many cities. It's not just the city of Anaheim, which houses the Angels baseball team, the Anaheim Ducks, and Disneyland. The county has a diverse population of about 3.5 million people whose incomes range from the poor to the extremely wealthy. The county is known for its large number of Asian and growing Hispanic populations. The city of Westminster even has Little Saigon running down the middle of its borders, with an adjoining city having Little Korea town.

for me to intercede, but I was only allowed to investigate the case and submit it to the jurisdiction where the victim lived for further processing and hopefully a criminal filling.

 Now you might think this was an unusual situation, and we only got involved because the victim was a celebrity. That's not so. Chief Andrew Hall, who retired as Westminster's chief of police a few years ago, developed the concept for the Family Protection Unit (FPU), which was the specialized detail I was also assigned to at the time of this incident. His policy was to help the victims of stalking and domestic violence no matter where they lived. I was loaned out to various agencies, such as the District Attorney's Office, to assist on cases whether the victim was a celebrity, a political figure, or just an average person needing help. (The FPU will be discussed more when we get into the portion of the book that deals with how we investigate stalking.) It was not uncommon for specialized threat assessment units like the Los Angeles Police Department's Threat Management Unit (TMU), the Los Angeles County District Attorney's Target Crimes Division (which is comprised of special prosecution units targeting stalking, criminal threats, crimes committed against peace officers, arson, and child abduction) or the San Diego District Attorney's Stalking Task Force to lend a hand to those in distress. Yes, these units are busy, but they will often get someone involved in the jurisdiction where the crime is taking place to assist the victim and consult when they can. *Contrary to a lot of crap that circulates about law enforcement, those that swear to protect and serve truly believe that is what they are supposed to do.*

Back to our example, I had talked briefly with the victim ("Tawny") on the phone. I asked Tawny to respond to the police department so we could conduct an in-depth threat assessment interview. (We'll detail our step-by-step investigative process further in the book.) When Tawny arrived she brought notes, photos, and other information concerning the case. The following is a synopsis of why we were concerned about this case and felt law enforcement should be looking into it. In some celebrity cases, there are many twists and turns, as you will soon see. You will also see why we are being nondescript about the identities of the individuals involved.

Tawny had been married to a member of an internationally well-known band. Prior to their marriage, she did not have a great deal to do with the other band members because she was working while they were touring. This was apparently also the case once she was married to this individual. They had no children together. In fact she told us her ex ("Charlie") did not want any children. Early on in their marriage, he forced her to obtain an abortion while he slept in the waiting room of the medical facility; telling her basically to get the kid taken care of and not to bother him.

Tawny said that once they got married, their relationship began to change dramatically. She soon found out Charlie had strange and bizarre sexual proclivities. Tawny complained that Charlie was a cross-dresser. He would force her to participate in some of his weird fantasies. When she threatened to leave him, he would handcuff her and hang her on a pole in a closet for a period of time. Tawny also complained about spousal rape. Tawny later discovered Charlie was into bondage pornography. Most disturbing of all, however, was his interest in child pornography, which included very aberrant behavior. Tawny was appalled when she found a large collection of his child pornography. (In regard to the child pornography, Tawny did not locate most of these items until she was estranged from Charlie.) Tawny strongly believed that neighborhood children were at risk because she found photos of these same children that Charlie had taken. She also uncovered digitally enhanced pictures that had been morphed on Charlie's computer. Some of the photos that had been altered (we won't describe how) involved some of shots Charlie had taken of the kids in the residential track they Tawny and Charlie lived in.* Some of these

---

* Morphing is where an individual takes one photo and attaches it to another on a computer. Example: Putting a cat's head on the body of a dog.

morphed photos also showed Tawny's head placed onto a variety of females upper bodies with digitized depictions of nude males from the waist down.   Tawny described a great deal more weird behavior that we don't need to discuss.

Tawny also revealed that Charlie would take any money she made and keep it, telling her he needed to pay bills. Tawny said Charlie admitted to being the victim of sexual assault when he was in his youth. This was in response to one of the standard questions we ask during our threat assessment interviews with DV/intimate partner stalking victims. It is not uncommon, especially when bizarre sexual behavior is present, that the stalker was a victim of early childhood molestation. This kind of abuse is very crucial information to have when dealing with stalking cases where children are involved, as in this one.

Tawny explained that Charlie was violent and, in her mind, "paranoid." On at least one occasion (probably more), he would rush out of their house with a sawed-off shotgun in the dead of night searching for people he felt were out to get him.

Not too long after their marriage, the victim had an affair with another well-known celebrity, which yielded a male child. The child lived with Tawny and her soon-to-be ex, Charlie. While the child was an infant, Charlie paid no attention to him. In fact Charlie wanted Tawny to get rid of him. While Tawny tried to raise her new infant son, she explained she was continually ill. Charlie forced her to live in the front of the house where the water heater was. Charlie lived in his studio, which was located in the back of the home and closed off by a door. Tawny eventually found out why she was so ill. Someone had partially blocked the vent on the water heater, causing her and her child to suffer from repeated exposure to carbon monoxide poisoning. This information was also submitted with the rest of our report to the agency handling the case.

When support money started coming in from the other celebrity, Charlie, who had lost his job in the band, began blackmailing Tawny for a good portion of that support money. Charlie threatened to reveal the identity of the child's father to the newspapers and television if she didn't comply. Because Tawny did not want to cause the celebrity any grief, she put up with the abuse and paid Charlie. Tawny said she couldn't work those first years with her newborn, and there were times she had to count on her family for assistance because Charlie was using drugs a great deal, and he would not help her or the child.

When Tawny was finally able to divorce Charlie, it was a few years later. The male child ("Sammy") had grown into an adolescent. For some reason, Charlie now took an extreme interest in Sammy. (Pedophiles usually have a specific type of child they are interested in. That might be an age group, body type, hair color, look, etc. Whatever the condition, Sammy had reached the age group and fit the profile of the type of child Charlie was interested in.) Tawny admitted she thought Charlie wanted to keep tabs on Sammy because of the money, but she soon realized, especially after the money stopped, that Charlie was interested in Sammy for the wrong reasons.

Tawny also realized that Charlie was now stalking her. He continually called her at all hours of the day and night. He followed her and her son and showed up unannounced at friends' houses. He even went to court with an attorney and, through a continual barrage of court appearances, got her to allow him "supervised" visitation with Sammy, whom Charlie had befriended with gifts, etc. You may be saying, how could she do that? Remember, we were dealing with the victim of an extremely violent and traumatic domestic violence situation. Charlie, now turned stalker, had controlled her for years via sexual, physical, and mental abuse. Once again, she lost control. Those of us that investigate stalking and domestic violence see it time and time again. (We will also discuss how stalkers use children to manipulate their targets, and how, a special program called Keeping Kids Safe (KKS) was developed by members of the Orange County Superior Court, Court Services Group, and it has greatly reduced problems with so-called "supervised visitation.")

The victim was terrified every time she had to leave Sammy with Charlie for a "controlled visit." Sammy was supposed to have a few hours of "supervised" time at a local YMCA, but Tawny found that Sammy was being left alone with Charlie for long periods of time. She would find rub-on tattoos on Sammy's arms and body when she got him back from the visitations. Tawny noticed that Charlie was continually taking photos of her son. On one occasion she found Charlie had placed several of these photos and some that he had apparently removed from her residence on his apartment wall. (Removal of items such as these photos from a target's residence is construed as a process we will refer to later as trophy collection.) They had been meticulously trimmed and arranged in what appeared to her to be an organized pattern on the wall. (This is called a shrine. We have seen shrines with photos, articles, underwear, or other items that belong to a victim. These items act as a continuous reminder to the predator of the person he or she is pursuing. Oftentimes we will locate the shrine in the stalker's bedroom. This allows the stalker to be reminded of the target(s) before bed and upon waking.)

Tawny unsuccessfully attempted to get the court-ordered visitations revoked. She went to the police department in her jurisdiction with her concerns, and got little or no relief. That was when she turned to us. Once we had completed our investigation, which included interviewing witnesses who could corroborate her statements, we wrote a fourteen-page police report and forwarded it to the necessary entities along with all the physical evidence we had obtained. We had evidence to back up a majority of Tawny's complaints, but we are not going to get into what it was. The information, however, was forwarded to the law enforcement agency where she resided. We strongly felt as did our in house FPU prosecutor that the information we had developed would hold up in court. Tawny obtained a copy and, through her attorney, was able to present it in court. We were told the visitation order was removed, and as for Charlie, he is what we in police work refer to as *in the wind* (ITW).

The Acquaintance Stalker (AS)

The acquaintance stalker, as a typology, is pretty much like it sounds. These are male or female individuals one might encounter in the workplace, while out shopping, or in any environment. In these cases, however, the victim actually knows the stalker but does not have a sexual or intimate partner relationship with that person. Whenever we ask about the AS in a class, we always get a surprising number of hands going up. This class of stalker can attach even if the victim and stalker have just gone out for drinks or coffee on occasion. Remember, this still doesn't count as an intimate relationship.

Example of an acquaintance stalker (AS): We were contacted in 2005 by a member of the Omaha Police Department in Nebraska. The woman whom we will refer to as ("Rebecca") was a crime prevention officer. One of her responsibilities was setting up meetings in neighborhoods and giving presentations about being safe, burglary prevention, and working with the landlords of vacant houses, which were not only eyesores but hotbeds for concealing criminal activity. On one such meeting in Rebecca's own neighborhood, she encountered a Vietnam veteran (—whom we will refer to as "Kevin"). Along with being one of her neighbors, Kevin had become heavily involved in the area's neighborhood watch program. Rebecca said, prior to any stalking taking place, she worked with Kevin in the watch program for over ten years. (He eventually became the watch's block captain.) Initially Rebecca didn't think much about their encounters, which all appeared to be what she expected it to be that of a business relationship; but not too long after her divorce did the worm began to turn.

Rebecca began to get repeated calls from Kevin asking for additional one-on-one meetings. He then sent her flowers with a card signed "Mr. A. Nony. Mous." Rebecca, whose intuition was telling her this guy was bad news, felt Kevin had sent the flowers and was later able to verify this. Kevin then began sending Rebecca rambling apology notes, which also created more ill feelings. Rebecca told Kevin specifically that she was not interested in him. This, of course, fell on deaf ears and didn't slow good old Kevin down.

Shortly after Kevin had been told to cease and desist, Rebecca was home cooking dinner, when she heard her front door open. Rebecca thought it was her ex-husband, so she called out to him. When she turned expecting to see her ex, Kevin was standing near the kitchen entrance staring at her. She rushed him out of her house, called the police, and had him arrested for trespassing. The next day she obtained a restraining order, which listed both she and her daughter as the persons to be protected from Kevin. Shortly thereafter Kevin once again called Rebecca at the police department. He left her a message this time telling her he loved her.

The next incident took place when Rebecca was in her driveway talking to a close friend, and Kevin, who had been formally served with the order of protection pulled into her driveway. This caused Rebecca to flee into her residence, secure her door, dial 911, grab her 357 Magnum, and ready herself for what she feared wound be is a forcible entry into her residence. We obtained a copy of Rebecca's 911 call. On the tape Kevin can clearly be heard in the background pounding on her front door and screaming in an enraged, high-pitched wail for her to let him in.

Prior to officers arriving on scene, Rebecca's neighbors came to her aid and confronted Kevin, who by that time was inside Rebecca's covered porch pounding on her inner front door. Rebecca's petite, female friend was punched, choked, and thrown to the ground by Kevin injuring her back. Kevin lay atop this small woman—whom we would later meet when we lectured— and continued to assault her until her husband was able to pull Kevin off of her. The husband and Kevin then struggled until police came on scene (cop speak for arrive). When police arrived Kevin was still pounding on Rebecca's door, glaring into her kitchen window, and screaming. As they approached, Kevin turned towards them and began yelling, "Reverse, I'm the bad guy!" He stretched out his right arm and pointed his right hand towards the officers, forming his black-gloved hand in the shape of a gun. (This guy was so lucky that, in the dim light, the officers kept their wits and didn't blow him out of his socks.) Still very combative he began swinging and kicking at officers. He even tried to remove the deployed Tasers out of their hands. Kevin was Tased and, according to Rebecca, became the first suspect ever to be shot with a Taser in Omaha, Nebraska. (Good for Kevin. We like it when a stalker makes it into the record books on those terms.) One of the arresting officers came to the conclusion that Kevin was "probably one of the most dangerous individuals" he had contacted in the years he had been on the force.

Kevin received a mental health evaluation, did his jail time, and was placed on probation. Information on Kevin indicated he was intelligent, did well in school, and may have had mental issues, although the type and treatment were not indicated to us. Kevin also received medical training, which he was not utilizing at the time of the stalking. At the writing of this book, Rebecca indicated she has not had any further problems with her stalker, even though he still resided in her neighborhood.

At the time of this incident, Nebraska's anti-stalking law only made stalking a misdemeanor, so Kevin got some local jail time and counseling. Our interaction with Rebecca prompted us to conduct a two-day training seminar for Community Oriented Policing Services (COPS), the United States Attorney General's Office, and in conjunction with the Omaha Police Department. Not too long after the training, Rebecca and others promoted a change in Nebraska's stalking law, pushing to make it a felony in certain instances. I was asked to present information to members of the

Nebraska State legislature, which I gladly did to assist Rebecca in her quest to change the law, which she was successful in doing.

Rebecca told us that most people, including herself, would consider her a pretty tough cookie, but the incident with Kevin was the most frightening thing that she had ever experienced in her life. Because of this incident, she has become one of the strongest advocates we have encountered for those individuals who are struggling with the terror of being stalked. We continue to consult regularly on cases she submits to us for review.

The following is another example of an acquaintance stalker. Fortunately this type of case is not that common, but it does occur. This is an example where the stalker himself is a police officer. This is the first one we have come across where the stalker, a recently retired cop, stalked another police officer and his family. You might also be able to classify this particular stalker as a retribution stalker (see definition later in this chapter) as well as an (AS) stalker.

We received an e-mail from a detective who we taught when conducting a seminar back East. He informed us that he and his family are currently being stalked by a medically retired police officer from an adjoining city. The officer apparently has a grudge against the detective because he testified against him on a case involving a dispute between the retired cop and his neighbors. According to the detective, the stalker began following his wife while she was driving. He shows up at the school where both the stalker and the detective's wife pick up their children. (This really can create issues.) The stalker makes his presence known to the victims in a variety of ways. He may even be using his previous law enforcement contacts to develop personal information on the detective and his family.

The detective filed a restraining order against the stalker, but he has violated it numerous times. The stalker was recently arrested for violation of that order as well as stalking; the case is still pending. According to all indications, that the detective has concerning this individual he appears to be mentally unstable, and there are reported instances of domestic violence issues at his home with his spouse. The detective is not only concerned for his and his family's safety but the safety of the stalker's wife as well.

We are currently trying to advise the detective and his wife in the hopes of avoiding the extreme potential for the violence that could easily transpire in this particular situation. From what we are told, we picture a disgruntled and angry man sitting at home and festering with nothing better to do than harass and cause emotional and perhaps physical damage to those he erroneously sees as causing his problems.

The Stranger Stalker (SS)

Stranger stalkers (SS) are at least initially considered the most frightening type of stalker that one encounters simply because the victim/target is hounded by an unknown entity. We said, initially because it has been our experience that on many occasions the SS, when unmasked, oftentimes turns out to be someone the victim knows, either intimately or casually. Of course there are those cases where when the stalker becomes known either through his or her own conscious efforts, or via law enforcement intervention. The victim (or "target") may have never heard of the stalker, or later on find out that it is someone they knew, but never suspected. We have had cases where the stalker went to high school with the victim but never made contact throughout their four years together (at least none the victim was aware of). Then, all of a sudden, he or she begins stalking the victim out of the blue years later. We have investigated and consulted on a variety of SS cases, and each has its own peculiarities.

Many times Stranger stalkers often start their campaigns by leaving cards and letters on a victim's vehicle. One case involved a man that would sit on a copy machine and make copies of his buttocks and genitals in various poses and positions. He then wrote messages to his target and left the pictures on her windshield while she worked in a fairly large strip mall. We surmised that he probably didn't draw any attention to himself by putting these items on her car because, in many mall parking lots, flyers are frequently placed on the cars of the shopping public. Needless to say, his flyers were just a tad different than an advertisement for a cheesier pizza. When the stalker was finally taken into custody, the victim had no clue who he was. The stalker had seen her at work and wanted to get to know her better. Obviously he was socially inept and lacked the necessary skills to make proper contact, which he hoped would then evolve into some kind of a relationship.

One type of SS scenario we occasionally run across is quite scary for the victim but difficult for him or her to prove to law enforcement. When called out to the victim's house, law enforcement might even think the victim needs to see a psychiatrist. This is when the stalker actually enters the victim's residence and begins leaving things behind that do not belong to the victim. Oftentimes there are no signs of forced entry which causes more concern for the victim. It also creates issues for the officers responding to the call. An example of this type of stalking would be if a woman goes through her underwear drawer and finds new panties she did not buy and which are at least one size too large for her. We had one female complain she found some of her undergarments with several "2–3 millimeter holes punched into the crotch." Other victims have found dolls or pictures from "some five-and-dime" they had never seen before hanging on their walls.

Of course, false reporting and false victimization syndrome may play a role in some of these cases but not all. Let us remind you that stalkers can be extremely adept at causing grief and terror in the minds of their victims.

I am currently assisting a Utah Police Department, which is located near Provo. (Just a point of information, we have been assisting a few agencies in Utah of late.) The detective in charge of the stalking cases has been using our stalking protocol to develop his cases with, according to him, great success. (By the way, whenever law enforcement contacts us to consult on a case, we don't charge. We want them to solve the case and help the victim.) Both of these cases are stranger stalkers. Both of the suspects are male. Yes, we can have females in this role, but it has not been a reoccurring theme, at least not in our experience.

The first case began in April and May of 2006. Our victim's family had moved into the area the year prior. The victim, ("Maya") was a young girl in her late teens or early twenties. She was a high school graduate who worked close to her home and still resided with her parents. When the stalking started, Maya was not dating anyone specific, and there was nothing else remarkable about her. During the first part of 2006, someone (they believe him to be the stalker) entered into the basement of Maya's residence and looked around. His clumsiness drew attention to his presence causing him to split. Obviously, this is not a good thing because now you have a "hot prowl entry" into the residence. (That's when a suspect enters a victim's house while the victim is inside. It's a scary and dangerous event.) In April and May, the stalker was actually first observed lurking at the edge of the property. He wore all dark clothing including a hooded sweatshirt. (That seems to be typical predator type attire.) He was seen for about six weeks, usually between 0200 hours to about 0500 hours. (For you civilians, that is between 2 and 5 a.m.)

Once Maya's father went after the stalker, they did not see or hear from him for about two years. Stalkers will deviate from their targets for a variety of reasons. They move out of the area, become sick or injured, become incarcerated on non-related charges, die, or begin stalking another target. In early 2008, Maya began seriously dating her boyfriend ("George"). A few months after George and Maya began dating, they decided to become engaged. This became well-known throughout the areas they frequented.

In January of 2009, the stalker again entered Maya's home. He took various articles of underwear from her closet and arranged them on her bed. (When I profiled this stalker, I advised the detective in charge that he probably laid out the panties to photograph them as a trophy.) Later in 2009 the suspect left a note on Maya's windshield while she was filling up at a local gas station. The stalker left the note just as Maya went into the cashier's office to purchase the gas. The stalker left another note when she was sleeping at a local recreation spot in a trailer. Maya found the note after being awakened by the stalker tapping loudly on the camper where she was sleeping. The stalker also called to her as he was tapping. He placed another note on the outside of her car when she was at work. The note indicated that the stalker now knew where she lived and now where she worked.

Maya's latest encounter with the stalker was when she and George were in a Cineplex in a neighboring town. The stalker sat in from of them and turned to stare directly at her. He then followed them out of the theater. Maya could now describe the stalker as a thin, 6'2" to 6'4", dark, olive-skinned male with short, black hair, an emo look, and a deep voice.* Maya said she had no idea who the stalker was or why he was stalking her and now George.

I explained to the handling detective that George and Maya's engagement may have triggered a resurgence in the stalking events. To date, the stalker has not made any direct threats toward Maya or George, but we cautioned that now George is in the mix, he could be seen as not only a suitor, but as direct competition to the stalker's perceived relationship with Maya. That could be a safety issue for George.

---

* Depending on whose definition you use, the term "emo" basically came from emotive hard rock/punk bands in the 80s, which often utilized confessional lyrics or songs about emotional life experiences. Kids who are moody and emotional, have sideswept bangs, and wear dark and what some would consider effeminate clothing are referred to as emo. Some may also wear dark eye shadow and other makeup.

The second stranger stalking from this agency involved a thirty-something, very attractive bodybuilder ("Kim"). The stalking began one evening in late 2009 when Kim heard noises coming from the area of her front porch. The subject then knocked on the front door. Kim had installed video cameras around the perimeter of her residence, and the one that looked onto her front porch showed a male dressed all in black with, you guessed it, a dark hoodie covering his head and face. She did not recognize the person at the door and made the correct decision not to open it. This same individual left and returned two more times that night. Kim became very upset and asked a male friend to stay overnight with her.

The next morning, shortly after her friend left, the same individual attempted to have Kim open her front door. Kim, who is used to a variety of men trying to make contact with her for dates, went to a gym she frequents to work out. When she came out to her car after the workout, she found a note on her windshield.

WOW	I'M	BE
! YOU	SHY,	HURT
ARE	BUT I	IF
SO	WAN	YOU
BEAU	T TO	STAY
TIFUL	MEET	WITH
! I	YOU	HIM
LOVE	FACE	...
THAT	TO	
YOU	FACE.	
STAY	DUMP	
IN	THE	
SHAP	JOCK.	
E.	HE'S	
DON'	A	
T BE	LOSE	
FRIG	R	
HTEN	AND	
ED OF	YOU	
ME.	WILL	

First note left on victim's car.

YOU	ON	DOES	LEAV
ARE	THE	N'T	E HIM
THE	MOST	DESE	NOW!
MOST	MEM	RVE	!! I
BEAU	ORAB	YOU.	DON'
TIFUL	LE	AND	T
WOM	EVEN	HE	MEA
AN I	ING	ISN'T	N TO
HAVE	OF	GOIN	FRIG
EVER	YOUR	G TO	HTEN
SEEN.	LIFE.	TREA	YOU.
I	I	T	I JUST
WOU	KNO	YOU	WAN
LD BE	W	HOW	T TO
HONE	THE	YOU	WAR
RED	GUY	DESE	N
TO	YOU	RVE	YOU
TAKE	ARE	TO BE	...
YOU	SEEIN	TREA	
OUT	G. HE	TED.	

Note left on victim's car after incident at her home with stalker.

The note, which was computer-generated, is included in the book. The note clearly indicated he was the subject who had been knocking on her door. It also indicated he wanted to date her and that individuals she was currently dating were not good for her.

Again, due to her concerns, Kim had a friend stay with her overnight. Once the friend left Kim got a call from her stalker. He told her he was watching her and knew the male friend was no longer with her. Kim's friend brought another big bodybuilder to assist him in tracking down the stalker, but once they both left, the stalker made another call. This call was a threat. He told Kim not to have her two associates stay with her, or someone was going to get injured. The next night the two males saw the stalker hiding near the front driveway of Kim's house and gave chase. The stalker apparently was like a gazelle, running through backyards, clearing fences, and chiding the two bodybuilders for not being able to keep up.

Later in the week, the stalker tore out flowers from Kim's garden and placed them on her porch. He also moved a chest next to her window so he could look in on her. The detective in charge on this case did an excellent job profiling the stalker and developing a threat assessment profile on this idiot. This is one thing we teach via our protocol. It can greatly assist the investigator in narrowing the search criteria for the stalker. (We will discuss this technique in the chapter dealing with how we investigate the stalker.)

After reviewing the detective's case file, we advised him that we believed the suspect was from or lived in the neighborhood. He was able to clear fences and moves around at night too well not to be. We also felt he was a potential threat to Kim's friends. We believed he was socially inept and could well have a shrine or photos of Kim. If he had a computer, it would probably have some type of diary or log on her and her activities. We felt this was not the first peeping scenario he was involved in. We were concerned he was in the developmental stages of a rape fantasy (rape ideations) and was sitting in his home or, worse yet, outside Kim's home festering. His next step could easily be entry into Kim's residence and then a violent sexual assault.

Since our first profile of the stalker, he has in fact entered Kim's house when she was not home, but he fled as she arrived. He has also come up to her closed garage door. (She was on the other side with a loaded handgun.) He fled prior to getting in. Even though law enforcement is very aware of the stalker, and they have a very quick response time, the stalker is still able to evaporate before they arrive. This adds more credence to the theory he's a resident in Kim's neighborhood.

As of the writing of this book, the detective in charge of the case contacted us and advised that he had run a record check on some of the phone calls that the victim had received. Although he wasn't able to get a suspect phone number, he was able to find out that when the suspect had called the victim and told her about what she was doing, he was doing same via a "land line." This means that the caller was not using a cell phone but a hard wired phone while talking to her. This also added credence to the fact that the suspect lived in the neighborhood and was watching her from nearby while he made some of his calls. Another piece added to the puzzle. Hopefully, it will just be a few more before the puzzle becomes complete.

While teaching in Utah, the handling detective took us out to the location where the stalking had been transpiring. We would love to do this on all the cases we consult on because actually viewing the area greatly enhances our evaluation process. Oftentimes we can go on Google Earth and get an idea of the area, but there is nothing better for an old detective dog than actually walking the area and sniffing the air where the stalker has been applying his or her craft.

Other Stalking Typology Subsets

Over the years we have discovered stalking typology subsets. These are other classifiers that can and sometimes do give us a little tighter fit on the type of stalker we are dealing with while still remaining under the umbrella of the big three: domestic violence/intimate partner, acquaintance, or stranger stalkers. Some of these subsets can overlap with the primary types. We do have to admit that a lot of unusual ideas do creep into our noggin whilst sitting in a quiet office hammering out book chapters one by one. (*Well, sometimes the office is quiet. I have too many grandkids and a miniature wirehaired Doxie, which is always trying to get on my lap, continually interrupting that calm.*) Is what we write up to interpretation? Absolutely. Remember what we said, we don't know everything about the stalking phenomenon. We encourage our readers to go online, type in "stalking typologies," and see what information comes up. Academic researchers in the field have many typologies to which they have assigned their names. We only want to throw out ideas and systems that have worked over the years for us and many of our colleagues and pupils. So these are ours, and those are theirs, and that is just fine. Don't get us wrong. We like some of the adjectives others in the field have come up with, but variety is what keeps things from becoming boring.

The other primary reason we have developed these other subsets is because it helps those we educate put a typology or descriptor to a particular stalking scenario. So when A is describing the type of stalker he or she is involved with to B all they have to say is that it is this type or that type of stalker to give that individual a better picture on the stalker they are discussing.

Triangle Stalker (TS)

When we describe triangle stalking, and those that perpetrate this type of stalking as being a triangle stalker, you might be saying to yourself, "Man, this simple guy has gone over the deep end." Well, not really. We want you to visualize a lot of what you are reading about. We know the minute you read the word "triangle," you immediately saw, what?

Yeah, that's right. A triangle, probably an equilateral one, popped into your mind. Maybe it was red, green, or blue. Some of you more mathematically oriented people may have seen an isosceles, right angle, or obtuse. For our purposes, and especially because we sucked in geometry, we will be using the good old equilateral triangle.

Triangle stalking occurs in DV situations. It is starting to appear in some celebrity cases as well. (For example, it happened in the Catherine Zeta-Jones and Michael Douglas stalking scenario.) When that stalking case hit the newspapers and television news channels, we received calls from the networks asking for our observations. Many in the media, at least initially, made comments like, "Jones is so gorgeous, I would stalk her too." What they didn't realize was that the female stalker in this case was only going after Jones to eliminate her from the picture. Her primary target was Michael Douglas. The same is true for the Sandra Bullock and Jesse James stalking episode, which we previously alluded to, took place in Orange County, California. The female stalker was after Bullock, so she felt she had to eliminate James from the equation so she could get to Sandra. She tried to do this by trying to run Jesse over with her Mercedes. Obviously, in each of these stalking scenarios, the suspect felt they had some kind of connection with the intended victim.

One example of a DV situation where triangle stalking became evident was a case we caught from a Crimes Against Persons (CAP) detective. He had an assault case he felt may have been stalking. A subsequent investigation revealed that a couple that lived in another county had been in a relationship that turned toxic. Especially, after the male in that relationship began assaulting the female. This caused the female in that relationship to begin dating a person from her workplace that lived in our city. When the estranged abusive male found out about this new boyfriend, he began following the other male. The stalker, who was wealthy had the time and means to conduct his stalking campaign because he only worked when he wanted to.

The male, now turned stalker, began a campaign of sending threatening and harassing letters to the male victim. He also stole his mail, which included his utility bills and paychecks for some consulting work he had done. The stalker attempted to get the male victim's power and other utilities turned off, and he sent an application to North American Boy Love Association (NAMBLA) in the victim's name. The stalker paid for gay magazine publications and had them sent in the victim's name to his place of business, which was a major government contractor where the victim possessed a high-level security clearance. The stalker then got a hold of the victim's work e-mail and began sending homosexual pornography and other sexually explicit material to this site that was monitored by his workplace risk management/security detail. The stalker took pictures of the outside of the victim's residence and his car, and he surveilled the victim's home throughout the day. He also placed an ad in a local *Penny Saver* stating that the victim's house was for sale, and he posted a date for both an open house and a garage sale. He even went as far as to contact a Realtor and posed as the victim in an attempt to get the victim's house listed. The last straw was when the stalker followed the victim and the stalker's estranged girlfriend to the victim's home. He forced his way into the victim's residence and chased him into his backyard as the female slipped out the front door to freedom. The stalker, a large, muscular man in his late forties, then beat the victim severely and he threatened to kill him if he didn't stay away from his once girlfriend.

Our investigation showed that our millionaire stalker had recently lost his mother. Apparently she was his rock and assisted him with many of his problems, even though he was closing in on fifty. The female, who left him after several years together, had taken over the responsibilities his mother used to help with, and the suspect could not handle losing her as well. We will return to this case when discussing why search warrants are such a critical aspect of stalking investigations.

We consulted on a triangle stalking case that involved a same-sex relationship. The stalker both threatened and beat the victim, who obtained a restraining order. The victim later dropped the order, however, in the hopes of befriending the stalker. (We see this all too often. In a variety of stalking cases, the victim feels sorry for the stalker, removes the order, and the stalking begins anew.)

When the victim got another live-in boyfriend, the stalker began dropping off gifts and letters and threatening the victim's new boyfriend. This caused the victim to obtain another order. This time, after reading my book, he prosecuted the stalker on each violation of the order. This victim also started receiving unsolicited newspapers and other items in the mail, which the stalker had somehow signed him up for. He also believed the stalker loaded child pornography on his computer, which caused an FBI investigation to be initiated. He was unable to prove how the stalker accomplished that feat.

For our last example we thought of this one that could very easily escalate into a TS scenario. We recently conducted training in southern California where we were contacted by a parole agent after we discussed this issue of parole and probation officers being stalked by their charges. She advised that there was a specific female inmate that, in her opinion, was obviously enamored with a male correctional officer (CO) that was married and had children. The CO had not exhibited any signs of favoring or coming on to this particular inmate. The inmate, whose outward appearance and conduct was that of being "sweet and nice" had made it clear to her fellow inmates to stay clear of this particular CO because he was hers. Unfortunately when the parole agent voiced her concerns about this inmate representing a potential threat, she was basically blown off by her supervisors, who thought this particular inmate's feelings toward the CO in question were funny or cute. (This kind of response can easily be corrected via training.)

This particular female inmate was paroled, stayed out of custody for a short period of time, and then returned back to the same facility she had recently been housed in due to another parole violation. Interestingly enough, when this inmate was put back into the main population, she was sporting a new tattoo across her chest. The tat was the name of the correctional officer she was fixated on. Once again, our very concerned parole agent voiced her concerns to staff. They again told her they didn't see a problem. (We did not ask the complaining parole agent how long between our female inmate's parole violations. We would guess it was probably not too long after she got out of custody. It was probably just enough time to get herself tatted up, violate, and get right back to her target, in this case the unsuspecting CO.)

When she asked us if she was blowing things out of proportion, our response was absolutely not. We advised her that we felt this was definitely a threat issue, and we were concerned that the CO's family could be at risk, primarily the wife. Why? There was a good likelihood the inmate saw the CO's wife as an obstacle to her perceived relationship. We thought about how all those that had dismissed the concerns of our wise parole agent would feel if the obsessed female inmate decided to show up at the CO's residence and do his wife or other family members harm. We told the parole officer that had just completed our training that this could very easily turn into a triangle stalking if there was no intervention.

Predator Stalker (PS)

You may be scratching your head and thinking, "Well, aren't all stalkers predatory, at least to some extent?" Yes and no. Remember we said not all stalkers threaten, but their actions can be construed by their victims as threatening due to rude, annoying, or bizarre behavior. Thus, in the victims' minds, they are predatory. This subset, however, deals with individuals that stalk their victims prior to inflicting violence. An excellent example of this would be a serial killer like Dennis Rader. Rader was the BTK (bind, torture, kill) killer, and he stalked most of his victims prior to violating and killing them. (For anyone who does not know much about this case, Rader lived in Kansas, and had a degree in criminal justice. He had air force military training, worked as a supervisor for a residential alarm company, was the president of his church council, and was involved in Boy Scouts. At the time of his arrest in Park City, Kansas, for killing ten people, he was a supervisor for the city's Compliance Department.) Obviously not all serial killers are like Rader. Also not all serial killers stalk their victims, but enough do to make an impression.

Another example would be that of the sexual predators, which includes pedophiles. These individuals have been known to follow, document, and plan their attacks prior to predation. In regard to the actual legal criminal definition of stalking, when these individuals conduct surveillance and documentation,

We consulted on a stalker/pedophile that kept logs on how much he wanted to have sex with a young neighborhood child but wasn't sure if he could kill him afterwards or not. He wrote that he definitely would have sex with him no matter what.

they tend to leave out one critical facet of stalking. They do not make contact until they perpetrate their violence on their intended targets. However, we think all would agree these victims are in fact being "stalked." Under our definition of stalking, if the targets do not know they are being followed or harassed, the suspects cannot legally be arrested for stalking. Why? Because there is no fear or emotional distress attached if no contact is generated. We would love to see stalking laws amended in this fashion. If through investigation it is revealed the person in question is stalking another with the intent of predation (say a pedophile who follows a potential target and then logs how he is going to sexually assault and kill that child), that person can be charged with stalking. So far, no such luck for those seeking to pass this type of legislation.

However, a California law enacted on January 1, 2009 appears to be a step in the right direction. The Surrogate Stalker Act makes it a misdemeanor to engage in surrogate stalking. In legal terms, this includes publishing photos, physical descriptions, and/or locations of children with the intent that another person would use this information to commit a crime against a child. The law was in response to the actions of a specific self-proclaimed pedophile who was researching places children congregated and posted descriptions of these children on his website.[*]

While in this section on pedophiles as predators, we thought we would introduce the reader to a fairly new security device designed for a child's safety when out and about. It is called the "i safe backpack." This backpack has an easily activated siren and strobe light built into the backpack. Once a child feels threatened, they can activate the device, in the hopes of both scary the potential attacker away as well as summoning help. The company has larger backpacks and other bags designed for high schoolers and above. For more info go to isafebags.com. If you like it you might want to get it. If not that is fine too, we are only bringing it to your attention.

---

[*] For more information on this act, go to: https://www.govbuddy.com/directory/press/CA/assemblyman-smyths-surrogate-stalker-act-signed-by-governor/11375/.

As an example of this type of behavior, the mother of a potential victim asked us to consult on a major case. The case took place in another Orange County community, and the pedophile, who was in custody for a psych evaluation at a state institution, was finally arrested on unrelated criminal charges to this case and successfully prosecuted. The mother of the victim contacted us to ascertain why the district attorney could not file stalking charges against the predator. The suspect had been following her child and began ledgering about wanting to have sex with him. Then he wrote about deciding if he could kill the child after having sex with him so as not to be identified. The child predator was so emboldened that he sent the woman letters from the psychiatric ward discussing his feelings about her son and chiding her for trying to get a law passed concerning his stalking behavior. In one of those letters he wrote, "I can fantasize all I want about (your son), and I do...I fantasize about (your son) every day, and there is not a darn thing you can do about it." At the end of the letter, the stalker/pedophile wrote, "Tell (your son) I said, hi."

Not having such a law is really too bad because those of us in law enforcement that have and continue to investigate predators have encountered these types of criminals. They follow, fantasize, and write about how they are going to molest, rape, and/or murder. Sometimes we are lucky and can find another crime to charge them with. This at least would get these individuals off the streets for a while, but there are those times when we come up empty-handed.

With that in mind, we should take this brief opportunity to discuss another aspect of stalking law. In California, People v. Norman, 89 Cal. Rptr.2d 806 (Cal. Ct. App. 1999), the appeals court found that, under the stalking statute, the victim's fear did not have to be contemporaneous (existing or happening at the same time) with the stalker expressing his threats and harassment. In this case, the stalker was fixated on a major motion picture producer. That producer was out of the country filming. When he found out what the stalker had done and was planning on doing to him, he exhibited a great deal of fear and anxiety. He enhanced his security profile and did other things to ensure he and his family was safe. The stalker, who had a violent criminal past, was later convicted and sentenced under California's three strikes law to twenty-five years to life. Once again, Los Angeles County Deputy District Attorney Rhonda Saunders made stalking case law as the prosecutor on this particular celebrity case.

The following is a shocking case in which a sexual predator/pedophile was also clearly a stalker. In the summer of 2010, I received a disturbing e-mail on my website from a woman who had just read my first book. She related a situation that had taken place in 2007 to her then-adolescent son. We include this example not as something that is sensational (obviously we are not about that) but as both a clear example and a warning to all parents reading this book. As usual we will not be using names or locations where these acts occurred.

The woman ("Greta") indicated that she was a highly trained and well-educated professional. When her child was old enough, she enrolled him in a well-known youth organization. Things were fine for about a year until he wanted to move to another branch of this same organization. That's when he came in contact with a pedophile. Not long after her son joined the new branch, things began to happen. Greta said she had been suspicious of the pedophile shortly after her son's move. She didn't like the man's behavior with the boys and some of things he did and was reported to have done. The day the forcible assault took place on her son, he had been working on an organizational project where the pedophile was in charge.

It took her traumatized child a few days to report the incident, which is completely not an uncommon situation. She immediately contacted the head of the organization with the allegation and was advised not to contact the police. She was told they would do their own investigation, and then if they felt it necessary, law enforcement would be notified. She advised them that was not how it was going to work, and contacted the local law enforcement agency. Once that happened the organization closed ranks apparently to try and protect themselves and their reputation. (Unfortunately we see this behavior expressed by organizations all too often.) Greta told us that according to the local law enforcement agency, certain high-ranking members of this group went so far as to alert the pedophile about what was going on. Almost immediately after she contacted the person in charge, someone (she cannot say for sure who) contacted child protective services (CPS) and filled out a child abuse recognition and reporting report (CARR). This form stated that both she and her husband had been molesting their boy. It said their son should be taken away from them and placed in a foster home. According to Greta the report was completely unfounded and dismissed once the CPS worker contacted law enforcement. (Be aware that once a CARR is filed, CPS has to investigate, and we completely agree with that policy.)

Shortly after law enforcement was involved, the boy decided to keep a tape recorder with him just in case he was contacted by the pedophile. He was contacted, and on tape the pedophile admitted to wanting to take nude photos of him to post on the Internet. Law enforcement obtained a search warrant, and after searching his computer and camera gear (he apparently took numerous photos of young boys), they reportedly obtained a great deal of damning evidence. The stalker was arrested, and a restraining order was placed on him prohibiting any contact with the victim or his family. Unfortunately not too long after pedophile's arrest, the young boy began getting blamed for the pedophile's arrest by other youths and parents in the organization. He was bullied in school and referred to as being "gay" along with other nicknames. The boy became depressed, very reclusive, and afraid to venture out of his own home. According to Greta, he was also wrongfully forced to leave the youth organization.

Incredibly the pedophile-turned-stalker began showing up at the boy's school, shopping malls where he and his family went, and would park in front of the victim's house. According to Greta, he regularly parked there, staring and making faces toward the house. Needless to say this type of behavior terrorized both the young boy and his parents. Greta said she would photograph the pedophile in the hopes of scaring him off. Greta contacted the police, who submitted all these instances of contact to the district attorney's office for processing and stalking charges. Those charges never came. According to Greta the stalker/pedophile probably violated the restraining order at least sixty times over the course of their ordeal. She also explained that on one occasion, someone dropped off a box with her son's name written on it at their home. The box contained a project the boy had been working on when he was still associated with the youth organization. It had been in the sole possession of the pedophile.

During another incident, the pedophile used a sixteen-year-old youth to call the victim and make statements about how they were going to be killed and die like "Jews." The pedophile could be heard laughing in the background. More than likely the sixteen-year-old had been coached by the stalker. We have experienced this type of stalking behavior in other cases. Greta said the stalker admitted to law enforcement that he had been with the youth and was laughing when the boy made the call to the victim's residence.

The pedophile was eventually sentenced to five years supervised probation. Once he was sentenced, he continued to stalk. Every time he violated the restraining order, probation was advised. The family notified the district attorney, but —for whatever reason no additional charges were filed. He even stalked when a GPS monitoring device was attached to one of his ankles. When Greta complained to probation, they would again verify the violation and submitted their findings to the district attorney.

The pedophile was not taken into custody again until 2009. He was found to have molested another child. Oh, by the way according to Greta from what probation told her, the pedophile also violated probation by using the city's public library to access child pornography, and then he was seen contacting young children in the same library. When he was arrested for the second time, the police found new compromising photos he had taken of young children. According to Greta, the probation department was vague as to exactly what they had found, but told her the photos were "proof" of new molestations. Amazingly the pedophile only received two years in state prison on his second conviction.

We verified that the pedophile in question is listed on the pedophile registry in the state where this took place. We also located several newspaper articles on his arrest and conviction. Greta wanted to let us know she felt the police and the probation officers cared and did their jobs. However, she felt the prosecution was not helpful at all. She also advised me that she related this story to us in the hopes that we along with those that we work with might strive to get a law that prosecutes pedophiles for stalking once they have have been found to be conducting this type of surveillance and documentation, even if they do not actually make contact with their targets. Obviously, in this case, we believe there is no doubt a campaign of stalking took place.

Third-Party Stalker (TPS)

Although we do not come across this type of behavior too often, there are those stalkers who have used associates to assist in stalking their targets. This is not the same as a viable threat being transmitted by a person other than the primary stalker. (Remember, in that case, Johan is stalking Mable. He tells a mutual friend that he hates Mable, and is going to wait until she is asleep, enter her house, and slit her throat. Obviously, this would be a direct threat that has been transmitted by the mutual friend to

Mable. It is a threat none the less even though Johan did not speak the threat directly to Mable.)

Third-party stalking actually involves "a" or in some cases more than one co-conspirator who is actively involved in the stalking of another. For example, we had a self-employed female Asian who was being stalked by her domestic/ intimate partner. He had abused her for years and threatened to kill her and her children if she did not get back with him and do a variety of things, which she could no longer tolerate. During the course of this abusive relationship, the estranged husband-turned-stalker would commit spousal rape four to five times a week. He would forcibly sodomize her, causing her severe pain. He would tell her to stop crying that she needed to be hurt. He said she "needed to be taught a lesson" for defying his wishes. When she attempted to refuse his assaultive behavior, he would threaten to wake up and injure their sleeping child. (We will discuss this type of behavior more in the chapter dealing with how we investigate stalkers.)

After she was finally able to leave the stalker, she began experiencing a series of expensive property damage incidents. Many of these crimes involved damage to her car while it was in a commercial parking lot. We decided to set up a video camera directed toward her vehicle while it sat in the parking lot during her nightly work period. The tape revealed a young Asian male carving up her tires and digging his cutting tool into the rear quarter panels of her vehicle. Once the suspect was taken into custody, he admitted to being paid by the primary stalker to damage the victim's car. He was also paid to make annoying and threatening calls to her residence throughout the night. The stalker was arrested and convicted for felony stalking, and his apprentice was charged and convicted on felony vandalism and felony conspiracy to commit.

In March 2009, the state of New Jersey enacted AB 1563. This new stalking legislation expanded the definition of "course of conduct" to include actions directly, indirectly, or through a third party that would cause a reasonable person to fear for his or her safety or the safety of a third person or would cause a victim emotional distress. The addendum also details additional prohibited behavior such as, "surveillance and monitoring, which includes the use of Global Positioning Systems (GPS)." It also prohibits the making of "indirect threats, interfering with a person's property, and actions committed by a third party."[59]

Through our website, we have encountered complaints about what has been described as "gang stalking." There are even some websites with information concerning this "crime." Unfortunately many of these complaints we have talked to have turned out to be conspiracy theorists or delusional. Others, however, claim that the stalking started with one individual and spread to the stalker's friends and/or associates. These cases have grown to where they believe a series of individuals are currently stalking them in shifts.

The problem we have is that we are not privy to all sides of the reported incidents and really have no way to prove if the individuals contacting us about this type of stalking are being truthful. Unless we are contacted by the assigned detective to the case (if any) and invited into their investigation, we are not privy to the entire set of facts generated in a specific case. To date, neither we nor any of our associates in this field have experienced the investigation or prosecution of this type of case. That does not mean it could not take place, at least on occasion. That being said, none of the literature we have reviewed or anything we have heard or otherwise experienced with stalking leads us in that direction. As we have indicated, we do understand there are instances of third-party stalking where one or more individuals are directed to assist. Perhaps we are discussing a semantics issue and could all be on the same page just with slightly different word usage. We would welcome a law enforcement entity contacting us and sharing a case that incorporates a gang stalking scenario. Unfortunately, until that takes place, this is where our exposure to this reported type of criminal activity takes us.

Recently, we had been contacted by investigators attending one of classes that have told us that they have had family members join into a series of planned stalking events targeting one individual. The way it was described to me was that it was almost like a tag-team wrestling match. Where one family member would follow, harass, and threaten the individual say from nine to five then another would take the swing shift, and yet another graveyards.

Of course, there is always a caveat to most everything. We suppose one could consider what is happening in the world of cyberbullying a form of gang stalking. As we will discuss in our section on cyberbullying, a victim can be stalked by individual(s) who want to physically hurt or emotionally damage a specific target via a variety of means. Most often at least initially this includes a digital component. There have been several reported cases where the cyberbully teams up with friends or associates to either assault, have them convey these damaging threats, or enjoin in a type of character assassination. Therefore, you do have a group of people actually ganging up on a target for the purpose of bullying, and in the process, they are committing the crime of stalking.

Another interesting, (Web victim case), we received via our website a request for advice from an American female who was working on a large cruise ship. She was being stalked by an Indian male. (From India, he was not an American Indian.) The stalker, who also worked aboard her ship, sent a multitude of e-mails professing his love, wrote upsetting graffiti on the equipment she utilized in her job, sent love letters, and left other messages on her cabin door. This all occurred after they had a relationship. There was one time the stalker assaulted the victim's roommate, and then he sat on top of the victim, forcing her to listen to his ramblings about his "sick" love for her.

The stalker was finally removed from her ship but was not fired. He then began sending his buddies to the victim as a tactic designed to make her go back to him. The victim said she now basically felt she was being stalked and harassed by them in place of her original stalker. This victim was also extremely upset with ship command and the fact nothing had been done under the company's sexual harassment policy. This is not to mention that most of the security personnel, including the "brass," were Indian. (As a point of information, we do get complaints from females being stalked in India. We try to help, but unfortunately Indian laws and law enforcement are way behind the times when it comes to domestic and intimate partner relationships. We will touch on this topic once again when we discuss how culture plays a role in stalking.) Even though her stalker is on another ship, he still calls and harasses her ship to ship. We don't know about you, but that would be extremely troubling. This woman has to live on a floating city with her stalker for at least a two-to three month cruise assignment.

Along the lines of crime aboard cruise ships, we should note, that according to research revealed by an Anderson Cooper 360 investigation aired in July of 2012, children and other passengers on cruise ships are at risk of being attacked either by predators that come on the ship as passengers or by crew members themselves. One of the consultants interviewed advised that this is not a rare occurrence, and that as many as eighty-five percent or even more of the cruise ships sailing have one or more of these types of individuals on board.* *Many of us love to cruise, but if this type of behavior, stalking and sexual assault is continuing to transpire it needs to be immediately addressed by cruise line executives with a mindset of aggressive prohibition and strict prosecution.*

Retribution Stalker (RS)

The retribution or revenge stalker is just that. It is a person who follows and harasses another for the purpose of retribution (to get even). They are not trying to control the victim, or pursue them out of lust, nor because they are fixated.

---

* Refer to www.cruiselawnews.com › Sexual Assault of Minors There are several other websites that discuss this type of crime transpiring on cruise lines.

Types of Stalkers

Their goal is to cause damage to their target's reputation, property, or physical being. We see many of these stalkers raising their ugly heads in workplace scenarios. Oftentimes when a contentious worker has been laid off or removed from his or her job, the person decides to somehow get even. The stalker does make contact many times in the form of threats as well as by performing acts of vandalism. The retribution stalker may try to stay anonymous only to avoid being caught, or in some rare cases because they utilize their cloak of anonymity as an added tool of terror. We have even experienced at least one third-party stalking embroiled in the act of retribution stalking, but so far that also has been seen as a rarity. Of course, this type of stalker can be considered fairly high up on the threat concern meter.

Not too long ago, we received a request from a police department we have dealt with in the past. They wanted us to evaluate and generate a threat assessment evaluation on a case. We do this on a fairly regular basis for the Westminster Police Department (our previous agency) and other law enforcement entities that contact us and request similar evaluations. This following case is a good example of an RS as well as a stalker that expresses paranoid behavior. (We will discuss mental disorders in this chapter as well.) The stalker was eventually evaluated by a mental health professional and found to be suffering from a paranoid personality disorder. That paranoia was perhaps a result of (or at least exacerbated by) reportedly doing a great deal of drugs. The drug suspected in this case was methamphetamine or another drug similar in makeup.

The detective in charge of the case had gone through one of our training seminars and followed the stalking protocol we had supplied his department. (This protocol will be explained in greater detail in the chapter about how we investigate stalkers.) At the time of the incident, our stalker ("Sid") had been placed on disability from a union job due to his strange behavior in the workplace. He had been at this job for several years. He feared he was going to be (of course, in his mind, unfairly) fired. This was a concern to us, and we expressed that fear to his employer. With all the other negative things Sid had in his life, he may have felt that supervisors or others in his work environment would cause him to lose his job. These beliefs could stimulate Sid into acting out against those people. This was of particular concern because Sid had access to weapons. Whenever you find an individual like Sid, that feels displaced by his place of work, coupled with all the other threat information we were developing on him, made his violence quotient climb higher and higher. This created a greater threat picture, which could increase the risk factors for his coworkers.

Sid was also going through a divorce, and due to his increasingly violent nature and bizarre behavior, he had a restraining order placed against him by his estranged wife. The wife resided in another Orange County city. She was very fearful of Sid and strongly believed he burned her car to cinders not too long before being arrested. (Although we can't get into it, there was good reason for this assumption concerning the arson.)

The investigation revealed that a few months before Sid came onto this police department's radar, he had purchased several hundred dollars' worth of surveillance gear from a spy-type shop located in the city requesting the assistance. Detectives believed, as did Sid's wife, he was using this gear to stalk her. The spy gear that Sid obtained included a GPS (global positioning system) device that could be placed on someone's vehicle and then tracked by whoever had access to its coded keyword. (Even though Sid was diagnosed as having a paranoid personality disorder, he could also fit under the delusional disorder of jealous type. He believed his wife was having an affair, and he confronted both her and the owner of the spy store. He had no basis for these allegations.)

Apparently, Sid's wife found out about this gear and later contacted the owner of the spy shop to ask if Sid had hired him to follow and document whatever she was doing. The owner told her he had merely sold the items to Sid and nothing more. The detectives felt that when Sid's wife contacted the store owner, Sid must have been in the process of following her. He must have seen her going into the store because shortly after that contact, Sid began a campaign of harassment against the owner and his son, who was an employee.

Sid confronted the owner and initially accused him of having an affair with his wife. but for some reason after that contact, he then began continually referring to the store owner as a homosexual. Sid was known to send over one hundred twenty text messages to the victim's phone in one day. Some of the texts would be threatening, such as, "What are your true thoughts before you go off to get your ass (blanked) in prison or I kill you faggot?" Sid would also send text messages talking about his .223 caliber scoped rifle and how he would use a tripod to get the best kill shot. Other text messages would be random and not make sense to the victim. Perhaps they did to Sid but not to the victim. Detectives indicated they had calculated that Sid had called or sent text messages over eight thousand times in a period of a few short months. Sid would also drop off threatening letters like, "Listen up U (blankin) Freek Queer Back THE (blank) AWAY LAST TIME No more breaks I'm done F--king around." Sid also damaged the victim's property by putting superglue into the business's door locks, and he was suspected of smashing one of the victim's rear windows.

Sid told people the victim and his wife had some way of communicating with the FBI and other divisions of the federal government. He felt they were also watching him. He said he had communicated or tried to contact the FBI. It's unknown if that is true. The detective did discover Sid had contacted some government officials with his complaints. When Sid was taken into custody, he admitted to much of the threatening and stalking behavior. He said he felt the owner of the spy shop was the bane of all his problems. Sid told the interviewing detective that he had between twelve and fifteen cell phones at home. He said the store owner was able to somehow use a device that shut off each phone after only one day of use.

Sid later wrote a note to the detective in charge of his case and had the jailer give it to him. In the letter Sid asked the detective how many cops worked for the victim off the clock. How asked how long he had known the victim and if he (the detective) was gay also. Sid also wanted to know if the store owner got better service from him than he did from the police department where he lived was because the detective knew the victim. (The only contact the detective had with the victim was via this case.) Sid's last question was particularly interesting; not that the others weren't. He asked if the detective knew a good civil rights attorney. Sid later pled out to felony counts and was sent to a mental health facility for evaluation and treatment.

As of the writing of this book, Sid just got back onto the street. The handling detective who was new to the case, contacted us to say that good old Sid had been released from the state penal institution. Since then he had begun stalking his ex-wife again, and he had been placing—morphing—pictures of her head pasted onto the bodies of other nude women throughout her neighborhood. (Sid was released from his job of many years.) He had also began shooting out the front plate-glass windows of the spy store. What Sid didn't know was that operation was now under new management, and the guy Sid was going after didn't work there. Sid was in the process of being evicted from his rental home, and his female landlord was terrified of him. Sid also obtained a loaner car from a dealership and reportedly did extensive damage to it.

When the new lead detective told us of the type of damage (trashing the expensive vehicle's onboard computer, tearing out the dash, drilling holes in the roof and quarter panels of the vehicle), we explained our theory.

Damaged Dash, Photo Courtesy of Westminster Police.

Smashed vehicle computer, Photo Courtesy of the Westminster P.D.

Holes drilled into roof of new car. Photo courtesy of Westminster P.D.

Sid had been diagnosed with paranoid delusional disorder, and he had done this damage in an effort to ensure that whoever he thought was monitoring him had not bugged the loaner. This would include drilling a hole in the roof so that he could occasionally peer out and watch for any type of air surveillance. The holes in the quarter panel were probably an attempt to locate any GPS tracking devices. After viewing more of the photos of the $45,000 loaner, we saw that Sid had also attempted to scratch off all the serial numbers and vehicle descriptions off its side front and back windows.

At his rental home, detectives found that Sid had also spray-painted portions of his windows black. This was an attempt to stop those radio waves and other monitoring beams from coming in. (At least no aluminum was found on Sid's windows.) The detective in charge said they would go after Sid probably for felony vandalism. He also told us Sid talked about the murder of a homosexual friend of his that took place in a neighboring city. The murder is still unsolved. The detective is going to look into that case and see if Sid either has information or was possibly involved in that case. We recommended he serve a search warrant on Sid's residence and his computer, which he did. A $100,000 felony warrant for Sid was issued. Hopefully the information gained from that search will get Sid off the streets for some more time.

By the way, the computer search showed that Sid made thousands of comments and inquiries about the store he had damaged. It also showed he had taken numerous photos of different license plates and put them into his computer database. We can only assume he took photos of these license plates because he erroneously felt vehicles were following or after him.

 We should note that this case also has elements of DV stalking. After all, Sid stalked his wife as well as stalking and threatening an innocent bystander. So you can see how the typologies can sometimes overlap. To those of us that investigate these cases, it really doesn't matter what typology the stalker falls into. We just want to do the job we are paid to do, which is protect the victim by hooking up the stalker and then assisting in his or her prosecution.

Another example of the retribution stalker would be this little gem, which was left on the front doorstep of a female victim by a stalker she had rebuffed. The stalker was actually videotaped placing the device and then splitting prior to the victim opening her door. Fortunately for the victim (and perhaps the stalker as well) the device was inert, but it obviously instilled a great deal of fear into the victim. The stalker was prosecuted and convicted on felony counts. This was another Orange County department case that the investigator sent over to us for review.

Fake explosive left by stalker. Courtesy of Westminster PD.

Even though the device depicted above was fake, others stalkers have used real ones. A victim advocate from the Boston area named Cheryl Darisse, LPN contacted us along with her organization, Feel Safe Again, Inc. (of which I am a proud consulting board member). The reason Cheryl got so involved in the issue of stalking was because her sister was executed by an acquaintance stalker with a device that was left on the sister's doorstep and detonated after she took it upstairs to open. The AS had incessantly followed and harassed her sister, a waitress at a local eatery, for a protracted period of time prior to killing her. Darisse has gone on to help change the stalking law in her state. This is just another great example of a victim advocate going to the mat to help future victims.

We should also take this movement to explain that women can also be listed in the retribution stalker category. In a recent contact, we consulted on a case with a young college-age student with a myriad of problems, including suicide attempts. She had been stalking a male student for a period of time with an unsuccessful outcome for her. Her stalking behavior changed from one of pursuit to acts of revenge designed to defame her target. The stalker would write a series of Internet slurs with fraudulent and harmful information about the male. At one point, she contacted a group he was extremely interested in becoming a member of, and by making derogatory and untrue claims, caused the male to be released from any further participation in the organization. Keep in mind, any group that is in the public eye, especially in these days of complete Internet exposure, wants to limit any (we repeat, any) type of scrutiny. In most cases they do not have the time, money, or manpower to vet claims made against individuals. Sadly it is much easier to drop the person than suffer any of the potential consequences.

Neighborhood Stalkers (NS)

Due to an increase in this type of problem, we thought we should at least talk about neighborhood stalking. This can and does create its own set of issues. Neighborhood stalking is just what it sounds like, which is a stalking scenario that develops between two neighbors. These types of stalking situations are oftentimes very aggravated, and they represent a challenge for law enforcement. This is why cops and their administrative supervisors need to be trained in stalking. Once brought up to speed the supervisors need to then encourage their troops to get involved. (As we will discuss in the chapter on how we investigate stalkers, this is not always the case.)

During a two-day training we conducted on a well-known university campus, we met a family that had been terrorized by one individual for a period of years. This is a somewhat unusual case, but it does graphically depict how out of control these types of stalkers can get. At the writing of this book, the stalking is still ongoing. It is transpiring in a city in California, although we cannot say more about the location of that particular city. The following is an overall synopsis of this case:

- The stalker is a male neighbor who rents a home next to the victim, a very quiet, middle-aged female. She lives in the house with her mother and father. Until his recent passing, her father was continually harassed by this neighbor. The stalker is of Middle Eastern descent and is married with several children. We only mention his background because, according to the victim, the stalker seemed to act fairly "normal" until after 9/11 when he suddenly changed dramatically. He shaved his head, started wearing Middle Eastern attire, and began intensely harassing the victim's elderly father (whom he knew to be a veteran). The stalker made comments about the father being a warmonger and involved with killing "his" (the stalker's) countrymen. (This is interesting seeing as how the father was a World War II veteran.)

- The stalker put up video cameras pointed directly at the victim's front door to monitor the daughter's comings and goings. He cut his hedges to get a better view of the house. Then he began following the victim when she shopped, went to work, and even when she went out on a date. On one such incident, he followed the victim to a hotel where she spent several hours with a male friend. He later confronted her and told her where she had been, how long, and with whom. When that same male came over to her house, the stalker exited his residence and began demanding information from him. Saying he was a friend of hers and the family, the stalker asked questions such as, "Are you her boyfriend in any way, shape, or form? Are you intimate with her?" When the male caller refused to give the stalker the information he wanted, the stalker got more detailed. "My question was specific.'Are you intimate with…?' Does she stay at your house a couple of days a week? I know you live in…"

- The stalker later confronted the victim and told her where her bank was, her account number, and how much she had in that account. The victim has had her car vandalized on multiple occasions, including having it keyed, urinated on, and doused with caustic chemicals that destroyed the paint.

- The stalker has called the victim's workplace. He parks his car directly behind hers, and when she comes out to her car, he emerges and begins making rude comments and hand gestures.

- The victim placed surveillance cameras on her home that captured the stalker trespassing on numerous occasions. The cameras also recorded a time when the stalker physically assaulted the victim, knocking her to the ground and breaking a bone in her arm.

- The victim obtained a restraining order. Unfortunately when law enforcement responds, they don't usually take a crime report nor take any type of action. To date they have yet to make an arrest on the stalker. The most recent development was that the handling prosecuting attorney advised the stalker to move. Supposedly he did, but it is believed he merely sublet the house to a series of tenants. He still regularly comes to the house and continues to harass the victim and her relatives.

- This has caused a great deal of mental and physical anguish for the victim. She continually carries a camera with her to document the stalker's behavior. She has placed additional exterior lights with motion sensors on her house, and she quakes each night in her bed awaiting the possibility that this stalker may enter her home at any time and once again assault her. She also strongly feels this stalker's harassment added to the early demise of her father, whom as indicated the stalker continually harangued.

What did we do? We had the victim submit her case to a Los Angeles-based agency that handles special prosecutions. They are in the process of reviewing the case. Hopefully some type of prosecution will result from this.

One of the strangest neighborhood stalking cases we have encountered was one that took place on the east end of the city located in Orange County. We started getting calls about a neighbor who was harassing an eighteen-year-old female who lived with her grandparents in the house directly west of the stalker. The young girl had been with her grandparents since she was thirteen years old, and she had blossomed into a gorgeous woman. At the time she worked for a restaurant chain known for hiring women with ample curves.

In his later forties, the neighbor was a male throwback to the hippie generation. He wore clothing akin to the time of Haight-Asbury in San Francisco, drove an old VW van, and claimed to be a devoted vegan. Then the victim began noticing him lurking in the shadows near her garage door when she came home at night. Later she noticed he was peering over the side fence of his backyard, which was close to her bedroom window. He would oftentimes sing old (possibly '70s) songs about being in love. Then she caught him sitting under her bedroom window late at night groaning, masturbating, and calling her name.

Further investigation revealed the stalker was the sole caregiver for his aged mother, who was bedridden with several ailments including diabetes. When patrol officers went into his house on a 911 call from the stalker's blind, bedridden mother, she made it very clear she feared her son and did not want him around her anymore. The patrol officers that contacted the woman had been in the area on a report of prowling once again by the suspect. Once they saw the woman, they called for medics, and detectives because it appeared to be an elder abuse case. She was rushed to the hospital. Both of her legs were so gangrenous they were later amputated. The stalker's mother died, so the detective in charge collected one of the legs and had it frozen at the police department. The involved agency wanted to file charges of elder abuse and perhaps even reckless endangerment leading to death.

During detectives' initial interview with the subject, we were told he began singing '60s and '70s rock songs in the middle of their examination. The elder abuse case was submitted to the district attorney, but much to that department's dismay, the district attorney refused to file any charges. He refused even after the detectives made repeated attempts to have him revisit all the facts. (There are times we detectives sit around and scratch our heads in disbelief.) The stalker later sold his mother's home after he could no longer make the payments. The investigation revealed he was living off of his mother. (Remember, some stalkers are parasitical in nature, and they do live off of relatives.) He began living out of a new VW van he purchased.

Not too long after finding out our boy wasn't going to be a member of county jail's hospitality, we received another complaint by another elderly female. She lived in a retirement complex close to one of our city's libraries. That library was where our stalker hung out most days, reading periodicals and debating with the elderly patrons. That was where the elderly woman and the stalker met. She then allowed the stalker (because she felt sorry for him) to begin living off and on with her. The victim had apparently been to a large bookstore in an adjacent community and heard about a recent book signing we had there. She obtained a copy of my book, read it, and decided she had to contact me concerning the most recent behavior of our stalker. (My life always seems to go like this. I wouldn't know what to do if weird didn't get weirder.)

When we interviewed the woman, she confirmed what we had feared during our first investigation with this strange male. The victim was in her late sixties, and the stalker (at least twenty years younger than her) kept wanting to have sex with her. Based on our threat assessment of the suspect at the time of his mother's death, we feared there was a good likelihood she had been molested by him as well. The woman claimed the stalker would complain about dreams wherein his dead mother came to him at night in a skimpy negligee.

The stalker was again confronted and advised not to contact that victim any longer. (He had been following her as well.) No additional charges were filed, and to the best of our knowledge, the stalker moved out of the area.

Surprisingly we get a number of neighborhood stalking complaints like the following web victim. This W/V said she lived directly across from a woman with known mental problems. (Their front doors opened up onto the same walkway threshold.) The woman continually confronted the victim. The victim was even hospitalized when the woman pushed her down the stairs, causing her to sustain significant injuries. Allegedly the woman had also threatened to kill her. When she obtained a restraining order, she was told by the locals (cop slang for local police) that because they lived right across from each other, there was not much they could do except suggest the victim try to avoid the stalker.

We told the victim there were ways the judicial system in her community could handle this particular stalker if they took a different approach. Once an arrest took place, the court should be able to order a mental evaluation and then progress from there. Of course, a certain amount of training on how to generate a case for this type of stalker is probably necessary.

Our last example of this type of stalking scenario involved a law enforcement officer being stalked by a dishonorably discharged policeman from another agency other than that of the victim's. The stalker lived next door to the victim officer, and would write long dissertations (a series of manifestos if you will) about how he was afraid that the victim was going to kill him (the stalker). The victim had no idea why. The stalker would also describe how he watched for the victim to come home. The stalker said he sat in the corner of his room with his gun and contemplated how he was ready when and if the victim ever confronted him. The stalker's ramblings went on and on. We conducted a limited consult for the victim. Because we only had small amounts of information about what the stalker wrote in his manifesto, the scope of our threat assessment was also diminished. However, one thing we did discuss with the victim officer was that due to the stalker's agitated state, coupled with and the fact that he apparently was still reeling from being fired, he may be considering suicide. Based on some of the stalker's statements, we suggested that this individual may not have the wherewithal to do the deed himself. He might be seeking confrontation for the purpose of suicide by cop. (For the layperson, this means he wants the still-employed officer, who the stalker knows is armed and trained, to kill him. In this way it is a suicide by cop.) Due to the fact, that when the victim and his wife decided to move and in fact did, the stalker/neighbor did not pursue tended to bolster our suspicions about the suicide by cop suspicions.

The victim officer took our advice and initiated specific steps to start the ball rolling to attempt to neutralize the former officer's stalking threat. We wished him luck.

How did we handle many of these types of cases? When we got a neighbor stalker, we followed a series of steps. First we arrested the stalker for every penal or municipal code violation of law that he or she committed. If we had the manpower, we set up a surveillance team on the stalker. It usually did not take much time for the stalker to commit a violation. When the stalker was convicted, we requested he or she have a GPS ankle device applied as part of probation. We also pushed for probation, to violate the stalker so if he or she slipped up, they would end up in prison. Keep in mind that if the stalker owns or is buying his or her house, it is difficult to get that stalker to move.

These cases can and are successfully prosecuted. A recent example of that is a Sacramento case that was reported on by the *Sacramento Bee*. According to the article, a sixty-eight year old male that had been stalking a neighbor couple for a period of years. In 2006 he was convicted of felony stalking and sent to prison. When he got out in 2009, he went back and began stalking them again until the summer of 2011. He was again convicted of felony stalking in June of 2012, and once again placed back to the joint for another seven years.[60]

Juvenile Stalkers

In the last couple of years, we have received many inquiries from law enforcement as well as victim advocates about kids in junior and senior high exhibiting stalking behavior. We have even had a couple of calls concerning elementary school situations. Sometimes this type of stalking is described as "puppy love gone awry," but other think it is an extension of bullying. Interestingly enough when we talked to Australian stalking researcher Rosemary Purcell, PhD, she referred us to a 2009 study published in the *British Journal of Psychiatry*. She and her fellow researchers were involved in the study, which addressed this very issue. (Again, researchers help us verify what we, the laypeople, observe on the street.)

The study's findings were very interesting. The study was conducted in Australia with a population sample of almost three hundred juvenile and adolescent stalkers. Like we said, the researchers found that most people viewed this type of stalking as rare and "harmless." What the study actually found, however, was that juvenile stalking represented "far higher levels of threats and violence than adult stalking." The stalkers almost exclusively pursued people known to them. Not much stalking was done as a result of being infatuated with the victim. Instead, it was more an extension of bullying. About three-quarters of the stalking victims reported threats. In about "15% of cases, threats of violence had been made against victims or friends as well." These threats included but were not limited to "explicit threats to harm, rape or kill." Over half the victims were actually attacked. Another interesting fact was that about "36 percent" of the stalkers were female, and they primarily focused their harassment on other girls. The study also found that many of these female stalkers enlisted friends to assist in the stalking. We seem to be seeing more and more of this kind of violence on the Internet. Girls are videotaping their assaults and putting them on the web, adding to the victims' shame and fear. The study indicated male stalkers usually pursued females.[61] Once again, this would indicate a more predatory type of stalking behavior.

We received a call from a detective lieutenant that supervised a detective division in a Midwestern community. He had heard we were coming out to teach a seminar he was going to attend, and he wanted to relate a case he found troubling. The lieutenant said he had a sixteen-year-old male suspect that was an athlete, Eagle Scout, involved in his church, and a good student. The boy had been conducting a very close documentation of a seventeen-year-old girl. One unusual thing he did was leave a note on her backpack describing exactly what the young girl had worn for the last seven days. The note went on to say that he knew she wanted sex, and he would give her some. He made repeated phone calls to her cell phone when she was home. He disguised his voice and didn't leave his name. The juvenile justice system eventually adjudicated the case. This is just another example of what we are talking about with the types of juvenile stalking we are seeing.

Studies show an ever-increasing number of our youths are falling victim to the realm of being unsupervised for longer and longer periods of time. This is oftentimes blamed on the breakdown of the nuclear family. We would tend to agree, but we also feel the recent burden of economic uncertainty is adding to the family's plight. This includes the diminished availability of part-time jobs for youths and loss of recreational activities. These are two things that tend to keep kids in a productive and structured environment, which even though they don't want to admit, they all need. In our opinion this sets them up for a higher degree of failure and ever-increasing entry into criminal enterprises from street crime to other criminal behavior.

Along these same lines, a case of cyberbullying/stalking took place in an upscale intermediate school in Los Angeles. A specific group of students in the school were encouraged, via an Internet blog by another student, to follow and assault only red-headed students on a specific day. The assaults did cause emotional and physical trauma, and arrests were made. The idea for this type of activity was supposedly generated by an episode of a popular animated television show, which talked about tolerance and bullying in a comedic fashion.

Another topic related to juveniles and even young adults is the ever-increasing use of violent or role-playing video games. We are in the midst of an entire generation of "gamers." I have two young adult sons who are completely immersed in playing online role-playing games. They are members of a "guild," whatever the heck that is. They utilize an entirely different language than I do. They tell me I need to get up to speed and learn the lingo. I have enough problems with English and a little Spanish, let alone' "game-ese." Entire social networks have sprung up around the video game genre. My kids and other like them take road trips to visit fellow guild members. Some begin dating those guild members. A Stanford University study found that males are more prone to get *hooked* on video games than females because the rewards portion of the brain is stimulated much more than in a woman's brain. Don't get us wrong. There are a lot of females in the gaming world, and the numbers grow daily. For more information about the effects of continued video game usage, go to www.SOSParents.org. Of course, just because Junior sits down and plays his video games for hours on end does not mean he is going to become a serial killer. Obviously not all kids on these gaming sites are impaired or go off the deep end, but as parents we need to be aware of what is going on in those noggins of theirs, which are not always wired the way we would like.

I will admit when my kids were younger and first got heavily involved in gaming, my wife and I both saw unfavorable changes in their personalities. They were quicker to anger, nonresponsive to our wishes, etc. We found a time-out for a few weeks actually brought the nicer kids we were used to back to us. Now they are older, those personality disruptions have decreased immensely. They still play, but it is at a different pace, and they respond in an appropriate fashion when contacted during game usage. Well as much as we feel they can even at this particular point in their lives. (This is the brain wiring we discussed. Studies have indicated that our brain mapping doesn't really complete until our younger adult years. In general, that is oftentimes why youth don't always compute things such as fear or common sense like us older folk.) To be fair, gaming also has been shown to produce better hand-eye coordination. This is also a useful skill for recruits of the military, which is going to more and more robotic and computer-generated warfare. Also some scientists are currently studying how specific video games can assist the elderly with cognitive brain behaviors, etc.

The problems law enforcement have experienced with this new genre of intensely violent gaming are complaints of suicidal or other violent behavior. This has caught the attention of some of the more responsible individuals in the gaming industry, who have assigned monitors on subscribers to their gaming sites. They watch for users who may be going south and contact local law enforcement with their findings. Occasionally we have been asked to counsel parents whose young adults have contemplated that road to abandon.

Many believe that constant viewing of violence tends to desensitize those involved, and some of the role-playing in these games can lead or direct certain kids and young adults on the path of violent behavior. Does that mean the youth already had a propensity for violence, and the game was a catalyst? Perhaps. We don't know all the answers. We are seeing, however, more violence associated with those who continually utilize some of these venues. When we were growing up (according to our kids, when dinosaurs roamed the earth), the role-playing game reportedly taking some into the abyss was *Dungeons & Dragons*. Now the blame has been laid at the feet of a myriad of other games. An example of this is the following case. It's a very unusual homicide that my partner and I worked along with other homicide detectives just prior to my formal retirement in December of 2004.

Some of the stalker's artwork. Courtesy of Westminster P.D.

The call initially came as a male requesting help from his home on the west end of the city in a middle-income housing tract. The dispatcher also related that a 927D (dead body) might be involved. When uniformed patrol officers arrived, they found a distraught male in his sixties in front of the house. Holding his head with both hands, he was whimpering. He told the officers "Teddy" was in the house along with his dead wife. When patrol officers entered the residence, they found a male in his mid-twenties quietly sitting on the couch. In the master bathroom they found his mother with a portion of her head blown off. They also located a recently fired 12-gauge shotgun on the master bedroom floor.

The investigation revealed some interesting things about Teddy. According to relatives he was thought to be suffering from attention deficit hyper disorder. When he was a child he tried to stab a neighbor child with a knife, which he kept next to his bed. He did not like the then-Governor Schwarzenegger and his wife, and he wanted them killed. According to his limited group of friends, the night before he killed his mother, Teddy had gone into a rant about the "immigrant" governor and his wife and wanted to "get rid" of them. Also Teddy had an extremely high IQ and was so proud of it that he had personalized plates displaying his intelligence quotient affixed to his vehicle. Teddy was heavily involved in a video game incorporating the ancient Chinese art of warfare. The game was designed to have players develop role-playing strategies to kill their opponents. This may have been why he continually talked about a book written in the fourteenth century by Luo Guanzhong. Called *Romance of Three Kings*, it discussed the battles and wars during the turbulent times of the Han Dynasty. Teddy was also heavily involved in prophecy and used to talk to his friends about hidden meanings in things such as the dollar bill. Apparently Teddy had not been sleeping or eating much but was instead cooped up in his room and playing the game for hours on end. This and Teddy's poor physical condition had caused his mother a great deal of concern.

(Again, when dealing with a stalker, it behooves the detective in charge to try to gather as much background on that individual as possible. This helps when conducting interviews. It also creates a picture of the stalker's mind-set for anyone who reviews the case in the future. This background would include mental health, parole, and/or probation.)

On the day of the shooting, Teddy did some unusual things. He first walked over to a female's residence. We later discovered he had been stalking this woman for several years. She was a researcher and had not contacted local law enforcement about Teddy because, due to her job, she was able to keep a safe distance from his unwanted attempts at contact. She had been aware of Teddy ever since high school where, according to the woman, he had wandered aimlessly around campus acting weird. She said Teddy had no real contact with her during most of their high school years. She had been home from a break from her job when Teddy showed up to her door with a strange note, which was given to her father.

After reading the note, he felt it might have been a type of suicide letter because Teddy had scribbled something about not living past his twenty-fourth birthday. According to the female's father, Teddy had also written about geological information such as tectonics, which was the research area his daughter was involved in. The father said his daughter had also recently received notes scribbled by Teddy through one of her girlfriends. In those notes, Teddy talked about how much he liked the man's daughter and that he had been tracking her via the Internet for months. Even though Teddy had written an explanation about why he felt he would die before he turned twenty-four (according to Teddy, he had a debilitating heart problem), the father still felt it was more like a suicide note. (Judging from what transpired later that afternoon, he could have been right.)

After delivering the note, Teddy went home and locked all the doors in the house. He shut off most lights and pulled the drapes and shutters closed. He did not answer the phone when his mother called repeatedly to check on his welfare. You see, Teddy didn't really care for his mother. She was the reported disciplinarian in Teddy's world, and Teddy had conveyed this dislike to his limited group of friends and associates. He felt she was too intrusive into his life. He also had a feeling, based on previous behaviors that not responding to his mother would cause her anxiety levels to increase exponentially. This would cause her to come home early and check on him. (Detectives later found out she was a very good person and very concerned about Teddy's well-being due to his various medical conditions.)

Teddy then went into his father and mother's master bedroom. His father had been staying in that room, and his mother stayed in another. This had been going on for a period of time. Teddy found a key and locked himself into the bedroom, knowing his father would not be home until later. Teddy then located a 12-gauge shotgun, loaded it, and sat in the corner of the bedroom. When his mother came home early from work to check on him, she unlocked the master bedroom door and began to walk toward Teddy. She only got a few steps when Teddy shot her in the head. (From all the indicators, the detectives involved in the case felt there was a good likelihood that our boy Teddy had planned a lying in wait homicide scenario.)

While Teddy was being taken into custody, I drove to the crime scene as I always did. I wanted to get a look-see prior to assisting another homicide detective in Teddy's initial interview. When I arrived, other detectives were assisting CSI in processing the scene. They directed me to a location near the living room. There, on the floor, was a lock of hair that had been tied. It belonged to Teddy's mother. It was later determined that the hair was in fact a trophy of Teddy's kill. That interview was one of the strangest I have ever been a party to. When we interviewed Teddy, he reminded me of a scalded monkey attempting to stay atop a hot plate turned to its highest temperature setting. He kept muttering about the art of Chinese warfare and how to disable his opponent. During his second jailhouse interview with the two other detectives assigned to the case, he finally copped out to killing his mother. He had initially said she was armed when he shot her, but he later admitted that was a lie. Teddy was convicted and sentenced to forty years to life. The judge commented that he thought Teddy was a whack job, but at the time of the murder, he knew exactly what he was doing. Teddy will need that high IQ to figure out how to stay one step ahead of the animals he will now be caged with.

Campus Stalker

Because we have just talked about juvenile and adolescent stalking, it is apropos to examine the ever-growing issue of stalking on our nation's as well as other countries' college campuses. A well-reviewed statistical study took place in 1997 and was published in 2000 as "The National College Women Sexual Victimization Study" (NCWSV). The following are some of that study's findings:

- 80.3% of victims knew or had seen their stalkers before

- 3 in 10 women reported being injured emotionally or psychologically during the stalking

- in 15.3% of the incidents, the stalker threatened or attempted to harm the victim

- 10.3% of victims said the stalker either forced or attempted sexual contact

- about 83.1% of the stalking cases were not reported to campus police or local law enforcement

- about 93.4% told someone else about being stalked[62]

The United Kingdom has found similar problems on their college and university campuses. A recent study entitled "The UK Hidden Marks Report Survey of 2010" found that of those surveyed:

- "12% have been stalked while at university or college;

- [In] 60% of these cases of sexual assault or stalking, the perpetrator was also a student;

- Only 4% of women students who have been seriously sexually assaulted have reported it to their institution;

- Only 10% of women students who have been seriously sexually assaulted have reported it to the police;

- Of those who did not report serious sexual assault to the police, 50% said it was because they felt ashamed or embarrassed, and 43% because [they] thought they would be blamed for what happened."[63]

Due to this study and others, Scotland's National Union of Students (NUS) has started implementing anti-stalking policies on their college and university campuses. It is hoped this will spread elsewhere throughout the United Kingdom.

Based on the number of complaints we get from both students and educators, we are sure the college stalking numbers have gone up since 2000. The following are some possible reasons given to us as well as from our own observations, why stalking has become more of a problem on our campuses:

- A college environment is somewhat cloistered and contained. This allows a potential stalker to view, follow, and plan his or her stalking with a good deal of ease.

- Student stalkers can easily gather a great deal of information on their victims via in-house data systems such as student registries. They can also talk to other students or friends of the target.

- Stalking victims often believe they can take care of the problem themselves through counseling or trying to talk to the stalker. In other words, because the stalker is a fellow student, he or she may not be perceived as that much of a threat. (This is a real problem that we experience all too often.)

- Oftentimes peer pressure, fear of being ostracized by fellow students, or fear of being blamed adds to the lack of reporting by victims.

- College and university personnel often lack the requisite training to handle a stalking scenario. In some scenarios we have been contacted about or consulted on, personnel may even tend to downplay the situation due to political pressures. They don't want the hassle or the bad publicity.

An excellent example of a campus stalking that went terribly wrong was a murder/suicide that took place on a December night in an apartment complex near a college campus. The case was profiled on an *E! Hollywood* stalking special we were one of the consultants on. A young, beautiful, and talented women's life was snuffed out by a twenty-four-year-old, troubled male friend. She was trying to get him help but was later stalked by him. The indicators for disaster were there, but due to inexperience and perhaps not be educated on the dangers presented by a stalker were not realized by the caring victim. The stalker was a student athlete, who had been suffering from bouts of depression after being cut from his baseball team. He had attempted to kill himself on two occasions, and the second time he almost made it. Ironically if it had not been for the female nursing student's quick thinking, the stalker (whom she was still trying to help) would have died. The young, desperate athlete called her after he had taken an overdose of sleeping pills. When she realized what he had done, she notified authorities, and they were able to save his life. Not too long after that incident, he called the victim and said he needed to see her. She reportedly did not want to see him, but she thought she would to tell him once and for all not to contact her anymore. Unfortunately he brought a gun, an argument ensued, and he shot and killed the victim before turning the weapon on himself. (In this scenario, local law enforcement advised they had no knowledge the stalking was taking place. Folks, if the cops don't know, they can't help.)

Keep in mind that one of the things that certain stalkers will do is feign committing suicide in order to get a response from their target. In this particular situation, the stalker, not only called the victim to let her know what he was doing, but also texted her with information about his suicide attempt. Without knowing more of the facts as to the amount of drugs he took, length of ingestion time, etc, we could not speculate if this ploy was in this particular stalker's mind at the time of the incident.

All too often, we see a college victim such as this. The victim wants to think the best about everyone and help but is somewhat blinded by factors that can spell danger for her. In this case, from what was portrayed, she knew her assailant from high school but never dated him. Once they were both at the same university, they did have a brief dating relationship. It was obvious to others he was becoming increasingly fixated with our young nursing candidate.

(From all indications, she was one of those people who shine so brightly that everyone is drawn to her.) Once she broke off their relationship and told him she wanted to be just friends, he began to stalk her. He followed her and ended up at the same places she did. Remember, this is not that difficult on a college or university campus. He would contact friends to see where she was. He would continually call. All the while he was becoming more and more depressed, suicidal, and unstable. These were

all things the victim saw but apparently didn't compute as red flags. This is just another reason why student and faculty training about stalking is so important. *

In another case, April 16, 2007 was a huge wake-up call not just for Virginia Tech. but the rest of the world. Cho Seung-Hui engineered the largest mass murder to take place on any college campus in US history, which left thirty-three dead. Behind all the carnage was an extremely troubled South Korean male diagnosed with a rare mental disorder called selective mutism. This disease reportedly only manifests itself in less than 1 percent of the population. He was diagnosed with the disorder while in secondary school. According to the *DSM-IV-TR*, someone with selective mutism can present with, "excessive shyness, fear of social embarrassment, social isolation and withdrawal, clinging, compulsive traits, nega-

---

* In October of 2012, I had the opportunity to present two seminars at the very campus where this poor victim was murdered. The class revolved around victimology and campus stalking. When we discussed this particular case, you could hear the audible gasps coming from some of the attendees. Obviously a very poignant example of how stalking can affect the lives of those remotely involved with the incident.

tivism, temper tantrums." The subject may also experience severe impairment in school and social environments.[64]

Although a tremendously tragic scenario, as those involved in the world of threat assessment, we were much more concerned about the events which led up to this murderous outburst. Cho was definitely a stalker. He reportedly stalked at least two females prior to the April event. This and his other extremely unusual and strange, and at times very bizarre behavior caused concern among both faculty and students. If interested go onto the Internet and Google the Virginia Tech incident. There is a great deal of information concerning the before and after events, who was supposedly contacted concerning Cho's behavior, and how it was or wasn't handled. We were not part of the investigation or the after action evaluation. Therefore it would be speculation on our part as to speak to how the events unfolded either before or after the incident. I did, however, contact some of the VT faculty and provided them with copies of my previous book as well as my condolences. They expressed both via letter and e-mail that these efforts were appreciated, so in times such as these, we were glad to be of some assistance.

I contacted two of Cho's roommates. They told me the following information. Cho created a character he referred to as "Question Mark." He started using this alter ego on Facebook.com. They told me Cho made a drawing, which he placed on his Facebook profile. (A roommate sent me this drawing. See to the right of page.) Cho then began using

*Picture of Cho's alter ego,
received from Cho's roommate.*

this identity when he talked on the phone, and according to the roommates, he progressed to taking on this persona altogether. The roommates advised he initially claimed that Question Mark was in fact his brother who lived on the sixth floor of the building. (The roommates said there was no sixth floor.) His roomies also said that Cho's alter ego "had an obsession with being cool." When we asked what music Cho listened to, we were told Cho would listen to the Beatles, The Who, and Nirvana. On one occasion he wrote lyrics on the common's wall from the Nirvana Song "Smells Like Teen Spirit." He wrote, "Load up your guns, bring your friends, it's fun to lose and to pretend." We wanted to know what television programs he watched. They told us he watched a lot of Spike TV, primarily wrestling, and a Japanese game show where the contestants attempt to get through various hazards.

We were told Cho did not appear to read for pleasure but frequently carried around a large book of Shakespeare. One roommate said Cho wrote on one of his female stalking victim's door, "By a name I know not how to tell thee who I am: My name, dear saint, is hateful to myself, because it is an enemy to thee; had I written, I would tear the word." The roommates said Facebook, instant messenger, and VT (Virginia Tech) people search were Cho's primary ways of researching and then stalking females. They also said Cho would sit in their room doing lengthy data entries into his laptop. They did not know what he was writing about. They said he would communicate with them but was very quiet most of the time.

Since that horrific event, many college campuses have begun to earnestly generate better plans of attack against threats to students and faculty. We applaud their efforts. That being said, we are still contacted by people who are concerned about their college or university's approach to threat assessment. The following is one such example.

Not too long ago, we received a request for assistance. The case concerned a female stalker going after the requestor's W/V son, who was a varsity athlete at an elite university/college. (We will not use identifiers or get into all the case specifics for the privacy of this individual and his family.) Due to the nature of the case, we actually called and talked to the requestor. Normally, unless it is a law enforcement agency, we just make our comments via e-mail. Just from the brief amount of information we received from the requestor, however, we could see there may in fact be clear lethality issues involved.

Once we talked to the requestor on the phone, those fears were confirmed. Over the course of several months, the female stalker had fixated on the requestor's son, whom the stalker reportedly had feelings for. The female was associated with his sports team. When a coaching change took place, the position fulfilled by the stalker was eliminated. Somehow the stalker felt the athlete had something to do with her removal. According to the requestor, that was never the case. (Even if it had transpired, that would not be a cause for a stalking to take place.) Once the removal took place, the female began the usual course of stalking, which included surveillance. She would also call and send notes to the college/university and the student athlete.

The victim even saw one of the stalker's relatives show up to a closed practice and watch him. This was of concern because when we asked if there had been any threatening e-mails, phone calls, or letters, the requestor said the stalker had contacted the school administration concerning how she felt about the victim. Reportedly numerous calls came in, and they were tape-recorded. In many of the calls, the stalker said either she or one of her family members would eventually harm the victim. Both direct threats and indicated threats of violence were made toward the victim. This took on a more sinister tone when we asked the requestor if he/she knew whether the stalker had been seeking out a mental health professional. The requestor said on one occasion the stalker did contact the victim telling the victim that she was seeing a therapist and had just purchased a handgun.

The requestor had not gone to the local police department because he/she was concerned that if law enforcement contacted the school, they might just cancel the requestor's son's scholarship, thus eliminating the problem that they were presented with. We explained that it was unfortunate the requestor felt that way, but we also advised that we had heard of that type of response taking place. We strongly advised the requestor to contact law enforcement and get them up to speed. We told the requestor, based on all the information, we were presented with this stalker had probably stalked another male before. The requestor said this had recently been found to be the case, and the victim in that scenario was currently undergoing mental health counseling. We got the impression after our conversation that the requestor now felt that his/her son could be in serious danger and would go to the authorities. It is unknown if that ever took place or not. It is indeed tragic that the vibes a school puts out would cause a parent to have safety concerns about his or her child in that particular school's environment. In other words, one would hope; especially in this case, that the institution would eliminate the threat as well as the stalker not the student-athlete and victim.

We along with Los Angeles County District Attorney Rhonda Saunders, Resident Coordinator Grant Burlew (now Resident Director at the University of California Santa Barbara), Assistant Director for the Center for Women and Men Todd Henneman, and others were part of the Stalking Policy Advisory Committee for the University of Southern California's College Consortium Project. This program was designed to handle stalking and threat assessment for USC and other universities and colleges in the Los Angeles area. This study was funded by a Department of Justice grant from the Office of Violence Against Women. The study produced a program, which at last contact is undergoing final review. It is designed to greatly assist faculty, staff, campus law enforcement, and students, to better address the stalking issue on campus. This will be accomplished through clearer reporting, better education and awareness, coupled with an aggressive, two-pronged approach in dealing with campus stalking. This dual system includes a direct law enforcement approach as well as the availability to handle an issue administratively if necessary. The program also looked at to increase the speed in which counseling services were made available to the student/victim after a stalking event took place. We feel counseling is very important for the victim and should be made available if at all possible.

What the study uncovered—as previously indicated— was that many students are reticent about contacting campus authorities for fear of retribution, peer response, or a feeling that nothing would or could be done. Another factor that came to light was the students lacked easy access to a reporting tool. These tools would allow them not only to make easy contact with the proper school staff, but make it simpler for them to log in and record the progression of the stalking incidents such as unwanted contacts via cell, e-mail, texting, or otherwise. The fact that some stalking begins elsewhere and ends up on the campus grounds was also addressed as a concern to be dealt with. Educating the student body and staff on the stalking issues was also stressed.

Along those same lines, in January of 2010, California passed SB 188. This amended Section 527.85 (a) of California's Civil Procedures code and stated that "any chief administrative officer of a postsecondary educational institution, or an officer or employee designated by the chief administrative officer to maintain order on the school campus or facility, a student of which has suffered a credible threat of violence made off the school campus or facility from any individual, which can reasonably be construed to be carried out or to have been carried out at the school campus or facility, may, with the written consent of the student, seek a temporary restraining order and an injunction, on behalf of the student and, at the discretion of the court, any number of other students at the campus or facility who are similarly situated."[65] We like this law and hope that most institutions of higher learning that have not already adopted this procedure will take a similar stance for the safety of the student concerned and for those that might become collateral damage.

The National Center for Victims of Crime, via their stalking resource center, and the California Coalition Against Sexual

Assault have just developed a model campus stalking policy, which can be obtained by going to the stalking resource center of the National Center for Victims of Crime, scanning for the publications section and look for the Model Campus Stalking manual. This policy manual outlines a great deal of information concerning how to deal with campus stalking.

Now we have discussed campus stalking and the campus stalker, which included threats at the college level, we must talk about the same scenario at the high school level. Due to several recent events in our country and abroad, there has become a greater emphasis placed on better securing our high schools from threat. Several research studies funded by the government and some private firms have tackled this issue. Those studies have spawned various training scenarios that are currently taking place throughout the United States. This is all good stuff, but a lot more has to be done. There is still way too much complacency taking place in our kids' schools. The old "it could never take place here" syndrome is still very much well and alive. Stalking, bullying, and other forms of predation regularly take place on our secondary school campuses.

Even before Columbine, we were concerned about the lax behavior we were seeing. There were glaring security issues at our children's high school, which was in an upscale community and presented with that very syndrome we were discussing. Being in the business of threat assessment caused us to take action, so we wrote a little ten-page paper entitled "Harden the Target." We then began submitting it to school districts in the area. For the most part, we got back a "thanks but no thanks" response. During one meeting with a city administrator about these and other issues, we were told the committee tasked with viewing this information felt we were trying to get a foothold in order to consult and make money. That was interesting seeing as how the information was completely couched as coming not from a consultant, but from a very concerned parent.

There are communities out there that take a very strong approach towards their students' safety and security. The Los Angeles School District has its own formal police department. There are other school districts around that have well-trained, armed school officers. For the most part, though, it has been our experience that the average school district either feels these entities are too costly or unnecessary. One extreme is the Israeli school system, which has heavily armed school security officers, and their school plants are built in a secure fashion. (We realize they have some different and more immediate issues than do most of our schools. However, trust us, when we describe their security as "extreme," we do not mean that in a bad way.) That being said we are seeing a growing number of school districts that appear to be getting up to speed, but too many are still lagging. Without going too in-depth into the entire content of "Harden the Target," the following are a few things we suggested all campuses do:

- Train security staff to be more aware of their surroundings. Take note of suspicious people and vehicles. Think about carrying a digital camera that allows them to photograph things they belief are suspicious. Keep a daily log to record any anomalies.

- Encourage the community's law enforcement officers to start coming on campus and communicating with students in a casual way. Lunchtime is a good opportunity. It will take a little while for students to get used to having officers on campus in a nonofficial capacity, but trust us. Kids will warm up to them after they realize they are parents, coaches, and oh yes, human beings as well. When I came on campus either in uniform or as a detective, once accepted, the amount of information I received about problems both on and off school grounds was incredible. We and others in the department would hand out our business cards, and we could not believe the leads (anonymous and otherwise) that were called in. Because we had personalized our contacts, these students had a name and a face they could call instead of a potentially confusing entity.

- Along these same lines, administrators, push your staff to get out regularly among their students instead of retreating to their offices. Again, more information will be shared this way. Make sure you have an open-door policy for students to be able to come to staff (without retribution) to discuss issues they or some other student may be having. I was a credentialed secondary teacher before I went into law enforcement. Therefore, I wrote the school resource officer pilot programs for the two major school districts our police department and two others serviced. For about three years after that, I taught police science in uniform and in plain clothes at two high schools, so I know this approach can work from both the standpoint of being a teacher as well as a cop.

- Designate a staff member to act as liaison with a member of local law enforcement. The member of law enforcement can be a school resource officer or designee. Have regular meetings and trainings concerning any and all security issues, which should include stalking and bullying. Get used to exchanging information about ongoing issues. Eliminate the "head in the sand" phenomenon. Include your on-campus security teams in the meetings, and be open to their input.

- If at all possible, try to hire retired law enforcement in staff positions such as dean of students. There are a number of law enforcement officers with a teaching background or degrees in psychology or sociology. Being former law enforcement, they can better implement policies between school and police. This increases the effectiveness of those programs. Former officers are often more adept at advising school administrative staff about the criminality of any ongoing problem taking place on campus.

- Develop an emergency plan. Discuss this with your law enforcement liaison. Find out exactly what is going to happen if you have an active shooter on your campus. What will be law enforcement's response? Practice your lockdown and evacuation drills regularly. If you don't practice, those plans are useless when the real need arises. While teaching in Norway, we discussed "Harden the Target." We said we liked students, when a suspected predator came on campus, to stay in a locked classroom behind a steel door and behind brick or block walls. One of the class participants brought up the point that many school facilities in his country were made of wood. Lesson learned. Prior to spouting all your great ideas, find out the lay of the land before you open your mouth.

- Whenever a new campus is in the planning stage, get law enforcement involved prior to building. This way they can have some input about entrances, exits, and other security issues. We have seen some school plans that would be disastrous under the right set of circumstances.

There are many other suggestions such as installing security cameras or a certain type of fencing. These are all contingent, however, on budget. Just doing a few of these things can make a big difference in the safety of a campus. We don't want to make your kid's campus look or feel like a prison. We just want them safer.

During the presentation of this program to a school we were concerned about, they basically gave us the cold shoulder. That was until we advised that cameras would definitely help mitigate potential lawsuits. It's funny how those cameras miraculously appeared. It makes no difference to us what tactic is applied as long as there are positive results.

 Before we get into our next discussion about stalkers and the mental disorders they may exhibit, we need to discuss some alarming facts about mental health issues we are facing currently in the United States. The editors in the March 2012 edition of *Scientific American* brought forth some interesting statistics about this very issue. Those who work stalking cases and the increasing number of the mentally disabled left to wander our streets (or who are warehoused in our jails) will agree with their findings. According to the editors, "nearly one in two people in the US will suffer from depression, anxiety disorders or another mental health ailment at some point in their life."[66] The article goes on to state that mental illness is woefully undertreated in this country, and this adds to an ever-increasing risk of suicide, especially in our younger generation. (From our experience, they do seem to be struggling much more with these maladies than did past generations.) In our opinion this is because they lack or have not been able to develop the requisite coping mechanisms to fight off these debilitations. They seem to also have greater difficulty when confronted by social interactions that don't involve sending e-mails, tweeting, or going on other social networking sites.

We would agree we need more treatment facilities if for no other reason than to get people on a better track. Another benefit is removing those individuals that can harm both causing injury to themselves and/or others from a sea of potential victims. Many of us in law enforcement tend to feel that treating the mentally ill is somewhat of a crapshoot. You throw the dice and hope you win. We see those who have crapped out way too much on the streets. Most of the time, we are told by the physicians who treat these people, "If they don't take their meds, there is not too much we can do."

Some Mental Disorders Exhibited by Stalkers

Now we have discussed stalker typologies, we need to address another facet of the world of stalking. This is the mental disorders we often encounter when dealing with this breed of criminal. Sure, other criminals can have mental health issues, but many of the stalkers we encounter seem to pop right out of the pages of the *Diagnostic and Statistical Manual Of Mental Disorders (DSM-IV-TR)*. This is so much so that when we teach, we strongly suggest the detectives and probation officers assigned the task of dealing with these yahoos get copies and keep them on their desks. We are not saying you must have your medical degree or a PhD to work this species of criminal, but the knowledge truly does help when compiling a threat assessment profile on your stalker. It also greatly aids in the investigation if you know what type of stalker you are dealing with, and if at all possible one, if they are suffering from a mental disorder, and two what kind is it. This will indicate how best to approach the investigation and tell you the necessary tools. Just a word to the wise, if you are like us, it's a good idea to invest in a desk copy of a good college dictionary or even one that defines psychological terminology. *The Dictionary of Psychology* by Raymond J. Corsini is a good, quick read dealing with mental health definitions. These references will help explain words such as "ideation," which is the process of forming ideas and images, and others. Also be aware that mental health experts we talked to advised that stalkers can and do exhibit more than one form of mental problem. It is like the joke my wife told me. Why is a man like a box of chocolates? Because you never know what you are going to get, and most of them are fruits or nuts. Plus, whatever you pick, you'll regret it later. It's kind of like that with stalkers. You have to peel back the layers to see what is really underneath.* (Because we like the layout of the *DSM-IV-TR* and its ease of use, we tend to review it more than other reference guides. If you find a specific disorder you are interested in or need more information on, please feel free to search the web. We always try to find as much information on a specific topic we are interested in as possible.)

For example, if you encounter a stalker with an obsessive-compulsive disorder commonly referred to as OCD, which is different than an obsessive-compulsive personality disorder, we have found the nature of that disorder often prompts that person to keep logs about almost anything and everything. We love these guys. When you find an individual like this, as an investigator, it is usually a

---

* One place to find articles on the mental health issues of stalkers is the online Bioinfo Bank Library at http://lib.bioinfo.pl/pmid:11929447. We are sure there are others, but this is a good place to start.

gold mine. When you serve a search warrant, you generally find all kinds of information concerning his or her stalking behavior. This includes things like where they stalked, when they stalked, and sometimes why they stalked their victims. Their logs are thorough and usually have dates and times. They are true evidence bonanzas.

Now we will endeavor to discuss some of these disorders. Obviously we are not medical doctors, nor do we have advanced degrees in psychology or psychiatry. Therefore, you will once again see some endnotes so we can give the well-deserved credit to those that have put in years attaining these degrees as well as continuing research in their specific fields of endeavor. It is still important for anyone reading this text to understand some of the maladies' that we encounter when dealing with the stalker.

According to Dr. Debra A. Pinals, MD, "research suggests that a substantial fraction of stalkers suffer from delusional disorders or other severe mental illness, and many defendants charged with stalking adduce (to give as a reason) irrational beliefs to explain and justify their behavior."[67] We met Dr. Pinals at a conference in held in the area of Boston, Massachusetts, where we both delivered presentations. Dr. Pinals, a psychiatrist, has dealt with a variety of stalkers. Although there are many delusional type disorders, which includes erotomanic type, grandiose type, jealous type, persecutory type, somatic type, mixed type, and unspecified type. We will say that the vast majority of stalkers we have dealt with know what they are doing. This is true even though they may be suffering from some type of mental disorder, which is usually a class of personality malfunction. The people with diagnosed delusional disorders that we run across the most seem to gravitate toward the instances of celebrity side of the stalking equation. Having said that, in our noncelebrity cases, we do see the jealous type and erotomanic type more than any other kind of delusional disorder. Also keep in mind that even though we do actively work and consult on a variety of cases, just because we may not come across these other delusional types doesn't mean they are not seen in other ongoing stalking scenarios. Keeping an open mind is the key to any good investigative process.

In early 2011 we were asked by a member of a large police agency to review a celebrity stalking they were dealing with. The case involved an attractive radio disc jockey for a well-known station in their community. After reading information generated by the stalker and discussing the case with the requesting party, we came to these conclusions.

First of all, the stalker believed he had a direct line to God, and he felt Jesus Christ was going to assist him in gathering up a specific group of women to take care of him for the rest of his life. This man was probably suffering from a grandiose type delusional condition. (Of course, we advised the individuals requesting this evaluation to run our findings past a mental health professional for verification.) The stalker also believed he was the greatest rock star that ever lived. He also believed the victim he was stalking was completely in love with him, even though he had only met her on one occasion when she was appearing at a public venue. (At that public venue, the stalker made it a point of hugging the victim. When he attempted to do it multiple times, event security stepped in.) The stalker talked about all the churches he visited and quoted a great deal of Bible verse. He may have been conflicted sexually and felt he had been a bad person in the past but could do no wrong now.

From the facts we were privy to; it appeared the stalker was extremely full of himself and very verbose. (There was a great deal of information in the provided data that we are not able to discuss.) As we indicated, anything a stalker produces can be a gold mine of information. Those charged with investigating a stalking case should never gloss over a stalker's letters, e-mails, texts, blogs, or other scribblings.

We advised the investigator to do a background check for previous victims. From information transmitted to us, we felt he had at least one other victim perhaps as many as three. We also advised that when they conducted a search of his residence, they would probably find ledgers with Bible verses, and they would most likely be written in a random fashion. They would probably mean something to the stalker but not necessarily to anyone else. He would more than likely have some type of shrine concerning his newest target along with other items concerning his other victim(s).

Because of the chances that a mental disorder might be in play, we probe our victim when conducting a threat assessment evaluation. (This topic will be discussed in the chapter on how we investigate a stalker.) Specifically we ask about the behaviors exhibited by the particular stalker. Once that information is obtained, we have an in-house mental health case worker who can assist in diagnosing the stalker. This gives us a better direction as to how we plan our investigative approach of the suspect. LAPD's threat management team and other units designed to work threat assessment also have this mental health evaluation system in place.

These are some types of disorders we commonly see when dealing with stalkers: obsessive-compulsive disorder, obsessive-compulsive personality disorder, narcissistic personality disorder, antisocial personality disorder, and a few types of delusional disorders. Many researchers we know and have reviewed would also include dependent personality disorder, borderline personality disorder, and paranoid personality disorder.

Another example of a stalker suffering from a delusional disorder involved a stalker we were recently asked to consult on from a W/V residing in Arizona. Years before, the victim had been engaged to this individual. For some unknown reason, he broke off their relationship. She did not hear from him for years, got married, had children, and then moved away from her home state. Out of the blue, she began getting letters attempting to rekindle their relationship. There was only one problem (other than her being happily married). The stalker told her he was not able to contact her over the years because he was a secret agent. (That is probably as good a reason as any.) The stalker said he had been working with covert operatives, hit men, and people close to a specific president that were involved in national espionage. He also advised her he was currently working as a long-haul trucker as his new cover story.

There are stalkers diagnosed with schizophrenia. When we teach, we ask if the class knows what schizophrenia is. We had one student tell us, "Yeah, it's what the guy on the street who jumps out of the cardboard box at you when you walk by, and he starts yelling and screaming about something you are clueless about." Well, that individual could be suffering from a form of schizophrenia and be having auditory or visual hallucinations. We had several people who used to frequent our local fast-food joints. Each sat in the back of the room, drank coffee, and talk to themselves for hours. These individuals might rub one portion of their body continually. For example, Andrea Yates (a diagnosed schizophrenic) was the woman who drowned her children in 2001 after hearing voices telling her to do so. Reportedly she used to sit in a chair, stare out into space, and rub her head until raw. The individuals we were talking about were known to have some form of schizophrenia, but they never bothered (let alone stalked) anyone. The key here is that there are a lot of schizophrenic disorders, even though we are not going to get into them. The point we are trying to convey by giving you just a few definitions and examples of these mental disorders is that some (not all) stalkers can suffer from one if not more of these afflictions, so just be aware of that. †* Those that actively work a number of stalking cases will invariably run across people diagnosed with some type of schizophrenia.

---

* Besides taking the time to go on the Iinternet, one of the best reference materials on mental disorders to have at work or home is *The Diagnostic And Statistical Manual of Mental Disorders* (*DSM-IV-TR*).

We have been contacted on so many occasions by people suffering from a variety of disorders that we pretty much know before we even open the letter or package what type of person we will be dealing with. These people often want to ensure you get the package, so there might be too much postage. Oftentimes they will label it multiple times. Whatever is sent, we don't even want to open it anymore because there is often not much we can do for the poor person sending us the information. We just contact their local law enforcement providers in the hopes they can get them some mental health assistance.

We currently have three such individuals venting to us about three or four times a year, and many more who unfortunately communicate almost daily on our website; even though we rarely if at all acknowledge them. Sometimes we can contact someone in his or her jurisdiction who might help that person, but oftentimes they don't include return address or e-mail. Perhaps the person knows we cannot really do much for them. Many times, we just let them vent, store the letters in a file, and move on with life. Of course, if they talk about trying to kill or injure someone including themselves, we try our best to locate them.

We will now define some other mental conditions seen in stalkers. Again, be aware these disorders may pop up on your stalker radar, but it is always best to get in touch with a professional with extensive knowledge in the mental health field. You will need someone to talk to you in language the average person can understand if such a consultation becomes necessary.

Obsessive-Compulsive Disorder (OCD)

Obsessive-compulsive disorder (OCD) is "a diagnosis of patterns of behavior which interfere with the ability to function, characterized by obsessions, compulsions, or both."[68] (This is also classified under anxiety disorders.) You may have seen someone like this. They obsess about door not locking and are overly concerned about life problems such as what is happening at work or school. Their compulsions might manifest as excessive hand washing. We have had prisoners enter our jail and begin repeatedly cleaning not only their hands but the surfaces around where they wash their hands. Some pray incessantly or appear to mouth or repeat the same word or phrase over and over again. These compulsions are designed to reduce the stress or anxiety the individual is experiencing. A person with this disorder is cognizant that the thoughts and obsessions are a product of their own minds and not forced on them by some other entity. They are not happy they have these compunctions or obsessions.

Obsessive-Compulsive Personality Disorder (OCPD)

Obsessive-compulsive personality disorder (OCPD) is "a persistent personality pattern characterized by an extreme drive for perfection, an excessive orderliness, an inability to compromise, and an exaggerated sense of responsibility."[69] These guys are into details, rules, laying out things, and scheduling. We once knew a contractor that expressed these and other traits of this disorder. He was a perfectionist to a fault. This meant he could never get most projects completed due to his incredibly precise and strict standards, which were never met by him or anyone else. When he drew plans for a project, he would meticulously draw in every bracket, stud joist holder, and even where the nail placement should be. You needed a wheelbarrow just to carry around the blue lines (contractor slang for building plans).

Other traits of this disorder include an inability to delegate, lack of many friends, and inflexibility, especially when it comes to morality or what they believe is an ethical situation. This type individual can become conflicted when he or she stalks because he or she knows it is wrong but keeps on doing it. We have had a stalker with this malady write in the margins of his logs that he knew what he was doing was stalking behavior, and it was wrong. We even had one write, that I (Detective Proctor) would be upset with him for what he was doing. Obviously these people usually display a very stubborn side as well. We have even encountered some that are unable to throw away well-used items. They say these things don't really mean anything to them, but they don't feel the need to get rid of them. (We have no idea if this is a condition a hoarder might have. It really wouldn't concern those involved in a stalking investigation.)

Here are some things one of the stalkers diagnosed with this disorder wrote in one of his ledgers: "Masturbated today, looked at porno magazine rack at liquor store, calling Verizon excessively, spending money uncontrollably, threw away my pornographic books today and did not masturbate, did not call Verizon operator to jack off, had one cup of coffee at 7-11, put away coffeepot, don't need caffeine." This particular stalker seemed addicted to coffee not to mention having obvious issues with how to utilize his cell phone provider's service plan.

One of the last stalking cases I was the lead investigator on just prior to retiring was a stalker diagnosed with an obsessive-compulsive personality disorder. This individual met his victim in a church environment. He had a previous history of stalking and was arrested and convicted for a stalking and arson he did in an Orange County beach community. Our boy, who was in his late twenties at that time, had gone after a female in her late seventies. She lived in a mobile home park, and he demanded to have sex with her. When she refused, he tried to burn her mobile home with her in it.

In our case he began stalking a woman he befriended in a nondenominational church. After a short relationship, due to his strange behavior, she told him to stop coming around. The stalker then began threatening to kill her. He tried to push her down the stairs, and he didn't like she had a young boy who kept getting in the way of his aspirations for the victim. On one occasion while following the victim in a store, he confronted the boy and threw him down a store aisle. He also wrote about how the boy was taking up too much of his victim's time. This meant he (the stalker) did not have more of an opportunity with the victim. We felt he was a threat to the boy because of these issues. The stalker made comments to the victim, such as, "You probably don't understand how I can care about you so much and still want to kill you…I am hurting so bad; I want you to hurt too!" During the course of our investigation, we also found the stalker had a fetish for women's shoes (retifism). (We don't have to make this stuff up. Stalkers are an unusual group. That is one reason we like investigating them.) Our stalker would put a pair of new stilettos in the corner of his room and stare at them for a period of time while he masturbated. Then he would wear the shoes around. It is unknown if he was also a cross-dresser, which we have also encountered in the weirdness of stalking. We had one guy who dressed in female attire in order to follow his target into the women's bathroom. Along the line of fetishes, we had one stalker recently brought to our attention that had a fetish for stalking women with only one leg. We are still waiting for the case information to get to us for an evaluation.

When our stalker was taken into custody, he was given a public defender. He would call the public defender about twenty to thirty times a day, and then he would call his supervisor. The public defender told the prosecutor he had what we refer to as LOCC, or lack of client control, with this individual. Due to this condition, they were going to have to go to trial because the stalker would not accept a plea bargain. The judge had offered the stalker nine years if he pled guilty. He refused, went to trial, was convicted on multiple charges, and ended up getting nineteen years. You learn fairly early on, about not pissing off the judge. Oh well.

Because of this particular stalker's disorder, we knew the type of things we would find during the search. We expected to find step-by-step accounts of his actions during the day while stalking the victim, and were not disappointed. We have included a few examples of items found in the search.

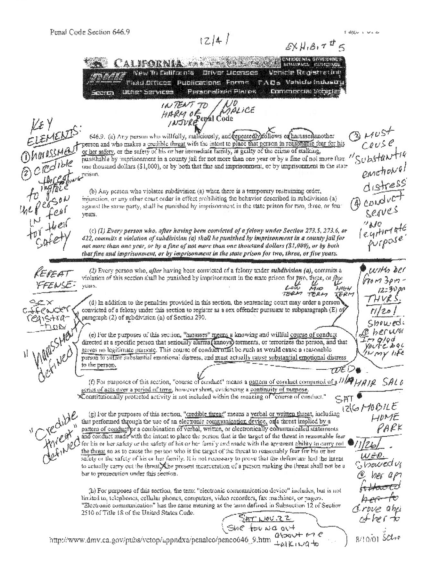

Stalker had made notes along borders of a page from the California Penal code.
Courtesy of the Westminster P.D.

The life of an obsessive
compulsive person.   EXHIBIT #7

DECEMBER

SUN 14 - went to first service, sat with
___ went to Norm's afterwards w/ ___
I started crying at breakfast about ___
I was in a hurry to get to 3rd Service @ Grace.
I called ___ from pay phone @ Seal Beach.

(FIRST CONTACT IN 3 WEEKS)

her - first contact with her in almost 3 weeks
since she shut the door in my face the day
before Thanksgiving. I went to apt. that
morning to ask her to forgive me for talking
to ___ I waited for her
to come out to take ___ to school. When
she did I startled her ___ said, "___
what are you doing her?" I called her ___
the night before and she was on the phone.
She said she would call me back but never
did. I asked her why and she said, "I
changed my mind" flatly. She got in the car
with ___ and drove off down the street.)
I tried to get to ___ school ahead of

(NOT HEALTHY BEHAVIOR)

her to talk to her but I didn't see her there.
I think she knew I was going to do that
and outsmarted me dropping off ___ somewhere else but I don't know for sure.)
She says 1/2 dozen of her friends
think I'm "stalking" her. She knows I called

(* KNOWS TOO)

the ___ Senior Center inquiring about
being a friendly visitor and saying she was
my ex-girlfriend and that I wasn't
comfortable talking to her.

Stalker documented this in his diary concerning his victim and her son.

Narcissistic Personality Disorder (NPD)

Narcissistic personality disorder is "A clinical diagnosis of a disorder characterized by grandiose ideas of self-importance, need for attention and admiration, feeling entitled to special favors, and exploitation of others."[70] When we contacted our mental health professionals that we deal with on a regular basis, they simply said this disorder is a dramatic personality disorder. It causes one to exhibit a distorted self-image, extreme interest with success and power, and a great deal of self-love. (These people need to be regularly told how wonderful they are.) It has been both their and our experience that these individuals try to hide their insecurities and self-esteem issues. Other symptoms we have experienced exhibited by those that have been diagnosed with this disorder are that they demand attention, express many talents they don't really have, and are very self-centered. They could not, for the most part, care less about the feelings of others, and as indicated in the definition will oftentimes take advantage of people around them to get ahead. We have also found they are fairly thin-skinned and do not like to be criticized. (A quick check of the Net should back up these observations.) Those in the mental health field that we contacted, also advised there is no known cure for the disease. Of course, they recommended seeing a psychologist or psychiatrist if one suffers from this disorder. I guess I should see one because my wife says I fit many of the parameters described in this condition.

We tend to see a number of these individuals in our investigations. One was a retired professor from a local college. In that case he dated a woman who was married, took her to a motel room, had sex with her, and (unbeknownst to the victim) videotaped the segments. We figured he was using the tapes to judge his performances, but we were never provided with copies of these videos. The suspect, who had a heavy foreign accent, was also married, and he felt he was the cat's pajamas (irresistible to women). Then he began going after his first conquest's sister, who completely blew him off. I guess she didn't like the accent as well as some of his other dalliances. When the sister rebuked teach, he began stalking the videotaped sister. (Her husband found out about the affair, causing her to end it.) We also found out that when the victim first attempted to break off the relationship, he called her and threatened to send e-mails to her husband and other relatives telling everyone about their affair. When my partner and I conducted a threat assessment interview with this woman, she initially appeared conflicted about her situation. She admitted that what the professor was doing was stalking, but she still had some feelings for him. When we told her we could not continue our investigation because of this issue, we stopped our processing. You have to understand that if the victim does not express fear, concern, or emotional distress, ours and most district attorneys that we know of will not file a case for stalking let alone endeavor to prosecute the suspect.

About a month passed, and the woman re-contacted the Family Protection Unit (FPU). She was now very upset and concerned. The stalker was now calling and talking to her about how much he liked her teenage daughter. This sent a chill down her spine, which it should have. We dealt with the case by making contact with the stalker, who decided it would be best to cease any further contact with the victim, her sister, or any other family members. He was not happy we were starting to contact his family or others he associated with during the course of our investigation.

While profiling this particular individual, we found he was definitely into documenting. He kept a detailed record of all his bowling scores for the past fifteen years. (He bowled seven nights a week.) He also spent a great deal of time on various chat rooms, wrote down every bill he had paid since 1965, and kept one sheet of every stamp printed in that same time period. He collected over seven hundred stuffed animals, had some three hundred plus shirts, reportedly was a "clean freak," was obsessed about how he dressed He also was extremely emotional, frequently cried, sent Bible scriptures, did not like to be criticized, made repeated phone calls to the victim (thirteen in less than two hours), and texted her numerous times a day. The subject had threatened to commit suicide and was under a doctor's care who had prescribed some antidepressant medication. (If you're saying he also sounds somewhat obsessive, we agree. Remember, certain stalkers can exhibit multiple, simultaneous personality disorders at the same time. We have found some to be real potpourris of disorders.)

We have had other stalkers with this illness who can't walk past a mirror without checking themselves out. Others dye their chest and pubic hair to match their freshly coiffed hairdos. (Now, that definitely would not be me. I wear camouflage pants or shorts, T-shirts from Cabelas and other "redneck stores", along with military combat boots as normal attire. It tends to drives most of my upscale friends nuts, which is probably one of the reasons why I do it.)

Antisocial Personality Disorder (APD)

According to the *DSM-IV-TR*, this disorder is "a pervasive pattern of disregard for, and violation of, the rights of others that begins in childhood or early adolescence and continues into adulthood."[71] The authors of this manual have developed the following criteria for this disorder:

> "A. There is a pervasive pattern of disregard for and violation of the rights of others occurring since age 15 years, as indicated by three (or more) of the following:
>
>> (1) failure to conform to social norms with respect to lawful behaviors as indicated by repeatedly performing acts that are grounds for arrest
>>
>> (2) deceitfulness, as indicated by repeated lying, use of aliases, or conning others for personal profit or pleasure
>>
>> (3) impulsivity or failure to plan ahead

(4) irritability and aggressiveness, as indicated by repeated physical fights or assaults

(5) reckless disregard for safety of self or others

(6) consistent irresponsibility, as indicated by repeated failure to sustain consistent work behavior or honor financial obligations

(7) lack of remorse, as indicated by being indifferent to or rationalizing having hurt, mistreated, or stolen from another."

B. The individual is at least 18 years of age.

C. There is evidence of Conduct Disorder (see p. 98) with onset before age 15 years,

D. The occurrence of antisocial behavior is not exclusively during the course of Schizophrenia or a Manic Episode."[72]

Even though this disorder may start to manifest around age fifteen, the authors says it really cannot be diagnosed until the subject is about eighteen, and the behavior can continue later into that person's life. Please note, this disorder used to be referred to as sociopathic behavior.

Substance abuse (alcohol, cocaine, methamphetamine, etc.) tends to heighten the type of behavior exhibited by individuals with this disorder. Therefore, if drug usage is occurring, one can expect more high-risk behavior out of these people.

We had a large-framed fourteen-year-old boy stalk a young female in an upscale portion of the city we used to work for. When he decided it was time to rape the girl (reportedly following in another family member footsteps he entered her residence at night. This was after conducting several nighttime vigils in previous weeks. For whatever reason, he did not assault the sixteen-year-old girl. Instead he went into her mother's room and began to fondle her. When she awoke, he stabbed her to death with a large butcher knife he had obtained while in the residence. When interviewed the stalker exhibited no visible signs of remorse. He had no expression of emotion whatsoever as he matter-of-factly related to my partner and me all the gory details of the crime. Further investigation revealed he had been involved in a previous arson and had conducted other hot prowl burglaries (entering when the residents were home).

Another example of an individual my partner and I confronted who exhibited signs of this disorder concerned an attempt murder investigation. The subject who was known to the victim, entered her residence and while sexualizing her from behind put on a pair of gloves, pulled out a knife, and calmly slit her throat. The victim commented that the subject seemed to be in a trance until she screamed after having her throat cut. When we interviewed the suspect, he was very unaffected, showing no concern for the victim or what he had done.

Dependent Personality Disorder (DPD)

The essential feature of dependent personality disorder is "a pervasive and excessive need to be taken care of that leads to submissive and clinging behavior and fears of separation."[73]*

According to the *DSM-IV-TR*, the following are other symptoms exhibited by those having a dependent personality disorder:

1. "has difficulty making everyday decisions without an excessive amount of advice and reassurance from others

---

* Another good site to review concerning this and other personality disorders is the Cleveland Clinic: http://my.clevelandclinic.org/disorders/Personality_Disorders/hic_Dependent_Personality_Disorder.aspx.

2. needs others to assume responsibility for most major areas of his or her life

3. has difficulty expressing disagreement with others because of fear of loss of support or approval. **Note:** Do not include realistic fears of retribution.

4. has difficulty initiating projects or doing things on his or her own (because of a lack of self-confidence in judgment or abilities rather than a lack of motivation or energy)

5. goes to excessive lengths to obtain nurturance and support from others, to the point of volunteering to do things that are unpleasant

6. feels uncomfortable or helpless when alone because of exaggerated fears of being unable to take care of himself or herself

7. urgently seeks another relationship as a source of care and support when a close relationship ends

8. is unrealistically preoccupied with fears of being left to take care of himself or herself." [74]

Even though the literature on DPD states this order afflicts men and women equally, we have seen it more with female stalking suspects. We investigated one case where the stalker's significant other came home to gather up his property and leave, and he encountered her lying on the side of their bed. She was upside down and naked with a gun next to her head. She said she would kill herself if he left. When the victim did leave, the female began a campaign of stalking. She showed up at his place of work and sent numerous cards and letters, all begging him to come back. She said she could not eat, was lost without him, was becoming increasingly depressed, and could not stand being alone. She would also send various photos that she took of her private parts to the victim and his coworkers. We surmised this was an attempt to embarrass the victim and force him to return as so to stop the behavior.

While investigating this case, we were contacted by a security specialist working for the female's company where she was an executive. There was growing concern about her behavior at work, and they wanted to know our opinion about letting her go. Remember, as threat assessment people, we try to assist with all components involved in a stalking, and it is not unusual for us to get involved with either the victim or the stalker's workplace.

We suggested that the best way to handle this particular subject was to release her with a fairly good severance package. That way it looked, at least on the surface, that the company was showing good faith. They would send off the troubled employee on "good terms," thus giving said employee less reason to come back on them in whatever form that might take. They were more concerned about a violent workplace confrontation than any type of civil action. The severance they provided allowed the subject to move out of state, so both they and our victim were assisted by this corporation's shrewd decision making. Of course, during our threat assessment evaluation, we found that this stalker wanted to move out of state to a relative's house, but did not have the funds to do so.

Paranoid Personality Disorder (PPD)

The essential feature of paranoid personality disorder is "a pattern of pervasive distrust and suspiciousness of others such that their motives are interpreted as malevolent."[75] The authors of the DSM-IV-TR have developed the following diagnostic criteria for this disorder:

> "A. A pervasive distrust and suspiciousness of others such that their motives are interpreted as malevolent, beginning by early adulthood and present in a variety of contexts, as indicated by four (or more) of the following:

(1) "suspects, without sufficient basis, that others are exploiting, harming, or deceiving him or her

(2) preoccupied with unjustified doubts about the loyalty or trustworthiness of friends or associates

(3) is reluctant to confide in others because of unwarranted fear that the information will be used maliciously against him or her

(4) reads hidden[,] demeaning[,] or threatening meanings into benign remarks or events

(5) persistently bears grudges, i.e., is unforgiving of insults, injuries, or slights

(6) perceives attacks on his or her character or reputation that are not apparent to others and is quick to react angrily or to counterattack

(7) has recurrent suspicions, without justification, regarding fidelity of spouse or sexual partner."

B. Does not occur exclusively during the course of Schizophrenia, a Mood Disorder With Psychotic Features, or another Psychotic Disorder and is not due to the direct physiological effects of a general medical condition.

Note: If criteria are met prior to the onset of Schizophrenia, and "Premorbid," e.g., "Paranoid Personality Disorder (Premorbid)."[76]

In regard to this type of stalker, we have had some unusual cases. In one scenario the female victim complained her spouse would call her numerous times a day to find out what she was doing or where she had been. He would contact coworkers to verify her statements. He would time her from the point when she left work to the time she got home. He would then conduct an "interrogation" about what she had done during the day. It got so bad that he had started making her strip so he could check her panties to see if she had had sex.

We may have discussed other cases similar to this one in other works where the stalker utilized a variety of devices to conduct an almost CSI approach to searching his spouse. This including doing a routine search of her car. What is next doing a fingernail scrape, and then sending it out to a lab to run DNA?

Borderline Personality Disorder (BPD)

According to the *DSM-IV-TR*, under the diagnostic criteria for this disorder, an individual who may present with this specific disorder may exhibit a "pattern of instability of interpersonal relationships, self-image, and affects, and marked impulsivity beginning by early adulthood and present in a variety of contexts, as indicated by five (or more) of the following:

(1) frantic efforts to avoid real or imagined abandonment. **Note**: Do not include suicidal or self-mutilating behavior covered in Criterion 5.

(2) a pattern of unstable and intense interpersonal relationships characterized by alternating between extremes of idealization and devaluation.

(3) identity disturbance: markedly and persistently unstable self-image or sense of self.

(4) impulsivity in at least two areas that are potentially self-damaging (e.g., spending, sex, substance abuse, reckless driving, binge eating). **Note**: Do not include suicidal or self-mutilating behavior covered in Criterion 5.

(5) recurrent suicidal behavior, gestures, or threats, or self-mutilating behavior.

(6) affective instability due to a marked reactivity of mood (e.g., intense episodic dysphoria, irritability, or anxiety usually lasting a few hours and only rarely more than a few days).

(7) chronic feelings of emptiness

(8) inappropriate, intense anger or difficulty controlling anger (e.g., frequent displays of temper, constant anger, recurrent physical fights).

(9) transient, stress-related paranoid ideation or severe dissociative symptoms."[77]

Stalkers diagnosed with this type of disorder have a lot of problems with abandonment issues. They oftentimes talk about suicide. Some do take their lives, and some cause other injuries to themselves. We believe they do this to draw attention to themselves. Many we have encountered feel they are being mistreated. They tend to go out of their way not to be alone. Those in the mental health field say that those suffering with BDP can have other disorders, which can create a minefield for the stalker and those exposed to them. Like we said, many of these disorders can and oftentimes do join forces.

A recent consult revealed a stalker with a diagnosed borderline personality disorder. We were contacted by a psychologist who had been dealing with a female patient-turned-stalker. The psychologist said she began working with a young female who began expressing suicidal thoughts along with abandonment issues. According to the therapist, the women wanted to expand the boundaries of therapist and patient. She tried to obtain more and more personal information concerning the therapist, which the therapist resisted at every request.

The therapist noted that the client said she had purchased a handgun, and on one occasion she expressed a desire to bring it to the therapist's office. Of course, the therapist refused. She contacted local law enforcement and had them get involved in a criminal investigation. During that time, the female client, who was versed in medical procedures, would send the therapist photos of herself using IVs reportedly filled with drugs that could kill her. The woman also sent descriptions of how she would hang herself. This stalker is also believed to have been able to hack into the therapist's social network, allowing her to show up at social gatherings the therapist was attending with family and friends.

When the stalker would show up to formal proceeding or was seen in another setting, she would be wearing the "exact same [type of] clothing" as the therapist had worn on previous occasions. The stalker had been known to try to impersonate her victim. The stalker was finally arrested and successfully prosecuted on multiple charges related to stalking, but to date stalking itself has not been filed. Efforts are still afoot to get stalking charged as well. Hopefully that will eventually come to fruition.

During this stalking scenario, the therapist evolved into a stalking victim advocate. She is currently pushing for additional stalking legislation in her state. As always, we volunteered to send information to and contact the state representatives she was dealing with. However, as the victim advocate, she does all of the legwork. It looks like she will eventually prevail. We wish her all the luck in the world.

Since our first set of consults with this victim, this same stalker has been sent to additional therapists for court-ordered treatment. Those therapists have been stalked by our girl. One of the therapist's home was broken into by the stalker. Unfortunately the defense attorney in this case once again has asked the judge in these two new on-going cases to have his client reevaluated prior to sentencing.

Hmm, let us see how this works. You are a serial stalker diagnosed with a mental disorder. A big part of that disorder causes you to identify with your caregiver, and when that caregiver can no longer deal with you as a client, you feel abandoned thus you stalk. So your defense attorney asks a judge to once again put another therapist in harm's way instead of throwing you in the slammer. It is our opinion this circle needs to be broken.

We recently consulted on another stalking scenario in which a mental health care professional notified a therapist that a stalker (whom the therapist had advised she could no longer treat) still was obsessed with her. This stalker presented with gender dysphoria (unhappiness about their assigned gender role, say a man wants to be a woman, or a woman wants to be a man) along with a litany of other psychological conditions, including borderline, grandiose, and narcissistic personality issues. Yes, we do seem to run across a good number of stalker's with sexual proclivities. Believe it or not, we have investigated and consulted on cases where the stalkers can't figure out what to wear when they get up. What we mean is what type of gender-specific clothing they should wear that day, even down to the type of shoes. This can go both ways, but we seem to encounter more male stalkers conflicted about their feminine sides. Many times the stalker does not appear to be involved in a homosexual relationship; at least not at the time of our evaluation of the subject.

What we have found interesting about mental health providers, including the private sector therapists we have dealt with, (on a truly professional basis, mind you) were their requests. One, they wanted to know when we were going to lecture next and where, and two, they wanted to know when our next book was coming out because they had our first one and wanted more information. (We always find it interesting that even though we write in basic simplistic fashion, how many very intelligent and professionally trained therapists, psychologists, and psychiatrists actually utilize our book(s) and articles.)

When we explain we would be nowhere as technical and eloquent as some of the academics (Sheridan, Purcell, Pathe, Mullen, or Meloy) their response was quite direct. They would review those works for additional information, but when it came to being helped with stopping the fear associated with stalking, they wanted someone who had eliminated the stalking threat in a variety of scenarios. They wanted that someone to give them a plan of attack in the hopes their pariah would hit the bricks. We can appreciate this point of view. These comments are precisely why we have decided at this particular portion of the book to discuss some safety ideas specifically directed towards therapist.

Safety Strategies for Therapists

For those readers not involved the world of counseling, there are a large number of single-person (meaning only one person in the office) therapists. Some are tasked with court-ordered psych evaluations for presentencing reports. Many of these interviews and evaluations are not conducted in a secure jailhouse or otherwise environment, and many of these individuals are not in custodial situations when they are evaluated. Therefore they end up in the therapist's private office. Many other therapists that deal with what we would refer to as "off-the-street" patients have similar private office setups. Therefore, both classes of therapist potentially run into a lot of loose cannons.

Many private sector therapists complain that when the subject-turned-stalker is turned away, and the care is terminated (for a variety of reasons), the subject will not stay on his or her medication and becomes extremely dependent on the therapist. This is by and large the primary problem encountered by the therapist. In many of these encounters, this is because the subject has abandonment issues and has become infatuated, or forms an attachment with the therapist, who expressed concern and empathy for that subject. Once that attachment is developed and then severed, that individual begins a course of stalking.

Besides the following, harassing, and other stalking behaviors, the stalker sometimes will file a series of complaints to the various state licensing boards, which have review powers over the therapists. Many will then follow up with civil lawsuits against the therapists, costing them hundreds to thousands of dollars in attorney fees.

The therapists that we have talked to who work with presentencing subjects have confided they too have been stalked because the subject-turned-stalker (for whatever reason) has fixated on them. Some have experienced more threatening behavior being generated towards them due to the outcome of their evaluations. It is a sad truth, but those of us that work with stalkers are oftentimes ripe for becoming their new targets. It is just an occupational hazard.

Suggested strategies to deal with a stalker:

- If you are a one-person office therapist, design the office with a foyer or entry space. This way, when the client enters, he or she activates a button or a switch that alerts you to the person's presence. We would suggest an intercom and a device that allows you to watch and listen to your client before letting that person in. This way you can observe the subject's behavior prior to that individual coming or going.

- The door that separates your inner office from the interview room should be a solid core door with a heavy-duty dead bolt lock on same. If you cannot exit from that portion of the office to the outside (—which unfortunately most of these offices are designed not to allow you to do—then you should have some way to communicate with the outside to summon assistance if necessary. Please note, we strongly suggest going into some depth about why you need these changes done to your office when dealing with your landlord. To eliminate issues, you may want to advise the landlord you will pay for the renovations, and when/if you vacate the premises, you will put it back the way it was. Most landlords will usually be open to this, especially if it is written into the rental agreement.

- Think about the furniture you have in your outer office. (Look to the simple sketch we have drawn of a typical therapist's office.) Place a couch along a wall that is some distance from you. Purchase a couch that is relatively soft and which causes the client to actually sink into the cushions in such a fashion as their backsides kind of slip into the crack of the couch. Why? It causes the clients to relax more, and it is more difficult for them to stand up if they start to come at you. All this gives you more time for escape. Attach quality carpet rollers to your chair (that you sit in—preferably behind a desk). Again, this gives you a chance to move out of harm's way if confronted. The desk can also be used as blocking device while in the process of escaping to the back office. (Remember, it is the little things that may save one from injury or worse.)

- When you do meet with a client, you might want to have some type of pepper spray or stun gun close at hand, so if the need arises, you can protect yourself. You are not necessarily trying to disable the threatening individual, but using such a device as a diversion allows you to safely leave the premises. (Obviously you should be comfortable with and trained with the use of such devices. You also need to check on your state, county, or city laws about the use/ownership of these implements.)

- Install a panic button. Many alarm companies commonly install a panic button protocol into their alarm panels. If one has an intruder, a press of the panic button will eventually summon local law enforcement. If you don't have an alarm company, and you share an office space with nearby tenants with similar office hours, get together and install a device that, when activated, beeps or activates a light in their offices. Make sure you are on the same page about the device, so the only time you activate the alert button is to call law enforcement, or that you need assistance immediately. While on the subject of lights. Obtain a flashlight and have it available. Also you might want to avail yourself of these small battery operated motion sensor lights that can be either screwed or affixed to most surfaces with the sticky tape that comes with the device. Whenever you have a power outage, or enter or leave your office in the dark, these lights will activate giving off an incredible amount of light. We utilize them on our property, and love them. The brand name we most prefer is "Light It!" by Fulcrum.

- Many therapists that have contacted us only take notes when talking to their clients. We suggest, unless there is some legal reason you cannot, tape-record your sessions. We like digital video. Why? If there is a problem that is later going to be litigated, you have a clear and concise record of the incident. This would include both civil and criminal litigation. Make sure the client is informed he or she is being either video or digitally recorded, and have that person sign a release. (Always consult with your attorney concerning this issue.) Many therapists have told us that if only they had recorded their encounters, either digitally or on tape, they would have had a much easier time dealing with their stalkers. For example, say a client leaps from his or her chair, leans across the desk, and exclaims, "Because you are stopping me from being your client, I am going to slit your throat!" This would have a great deal more impact if it could be heard on tape or seen and heard on video than if the therapist just wrote it in his or her notes. If you do opt for a video camera, install it in such a fashion as not to draw your client's attention to the device. If noticeable, it could serve as a distraction to the flow of information during the course of your session.

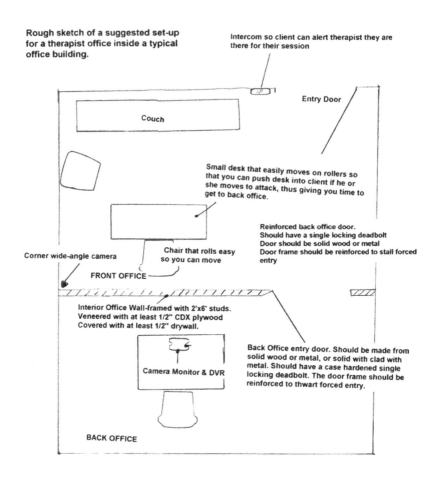

Rough sketch of a suggested set-up for a therapist office inside a typical office building.

Intercom so client can alert therapist they are there for their session

Entry Door

Couch

Small desk that easily moves on rollers so that you can push desk into client if he or she moves to attack, thus giving you time to get to back office.

Reinforced back office door.
Should have a single locking deadbolt
Door should be solid wood or metal
Door frame should be reinforced to stall forced entry

Corner wide-angle camera

Chair that rolls easy so you can move

FRONT OFFICE

Interior Office Wall-framed with 2'x6' studs.
Veneered with at least 1/2" CDX plywood
Covered with at least 1/2" drywall.

Back Office entry door. Should be made from solid wood or metal, or solid with clad with metal. Should have a case hardened single locking deadbolt. The door frame should be reinforced to thwart forced entry.

Camera Monitor & DVR

BACK OFFICE

Try and get an office on first floor so that your back office has acess to a door or window. If not make sure you have some way of monitoring your client when they arrive. Also have a way of alerting someone if things go wrong.

Rough diagram of an example of what the inside of a one person therapist office can look like. Drawn by author.

While on the topic of therapists and their safety strategies, we should discuss therapists that work with victim advocate groups. These therapists travel to various domestic violence shelters to consult with staff and victims that are being housed and protected there. These therapists are not <u>usually</u> at risk of being stalked, but there is a risk of being assaulted by the stalker, who is attempting to gather information on the individual the therapist is dealing with. (In most cases the victim will be the stalker's spouse or significant other.) Therapists usually do not have to worry about threats while inside a facility, but they are at risk once they have left. Many have complained to us about their fears and asked for counsel. We have suggested the following security measures be implemented in their particular situations:

- Have the facility in question install security cameras in the parking area. These are only going to help, however, if someone inside the facility is actually monitoring the cameras when the therapist (or other employees) walks to their vehicles. If approached, they can summon law enforcement or other assistance. As a point of interest, security cameras have come a long way. They now have a system where the person monitoring the camera can hit a key and talk to the person who is in the parking lot. Wouldn't this be a great thing? "Mary, are you all right? etc."

- Have an escort service available to walk the at-risk individual to his or her car. Armed security would be nice, but many of these organizations do not have insurance that covers that type of security. More often than not, they also do not have the funds for that type of service.

- Have each therapist carry a panic alarm button as he or she walks to his or her car. Once again, if no one is monitoring the exit, then setting off an alarm is useless, unless of course the alarm siren could wake up the dead.

- Many women, including the women in my family, carry Mace or other devices designed to fend off an attacker. Of course, training, reviews, and compliance with the laws of that facility's city and/or state all have to be taken into consideration.

We are continually looking for information about potential problem solvers for those that work in the criminal justice system on how science is developing new tools to stem the tide of mental issues. To that end, there was an April 2010 article in *Scientific American* written by Dr. Thomas R. Insel (a psychiatrist and neuroscientist). Entitled "Faulty Circuits," it said that "Neuroscience is revealing the malfunctioning connections underlying psychological disorders and forcing psychiatrists to rethink the causes of mental illness." The article indicated that this did not currently pertain to all mental illnesses, but it did talk about schizophrenia, obsessive-compulsive disorder (OCD), and a variety of other mental disorders that could be caused by biological factors (rather than environmental or other previously suggested causes of these disorders).[78] I found the information in this article fascinating and look forward to seeing if new brain mapping and other technology can assist those that have to deal with these debilitating diseases.

We do not have the necessary training to comment either way about Dr. Insel's findings, but we have observed another interesting phenomenon with stalkers and others with diagnosed mental disorders. While conducting background evaluations on these individuals, we always try to contact their family, friends, or significant others. In several instances, people have observed the onset of these maladies after a bout with a severe disease or significant head trauma, which caused hospitalization for at least some period of time. Medical science is aware of this type of change in personality, but people investigating stalkers should at least be cognizant of this when dealing with a case. The more information one has on a suspect, the better.

There is another interesting study that may eventually impact a certain variety of stalker. Scientists at the University of Cambridge are beginning to look at biomarkers in the blood of people having or suspected of having mental disorders such as schizophrenia and depression. They are using this information as a way of predicting or diagnosing these disorders (and hopefully other mental health conditions) more precisely and perhaps even at an earlier stage in the subject's life. As these types of tests are perfected and become cheaper, we hope more of these diseases can be successfully treated, thus eliminating some of the causative factors that lead to someone afflicted with one of these ailments becoming a stalking behavior.*

Yes, folks. Regardless of how some well-known politicians characterize those of us who drive pickup trucks, tote guns, listen to country as well as classical, and New Age Christian music), and say "howdy" when we meet you, we do read scientific journals. As well as study literature, speak in more than simple word phrases, and attempt to learn as much as possible about those areas that impact our given field(s) of endeavor.

Mental Disorders as a Stalking Defense

Mental health experts and prosecutors who handle high-risk, high-profile as well as "normal" stalking cases (such as Rhonda Saunders and Jane Shade, former Orange County prosecutor and current superior court commissioner) tell us that when a psychiatric defense is broached; proving the stalker planned extensively during the course of the stalking eliminates that defense when the case is put before the jury. Others advised us not to confuse the issue of sanity (whether the charged stalker is able to aid in his or her own defense and stand trial) with mental illness. The accused can have a mental disease and still be competent to be tried. This has also been our experience with the courts when we brought a case before a judge where the defendant allegedly suffered from various types of mental health complaints. In some high-profile celebrity cases tried in Los Angeles, even though defendants could utilize the psychiatric defense, they opted out for fear of later being institutionalized for an additional period of time. This would be under California's civil commitment laws for sexually violent predators, and others. To us, this demonstrates that, at least on this issue, these guys were firing on all cylinders.

---

* If interested in this area of research, look up a short article in the May 2012 edition of *Scientific American* entitled "Blood Tests for Mental Illness."

While on the subject of civil commitment for these predators, we thought we should probably discuss it a little. (Do not confuse normal civil commitment laws concerning those that are or are considered to be mentally ill with the mentally disordered [MDSO] sex offender laws we are currently discussing. They are not the same.) As of 2010 there were twenty states in the United States with civil commitment laws involving sexual predators. These laws are designed to further hold or detain potentially dangerous, sexually-based criminals for a longer period of time than their initial prison sentences.

Some other countries have similar civil commitment laws to the States. They may not be exact replicas, but they appear to have many of the same goals and processes designed to protect their citizenry. For example, according to the consultants we deal with in Norway, they have a section similar to the civil commitment laws in the United States. This allows them to keep individuals that are unable to stand trial due to mental defect, and deemed extremely dangerous off the street for an unspecified length of time. However, the crime does not have to be based on sexual perdition. The prosecution in the case of one Anders Breivik hoped this law would apply for his terrible criminal actions in that normally calm society. (We are, of course, talking about the bombing of government buildings and the slaughter of innocent camp-goers perpetrated by Breivik in 2011.)* (Note: Breivik was found by the Norwegian court to be "sane" and sentenced to twenty-one years in jail in August of 2012.)

The following is Minnesota's civil commitment law, Minn. Stat. 253B.185. Under this law, "Any person who has been determined by a court to be a 'sexually dangerous person' may be involuntarily

---

* We recently attended the 2012 ATAP (Association of Threat Assessment Professionals) in Anaheim Cal. One of the topics presented was an overview of the Anders Breivik scenario. The presenters, J. Reid Meloy, PhD, Bram van der Meer, M.A. and Jens Hoffman, PhD, painted a very informative forensic picture of what transpired before, during and after the incident. If you get a chance to attend conferences like these, the information gleaned can be quite helpful.

committed…There are three elements to the definition of 'sexually dangerous person.'

- First, the person must have engaged in a course of conduct of 'harmful sexual conduct' in the past. Sexual conduct is 'harmful' if it creates a substantial likelihood of causing serious physical or emotional harm to another person. Certain crimes are presumed to cause such harm, unless proven otherwise in a particular case. For example, felony-level criminal sexual conduct crimes are presumed to qualify as 'harmful sexual conduct.'

- Second, the person must manifest a sexual, personality, or other mental disorder or dysfunction.

- Third, as a result of this mental disorder or dysfunction, the person must be likely to engage in future acts of harmful sexual conduct."[79]

As a special note for those readers living in Minnesota, your stalking law used to be labeled as harassment, but as of August 1, 2010, it was renamed to "stalking." We just thought you might want to know.

In regards to stalking and these civil commitment laws, one would have to review each of their particular states' civil commitment language to see if it would apply. First, there would have to a sexual element involved in the stalking. Remember not all stalking has this as a component. Then the judge hearing the case would have to make this decision based on all the expert testimony about the stalker's mental condition. An excellent example of this was the Los Angeles stalking case involving gold medalist Shawn Johnson's stalker. (We don't like giving stalkers credit, so we won't use their names.)

Johnson's stalker had degrees in science related subject areas. He reportedly sustained an injury and began taking pain medications for same. While recuperating, he sat in his Florida home watching the Beijing Olympics, at which time he was drawn to Johnson. During this period in his life, he began hearing voices, one of which he believed was Johnson. He believed she communicated with him via the television.

According to reports, the stalker felt he and Johnson had telepathic children together and were destined to be together. When the voices began telling him that Johnson was in trouble and needed his help, he decided to come to California to contact his *beloved*. The only problem was that he brought weapons and duct tape along with other items that could be used to secure Johnson, along with several license plates from a variety of states. These items were to somehow aid him in his "rescue" attempt. The stalker also brought gifts for Johnson's mother to persuade her to allow his relationship with her daughter. (There is more information concerning this stalker's bizarre behavior, but it is not necessary to present for this example.) LAPD detectives commended network television security personnel for their very professional and timely handling of the stalker when he arrived at their studios searching for Johnson. (Again, it is so incredibly important that all those charged with the protection and safety of others are well-trained, as were these security officers.)

Both detectives from the Los Angeles Police Department's Threat Management Team and the experienced Los Angeles County District Attorney assigned to prosecute the case did an outstanding job as well. In June of 2010, the stalker was convicted and sentenced to a state mental health facility. He will serve time there and periodically be evaluated by mental health professionals. In this situation, the stalker will probably be off the streets for a longer period than his initial criminal sentence would have allowed. Therefore, having this type of adjudicated outcome involving the commitment process appears to be beneficial for all concerned. (For more on this type of commitment, refer to California's Sexually Violent Predator Act, Welfare and Institutions Code Section 6601.) If you want more information on Shawn Johnson's stalker, there is a great deal on the Internet.

While discussing this particular incident, we should advise you of an outstanding group of individuals that work hand and glove with the Los Angeles Police Department's Threat Management Unit as well as other members of the greater L.A. law enforcement community. That would be the Case Assessment Management Program CAMPS. This unit investigates and assesses persons that may have a diagnosable mental disorder in an effort to limit their impact on the community. If a law enforcement entity within CAMPS jurisdiction needs an evaluation or a consult, they call in this team who has a variety of tools at their disposal that law enforcement doesn't that can be brought to bear to eliminate a threat or potential threat, or as the unit indicates to assist people in crisis. CAMPS is a great model for other law enforcement entities to review. They realize as do we that most agencies cannot support a complete CAMPS type division, but those that review how they do things can utilize some of their techniques on a smaller scale, and perhaps generate assistance from within the mental health professionals in their specific communities.

We recently had the opportunity to talk to Tony Beliz, PhD, the deputy director of Los Angeles Counties' Department of Mental Health DMH, who is in charge of the DMH field response team, in which CAMP is housed. He advised that CAMP utilizes innovative approaches to working with the mentally disordered offender MDO groupings including threat driven predators. These solutions would include using a civil commitment approach when available; even though some of the commitment solutions must be monitored and/or reevaluated on a regular basis. Dr. Beliz also advised that when possible, their team may obtain a Lanterman-Petris-Short (LPS) conservatorship commitment for an individual. This type of conservatorship must be monitored on an annual basis.* Dr. Beliz went on to say that in his county, they were fortunate to have a great deal more resources than most, but with such a diverse

---

* For more on this type of conservatorship go to: http://www.disabilityrightsca.org/pubs/508201.htm

population with over twelve million people those assets are greatly needed. If interested, you can contact the Los Angeles County Department of Mental Health for further information. (*What we want to get across, is that law enforcement in conjunction with mental health represent a good approach to attempting to maintain the violent offender with mental health issues, whether or not a sexual predation element exists.*)

This doesn't mean jurists don't still send off stalkers for a psych evaluation and then return them for trial. We had one female stalker who, when asked a question by the judge, turned to the wall and started talking to her shadow. She was sent away for a ninety-day evaluation, came back, found competent to stand trial, pled guilty to felony stalking, did her prison time, and then began stalking her parole officer. This is just another example of a stalker stalking those involved in his or her case, and as this case shows, this can include parole and probation personnel.

Female Stalkers

Female stalkers, although fewer in number than male stalkers, are worth discussing. We have arrested and consulted on our fair share of women involved in the stalking trade. We were fortunate enough to have been at an Association of Threat Assessment Professionals (ATAP) conference when we were writing our last book. One of the presenters was Cynthia Boyd, PhD. Boyd had just completed her dissertation and, along with Reid Meloy, PhD, had finished an excellent study entitled "Characteristics of Female Stalking Perpetrators: Behavior, Psychology, and Violence Risk." We were able to question Dr. Boyd, who gave us an extensive interview that was published in our first book, *How to Stop a Stalker*. Their study, which included some of our cases for review, contained samplings from the United States, Canada, and Australia. Some were media-oriented stalkers. Here is a brief synopsis of the information derived from our interview with Dr. Boyd:

- Many of the women in the study exhibited personality disorders, and most did not show or express being psychotic at the time of the stalking.

- A good number of female stalkers had college or advanced college degrees.

- In the study, the stalkers were divided into four categories: acquaintance, prior sexual intimates, strangers, and family. The highest rate of stalkers that expressed violence was in the prior sexual intimate category.

- Female stalkers tended to send e-mails, send faxes, make phone calls, and utilize other forms of contact than pursuing or following their targets.

- Dr. Boyd said that one of the most important findings from her and Dr. Meloy's research was that "males tend to pursue to maintain intimacy, and females tend to pursue to establish intimacy."[80] (Keep in mind that if you do go to Meloy and Boyd's completed study, some of the information she gave us may be slightly different than what is projected in the finalized work. We have not availed ourselves of the completed study. For more details concerning this study, including percentages, go online and look up these two well-qualified researchers' study.)

Even though the female stalking population studied by Dr. Boyd and Dr. Meloy indicated that female stalkers tended to use e-mails and other forms of contact when stalking, rather than following their target's; the vast majority of the female stalkers we have investigated or consulted on did pursue their targets in some fashion. They followed or surveilled. They showed up where the victims worked, ate, and played. Some made contact with family members or other females the male target had some type of relationship with. They also did many of things described in the study. This included faxing, e-mailing, texting, and calling in combination with the surveillance tactics we observed.

The following is an example of a female stalker we feel is somewhat unusual. I was contacted by an Orange County supervising district attorney. This particular district attorney had attended one of my training seminars designed for prosecuting attorneys and had read my first book. This was extremely helpful. Once trained, these district attorneys are much better equipped to triage cases that come across their desks. We were notified that a female stalking scenario had transpired, and he ask us if we could get involved.

The issue, once again, was that the crime of stalking was taking place in two Orange County cities, which were about forty miles apart. Trust us, it can be tricky when one detective from some uninvolved jurisdiction tries to insert him or herself into another police department's case. You must use kid gloves and attempt to make contact with your hat in your hand. Being invited is a must. Fortunately we knew one of the homicide detectives, who was now a lieutenant in charge of one of the agency's detective division. We contacted him and got an introduction to the detective in charge. This investigator turned out to be very cooperative, and he allowed us to openly assist him in his investigation. This included open and continued access to his victim. The other involved department was not so open. In fact, they called our detective commander and wanted to know who the hell we were, and why we felt we could help them. (Keep in mind; we were not the one trying to get involved. The supervising district attorney was the entity requesting assistance.)

The stalking was somewhat convoluted as many can be. It started with a prominent doctor who practiced in the city that was upset with our involvement. At first the doctor had a casual business relationship with the stalker ("Rose"). Rose knew he had a business affiliation with a surgery center in another city. One day, she showed up unannounced and unauthorized and began questioning all of his staff about their duties and their relationships to the doctor. The doctor did have a brief dating relationship with Rose, who was in the United States on a work visa. She worked as an engineer for a neighboring city to the doctor.

On one of these dates, Rose found the doctor's cell phone, called a previous female he had dated, and told her the doctor no longer wanted to have anything to do with her. Rose said she would be handling all of his affairs, including his office staff. She also told the confused woman not to come to the office or communicate with the doctor or his office personnel in any way. She then proceeded to wipe his phone clean of any number involving this and any other female that was in his phone's contacts. When it became evident to the doctor that Rose was becoming increasingly possessive, he tried to sever their relationship. Shortly after the doctor attempted to break off any contact with Rose, she made a call to his office manager. Rose said something to the effect of "everyone should watch their backs." She then called another staffer and told her, "You're all dead!"

Then Rose began stalking the doctor in earnest. She went to the home of his mother and sister and demanded to see the doctor in order to get "closure." The next time the doctor encountered Rose was at an open-air concert he was attending with friends. She came out of nowhere and confronted him. He then began seeing Rose everywhere he went. After a lady friend's vehicle was vandalized (scratched with a key) in front of the doctor's residence, the cell phone calls began. She made fifteen calls in a short period of time. There were thirty-one calls on his answering machine. The doctor lived in a gated community, but somehow Rose got through the gates. We asked the doctor's office manager to develop a stalking chronology. (See this example in Chapter 5: Our Approach to Investigating Stalkers. All the names have been changed so they can be entered into this book. We will discuss stalking chronologies at greater length in chapter five as well.)

The good doctor's Porsche and Hummer SUV were the next vehicles to be keyed. Dirt was ground into the paint and spittle detected. While on a date, Rose followed the doctor in a vehicle the doctor had never seen before.

Rose then rented a car and began not only following the doc but his girlfriends as well. Once she found out where the women lived, she vandalized their cars, homes, and other property. She overturned planted plants and formed the soil into little graves. She spray-painted rude sayings on the victims' garage doors, calling them whores, sluts, etc. Rose also sat outside their residences and watched them. Once Rose began stalking these females, she entered into the jurisdiction we were beginning to assist.

When we conducted an interview with the one of the female victims, she was extremely upset. Throughout the interview, she shook, wrung her hands, teared up, and expressed the fact that she was terrified for both her and her children because of Rose's actions. The victim presented with dark circles under her eyes and looked worn. She complained of sleep deprivation ever since Rose started stalking her. She believed Rose would harm or kill her and her children. As a result of Rose stalking her, the victim had purchased a monitored burglar alarm system and had not gone back inside her residence since Rose had been seen outside her house in a rented sedan. As it so happened, the victim was a secretary for a major security company, and they assisted her when she expressed her protection needs. (For those cops reading this book, write in your reports everything you see your victims do. This includes things such as getting a security system or buying a gun, pepper spray, or a Taser. These observations all go towards showing the victim's state of mind. As we will discuss later, that is why we teach law enforcement to videotape the victim's threat assessment interview.)

We conducted a threat assessment interview. The results were included in the detective's crime report and charging form. In a portion of the assessment, we stressed that Rose was a serial stalker that could not handle rejection. It was our feeling she would continue stalking those that broke off any kind of dating engagement.

She would also stalk anyone she deemed to threaten her relationship with the male she was currently targeting. (Rose is a triangle stalker.) The threat assessment helped the detective in charge get a bail enhancement when she was finally taken into custody. At the time, she was in, you guessed it, another rental vehicle. (We knew exactly what day she was stalking by checking her credit card receipts for the days she obtained rentals from the same rental company.)

We told the detective we were working with to check Rose's criminal history. We were sure this wasn't the first time she was involved in stalking. Sure enough, the city's police department where she worked had arrested her for stalking another male in the same fashion as our doctor. When she was rebuked, Rose would rent vehicles, follow that victim and his girlfriends, threaten, and damage their property. In that case, the charges were reduced to misdemeanors. Because Rose was in the United States on a work visa, we contacted immigration. Immigration advised me and the handling detective they would not deport her until she committed and was convicted of a violent felony.

When Rose was arrested and brought to trial, the judge at sentencing said he had never seen a stalker like her. She was a talented engineer during the day and a stalker at night. She was found guilty of felony stalking and sentenced to three years in prison. She was slated for deportation as soon as she finished her prison term. Last we heard, Rose was allowed to stay in this country because she or some family member said they supposedly had information that was deemed to be beneficial to our countries national security. We were never advised exactly what that was.

Genesis Victim

Over the years, we have noticed an unusual occurrence when conducting stalking investigations. We refer to this phenomenon as the "genesis victim." (We did not coin this phrase. That is for researchers, and we are merely observers who decided we needed a name for what we were dealing with.) This phenomenon has happened enough that when we conduct our threat assessments/primary victim interview, we try to ascertain if the person we are talking to is a genesis victim. If that is not the case, our line of questioning with this particular target may lead us to the genesis victim that the stalker had been involved with.

Simply put, a genesis victim is a victim that the stalker, for whatever reason, keeps returning to, even if he or she has found another target to stalk. Say a man is stalking victim A. Some type of intervention takes place which forces him to stop stalking victim A, so he moves on to victim B. Then something happens to stop him from stalking victim B, but instead of trying to locate another target, he returns to victim A and begins stalking him/her again.

We had one stalker that returned to his genesis victim over five times in a period of several years. We try to find out what the draw is to that victim. In the case of this last example, the stalker felt he was married to the victim, even though that was not even close to reality. We had another stalker that continued to return to his genesis victim because, according to both stalker and victim, she was the first to allow him to sodomize her and conduct other specific sex acts. After he stalked her, he attempted to have all the females he stalked or had a relationship with do what she had allowed him to do. Most of the time, they would kick him to the curb, and this caused him to begin his stalking routine until some type of intervention took place. Then he would once again begin his search for his genesis victim.

When we locate a stalker's genesis victim, we often get an extremely negative response because that person has been terrorized so many times by the individual. We look for them to add information to our case because, in a California stalking trial, prior bad acts can be presented to the judge and allowed as information in that proceeding. (This is under Section 1101 of the evidence code, evidence of character to prove conduct.)

We commonly find this type of victim when the stalker is male, and the victim is female. We did find this in some cases of lesbian stalking, where the female stalker would continually come back to one specific female and continue to stalk her after she had left another target. One of the last cases I investigated involved such a case. The female stalker was involved in the medical profession, had a substance abuse problem, and relentlessly followed, harassed, and demonized a previous female intimate partner. Once my partner in the Family Protection Unit (FPU)—I had one there and one in homicide—got involved in the case, we were able to file numerous counts for a variety of crimes, including stalking. Shortly after my retirement, a warrant had been issued for the female's arrest. My partner called me and said, "Hey, Duck, you recall so and so?" When I told him I did, he said that the case had been closed, and there would not be any prosecution. I was confused. He said that when the stalker found out we were looking for her, she drove into San Diego County, got a motel room, and hung herself.

We have only encountered one male stalker having a male genesis victim. These two individuals were involved in a homosexual relationship. When we contacted LAPD's Threat Management Unit (TMU), they said they could only remember one such stalking event. We also checked with members of the San Francisco Police Department's Domestic Violence Unit (charged with handling most stalking cases in that community), and they said that, due to the way cases were dispersed within their division, they had no way of gleaning that information. This does not mean it doesn't take place more often, but so far we have not had a number of documented events with a male stalker having another male as a genesis victim.

Chapter Two Summary

- There are numerous stalking typologies in existence. The three we use most often are domestic violence/intimate partner (DVS), acquaintance (AS), and stranger (SS). Stalking typology subsets that we use; include triangle, predator, third-party, retribution, and neighborhood Stalkers.
- Stalkers *may* have a myriad of mental disorders such as obsessive-compulsive personality, narcissistic personality, antisocial personality, borderline personality, histrionic personality, or paranoid personality disorders. They can exhibit additional mental illness such as a type of schizophrenia or a delusional type disorder.
- According to a study conducted by Meloy and Boyd, PhDs, female stalkers can threaten and commit murder, but they usually use letters, notes, e-mails, faxes, pages, and other electronic devices to stalk rather than follow and pursue their victims. According to this same study, "males tend to pursue to maintain intimacy, and females tend to pursue to establish intimacy." Many of the female stalkers we have encountered have followed and pursued their targets.
- Genesis victims are those that stalkers reinitiate contact with after an intervention has taken place with another person they were stalking. Female genesis victims with male stalkers are the most common, but a female stalker may have a female genesis victim as well.

- There is an increase in juvenile type stalking. A study indicates that girls in this category stalk more than boys. These stalkers tend to be more violent overall than their adult counterparts.
- Stalking on our college campuses is a growing concern. Education and better methods of reporting are ways to start stemming the tide of these campus predators. High school/secondary school campus security needs to a higher priority.

Chapter 3
A Stalker's Bag of Tricks

Now we have discussed the different types of stalkers, it is time to enroll in what we call "Stalking 101," or "Intro to the Tools of the Stalking Trade." Remember, each stalker is different, and so are the tools and devices he or she brings to bear while stalking. In this chapter we will discuss the myriad of tactics we have experienced stalkers employ. Again, these techniques depend on the type of stalker encountered.

Before we get into the bag of tricks, however, we should discuss what all these things tend to do to the stalker's targets. Unfortunately most people who have never been placed into the inferno of stalking have little or no concept about what most all women and a great deal of men experience when being stalked. Many of the victims I have dealt with are at the end of their emotional tethers. Some have told me they would rather be dead than try to survive another day. They are physically and emotionally drained with no concept of future. When we have sat across from them during their first threat assessment interviews, we have experienced their terror, their tears, and all of their deep pain. Some have made out wills. Others have armed themselves. Others still have become prisoners in their own homes, terrified to go out in the world for fear of what the stalker will do next. We have seen and had reported to us the following issues and maladies expressed by female stalking targets:

- Extreme mental and physical stress

- Lack of sleep coupled with bouts of complete exhaustion

- Depression, fear, and anxiety

- Disruptions in menstrual cycles

- Skin eruptions, rashes, blotchiness, etc.

- Some have been diagnosed with P.T.S.D. (post-traumatic stress disorder (PTSD) seen in some men men as well)

- Fear of leaving their homes or going out in public

- Loss of jobs, or loss of work days

- Isolation from friends and family

- Weight loss

- Pressures on their economic and medical resources

- Moving back home

- Blame themselves for what the stalker has or is continuing to do

- Whole life disruptions due to moving to a new state/country in an attempt to flee the stalker

Male stalking victims also expressed and exhibited depression, anxiety, loss of weight, (at times) isolation, and economic pressures. Researchers such as Michelle Pathe, PhD, and Paul Mullen, PhD, have done extensive studies into what happens to victims when they are stalked. One such study was entitled "The Impact of Stalkers on Their Victims" in *The British Journal of Psychiatry. 170: 12-17 (1997).* Jumping on the Internet and conducting a simple search will bring up the relevant information. Of course we should mention stalking can also result in physical and/or sexual assault.

First Contact

Many stalkers may start their contacts with a series of gifts and/or notes. Most of the time, these initial gifts and notes are benign, but depending on the mind-set of the stalker, they can change over time from nice to sexually explicit to threatening.

One of the overarching themes of the violent and possessive stalker is, **"If I can't have you, no one else will!"** We have seen this written in almost every language, including, if you can believe it, Russian. That was a very interesting case because we had to find a translator for a Ukrainian suspect. (Trust us; having to do any kind of criminal interview with a translator is a bitch. There is a whole lot lost in translation.)

Note sent by stalker to his victim. Courtesy of Westminster P.D.

We have seen notes accompanied by nude photos of male genitals. We have even seen these same types of notes sent by female stalkers showing close-up photos of their breasts and vaginal areas.

In an acquaintance stalking that was profiled on an *E! Hollywood* special mentioned earlier in the book, the stalker would leave his lip print on the windows of the victim's vehicle as his calling card. We have seen this type of behavior in other cases. People have also left feces or

Drawing female stalker sent to her young target. Courtesy of Westminster P.D.

195

other bodily fluids on a victim's property. One of the strangest gifts left by a stalker (who started out as an SS but was later identified) was a series of used condoms on the victim's doorknob. Judging by the size of the condom, he didn't have much to brag about

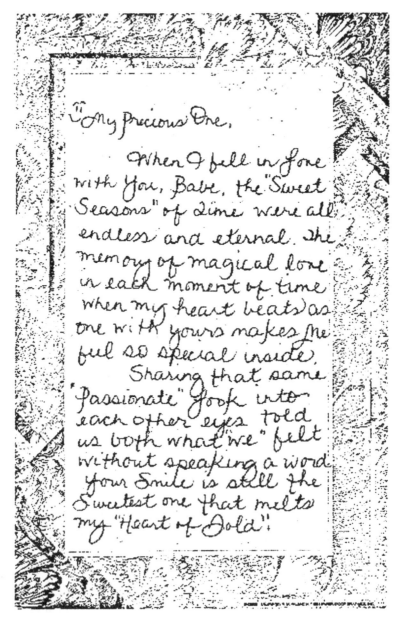

Love note sent by persistent female stalker to her male target.

We have had stalkers make detailed collages that have taken several hours to manufacture. Others write rambling notes that seem to only mean something to them. Some of these cards and notes contain Bible verses that seem random and disjointed until you interview the stalker, who eventually makes sense of them (kind of). Other stalkers send tape-recorded music with lyrics about cheating, getting even, or their unrequited love for the victim. Some of our stalkers write threatening notes and letters. This includes the Asian female stalker who wrote to her estranged husband about wanting to burn his house down. (For some reason, a lot of stalkers want to burn things such as houses, cars, clothes, cell phones, and even certain portions of the victim's anatomy.) The stalker went on to say, "I just throw the boy [their young son] into the trash and bury him...I will (do certain things to his body) until he coughs up blood and dies." There were other horrific comments about what she would do with the victim's new girlfriend such as grinding up parts of her and feeding it to her dog. (We don't know what it is about stalkers wanting to grind up their victims into dog food, but we see that expression over and over again.) Others write notes and letter expressing their undying love. Keep in mind, the female stalker who wrote the displayed love note was also the one that threw softballs through the front window of the victim's apartment when he was sitting on the couch with his soon-to-be wife. That was after she stood by a chain-link fence and groped herself in a very sexually explicit fashion while her target and another male attempted to play tennis. The stalker that drew the picture of the partially clad woman sent it off to a young male she was currently stalking. While conducting our investigation, we found that this same female, who used to dye her hair in a variety of different colors regularly, had been extremely violent with a previous boyfriend in a neighboring city. Her weapons of choice were large cooking knives that she liked to intimidate her estranged bows with. The agency we contacted said fortunately this male he had just stepped out prior to this stalker entering his apartment, or he may have been flayed.

On a case we consulted on in the Southwest, the stranger stalker sent endless cards with no name or forwarding address to a happily married, stay-at-home mom with three kids. The cards had sayings such as, "Everything about you is everything I love," "I am Crazy about you," and "What I am trying to say is that I love you." Even though these cards just kept coming, and the woman was becoming increasingly fearful, she complained she could not get law enforcement to take her seriously.

During the course of one of our stalking cases, we worked with a fourteen-year-old female victim who looked like she was in her early twenties. Her model good looks had caused her problems with older suitors over the past several years of her young life. When we got the case, she was actively being stalked male in his late twenties, who our investigation revealed as having borderline personality disorder. He was a cutter, meaning he would take a large military assault knife, which he carried with him, and cut slits into his forearms. He talked about committing suicide and had major abandonment issues. These were all bad indicators for the safety of our young victim. When we show this stalker's letters and drawings to those that attend our seminars, we ask how old they think he is. Most in the audience estimate he's a high school student that's no older than seventeen or so. From the letters and notes we gathered, that is probably the age he is stuck in. He is, however, quickly approaching thirty. Fortunately most of the stalking took place in a neighboring jurisdiction where we had recently trained. They took the case and obtained a successful prosecution of the subject. It was none too soon either. They found items in his truck that could be used to kidnap the female, which was an immediate concern for all those involved with the case.

Over the course of the stalking, gifts can turn to the dark side, especially when the stalker feels rebuked. We've seen bouquets of black roses, stuffed   with nooses around their necks, a child's doll with the eyes poked out, etc. Then you get the stalker who sends letters and notes from a mental institution where he or she is receiving a court-ordered mental evaluation. We received letters from a victim who had been stalked repeatedly by an estranged boyfriend. (He finally ended up in a southwestern prison.) Even though she still had a valid restraining order against him, and he was behind bars, he continued to stalk her by writing notes and letters. In one of the letters, he talks about how much he loves her, and in the same letter, he calls her a "slut," "bitch," and "whore." He then asks her to "please visit and dress [in] your sexy dress and no panties." We have had a few stalkers send threatening letters from prison that are actually prison poems. One such letter got our stalker a rave review of an additional two years in the joint. Oh, the price of showing off your literary talents.

Vandalism

Stalkers are experts at screwing up the victim's property and life. They have superglued doors, padlocks, and car door locks. They have cut brake lines and punctured tires in the sidewalls so the tire cannot be repaired. They have put rice into the radiator of a car. That way, after the car runs for awhile, the rice expands and blows the radiator casement. This often damages the engine itself. They have urinated on victims' computer keyboards, clothes, and bedding. They have smeared feces on the victims' walls and elsewhere throughout the abodes. They've even defecated in various parts of their homes. Please note, when stalkers leave items like these behind, we realize it is foul, foul, foul, but it also provides these clowns' DNA.

We recently encountered a stalker that would place extremely sharp nails, forced through a thin piece of wood, behind the rear tires of the victim's parked vehicle. The wood would keep the nails in their upright position, guaranteeing they would do their worst when she backed up.

Surveillance

These stalkers utilize all forms of surveillance techniques and equipment. Let us talk about some of these tactics.

- *Following*: Stalkers often will follow victims in their vehicles. They find out where you work, where you eat, where your boyfriend or girlfriend lives, where you shop, and where you go to church.

Speaking of church, I was recently contacted by my pastor (yes, even though I realize it is hard to comprehend, I do regularly attend church whenever they decide it is OK to let me in) about a stalking victim that needed help. The pastor was surprised that stalkers continually prey on victims in churches. The primary reason is that, when people go to church, their guards are down. They believe everyone at church is there for the same reason. Most are there to get stronger in their faith, so they talk freely about themselves to the rest of the congregation. We have had multiple stalkers find their victims via religious contact-oriented publications or by attending churches in their area. We have had more than one stalker use a church's outreach facility to get food, clothing, and older females to live off while stalking other people. When we come in contact with the victims of these parasitical relationships, they tell us the stalker made them take him wherever he wanted, give him money and food, and give him access to their Internet accounts and telephone. Some of the victims were beaten or, at the very least, threatened, and they were so glad we had taken the stalker out of their lives they were beside themselves. Keep in mind, they were not the stalker's target. They were merely his hosts. Does that mean we should run a record check on everyone we encounter in church? No. Simply be aware of what you are revealing about yourself and to whom, especially on the first couple of encounters.

While on the subject of following, there is a group that seems to be getting increasingly out of control. We are talking about the paparazzi. Celebrities used to have their photos taken either upon request or by the few celebrity photographers. These photographers were known to most of the famous and for the most part were accepted. These photographers even had a code of ethics. This is obviously not the case anymore.

In our last book, we talked about the need for regulation after the tragic death of Princess Diana in 1997. Since then the paparazzi (at least in California) have gone off the deep end. Many of these guys think having a camera gives them a pass on stalking and harassment. Groups of paparazzi have turned to sophisticated tracking information to follow their intended prey. They gather information better than some criminal investigators. Some set up teams with cell phones and walkie-talkies or cell phones, and then move like schools of piranhas in search of food. In an erratic and dangerous fashion, they continually follow celebrities as if they are in pursuit of a fleeing felon. They lie in wait, hide in trees, trespass, and cause emotional distress in many of these celebrities (dare we say victims). Of course, sometimes celebrities are their own worst enemies by tweeting and making other announcements that alert predators (among them, paparazzi) as well as their fan base.

As such California has passed a strong civil anti-paparazzi law with Cal. Civil Code 1708.8 (a). Essentially this law gives the plaintiff the right to sue an individual who "knowingly enters onto the land of another person without their permission or otherwise committed a trespass in order to physically invade the privacy of the plaintiff with the intent to capture any type of visual image, sound recording, or other physical impression of the plaintiff engaging in a personal or familial activity, and the physical invasion occurs in a manner that is offensive to a reasonable person."[81] The verbiage of this law is lengthy, so referencing the given URL in the previous endnote will aid the reader who wants to delve into the law in its entirety.

Governor Schwarzenegger first signed this bill into law in 2005, but Governor Pete Wilson actually signed the first anti-paparazzi law into effect on September 29, 1998. In 2009 Schwarzenegger signed into law an amendment to the legislation Wilson initially put to pen to. That allowed harmed parties to sue media outlets that published snapped photos in violation of this law. (Appears to have been enacted on January 2010) Several bills from members of the federal government have been proposed, but to date nothing has been passed along the same lines as California's legislation. Many suggest this type of action creates an issue with the United States First Amendment. At the writing of this book, the California legislature was putting forth another amendment designed to add increased sanctions against the paparazzi. If these new laws passed, it would make it a crime of trespass for paparazzi to loiter outside the personal residence of a celebrity. It would also add a specific section to the California anti-stalking law concerning the following and harassment of a celebrity, allowing law enforcement to make an arrest for stalking.

While recently travelling to Europe, we talked to a major magazine photo editor who was heading to London for a shoot. He said in the United Kingdom, especially in the greater London area, they have a huge problem with the paparazzi as well. So even though Hollywood seems to get the most attention when it comes to media hounds (or in many cases, media vultures), anywhere celebs show up, so do the paparazzi and many of them are out of control.

- *Global Positioning Systems (GPS):* GPS is an excellent tool passed down to the public by our military. We love GPS because we don't get lost anymore. (Well, my partner whom we refer to as the Polish navigator because of his last name occasionally still does.) It is touted on the Internet as a way for companies (transportation, trucking, and others) to continually monitor their rolling stock. You can purchase GPSs, which are getting smaller every year, on the Internet and elsewhere. For all the good GPS does, it can also be used for the wrong reasons. Stalkers are beginning to use it more and more. The first prosecuted case we know of was in Los Angeles, California. A stalker put a GPS-enabled cell phone on the undercarriage of his target's vehicle and then was able to track her movements.

Now a stalker can follow a victim's every move from a laptop or, in many cases, a smartphone. Those of you with cases where your victim complains that his or her stalker knows wherever he or she goes at any time, conduct a vehicle search to locate the suspected device. There are two types of GPS on the market. The passive device is one that, when installed, keeps a record of everywhere the driver has gone over a period of time. The real-time tracking devices send information to a database that can be accessed by the user from the Internet. (By the time this book is published, there may be more types. We just can't seem to keep up. This will be true for most, if not all, electronic and cyberstalking devices we will be discussing.)

One of the GPS trackers available on the Internet is advertised as having the world's smallest GPS tracking file so its users can track people without their knowledge. In defense of the manufactures of these types of devices, they can be used for good as well as bad. Some have emergency activators that, when pushed, send out a distress signal that can be tracked by emergency personnel. Like many other products, it is all in how it is utilized. Due to the increased GPS usage by stalkers, states such as New Mexico (under

SB 166, which is also known as Jodi's Law) have included in their stalking laws a provision against the use of GPS surveillance. (The addition to the New Mexico stalking law went into effect on July 1, 2009.)* More and more states are following suit in regard to this type of legislation. Like most everything else we are covering in this text Remember, refer to your state's stalking law and see if it applies.

If you have a GPS, we strongly advise not setting your device's home setting. If you want to put your home address in, don't. If your stalker or a random crook is able to access your device, he or she can easily obtain that information. Instead, we advise people to do if they want to list an easy way to follow the crumbs back to your home is to list the address of a store or park that is close enough to your true home address to get you back into the area.

Note: Law enforcement used to be able to place a GPS monitoring device on a suspected criminal's vehicle without obtaining any kind of warrant or subpoena. Recently the United States Supreme Court found that law enforcement now needs to obtain a warrant in order to affix a GPS monitoring device to an individual's vehicle.

- *Cell Phone Spying:* This is a phenomenon that is just starting to really catch on. There are Internet advertisers offering downloads and software that allow the user to monitor someone else's cell phone under the guise of checking on your spouse to see if he or she is cheating, check on your daughter to see who she is dating, or see if your business partner is making clandestine deals. According to the providers we talked to, all new digital cell phones have GPS chips so, depending on circumstances, can be tracked. According to the experts, satellites allow one to track the location of your target, monitor text messaging, and, in some cases, actually listen to what is going on around the person with the phone.

* Jodi Sanderholm was kidnapped, raped and murdered in Kansas in January of 2007.

From all we can find out, for someone to monitor your phone, that person either has to supply you with a phone capable of doing all these things or have access to your phone to download the spy software. This kind of software has been utilized by law enforcement, but it is currently available on the Internet. The way technology is changing; all this crud may soon be downloadable to your phone via a random text or e-mail. Every time a phone number we are unfamiliar with shows up on our phone, it is deleted. If the sender is legitimate, that person can leave a message.

If you feel spyware has been placed on your smartphone, experts will tell you to look for the following symptoms:

- If your phone is off, but you pick it up and find it is warm to the touch or continually drained, you may have a mechanical issue, or someone has been using your phone without your consent.

- If your bill shows additional charges you are not aware of, someone might be using your phone without consent. (You should be reviewing your phone bills for suspicious charges anyway. Suspicious charges might be fraud and have nothing to do with your device being hacked.)

- If your phone flashes from time to time while sitting idle, your device might be compromised.

We are told that trying to run down a smartphone infection can be pretty costly, and it is difficult to do, so good luck with your investigation. With the ever-increasing number of smartphones sold daily, hopefully some genius will develop a program that finds spyware at a reasonable price.

Along those same lines, we should talk about Bluetooth devices, which can also be monitored within a certain distance. Those of us with Bluetooth love it, but beware they can be monitored by unauthorized people. We recently purchased a vehicle with

Bluetooth hands-free operation for our cell phone. We later found that because we use a business-oriented smartphone, we cannot get text messages to appear on the vehicle's information screen like we could with phones we had in the past. The reason the carrier gave was that people in the proximity could also view our text messages if they were downloaded to the vehicle's onboard computer. Oh well. If the hackers want to see a text from my wife telling me to pick up a gallon of milk or my kids asking for more money, hopefully this will frustrate them as much as it does me.

While we are discussing cell phones, we should talk about a fairly new phenomenon emerging with the use of cell phones with cameras. This is something that has been coined "sexting." Sexting is when individuals voluntarily or through coercion or peer pressure take risqué photos or video of himself/herself and send them to whomever for whatever. The visual media is often accompanied by highly sexual text. Sexting is done in the hopes of having or attempting to have a sexual relationship with the respondent or as a voyeur type display. Unfortunately younger and younger people are sexting. Some law enforcement agencies have prosecuted the sender for child pornography. In fact, one segment of society, pedophiles are continually soliciting youths to send them photos of themselves. Of course, the child does not realize it is a pedophile encouraging this type of behavior. Our young folks seem to believe because it is a digital photo being sent from a remote location there is no harm to anyone involved. They trust in what they believe is the anonymity of their actions. (www.WiredSaftey.com has a section on sexting that you might want to review, especially if you have kids.)

- *Spy Cameras:* Yes, we are going to discuss spy cameras. We have had stalkers enter into a target's home and install these tiny Minicams that can transmit to a laptop or smartphone from a specific distance. These cameras can have their own power supply, or they can be attached to a fixture in the victim's home. Some refer to this as "video voyeurism." This type of surveillance is used as an information-gathering tactic that the stalker then uses to contact and create fear or emotional distress in the victim. If the person doing the viewing never makes contact with the victim or never threatens him/her, then it cannot legally be deemed stalking. We would like to see this changed. Video voyeurism has become a legal violation in a growing number of states such as Louisiana (Louisiana Penal Code Section RS 14:283.1) and Idaho (Idaho Penal Code Section 18-6609). For additional video voyeurism laws in the United States, go to http://www.ncvc.org/src/AGP.Net/Components/DocumentViewer/Download.aspxnz?DocumentID=37716.

Along the same lines of installing surveillance devices, we had a stalker enter the victim's house and place a digital tape recorder in a woman's bedroom bookcase. He then reentered the house and retrieved the tape recording until, on one occasion, the victim found the recorder. Each time he went into her house, it was a count of burglary. In California, this is a part one felony Strike count. Under California Penal Code Section 459, if you enter a person's residence for the purposes of committing grand or petty theft or any other felony, then it becomes burglary. So if your stalker enters your California home for the purposes of stalking, and that can be proven, he or she goes down for burglary and stalking. Being a felony, stalking allows the burglary to attach and be charged. We used to love charging the stalker with this in addition to all the other crimes we could prove up. This was especially fun because, in California, as indicated, burglary is a part one felony. Therefore, it has additional time attached to the perpetrator's sentence. Other states may have similar charging sections, but we believe if they don't, they all should. In this, we include all countries that currently have stalking laws or are considering them. The only problem any state or country would have is making sure the stalking law is chargeable as a felony and not a misdemeanor. Without this provision, depending on what transpires inside the victim's residence, it may only qualify as a criminal trespass.

- *Caller ID Spoofing:* There is software that allows a person (in our case, a stalker) to anonymously call a victim's home, even if that home phone is protected with caller ID. Normally if the victim has blocked the stalker's number, it stops the call from coming in, or at the very least, it warns the victim. With this software, the stalker can make the call from his or her phone, which should be blocked, because the software sends a random number to the victim's phone, disguising who the caller really is. This obviously, allows a stalker to contact the victim and ascertain if he or she is at home. Also it allows the stalker to harass the victim for however long it takes the victim to hang up. One of the advertisement come-ons was, "I just don't want them to know it's me calling." Much of this software is marketed as a tool for: private investigators, attorneys, law enforcement, and skip tracers (those looking for people who have absconded from posted bail, allowing them to get out of custody).

 We can't list every spying or tracking device, and, as indicated, by the time this book is published, there probably will be others. As long as there is some type of demand for the technology, it will be developed. Once the technology is available, it will not always be used in the intended way, and it will also be subject to hacking. If you are concerned, get up to speed on what is going on. Every time we teach at a conference or seminar, someone raises his or her hand and asks me, "Well, have you heard about this or that?" Not really. Number one, I am not a techie. For the most part, I can barely turn a computer on or off, and if I need something fixed, I grab a kid or the Geek Squad. Therefore, I have to do what you do and keep up as best I can. Go to sites such as www.WiredSafety.com, Working to Halt Online Abuse (WHOA), or other similar web locations. These sites do an excellent job of staying ahead of the curve on a great deal of this stuff. So go online and use them. Once you see what they have, go on your own and do more research. Information is flowing all around us now, and all we have to do is reach up and grab some of whatever we need.

- *Family and Friends:* You may be saying to yourself, what is he talking about? How are family and friends involved in surveillance? Stalkers will often make contact with family members and friends to try to gather information on their targets about what they are doing, where they are going, and who they are seeing.

Deterrent: The key to eliminating family and friends as unwitting participants is to clue them in as soon as you (victim) are aware you are being stalked.

- *Children:* Unfortunately, all too often, children are casualties of the stalking war. We personally hate to either investigate or consult on cases involving children for a variety of reasons. Stalkers will use children as conduits to gather information on their targets. We have had stalkers grill their kids on the day-to-day activities of the stalking victim. Stalkers have convinced their kids to leave doors unlocked in the house. This way, they can gain entry to vandalize the home or gather information on their targets. We had one case where the stalker took his young son to his ex-wife's house and had him climb through the doggie door to unlock the house for him. Sometimes children are so traumatized that they run into neighbors' homes and hide under beds when they are told the estranged stalker/ ex-husband is en route to pick them up for a visitation, which they know will be more like an interrogation.

While on the topic of children as it pertains to stalking, we are going to take this opportunity to discuss other issues involving children and the crime of stalking. One of the most egregious things an investigator has to deal with in a stalking scenario is when stalkers sexually molest the stalking victim's children. (The children can belong to the stalker and the victim or just the victim.) That is why we ask in our threat assessment interview if the suspect has ever talked about being molested or sexually assaulted as a child. After all, if the stalker was a victim of molestation, there is a good likelihood he or she too will be a molester. Too many times we have seen the victim's face take on that look of abject terror as if a two-ton weight just landed on their backs. That look comes when they realize what they didn't want to believe was probably true. Stalkers will molest as a tactic to get at the victim, or in some cases, they have admitted to fantasizing about the victim during the course of the sexual assault.

Deterrent: There are two specific tools that we are able to utilize in Orange County to assist law enforcement when child abuse and/or stalking is suspected by a detective. The first is a program called

Child Abuse Services Team (CAST).* This team is designed to handle sexual assault and abuse cases in a one-step approach. The detective assigned to the case has the suspected child victim come to the CAST center. The child victim is then interviewed by a child abuse specialist in a room designed to be

Westminster P.D. Scott Storey viewing a CAST interview. Author's personal file.

comfortable to the victim. The room has a two-way viewing window so the on-call deputy district attorney and the handling detective can watch the interview, which is also tape-recorded. Once the interview is complete, the victim is then examined by an in-house nurse practitioner in a specialized exam room. Counseling ser-

---

* To learn more about CAST, go to: http://www.ocgov.com/ocgov/Child%20Abuse%20 Services%20Team%20(CAST)

vices are also made available. Maricopa County, Arizona, has a similar program to CAST. The San Diego Stalking Task Force utilizes this type of one-stop center as well. When we recently taught a seminar for the Michigan State Prosecuting Attorneys Association, a group of advocates attending the seminar said they had a similar program. We are also told the SOS, Inc. group of Kansas has a program similar to CAST as well as the court services program we will be discussing.* (This was verified when we taught for SOS in Emporia Kansas in October of 2012.) We are sure there are others in the United States and abroad, but we are not aware of all of them. If you are curious or need these services, contact your local law enforcement or county social services division.

The second tool we utilize in Orange County is the Keeping Kids Safe (KKS) program. We have found this very beneficial in slowing down the harassment of children involved in domestic violence and stalking scenarios. I had the opportunity to evaluate this extremely positive process. The program was designed in response to problems associated with court-ordered visitation, which is commonly referred to as "supervised visitation." When a family court judge would order this type of visitation between estranged spouses (usually involved in some type of domestic violence scenario), the visitation was given over to a grandparent or some other supposedly neutral person to watch the parent (usually the male) when he or she had assigned time with the children. Abuses often occurred during these visitations such as demanding information about the spouse or estranged partner, physical abuse, sexual assault, and/or continual berating of the victim by the court-ordered partner. Another problem was where the exchange of the children took place. It was usually done in the parking lot of a police department, and confrontations oftentimes arose. This was quite a burden on law enforcement, who ended up babysitting and refereeing between combatants. (Trust me, when

---

* SOS, Inc. is a group in Kansas dedicated to assisting victims of domestic violence, child abuse, and sexual assault.

I had to work the desk, I hated when both hostile parents came to the front counter of the police department to do a child exchange.)

Finally an innovative group involved with Orange County Superior Court Services Division came up with KKS. The program does the following:

- The program forces the court ordered respondent to fill out paperwork agreeing to a variety of restrictions. The respondent must also pay for the visitation service, so the taxpayer is relieved of the cost.

- The respondent must go to a designated visitation location and park in a specific parking area. The respondent will then go to the visitation room where his or her child is already waiting with a trained technician. Some of the visitation centers are also set up with video recording devices, so the visit is also videotaped. The technician fills out a report and submits it to the court. If the respondent violates the court's orders, his or her visitation privileges can be terminated.

- The non-respondent (usually the woman) is told to drop off the child fifteen minutes prior to when the respondent is allowed to be at the visitation site. Where she drops off is completely different than where the respondent is allowed to park. This eliminates confrontation both at the center and the parking lot. Law enforcement loves this program. It takes them out of the loop of having to be a babysitter for estranged parents trying to drop off their kids to one another in the lobby or parking lot of the police department. It also stops the respondent from being allowed a so-called monitor, which was usually another family member or other unqualified, biased proctor. (A proctor is a term from the English for someone who monitors.) Of course, the police will respond if something during the process goes awry.

- The respondent is not allowed to give gifts, coerce, or try to gather information on the spouse during these visitations.

KKS has had outstanding results. My role in regard to this project was threat assessor. I was charged with evaluating the planned sites, commenting on the safety of staff and participants, and designing a layout of the properties. I also reviewed the entire program as to generate any suggestions concerning enhancement of same. The system completely eliminates the potential stalker from belittling his or her child and forcing them to give up information details about the target. (We have included much of the information the respondent is responsible for in the appendix. This is in the hopes that other agencies here and abroad might adopt this type of system for their use.) *We are finding out as we travel, teach, and consult, that more and more counties in other states have organizations that deliver programs similar to KKS. That is always good to hear.*

While we are in this section, we would like to discuss how family court can better assist victims and detectives handling stalking investigations. Unfortunately, it has frequently been our experience that family court judges/commissioners do not always see all the dynamics of a case involving a potential stalker. For example, we have had family court judges modify protective orders already in place in a stalking case. They will sometimes allow respondents (who are also stalkers) to have unmonitored phone calls with their children. This is where they attempt to gather information on their targets. Judges sometimes will modify specific items in the criminal stay away order, which can indirectly put the victim at risk. We have found the better educated everyone in the court system is about stalking behavior, the smoother things seem to go.

We strongly suggest that those detectives involved in a stalking case where children are present contact the family court commissioner or judge's assistant and get them up to speed about what is going on.

Targeting Animals

To many people their animals are much like their children. They are babied, groomed, taken on trips, and placed in positions of high esteem within the family. Stalkers know this. They may kidnap an animal and demand the victim gets back together or does a specific task to get the animal back. The stalker may also execute the animal in a terrible fashion with the intent of terrorizing the victim. We were apprised of a stalker in the Midwest that would poison the target's dogs and then call her up asking how they were doing. We suggest you have your veterinarian install an identification chip into your animal. This way if it is found by someone, the chip can be scanned, and the animal can be returned. There are GPS tracking devices such as *DogTracs*, but you can see these devices on the animal, and the stalker can easily remove them. More than likely this type of technology will be miniaturized so it too can be placed inside a small skin pouch on the animal. We also suggest taking a good photo of your pet just in case it is taken.

Burglary/Trophy Collection

Stalkers will enter a victim's home to gather information and take personal items as trophies. When a victim comes home, he or she often knows someone has been in the house but doesn't really find anything missing. Patrol officers and other first responders to a stalking scene are trained to ask (female) victims to check their lingerie drawers to see if anything is missing. They should also instruct the victim to check if any dirty lingerie is missing. Many times the stalker goes after soiled clothing as a trophy. The same can be true for sexual predators in the process of doing what we refer to as a "panty burglary." It has been our experience that most women can quote chapter and verse about the types of undergarments they have, including when they got them and even if they were gifts. This can help the investigator know if any of those items are missing and if they eventually turn up on a search. We find men, on the other hand, are pretty much clueless about their underwear, except maybe knowing they might have holes in them.

We had one case where the stalker took the victim's antique dolls and placed them in sexual positions. Stalkers will purposely damage a victim's collections to harass him/her. In another case, a stalker paid the victim's apartment maintenance worker for a duplicate key to the victim's residence. He would then enter the apartment on a variety of occasions and do things such as turning her heater up to maximum temperature while she was out working. When she came home, her house was sweltering hot. If we had been working the case, both the stalker and the idiot maintenance worker would be doing jail time.

Another subject of discussion is having an open house. We continually advise stalking victims that have decided to sell their homes to be aware of this type of surveillance technique. The stalker casually enters into the target's home and calmly roams almost anywhere he or she wishes, all the time gathering as much data as possible about the target. This includes taking photos of the interior and items inside the residence with a cell phone camera. Some were even able to do some videotaping while in the target's abode. If you have an open house, ask your Realtor to have a guest sign in list. The stalker may refuse to sign the list or give a false name. However, it may stop him or her from coming in, and some of these individuals are so blatant that they will sign their true name. They may see this as another way to frighten their victims. Either way, you now have a record of your stalker being there.

Most Realtors don't want you at your home when it is being shown. We might suggest, if you have a photo of your stalker, you provide them with one. This way the Realtor can report that the stalker showed; as well as pay more attention to them when they are in your dwelling.

Another frequent occurrence is when the stalker takes a target's checks. The stalker usually takes them out of the middle of the checkbook or from a group of checks that will not get used for a period of time. They take these and other financial records to commit various acts of identity theft, which is another way of harassing the victim. We worked a case where the stalker took checks from his estranged girlfriend. He then located a group of crooks who washed checks (used various chemicals to remove amounts on the checks); put new dollar amounts on the checks, and cashed them. This amounted to hundreds of dollars in losses to the victim. When arrested, he advised us that he just wanted to "screw" with his "old lady" because no woman ever left him.

A term we are starting to hear when we talk to certain stalking victims is "gas-lighting." From the definitions we can find, to gaslight someone is to use deception and manipulation to try to drive their targets insane or to cause the victims to have doubts about themselves or their abilities.

Gas-lighting could take place in the workplace. A superior or a colleague-turned-competitor leads the target to believe he or she is spreading rumors about him/her, and when the target complains to fellow workers, they look at this individual like he or she is delusional. They say the perpetrator has only said wonderful things about him/her. In a relationship, the gas-lighter makes statements or innuendos over a period of time that cause the partner to start to doubt himself/herself or begin seeing things in others that normally he or she would not have believed. Unbeknownst to the target, what he or she is now experiencing is a result of the gas-lighter's "continual conditioning." Gas-lighting has been studied and written about by individuals such as Robin Stern, PhD, who wrote *The Gaslight Effect*.

We bring up the phenomenon of gas-lighting in the burglary section as an introduction into another situation that is increasingly being reported. This situation falls into the "drive the target nuts" category. For example, the stalker may enter the target's residence and subtly move something in the residence. The stalker may place something in a cosmetics drawer that the target did not purchase and would not use. The stalker might add something such as another person's business card or other personal item into a piece of the target's clothing. Victims complain this does not happen just one time but on a regular basis. We have had other complaints where the victim finds items such as stuffed animals moved, or a drawer has been left open when the target was sure he or she had closed it.

We have had instances where the stalker is able to enter the victim's vehicle and add or rearrange items in the car. During one such episode, the victim found her mirrors and seat had been adjusted to a position that would fit her stalker, if he had been driving her car.

Of course, one has to take into consideration that the person reporting this could have mental issues, but as a victim advocate or person in law enforcement, looking into these allegations with an open mind is crucial. We have found stalkers to use many diabolical types of harassment techniques to ply their "stock" (not a play on words) and trade.

If you are in a relationship, do not take photos of yourself and/ or your partner that could come back later to haunt you. We hear and see it all the time. The stalker enters the victim's home and takes photos, drawings, or even worse, video of the victim in the nude or very private situations. Now those things can be posted on the Internet. (Before we would find them posted on telephone poles with the victim's phone number, or sent to a variety of locations the target might frequent or be known.) So if you are going to document your sex life, secret that documentation somewhere where no one can find it.

In regard to pictures, stalkers are using sophisticated computer programs to create a new phenomenon referred to as "morphing."

(We have already discussed this process in one of DV stalking scenarios, but bears a little more discussion.) The stalker obtains a photo of his target. He or she then scans it into a computer program that allows that person to alter or morph the target's photo. Some put animal bodies on the victim's head. Others alter the target's appearance in a variety of rude sexual ways. The stalker then sends these photos via e-mail, text, snail mail, or hand-distribution to a variety of people or locations. Sometimes it is where the victim works, where he or she frequents, or the schools his or her children attend. This is obviously done in an attempt to embarrass or discredit the victim.

Now, this isn't really a new form of harassment. I used to have fellow coppers paste a photo of my head on some bodybuilder or the body of the Incredible Hulk and hang it on the department bulletin board. I just chalked it up to pure envy.

When and if a stalker enters your residence, he or she may also take this opportunity to install a keylogger (refer to cyberstalking for definition) and some type of spyware on your cell phone if available. Obviously not all stalkers are that computer savvy, but we want you to be cognizant of these types of things.

Of course, if your stalker is a drug abuser, he or she may steal money, jewelry, or other valuable items from you besides doing all of the above.

Deterrent: To counter this harassment, we will discuss burglar alarms and other items in the chapter on stalker protection.

Disruption of Services

Stalkers have been known to get victims' utilities such as water and power terminated. They accomplish this by stealing the victim's mail, which would include utility bills. The stalker then contacts the various agencies with the victim's account numbers, feign being the victim, and have the utilities turned off. We had one female stalker do this at least twice to her female victim. She called the utility company claiming to be the victim, and once she conned the service agent, she got a stop date on whatever service she wanted turned off. When mail is stolen, the stalker can gather a tremendous amount of information concerning the target. This also applies to "dumpster diving." What you put in your trash is fair game to these information gluttons. So if it is something important, shred it.

Deterrent: We strongly suggest that if you are a victim of stalking, you do the following:

- Obtain a shredder. This is something you should do even if you are not a stalking victim. This will help you avoid becoming a victim of identity theft. Buy a good shredder that cross-shreds rather than makes strips. Strips can be reconstituted.

- Get a mailbox. We like the private mailbox system such as a UPS Store or Aim Mail Centers. We suggest this because, unlike a post office box, you can receive all kinds of mail from various providers, even ones requiring signatures. The United States Postal Service does not allow UPS or Federal Express mail or packages to be delivered to them. We also like the other features such as packaging, faxes, and computer-generated copies that these facilities provide. The victim can also use a suite or unit number as part of the address, which the postal service does not provide.

- Through their Secretary of State's Office, many states (such as California) have a program like Safe at Home. This allows victims of both domestic violence and stalking to have mail sent (not boxes) to them. Once it is received, it is transferred to a safe address specified by the victim, thus stopping the stalker or abuser from tracking the victim via a mailing address. (As of January 1, 2011, California extended the victim's confidentiality program indefinitely.) This service also provides under

SB 489/98 confidentiality for marriage applications and voter records. Many states are also limiting the information that can be found out from a victim's driver's license and vehicle registration. (Arizona and Delaware just adopted victim confidentiality programs as of 2011. For more information on these states and others, go to the stalking resource center's website.)

Especially lately, we have seen an increase in the stalker contacting the victim's cell phone and Internet provider and causing havoc. In regard to cell phone disruption, we had a female stalker go after any woman that was involved with her estranged husband. (This particular case would not be considered a triangle stalking because the estranged husband did not want to get a divorce and the stalker—his estranged wife—wasn't trying to have a relationship with him. She just didn't want him to have a relationship with anyone else.) Our investigation showed that even if the estranged husband had divorced the stalker, it probably would not have mattered. She would have stalked his girlfriends anyway. This suspect would continually call the victim's cell phone provider until she got an agent she could work. It was usually one that was fairly new on the job. She would then give some song and dance about forgetting her password. Once she was able to access the victim's account, she would actually monitor her phone calls and text messages. Eventually, on a couple of different occasions, the stalker had the victim's cell phone turned off.

In one of the cases we consulted on, another stalker got the victim's phone shut off by three different cell phone providers. One stalker was able to get the target's phone bills mailed to an address where she (the stalker) could pick them up. Remember, stalking has become these people's primary task in life. If they would just put this type of energy into something positive, can you imagine what could be accomplished?

As for the Internet provider scenario, stalkers are becoming increasingly computer savvy, as we will discuss further in our section on cyberstalking. The stalker will find out as much as he or she can about the victim in a variety of ways, not the least of which is conducting extensive Internet searches. A stalker might even hack into the victim's social networks and then contact the Internet provider, conning an agent into changing the victim's e-mail password. The stalker will then give an e-mail address set up specifically for this purpose, which is not readily traceable to the stalker, and have all password confirmations sent there. This completely trashes the victim, who often does not realize the password was changed for a period of time. (We have no idea how this is done, but the detectives we dealt with on these cases sent the information to their forensic computer people for evaluation.)

Citizen Harassment

As indicated previously, we have worked cases where stalkers place ads in local newspapers announcing that the victim's house or car is for sale or that they are having a large garage sale on such and such a date. Imagine your surprise when a cadre of vehicles shows up to your home to buy what is in your garage, or because a "for sale by owner" ad for your home or car was entered into a local newspaper. This is even more disconcerting when the lookie loos banging on your door are incensed because you are not actually selling any of your property.

We have also seen someone place an ad in a car magazine with the target's phone number. After an onslaught of calls at all hours of the day and night, the victim finally figured out what was going on and was able to remove the ad. (Remember, that removal is not instantaneous. Therefore, the target still has to put up with the calls until the next issue or posting comes out without his or her information on same.) Yes, the stalkers have to pay for these ads to be placed. They also pay for unwanted magazine subscriptions to ensure your postal worker, friends, and relatives see that sex or other deviant periodical.

Deterrent: There is not a great deal one can do to stop this type of activity until it actually happens. Once it does, notify local law enforcement and the newspaper or periodical running the ads to get them stopped. If it is an unwanted magazine sent in your name, contact law enforcement so they can track down who got you the subscription. We would often contact the magazine on behalf of the victim and let them know what was going on. At the same time, we'd gather as much information on who started the periodical subscription in the victim's name as possible.

Court Harassment

This takes place when the stalker continually files small claims or more egregious civil actions against the victim. This causes undue stress, time away from work, and attorney fees (if the victim responds to the malicious and unwarranted lawsuits). The stalker knows this is harassment. He or she also knows that by forcing you to come to court, he or she will once again get to see you. Again, a power and control technique evolves. We have had stalkers with orders of protection against them file these types of nuisance suits. They do this to see the victim and attempt to harass him/her in spite of the court-generated restraining order.

Deterrent: We have the district attorney appear instead of the victim to explain the problem to the handling judge. We consulted on a Midwestern case where the stalker was an attorney, and the victim showed he was filing malicious civil actions. The case was submitted to the state board for disciplinary action and is still pending. Unfortunately, unless the attorney involved has done something really outlandish, most state judiciary boards seem reluctant to take much action. Of course, that is just our observation.

Speaking of this, we consulted on another case which involved a civil attorney who continually stalked his ex-wife and a well-respected health care practitioner over several years by filing continual harassing lawsuits against her. It was so bad that when she finally got the state's supreme court to review her case, the lawyer was disbarred for a set period of time. The court claimed the attorney in question was guilty of filing "frivolous claims," which caused the victim "substantial emotional injury" and over $200,000 in legal fees. The court suspended the attorney for a specific period of time and issued him a set amount of probation. To our knowledge this is the first time an attorney accused of using the judicial system as a stalking tool has been sanctioned by the state he or she practices in. (So we guess it can and did happen but at a tremendous financial and emotional cost to the victim.) This individual has not been charged with stalking by the law enforcement entity where the victim resides. It is unknown if that will transpire.

Identity Theft

Stealing someone's identity has become a multi-billion dollar industry. According to FreeCreditScore.org, "Every 3 seconds there is a new victim." The reasons are simple. Obtaining information about someone is getting easier to do, and the crime itself is difficult to stop. Once the crook has done the deed, the penalties he or she suffers are minimal compared to the grief the victim sustains (sometimes for years). This is why companies are springing up all the time that claim to protect your identity by monitoring your transactions and the information placed on your credit reports. More and more states are allowing residents to place freezes on their identities. When a person places a freeze on his or her credit, a lending or financial institution cannot allow anyone, including the rightful owner of that identity to open any kind of account. This includes the purchase of a house, a car, or other type of product requiring a credit check without first notifying the person who placed the freeze on his or her credit report and having that person remove it. We are told by our bankers that the fee for unfreezing one's account runs from about eight to twenty dollars.

Identity thieves can develop fraudulent accounts from obtaining death records as well as information from birth certificates. They can gather a tremendous amount of information on a target via a public records search on the Internet. According to one article in Association for the Advancement of Retired People (AARP), in 2004 about 400,000 checking accounts were opened in the names of people who had died. One of the best places to obtain information about identity theft is the Identity Theft Resource Center (ITRC) at http://www.IDTheftCenter.org/index.html.

In early 2012, we were interviewed for a webcast show hosted by Mari J. Frank, Esq., one of the leading identity theft experts in the country. Going to her website, www.identitytheft.org should give a great deal of information as well as where to go for more.

One of the investment group newsletters I subscribe to talked about another Internet site you can check to see if you're at risk of becoming a victim of identity theft. This site runs your name and date of birth through a database to look for unusual activity. They look for more than your name attached to your social security number or several applications for credit cards made in your name with a variety of addresses attached. According to the newsletter, you have to give the (free) site your name, date of birth, and if desired, your social security number to run the profile. We are still very reluctant about putting that information on the Net, but then again, we have not used these services. This is just information for you to view and then to decide for yourself. Please note, this newsletter said their research showed that in 2008 alone over ten million Americans were affected by identity theft issues.

We should also note another investment periodical developed by Kiplinger (a company designed to make investment, forecasting, and management decisions) insight, advised by 2020 cash will be used rarely. Apparently there is a push in the technology field to develop machines that can scan your personal bar code or fingerprint when making purchases. Also the development of the near field communication (NFC) chips that one can carry on a key fob or in a smartphone can be tied to one's credit card(s) or checking account(s). There are applications available for smartphone users that allow them to click their smartphones over a scanner, debiting their accounts so they can make their purchases electronically. Although we have seen it done, we are not personally interested in the application (call us stodgy). Of course, the identity thieves will have to go more high-tech to steal one's information, and they will so that will force another layer of security to have to be developed.

A stalker steals a victim's identity to further harass that person. We have had stalkers buy cars and list their targets as their spouses on the credit application. Others have opened credit card accounts and initiated charges, while others have gathered enough information to be able to impersonate the victim and have utilities, cell phones, or other services terminated or monitored.

One of the newest scams (they seem to come out of the woodwork daily) is to obtain credit card information fraudulently and make very small charges on the card. The crooks use false, official-sounding names with 800 numbers to try to mask the theft. Apparently it works very well because they have found many of us do not sweat the small stuff. So pay attention to those little charges. If you don't understand where they came from, challenge them.

According to an article entitled "Social Insecurity" in the June 2010 issue of *Consumer Reports*, in 2009 "40 percent of online US households" were adversely affected by an increase of virus attacks. At least "one million households lost money or had accounts misused" due to Internet phishing scams. The same article said that, due to computer viruses, in 2008 and 2009, "sixteen million households" sustained serious damage, and "1.8 million households had to replace infected PCs" due to these viruses incursions.[82]

Deterrent: When I teach, I instruct the attendees to follow some simple steps to avoid being a victim of identity theft, whether a victim of stalking or not. We have seen people's lives thrown into the dumpster over ruined credit and compromised identity.

- We suggest that on the back of all your credit cards, write "See cardholder's ID" instead of writing your name. We do that, and it is amazing how many times we are asked for our ID. It is also equally incredible how many times the clerk never asks to see your identification if your card is signed. Don't believe it. Try it some time. People are programmed. For some reason if your card tells the clerk to conduct an additional process like check ID, the chances are that person will. If there is no such request, the cashier won't usually check unless something else causes that person to be suspicious. According to a recent study done by researchers at the University of Cambridge Computer Laboratory, they have found that crooks can insert a "wedge" between a person's stolen credit card and the terminal it is being slid into. The criminal types in any PIN number, and according to the study, the reader believes the correct PIN number has been entered, allowing the transaction to take place. What the banks see when they review the reports are that the victim's PIN was successfully entered. From what the article said in *TG Daily*, some banks were disputing the transactions as fraudulent. So this is something you should also be aware of. (The study can be found at http://www.cl.cam.ac.uk/research/security/banking/nopin/press-release.html.) Again, if these guys would just work on saving the planet or world peace instead of ripping us off, it might be a better place to live.

    While on the topic of PIN numbers, research has shown that hackers can hack a four-digit PIN in a matter of seconds, depending on the computer and available software. The software security people we talked to advised developing PIN numbers or passwords with at least eight characters and included numbers, letters, and punctuation marks. This makes it a great deal longer and harder for the hacker to unscramble thing. We told these guys that idea was all well and good, but you have to have a separate location in your office with all these new PIN numbers and passwords. This would not apply to you if you are a genius with an identic memory.

- Another credit card scam is referred to as "electronic pick-pocketing." This is when a thief walks up next to you with a portable credit card reader. They concentrate on areas they believe you keep your credit cards and rip off the electronic information of your cards. These scanners work on cards that transmit via a chip imbedded in the card. The radio-frequency identification (RFID) chip can transmit valuable information. The scanner picks up your code and stores your data. This is done on credit cards designed to merely swiped over a card receptor surface as opposed to being placed in a credit card slot and swiped. According to *Consumer Reports*, these chips are found in United States passports, some driver's licenses, and a variety of credit cards. The covers of the United States passports provide fairly good protection, but the new passport cards used to go into Canada and Mexico need additional protection. There are metallic wallets, RFID-blocking shields, and other data blocking sleeves available that can shield your cards from this type of theft. As to whether they work to stop the electronic message from being scanned all the time, we have heard they do most of the time but not always. In another *Consumer Reports* article dated June of 2011, they said one of their reporters made a homemade security wallet with duct tape and an aluminum foil liner that worked better than "eight of the 10 commercial products" they tested.[83] (We have no idea how well this works.) Banks are also continually working on new credit card chips designed to defeat this type of theft. The best way to find out if your credit cards are susceptible is to contact your credit card provider. Also make sure you are covered when a theft of information takes place. Always report it immediately upon discovery. Your credit card company should spell out exactly what they will replace if this happens. Recently a group at the University of Pittsburgh started working on an on/off switch for credit cards with imbedded RFID chip technology. Check Google or your search engine for more information.

- When ordering checks, order them with your initials instead of your full name. This way if your checkbook is stolen, the thief will not have all your information. Along those same lines, if you have a PO box or mail service center, put that address on your checks instead of your home address. Some people put their phone numbers on their checks. It is not mandatory. We don't do it, but if you do, consider using a work number instead of a home number.

- When you write a check to pay off your credit card(s), and if you decide to utilize the memo line for your card number, we suggest only putting the last four digits. Your card company knows who you are, but the suspect shouldn't. Don't put your credit card information or allow anyone taking your check to put that information on the check.

- It is a good idea to scan or makes copies of the important information you carry in your wallet such as credit cards. Make copies of both sides of the items, and keep them in a safe place. We strongly suggest you do not carry your social security card or pin numbers in your wallet. In regard to social security information, many forms such as billing or doctor's information ask for your social security number. The fewer times you put that out in public, the better. If you have valid health insurance and present your card, most doctors' offices will accept that and understand why you are not giving out your social security number. Whenever we have left that box blank, it has never been asked for. If they do, it is up to you how you deal with it. The same holds true for filling out job applications. If your intended employer requires your social security number to run a background check, then deal with giving them the information at that time. Don't get used to putting it down on every application you do, especially if it is an online application.

- If you have your wallet or other information stolen, contact law enforcement, and file a police report. Once the report is done, get a copy. You will be sending it to those companies where your identity has been fraudulently used. Call the three national credit reporting agencies. Equifax is 1 (800) 525-6285 or 1 (800) 685-1111, PO Box 740241, Atlanta, GA., 30374-0241. Experian (formerly TRW) is 1 (888) 397-3742, PO Box 9595, Allen, Texas, 75813-9595. TransUnion is 1-(800)-680-7289 or 1 (800) 888-4213, PO Box 1000, Chester, PA., 19022. If you believe your social security number was compromised, you might want to call the fraud line at 1 (800) 269-0271. You can order your free credit card report by going on www.Annual-CreditReport.com or phoning (877) 322-8228. Just an FYI, if you suspect you have been contacted by some type of fraudu-lent scheme by mail, you can write the United States Postal Inspection Service, Criminal Investigations Service Center, Attn: Mail Fraud, 222 S. Riverside Plaza, Suite 1250, Chicago, IL, 60606-6100, call 1-877-876-2455, or go online at Posta-lInspectors.uspis.gov. Suspected online identity theft scams can be reported to the Federal Trade Commission via ftc.gov/complaint.

- If you have housekeepers or you have relatives with in-house care givers, beware. As a former cop I dealt with victims who had these individuals regularly in their homes, and they robbed them blind. If you have a cleaning service or other persons who work in your home, don't leave anything out or in easy reach such as bank statements, boxes of checks, etc. If you have relatives that are being taken care of by outside help, check them out, and keep tabs on them as best you can. My wife and I have been the victims of cleaning crews who have stolen items, including a flat badge I thought I had secreted in a bedroom closet. In regard to checks, check occasionally that someone hasn't taken one out of the middle of your checkbook or a group of checks out of the middle of a box you have not yet used. Reviewing your accounts should help you discover anything fraudulent, but smart crooks may not write large sums on your stolen checks in order to keep under the radar.

- Beware of any e-mails asking for information about your assets, social security number, birth date, or any other personal information. Cyber identity thieves are very sly. They have been known to send requests for information claiming to be the Internal Revenue Service, other government agencies, or a bank that you may be doing business with. These entities should never send these kinds of requests via the Internet. Even if you get a request in the mail, you should verify its authenticity. Don't give out any more information than needed to accomplish whatever transaction you have validated as being trustworthy. In short, be curious and safe and not oblivious and sorry. One of the more recent scams we have seen is an e-mail that says it is from the Federal Bureau of Investigation (FBI). The e-mail wants personal information, saying you have been going to illegal websites. When we checked with the Bureau, they said they have been getting complaints about this, and of course, they had nothing to do with this information gathering. They said that if they wanted to gather information, they have other ways of accomplishing that goal. (We would hope so.)

- Watch out for people who look over your shoulder at the ATM. Some of these guys have become very adept at gathering your pin numbers. Along those same lines, check your ATM card scanner, and see if it is securely in place and has not been replaced with a dummy card reader, which can copy all your information to a nearby person.

- When you use a credit card at a service station to obtain gas or other services, make sure you get a receipt. Some service station employees have been known to sell the information they have gathered.

- When eating out, make sure your server has returned your credit card and not someone else's. If possible, make sure they are not palming your card into a portable scanner. Servers have been known to use these to record all your card information off your magnetic strip.

- When buying online, use only credit secure websites, and try not to use a debit card when ordering. Your credit card usually has more protection as far as what you will be responsible for if your card is used fraudulently. Privacy Rights Clearinghouse has a site for additional information (www.PrivacyRights. org/fs/fs23-shopping.htm). There is a website generated by the United States government for more information on credit card fraud and costs to the person being defrauded. Go to http://www.FederalReserveConsumerHelp.gov/LearnMore/ Frauds-And-Scams.cfm. We also use a credit card encryption device that scrambles our credit card information when we slide it via a portable card reader when we buy online. This way your credit card information is encrypted as it goes into your computer and to the company you are buying products from.

- We always suggest that if you are getting rid of your old computer and are not going to give it to anyone, destroy the hard drive. If you are going to give it to someone, then use some type of hard drive wiping or information deleting program. Just pushing the old delete files button doesn't do the trick. According to a CBS News story from April 15, 2010, most all digital copiers (at least office types, it's unknown about your specific home copiers and printers) have a hard drive similar to the one in your home computer. This records all or most of the transactions done on the copier/printer. The study found that when companies returned their leased copiers, they neglected to either clean the hard drive or remove it from the device. This allowed pages and pages of confidential information to be accessed by anyone. We don't know about you, but this definitely came as a surprise to us. One of the companies trying to raise awareness about this issue (Digital Copy Security) has developed software, INFOSWEEP that can scrub these hard drives before they are resold. We do not know if there are other such programs out there, but research may reveal that information.

- For those readers in the United Kingdom, which has Experian. UK and Equifax.UK, go to the Information Commissioners Office (ICO) at http://www.ico.gov.uk/for_the_public/topic_specific_guides/credit.aspx. For listings of worldwide credit bureaus, try going to Credit Guru at http://www.CreditGuru.com/WorldAgencies.htm.

- Another scam is when the stalker submits a change of address to the post office, thus allowing your mail to be sent to a specified place only the stalker has access to. This used to be fairly prevalent when a person fraudulently obtained some type of loan on a victim's property. The criminal gave a mailing address other than the targets, thus allowing the crook to receive all the information and/or payments generated by the fraud. The home owner goes about his or her daily life with no knowledge of the problem until he or she is contacted by a collection agency wanting interest or other loan payments.

- We should talk to everyone on the social networking scene. According to several of the forensic computer cops we deal with, if you are on Facebook, MySpace, and perhaps other social networking sites such as Twitter, you should be aware of a "worm" or malware called Koobface, which is continually plaguing these sites. This virus works by entering your social networking account as an e-mail from a friend. The e-mail talks about a recent video the friend saw you in, and the e-mail directs you to an external site. Once there, you try to play the video, and it shows an error message telling you to download a new version of a specific flash component. Once you do that, it has you. It can then cause a great deal of havoc until you get it removed. We suggest you go to a site you trust such as your antivirus website and research it in more depth. We are told it can collect a great deal of personal data once it is imbedded.

- Finally as we have discussed previously about dumpster diving, destroy personal papers via a shredder (that cross shreds, not strip shreds) or by some other fashion that completely eliminates the possibility of someone gathering information via a paper trail or dumpster diving. We have friends that burn all their paperwork in their fireplaces. We'd have a fire going every day if that were our process.

Before we go on, this particular scam is so insidious we just thought we would throw it into the mix. According to a recent *Consumer Reports* article entitled "The Sneakiest New Shopping Scams" by the editors of *Shop Smart Magazine* (SafeShopping.org), the new scam to be aware of are "stripped gift cards." In this ploy, crooks go up to a display of not yet activated gift cards. They have a scanner (purchased on the Net) that allows them to scan the magnetic or scratch off strip on the back of the card. They put the card back onto the rack. You or some other unsuspecting shopper takes the card to the clerk, buys the card, and has X amount of money placed on the card via the computerized cash register. The scammers wait a few days and then begin calling the card company with the information they ripped off the back of the card. Once they find it has been activated, they spend away before the recipient can squeal with glee and rush to the store of his or her choice to make a purchase.

The best way not to become a victim of this kind of fraud is to purchase gift cards stored behind the store counter. Of course, that only works if the person behind the counter isn't the one using a scanner on the cards.

Cyberstalking

Over the years, this type of stalking has grown by leaps and bounds. As indicated in my last book, I liken going on the Internet to the feel of us older guys had when we used to be CBers (citizen band radio users). Those of us who had vans, pickups, or maybe even a home base station talked and talked without worrying about anyone figuring out who we were. I had a neighbor who was a true redneck. He had short, cropped hair, tats, and missing teeth. He was a nice guy, and just about every night, he could be found in his garage with a beer in one hand and a CB microphone in the other. We all had "handles" (nicknames) and were untraceable (unless, of course, someone from the FTC wanted to track us down with a portable triangulation device, but that was once in a blue moon). Friends, with the advent of the Internet, that ain't the case any longer. Too many people feel that what goes on the web is not traceable, and it just ain't so. Sorry. Pretty much anything that goes on the World Wide Web is there forever. That is probably why I could never run for public office. As my wife says, I speak my mind way too often, and I am not always politically correct. Truth be known, I rarely fit that mold.

 Cyber space can be an incredible place to visit. It can hold the wonders of the world and expose surfers of its vastness to the darkest reaches of the universe. One such incident comes to mind that illustrates this fact. That this case was not a stalking case at all makes no difference. It still involved a violent predator using the Net to create havoc in the lives of at least two innocent people. We share it as an example of the twisted souls of those who have access to way too much information.

In February of 2010, a man and his girlfriend, who lived in an upscale neighborhood in a western Orange County city, were contemplating retirement. They had both worked hard their entire lives and deserved the relaxed life they so longed for. The couple had listed their high-end sports sedan on a car website.

When they opened their front door to the stranger (a clean-cut man in his late twenties), they had no idea they had just invited death into their warm, safe home. Shortly after they sat down and presented the keys to their car to this man for a test drive, both of their lives were ended by this deranged harbinger of darkness. He calmly pulled out a 9mm semiautomatic handgun and shot them both in the head. The woman fell dead before she hit the floor. The man soon followed, but he was not dead (at least not to the point of being pronounced dead) even though the round had pierced his cranial cavity and scrambled its contents. Our cowardly predator was not unscathed. He had shot himself in the foot during his reign of terror. With house pilfered and car stolen, our male victim lay bleeding on that cold floor for over thirty-six hours. Our AWOL (absent without leave) naval seaman traveled to Las Vegas to try his luck. Tragically the victim died days later in intensive care.

Shortly after being in a casino, the clumsy killer's actions drew attention. Local law enforcement was summoned, the subject fled to the stolen car, a pursuit ensued, and our budding killer was caught. When he was questioned by police, he told them a tale of going on the World Wide Web and learning from a few websites how to kill his human prey and get rid of the evidence along the way. For his trouble, he will get the needle. Once again the web trained another to go astray.

This next comment just might get me branded as paranoid and a stuffed shirt, but here goes. I personally do not like social networks. I am continually harassed by friends who want me to get on so we can communicate. I explain to them that I have an e-mail, website, and a cell phone. (By the way, one of the newest studies on cell phone use has shown that using a cell phone may prevent or slow down Alzheimer's due to the magnetic resonance from the phone. Armed with this new information, I have been meaning to use my cell phone more, but alas, I have a tendency to forget where I put it.) If they want to use these social networks, I wish them well.

I ask them not to spread my information around. People who go on these websites continually offer up way too much information on themselves and others. Also the media continually reports that these sites are hacked on a fairly regular basis.

We were sitting with a friend in his late fifties having breakfast. He was complaining that his daughter had just signed him up for a social network, and he was now getting inundated with people he was clueless about wanting to be his friend. Another friend complained he had been having drinks with another associate that had his two daughters on her (the friends) network list and showed him what they were currently talking about. From the gist of our conversation, he felt it was what people on the web refer to as TMI (too much information). In his case, we believe it was way too much information. Some of the people on these sites pride themselves on their number of "friends." They compete for as many people as they can get to sign up on their sites. When it comes to stalking, we constantly tell people stalkers thrive on information. So keep whatever contacts you have simple. A recent Bureau of Justice Statistics (BJS) study said that out of the 3.4 million victims over age eighteen that are stalked annually in the United States, about one in four of these victims reported experiencing some type of cyber-stalking incident.

The last comment about the use of the Internet to stalk and gather information is that predators (not just stalkers) learn and evolve from scenarios that are described on the Net. What exactly do we mean by this? Whenever a tragic situation plays out over cyber-space, be it nationally or internationally, predators pay attention. One example of this was when a local milkman took over a small, rural, religious school in the eastern United States. During this terrible act, he sexually assaulted and killed students, but first he chained the school doors closed to stop any escape and to impede anyone from trying to gain entry in an attempt to conduct a rescue. This fact was blasted out over the airways and the Internet. When the Virginia Tech tragedy unfolded, we learned that its deadly perpetrator had chained the doors of the buildings he entered to conduct his deeds of death. Coincidence? Maybe, but we tend to doubt it.

As to how many of these predatory crimes evolve, seeing an incident on the national or international news media (on television or repeatedly on the Net) acts as a catalyst for predatory behavior. Time and time again, we tell our student base to watch. When one incident takes place, it activates clusters of predation throughout the country and, from time to time, in other areas of the world.

Before we get into the tools cyberstalkers use, we need to talk about law enforcement. Oftentimes we get complaints from victims that their law enforcement entity is not capable of helping them with their cyberstalking problems. (We recently received requests from advocates we deal with in the UK about this same issue.) These concerns also include issues stemming from the investigation of identity theft and other Internet-generated fraud cases. About ten years ago, most police departments were definitely in the weeds when it came to having any kind of expertise in regard to Internet cases. In fact the 2001 "Stalking and Domestic Violence: Report to Congress" complained about the lack of law enforcement response to cyber threats. However, in the same report it discussed how police agencies were beginning to develop divisions utilizing techniques to combat these problems. Since then, many agencies (such as the one we came from) have developed their own in-house forensic cyber teams. The Los Angeles Police Department and the San Diego County District Attorney's Office were some of the first groups to get organized. Others have a centralized group that either works out of the county sheriff's department or the district attorney's office.

Recently in Orange County, California, a combined cyber task force consisting of both local and federal law enforcement was formed. The unit was called the Orange County Regional Computer Forensic Laboratory or Orange County RCFL. The RCFL consists of detectives from the Westminster, Irvine, Fullerton, Newport Beach, Anaheim, Fontana, Santa Ana, and Ontario Police Departments as well as members from the Orange County Sheriff's Office, Orange County District Attorney's Office, and the Federal Bureau of Investigation.* The RCFL was originally housed in the basement of the Orange

County District Attorney's Office. It is now housed in the city of Orange.

The FBI has established sixteen Regional Computer Forensic Laboratories (RCFL) sites throughout the United States. The first one was in San Diego. If you wish to learn more about RCFL's please go to www.rcfl.gov.

Detective Finley at his work station at RCFL prior to moving into the new Orange facility.

We recently sat down with the detective from the Westminster Police Department assigned to the unit, Detective Glenn Finley,

---

* The lab is a very secure facility. Entry is very closely monitored. You are observed even before you get to the secure entry door, as evidenced by the photo on the previous page.

to see exactly how the unit was designed and functioned. Detective Finley said the unit's primary responsibility was to assist law enforcement agencies in the Orange and Los Angeles County, and other nearby jurisdictions with both their computer and cell phone computer forensic exams. When a department conducted a search that included a computer or other digital storage device, they sent those devices to the unit. The unit then ranked the case by priority. An ongoing stalking or a homicide was higher up the food chain. The unit also worked many identity theft and child pornography cases. However, Detective Finley cautioned that they did not monitor any active (monitored as it was occurring) Internet cases. They only searched through the digital media they were supplied with and reported back to the particular agency.

Once one of the RCFL investigators conducted a search of the potential suspect's digital devices, the detective in charge was invited to the RCFL to sit in a viewing room. That way he or she could view what the search warrant had revealed. If the handling detective wanted any of the data uncovered by the search, a copy was made by the RCFL investigator and later submitted to the detective. The detective could then prepare a search warrant return and present the newly found evidence to the court.

Finley said they currently had some of the most high-tech equipment available to sort through all the various investigations they worked. He said many of the stalking cases he had handled involved the stalker going online and going through various websites to gather as much information as they could on their victims. He said these individuals would oftentimes pay to data mine these sites. He said he recently worked a case where the stalker gathered a great deal of information on a stalking victim by being a "poser" (a term we use for someone who feigns being the actual victim). He would then use this information against the victim by making her out to be a less than virtuous individual to friends and even her parents. In other words he conducted a campaign of character assassination.

While on the topic of posers, we would like to relate a story that many of you may find interesting. While at a friend's restaurant in an upscale area of Orange County, I was contacted by a celebrity that once headed up a major "boy band." It doesn't matter which band (there were a few). The story is just another example of the lengths people will go to meet people they are obsessed with, celebrities or not.

While recently touring, our celebrity met a young women that he finally felt he had a connection to. (He still has a tremendous fan base that will travel from state to state to see his concerts.) He had dinner with this woman, and they seemed to hit it off quite well. They exchanged e-mail information. He, of course, is also on Twitter and other social websites. Over a period of several months, he conversed with this woman. He said that as the communications continued, they became more and more personal, and he felt a greater attachment to this person. He also talked to her on the phone periodically. She would send him photos occasionally, and thus began a very extensive cyber relationship.

While in a Midwestern venue, they decided to meet again. For a series of excuses she had provided, they could not get together prior to that. After a concert he sat in his hotel room anxiously awaiting the appearance of the woman he had grown fonder of over the past several months. When she initially didn't show up, he called, and she said she was en route but was having some difficulties finding the hotel. More time went by, and she didn't show. Then more time and finally she called saying she was in the hotel lobby but that he might be disappointed when she came up. This celebrity, who is known to be a pretty caring guy, couldn't really understand what was going on, but he told her she was already there, and she might as well come up. When she knocked on the door, and he opened it up, he was flabbergasted. Instead of the extremely attractive petite female he remembered, a heavyset, not so attractive young woman stood before him who he had never seen before. After talking for a few moments, he quickly realized this was the girl he had been communicating with for all those months, believing her to be the girl he had originally met and had dinner with.

This young woman said she was completely infatuated with our celebrity and had taken on her cousin's identity to communicate with him. The singer told me that even though he had been duped, he decided to take the girl out to dinner to try to make her feel better. He said he's now a great deal more cautious about pouring out his thoughts and dreams.

He recently contacted me, and he told me he now had an "ordinary" stalker perusing him. He has been touring of late, so we haven't been able to touch base so that I might advise him. *What did I say about being famous.*

A growing problem rearing its ugly head in the cyberstalking arena that we would really like to see addressed are the cyberstalkers that reside in other countries and set up blogs and other venues to stalk and terrorize victims in another country. We recently assisted a victim that resided in the United States. She was being stalked by a male she had once dated and who had moved to Scotland. He was now harassing her and her family by making false accusations and hacking into specific accounts, some of which are sensitive in nature. We were contacted by our victim advocates and Scottish law enforcement about this case, so we developed a stalking chronology and a minor threat assessment report on this particular case. We forwarded these to both the Scottish and the United States detectives in charge. During our evaluation, we were able to find out our stalker was possibly wanted in France for another stalking episode. That information was also forwarded along with the suspected name of the French victim. (The reader should know that France does not have an extradition treaty with the United States concerning the deportation of French nationals, which is interesting. The stalker knew this and flaunted that fact when he discussed his French victim with his American one. We thought that was strange as well, seeing as how to the best of our knowledge he was not a French national.)* By the way, France also does not have a specific stalking law. We are told by those advocates that have dealt with the French concerning the issue of stalking, that they like some other countries have concerns about limiting a man or for that matter a woman's pursuit of an individual in a "romantic" situation. Again, we cannot understand why law makers in these countries cannot differentiate between wanted and unwanted pursuit. In our humble opinion, all nations need to have some type of law that panelizes those that exhibit behaviors that amount to stalking as being a violation of law.

Along those same lines, I consulted on an April 2011 article in the London-based international magazine *The Economist*. The article described an account of a New York-based opera singer that was being stalked and demeaned by a stalker who was based out of the orient. It appeared this particular stalker was hell-bent on character assassination and making regular death threats to the victim, her friends, and family members. We were not able to assist this particular victim because of the location where her stalker resided. Countries really need to push legislation through allowing law enforcement the necessary tools to eliminate these types of issues. Of course, this is much easier said than done. When we talked to our forensic computer detectives, they said they are routinely frustrated with the lack of international laws about cyber crimes, including identity theft and stalking.

Detective Finley said that his organization is able to assist many agencies that are either too small or cash-strapped to have their own in-house digital forensic unit. We encourage more and more jurisdictions to look at developing their own regional units. In our opinion, it is no longer a frill but a necessity.

---

* If you are interested in all the other countries that don't have an extradition policy with the United States, go to Yahoo Answers and type in What countries do not have an extradition with the United States.

For those that surf the Internet for information, there is a growing cache of information on cyberstalking. We are sure it will continue to build due to an increase in people being stalked, harassed, and bullied on the Net. Just type "cyberstalking" into any search engine, and a multitude of sites will pop up. We don't claim to be cyber experts by any stretch, but we will try to give the reader the benefit of what we have been exposed to over the years when dealing with this ever-growing problem.

I guess I wasn't completely truthful when I said this would be my last comment concerning Internet crimes. I think the brain trusts that develop the worms and Trojans that completely trash our laptops so we have to drop kick them into oblivion or take them to some computer veterinarian at an outrageous cost of both time and money, when apprehended, should all be given a lobotomy medically or in some other more painful fashion. Then these drones should be shipped off to a recycling plant where they can sift through mountains of parts for the rest of their lives. (*It's just a thought*).

Cyberstalking Laws

Numerous states, the United States Federal Government, and various countries currently have cyberstalking laws. One of the better locations to review these laws is on the Working to Halt Online Abuse (WHOA) website, www.HaltAbuse.org, and the sister website designed to assist with cyber crimes such as cyberbullying directed toward kids, www.HaltAbuseKTD.org. Another is the National Conference of State Legislators (NCSL) website.[84]

In regard to the United States Federal cyberstalking law, it appears to be a bit sketchy about an actual law dedicated to cyberstalking. This frustrates those of us who consult with victims in the United States being stalked by individuals from other states and other countries through a variety of digital communications and the law enforcement entities involved in trying to prosecute these cases. Under the Federal Stalking Section, US Code 18, Section 2261A, (2) (B), anyone who "uses the mail, any interactive computer service, or any other interstate or foreign commerce to engage in a course of conduct that causes substantial emotional distress to that person or places that person in reasonable fear of the death of, or serious bodily injury to" is guilty of a cyber type crime, which could be construed as cyberstalking under the confines of the federal section. Under USC 18:41 and 875 (c), it is a federal crime punishable by up to five years in prison and/or a fine "to transmit in interstate or foreign commerce any communication containing any threat to kidnap any person or any threat to injure the person of another." Section 875(c) applies to any communication transmitted in interstate or foreign commerce, including threats transmitted via telephone, e-mail, and the Internet. The inherent problem with this federal law is that it must be an articulated threat. It does not include the normal course of conduct of harassment and annoyance associated with the definition of stalking. (We are aware that Section 875 has an (a) and a (b) section with different fines and penalties attached to each. For the purposes of this book, we are only bringing (c) to your attention.)

Another federal section that could be described as dealing with cyberstalking is US Code 47 U.S.C. 223. Under this statute it is a federal crime to use a telephone or telecommunications device to annoy abuse, harass, or threaten any person at that called number. This would include, among other things, making lewd or indecent comments. This code may be helpful as a starting point if the federal authorities are up to date about your current case. There are several websites to research this crime at length. (www.Law.Cornell.edu is a good one.) Just search for US Code 47, U.S.C. 223, and pick one of the sites that comes up. At this juncture, we could not find a definitive United States federal cyberstalking law on the books.

Like we have indicated, according to the National Conference of State Legislatures (NCSL), many states have now initiated cyber-stalking, cyberbullying, and cyber-harassment laws into their legislative bodies.* For example, California has these types of stip-ulations in their criminal threat section, Penal Code 422, in their stalking section, Penal Code 646.9 rude and annoying phone calls, Penal Code 653m, and even in their stalking civil code Section 1708.7. The states and countries without some form of cyberstalk-ing sections need to be encouraged to implement such legislation, as it gives their citizens one more tool to use against the stalker.

One other cyber law in existence in the United States should be of interest to those parents with kids on the Net. This is the Children's Online Privacy Protection Act (COPPA) of 1998.[85] This act, also classified as Title XIII-Children's Online Privacy Protection, pro-hibits any "operator" of a website or online service from collecting and distributing the following information on a child under the age of thirteen, as detailed in the following section: "(8) Personal Information—The term 'personal information' means individu-ally identifiable information about an individual collected online, including—

(A) a first and last name,

(B) a home or other physical address including street name and name of a city or town,

(C) an e-mail address,

(D) a telephone number,

(E) a social security number,

---

* Go to http://www.ncsl.org. Then type in "cyberstalking," "cyberbullying," or "cyber harassment." A list of state laws will pop up.

(F) any other identifier that the Commission determines permits the physical or online contacting of a specific individual, or

(G) information concerning the child or the parents of that child that the website collects online from the child and combines with an identifier in this paragraph."

This law is so important to parents and others is because kids thirteen and under are continually going onto social websites and lying about their ages. Once they post their information, it is out there for all to view. Recent studies have shown these children are being sexualized and bullied at an alarming rate. There is specific software available that will now allow you to monitor your kids' Internet and cell phone communications. We have never used this and could not recommend any. Again, if interested, you must do your own investigation about how well they work.

In the United States a new bill has been introduced in congress as an amendment to the Children's Online Privacy Protection Act. It is listed under H.R. 1895 and entitled the Do Not Track Kids Act of 2011. This bill, if passed, would allow parents to limit how their children are tracked online. In other words how companies follow what sites children go to online, thus allowing these entities to target these same kids with advertisements and other marketing ploys.

Queensland, Australia covers cyberstalking under their Unlawful Stalking law Chapter 33A, Unlawful Stalking, 359B (c) (ii), which states, "contacting a person in any way, including, for example, by telephone, mail, fax, e-mail or through the use of any technology" [in a threatening manner is unlawful.] [86]

According to WiredSafety.com (another good information site to research Internet safety issues), under the Malicious Communication Act of 1998 in Great Britain (England and Wales), "it is an offense to send an indecent, offensive or threatening letter, electronic communication or other article to another person." Also if e-mails cause the victim to fear that violence will be used against them, then law enforcement can choose to use the charging section under Section 4 of the Protection from Harassment act of 1997.[87] That might change depending on how the new stalking section (2A) of that act slated to become law relates to cyberstalking.

Methods Employed by Cyberstalkers

Webcam Hijacking: Yes, there have been recorded cases where women have allowed their computers to be "fixed" by alleged friends and/or associates. These individuals have installed spyware that allows them to remotely activate their built-in Webcams. This way they can record the victims by generating either photos or digital video. A nationally publicized case concerning Webcam hijacking and video voyeurism took place in Fullerton, California in June of 2011. In this case a twenty-year-old computer technician took in several females' laptops for repair. While completing the repair, he installed a spyware program that allowed him to monitor the females without their knowledge. He advised them to take their laptops into a "steamy" environment such as the bathroom while they took a shower or bathed in order to eliminate a problem on the computer's camera. Many followed his suggestion and were videoed in various states of undress. He was arrested and prosecuted for his crimes, which included collecting hundreds of thousands of images of the various unsuspecting female clients. We, on the other hand, would strongly suggest not taking anything like a computer into a steamy, wet environment.

According to several Internet security watchdog groups, millions of computers are currently compromised or "hijacked" without their owners' knowledge. (Obviously, this does not mean just Webcams but computers in general.)

The following is a note concerning our use of e-mails. Those of us that use the Internet to send e-mails know that, with the right software, they can be intercepted and read. We are told that one of the ways to really slow down that process is to obtain some type of encryption software that requires the hacker to be really good, which many of them are, or to have software that can decipher these encryptions. That is why all the experts we know keep reminding everyone that "e-mails are forever." In other words, once you have written an e-mail, it is supposedly in cyberspace for the rest of time. Most all of us have sent e-mails we shouldn't have, so just keep that in mind.

Spyware: Believe it or not, once upon a time, spyware was developed to check on "junior's" computer. Spyware can be sent to your computer via an e-mail or installed by actually having access to your computer. With the programs installed, the stalker can obtain personal information on his or her target. There are a multitude of anti-spyware programs now, and some are even free to the user. Most major cyber security program providers (such as McAfee or Norton) have programs with anti-spyware included in their packages.

Keystroke or Keyloggers: These are devices that used to be physically installed in the back of your computer or in the guts of your keyboard. Now they can come in via a Trojan horse e-mail or injected into your computer while visiting an infected website.

These keylogger programs are hyped as security for businesses to keep track of what their employees are doing. The more sophisticated programs can monitor e-mails, instant messaging, and chats. The person who has installed the keylogger into your computer can monitor from his or her computer all the information you have generated. They can capture credit card data passwords and other critical personal information. Keyloggers are extremely difficult to detect. If you feel you have one (your credit cards are compromised or someone seems to know exactly what you have been typing or said in e-mails), we suggest you contact an expert to assist in removing the problem. Having current computer anti-virus software installed tends to help.

Phishing: According to Symantec Internet Security, phishing is defined as attempting to hook people online through deceptive e-mails and websites that ask for private information such as financial passwords or bank account numbers. The individuals that generate these websites and/or e-mails try to make them look as official as possible, often fraudulently cutting and pasting copyrighted logos and data normally found on an official website. Many times these sites will say there has been a breach in security on your account, and they desperately need to confirm your identity to ascertain if your personal information is at risk. They then require you give all your personal information so they can check it against what they don't already have.

The newest of these scams is referred to as "smishing." This is where your SMS (texting) portion of your phone is accessed by these same types of scams. Security experts advise not to immediately respond to these texts. You can go online and see if the number you are being texted belongs to the official institution. We suggest calling a known service provider about your account and verifying any text from them prior to making a decision on what to do. When someone smishes your phone, they may also be able to download a Trojan. A Trojan (based on the Trojan Horse) is a program that is mistakenly downloaded by a user into a device. It can compromise or destroy files or send information to an offsite user. They have become quite sophisticated over the years. Unlike a virus they don't replicate themselves. They just stay in place and do whatever they are going to do. (One of the better places to look up definitions like smishing or other computer terminology is *PC Magazine Encyclopedia* at www.pcmag.com/encyclopedia.)

If banks or the IRS have a problem, they will send you a letter. If you get any kind of correspondence, always verify who you are dealing with prior to giving anyone anything. Another site to visit for more information concerning the ills of phishing is www.anti-phishing.org.

Pharming: Symantec advises that another thing to watch out for is "pharming." Pharming is where one goes to a website that seems to have amazing prices or, worse yet, a site the victim trusts is his bank's and enters his or her credit card data. Once the information goes in, it is immediately stolen, and the victim may not be aware of this for weeks. (Symantec has a site that you can go on to see to assess how much monetary value you represent to cyber-crooks. It's called Norton's Risk Assessment Calculator.) We went on it, and it said we were probably at medium risk, but then again, who knows for sure? The Internet can be a real minefield.

Geotagging: Most people don't realize that when they use their smartphones to send others photos, a few right clicks on that photo will yield enough GPS information to tell whoever is looking at the picture exactly where you were when you took the photo. Just think, you are taking pictures of your pet or a new TV you just purchased, and the individual you Tweeted or Facebooked with that photo knows where you live. A stalker can track your whereabouts by just monitoring the photos you send. You may be able to turn off this part of your smartphone software. Recently ABC News reported on this problem and interviewed the developer of "I Can Stalk U—Raising Awareness about Inadvertent Information Sharing." Yes, even though on the face of it; the site might sound like a stalker-oriented website, according to the interview, the developer is trying to alert people to all the information they are putting out for anyone with Internet capabilities to use. (We have not visited this particular site.) If you want more information on this, simply go on the Net and type in "geotagging." There are a growing number of locations to gather information on this particular issue.

One thing to keep in mind concerning the GPS information that can be developed off a photo is that it may assist law enforcement.

If an entity is perhaps looking for the individual that took the picture. Then they can gather the info and go to that area to begin a search. Remember what we keep saying, technology can and oftentimes is a two-edged sword.

We were recently contacted about a disturbing app that had made its way onto the market. The app (the name is not important as it was supposedly recalled by its manufacturer) allowed users on their smartphones or similar devices to obtain profiles of women who had posted on social websites. It showed a photo of the woman, her background, and where she lived in proximity of the one requesting the information. One of the nicknames the app got was the "stalker app," and it immediately received a great deal of negative press. Folks, there will be others. Posting information on social websites in our opinion is a huge concern.

Stalking by Proxy: This type of stalking is accomplished when the perpetrator goes on the Internet and feigns being the victim. The stalker usually goes into adult-themed chat rooms and posts provocative images of the victim (in many cases photo shopped with the victim's head placed on a nude body) or makes claims of wanting to be contacted for sex or other activities such as rape or bondage. Then the person who was online shows up at the victim's house and attempts or makes unsolicited contact with the victim, believing she was a willing participant. Thus the stalker has used people who are unaware that what they are doing is in fact rude, annoying, and threatening behavior. The Los Angeles Police Department reportedly had the first prosecuted case, which involved a security guard that was using the Internet to stalk his unsuspecting female target.

More and more interest is being paid to this type of stalking. There are groups of victim advocates including third-party stalking into their definition of stalking by proxy. States such as Washington have upheld third-party stalking where a primary stalker has used friends to follow a target upon his or her direction and then report back to him/her. As we said previously, we get many requests from victims that say they are being "gang stalked." In other words a group of people are being directed by a puppet master to follow and harass a victim. Many also refer to this form of stalking as stalking by proxy. We tend to differentiate third-party stalking from stalking by proxy as being committed by a stalker that personally directs his or her minions to follow or harass a specific target. Stalking by proxy, however, is done by a stalker through means other than conspiring with individuals to commit the act of stalking, causes through his or her actions others to contact and harass his target believing that person (victim) is welcoming their advances.

We had a case of stalking by proxy, in which a known gang member, known to have extremely violent gang ties, wanted to have a relationship with the victim's underage daughter. When the victim put a stop to his advances, he went onto several rape websites and posted a photo of her head atop the nude body of a well-endowed female. He then made comments about having rape fantasies and wanting to be raped. He also included her phone number and e-mail address. She contacted us, and when we were about to get an arrest and search warrant on her stalker, she told us, due to his violent gang ties, she no longer wanted to prosecute the individual. Sometimes these things do occur, and when they do, law enforcement's hands are tied.

Information Gathering or Data Mining: As we have discussed previously, the Internet can be your best friend or worst nightmare. It offers a tremendous amount of instantaneous information at one's fingertips. This is great for school research and general knowledge, but it is also a troublesome because of how much information your stalker can gather about you through casual and/or more defined searches being generated. For a few dollars, the stalker can enter the target's name and any other available information to gather an incredible amount of personal data off the web. This can even include an aerial photo of the victim's residence.

We have done search warrants on stalkers and their computers and found they have gone on various public record databases to find out background information on their targets. Prior to the development of the Net, these things were extremely difficult for the average person to obtain. These searches expose phone numbers, sometimes e-mails, residential information, and depending on the search, date of birth, and other pertinent information. More controls are being attached to some of these databases, but in our mind, it's not nearly enough. (Some of these websites allow you to remove your name and information. We have done this on a few sites, but there are just so many. You could spend half your life trying to eliminate information.) Using those same search warrants, we also discovered stalkers were able to obtain information on how to stalk and harass someone, causing them untold trouble. There are actually manuals available online to accomplish these goals.

IP Sniffers or Packet Sniffers: According to the experts we contacted, these little devils are utilized by companies to monitor their networks and gather information, but they can be used by hackers to gather personal information on their targets without the targets' knowledge. These hackers can also gather enough information to penetrate a network. According to one of our sources, the sniffer is "virtually impossible to detect, and can be inserted onto the network from almost anywhere." If you go on the Internet, you can find several sites offering these types of programs for sale.

Please note, according Club Symantec (who sends out updated cyber threat information to their customers), like us—getting rid of spyware can be as easy as doing a system restore, which means you go back to a date when you didn't have the spyware and reset your computer to that date. The only problem is that everything after that date will not normally be recovered or returned unless you do a data backup prior to doing the system restore. They also advised that some spyware can work around this option. Symantec's newsletter also said their research showed that one in six persons have become the victim of cybercrime.

They warn that most spyware is in the form of an executable file. In other words, when it appears on your computer in the form of a free download or check to see if your computer is protected, you have to ask it to come into your computer. (Legend has it that vampires cannot come into your home without first being invited, so it is kind of like that.) They strongly suggest that, prior to downloading anything you are not sure of, you read the end-user license agreement (EULA) prior to completing the download. Make sure you want what they are selling or giving you. One of your last options is to completely reinstall your operating system, which is a total pain. This is not to mention that you most likely end up with none of the downloads that you really wanted, and installed at an earlier date. From what we can tell, make sure you go on sites you know about, and use a top of the line malware or Internet anti-virus software package. Oh, yeah. Crossing your fingers is probably not a bad idea as well.

We like WHOA's website (www.haltabuse.org) as a reference about Internet harassment. Jayne Hitchcock, president of WHOA, lecturer, author, and researcher, is someone who is always working hard to gather helpful information. For example, here are some of the 2011 cyberstalking statistics WHOA has generated. Gender of the victims: female—74%, male—26%. Gender of the harasser: male—40%, female—33.5%. unknown—26.5% Did the victim have a prior relationship with the harasser?: Yes—41%, No—59%. What was the relationship with the harasser?: Victim's Ex—56%, Online Acquaintance—7.25%, Family—12.75%, etc. The primary way the harassment was initiated was by e-mail (32 percent of the time). In 80 percent of the reported cases, the cyberstalking escalated. Facebook was noted as being one of the areas many of the harassment scenarios transpired. The site went on to discuss the states with the highest rate of victims and harassers. California and Texas were the top two. They list Canada, England, and Australia as the top three countries outside the United States with the most reported cases.[88]

WHOA also has a good kids and teenager "not to do list" about what to watch out for and what not to post on the Net. This includes information on sexting, cyberstalking, cyberbullying, and other predatory type behavior. (Once again, go to www.HaltAbuseKTD. org.) We have mentioned WHOA previously in this book, but feel this is another place to bring them up.

For those of you with offsite or Cloud-type storage contracts, beware. The April 2011 edition of *Popular Science* article (April 2011, Volume 278 #4) had an article entitled, "Hacking the Cloud, Cyber-Security Just Got Scarier." page 68-72. This article talked about how hackers were just beginning to mine this valuable data stream for all kinds of information that could be used for identity theft and other criminal enterprises. So just because you have protected your files, photos, and other information from computer theft or fire, it doesn't mean your information is locked away in Fort Knox and can't be viewed by someone you don't want looking at yours and our stuff.

Cyberbullying

Cyberbulling is another form of harassment we are currently encountering at an alarming rate. A great deal of cyberbullying causes its victims to be followed, harassed, and emotionally and, in some cases, physically traumatized. Therefore, we feel stalking behavior is very much a part of this crime. That is why we tend to closely align the two. In the case of cyberbullying, the use of the Internet, cell phone, and other electronic transmission devices are utilized as in cyberstalking.

Here are some interesting statistics obtained from a 2009 School Crime Supplement to the National Crime Victimization Survey in the United States. "In school year 2008-2009 some 7,066,000 U.S.

students ages 12 through 18", (28%) of the students reported being bullied. About "1,521,000 said they were cyberbullied. We are told that since then the numbers have dramatically increased. [89]

A study conducted in the United Kingdom by staff at the Anglia Ruskin University, found that about one in five "young people" were cyberbullied. More girls about "69%"—which is oftentimes the case—than boys were the targets of these bullies. The studied indicated that the victims of cyberbulling, indicated having self-esteem issues, emotional problems, and many would not go to school for periods of time.[90] Those we have interviewed that have been bullied either as an in your face confrontation or via cyber-bullying admit to having the very same problems.

A study published in 2008 by *The Journal of School Health* was entitled "Extending the School Grounds—Bullying Experiences in Cyber-space." It was an anonymous, web-based survey with a population of 1,454 twelve- to seventeen-year-old youths concerning cyberbul-lying. The results indicated that within the last year about 72 percent of those who participated reported at least one incident of bullying. Of those 85 percent experienced bullying in a school environment. Most of this bullying took place via instant messaging. About two-thirds admitted knowing their harassers, and most did not report the incident to any adults.[91] Even though this study did not address cyberstalking, it suggested the ever-increasing use of the Internet to bully, which often leads to the act of cyberstalking and a possibly vio-lent outcome. At the very least it can take an emotional toll.

Cyberbullying is basically defined as the use of the Internet, cell phones, or other electronic instruments that can send, display, or post text or digital images designed to injure or embarrass another. Most cyberbullying takes place among teenagers and young adults. There have, of course, been recorded cases of older adults com-mitting this type of harassment for personal reasons, which have lead to violence. In at least one reported case, the cyberbully's tar-get committed suicide due to the intense harassment and embarrassment. (Some refer to the act of suicide by those that bullied or cyberbullied as "bullycide.") As has been reported in a growing number of situations, cyberbullying can and has led to victims attempting and unfortunately committing suicide. Cyberbullies do some of the following things:

- Take on the identity of another to create problems for the target (posing). This includes sending defaming or threatening texts to others via cell phones or e-mails under the guise of being the target.

- Spread lies and rumors that are damaging to the character of the target. This may be done on social networking sites.

- Set the target up for assault. Often these rat-packing (use of multiple assailants) beatings are videotaped and distributed to others or even displayed on the Net.

- Display embarrassing photos or images of the target without permission.

One of the major problems with cyberbullying is that it is looked on by many of the perpetrators as no big deal. Many view this type of activity (—lest the bullies that actually physically assault their targets) as a form of social interaction. It's almost like an after-school activity or the "everybody does it" cop out.

A cursory Internet search will reveal that cyberbullying is not just a problem in the United States but worldwide. There are German studies and news articles from Japan, the United Kingdom, and elsewhere. It seems that anywhere there is the combination of young adults and access to the Internet and cell phones there is this type of cyber crime/harassment taking place.

A cyberbullying that took place in the United States in early 2010, and it reportedly led to the young bullying victim taking her life by hanging as a result of her fellow classmates and associates continually and repeatedly bullying her. This particular incident made the national news. However, it is our belief that other young adults may have already succumbed to this type of harassment and have fallen through the cracks. Remember, many of our youths are ill-equipped to handle severe peer pressure, no matter how it is delivered. They have not developed the coping mechanisms needed to put up the proper defense. Obviously with the advent of texting, social websites, e-mail, and other digital communication, the amount of harassment can be extremely overwhelming, even to an adult who supposedly has more defenses in dealing with these types of onslaughts. There are more and more situations where this behavior is raising its ugly head.

Deterrent: There are a few things one can do to reduce the effects of cyberbullying. One of the easiest is to not perpetuate the process. If you get e-mails, texts, or images you do not feel are appropriate, don't send them on, and don't react to them. If you are the victim of this type of activity, contact a parent or trusted adult. If it persists, contact local law enforcement, and at the very least, document what is taking place. Obviously more education is needed. The National Crime Prevention Council (NCPC) has a website where you can gather more information on this type of crime. If you live in the United Kingdom, actagainstbullying.com and Bullying.co.UK are websites one can go to for information. Another excellent website for information about cyberstalking and cyberbullying is the WiredSafety site, which is located at http://WiredSafety.org/index.html. This is designed by law enforcement consultants and other specialists who compiled this information to prevent the crime and assist those that have been victims of it. Another good site to go to is the Cyberbullying Research Center, www.cyberbullying.us. According to the center every state except Montana have laws to address bullying. Fourteen states have laws that include cyberbullying.

New York State has passed one of the more stringent cyberbulling laws that will go into effect on July 1, 2013. Among the measures indicated in the law is that educators must be trained in identifying and trying to eliminate bullying incidents.

One of the consultants we deal with concerning kids and the Internet said that parents need to jump on their kids the first time they start tickling the keys on the keyboard. They said there are programs out there like MouseMail and MouseMail Maxx designed to guide the first-time web browser. With these types of applications, parents have the ability to review some of what is streaming into their kids. Some of these programs can be set up so that when an e-mail is sent to their children, they can be reviewed by the parent prior to them being sent off to the child. Many times the initial offering is a free download, which most of the time leads to having to purchase a more complete software package. There are even applications for the parents' smartphones that will allow them to monitor social networks that mention or contain their children's names. Again, there will be a cost attached to this. Reviewing the Internet for information about protecting your child will reveal numerous articles that also mention other cyberbullying and predatory software designed to head off these types of attacks. Some that were listed were CyberBullyAlert.com and SocialShield.com. We have no idea how well these software packages works. (Please keep in mind that I do not work for or have an association with any of the sites that contain these monitoring devices so look them over before you purchase or download.) We only bring it to the readers' attention as another way to hopefully protect their children. We are sure as the problem is expressed more and more, additional software will become available.

We are also hearing that, in the United States, congress may be leaning towards passing new legislation. This would allow law enforcement trapdoors (a method by which an individual can covertly monitor). In this way they could have access to certain social website communications. This would assist law enforcement in gathering information for prosecution of both cyberbullying and cyberstalking crimes. Of course, there have been concerns this type of information gathering process could be used improperly. We suppose that could transpire in any type of covert surveillance scenario.

Speaking of Congress, in October of 2011, United States senators called for an investigation into the so-called stalking apps. that can be placed on a target's phone. These applications are cell phone spyware. Many reportedly advertised as applications to track "her movements" and "see who she is seeing." The applications can track location, phone calls, and even the contents of text messaging. Now that it has been brought to the Senate's attention, advocates want to know if these applications are legal and, if not, request stern prosecution of their manufactures. As always with any governmental body, stay tuned.

Now that we have discussed some of the pending legislation concerning GPS devices let us retreat for just a moment. This is another time we need to mention the pros and cons (P&C's) of the technology that develops the devices that allows individuals to monitor people for the wrong reasons can also be used for good. Due to our aging population both here and abroad; companies have and are developing GPS devices that are utilized to check on Alzheimer patients, as well as your mom or dad that may be slowing down just a bit mentally. If your parents are anything like mine used to be, they didn't like you hovering or looking over their shoulder. It still would be nice to make sure they were still doing ok on a routine basis without calling and checking on them every moment of the day. We are told as the technology progresses the implantation of these positive devices will become less and less intrusive.

Workplace Violence Stalking

We thought this was as good a place as any to talk about stalking in the workplace. In order to do that, we will have to discuss workplace violence in general. The two kind of go hand in hand. It turns out this is becoming an increasingly hot topic. This is so much so that the Office for Victims of Crime (OVC) out of Washington, DC, (of which I am a consultant) had myself and Rebecca Dreke, one of the consultants for the National Center for the Victims of Crime (NCVC), which as we have indicated previously, houses the stalking resource center, conduct a one-hour online training session to answer questions from law enforcement professionals and victim advocates. That training can be viewed at http://ovc.ncjrs.gov/ovcproviderforum/asp/sub.asp?topic_id=129. See the questions and responses to the web forum on "stalking in the workplace." If you want to get further information on stalking in general or workplace violence stalking, simply go to the OVC site and put one or both of those phrases into the search section. (ovc.ncjrs.gov/webForumNotice/01190/welcom.html).*

We should also note one of the newer laws concerning workplace violence/stalking was passed in 2011 in the Australian state of Victoria. They liken workplace stalking to a form of bullying behavior in the workplace. The law has been referred to as "Brodie's Law" as it relates to the case of a female waitress who killed herself after being bullied/stalked in the workplace by fellow employees. If you are interested, go to http://www.abc.net.au/news/2011-05-31/brodies-bullying-law-may-go-national/2739524.

In regard to workplace violence, more and more companies and public entities are being encouraged to implement a policy. The reason is twofold. First and foremost, there should be something in place that aids in protecting your workforce. Secondly, workplace violence litigation is becoming a huge industry. (We occasionally conduct workplace violence training for businesses. We seem to be getting more and more inquirers from companies concerning this issue; both because it is a good thing to educate personnel, and the

---

* Be aware that, in the United States, the Occupational Safety and Health Administration is increasing its scrutiny of high-risk work settings concerning workplace violence. We are told they are monitoring them more closely than in the past.

worry of litigation.)For those readers who are responsible for these types of programs in your company or industry, we guarantee the first thing any litigator is going to ask your representative prior to trial is for a copy of your workplace violence policy. You do not (we repeat YOU DO NOT) want to be in the position where your response is, "Uh, what workplace violence policy?" If you do, you can expect to have just made that attorney's day and more than likely a few years of days. Just about every company we have dealt with has a sexual harassment policy. Why not add a workplace violence policy? *At this juncture, we would also like to advise you or your H.R. representatives to always being reviewing policy as it pertains to workplace violence issues, or even some of the new EEOC rulings concerning discrimination sections under Title 7 that come up when it pertains to hiring. They seem to have a life of their own, and to prevent problems you must be aware.*

Before we get into the different types of workplace stalking, we should discuss how to defend against workplace violence in general because a sound workplace violence policy should encompass workplace stalking. We suggest the following take place. We realize not all companies have some of the resources we are about to discuss, but it is no problem. The person reading this with a small business can review the information and still develop both a workplace violence policy and a valid course of action if it transpires in his or /her workplace environment.

The first order of business is to develop a workplace violence team or workplace violence prevention group. The name doesn't really matter. It is what the team does that counts. This team should consist of the following individuals:

- Human resource coordinator

- Security

- Executive or someone charged with reporting to the executive side of the firm

- Medical or nursing personnel, if available

- Risk management personnel, if available

- Employee advocate or, depending on the size of the business, a union representative

- We always like a threat management specialist, if available. If you cannot afford one, we suggest you contact a member of your local law enforcement agency to sit in on at least the formation of your policy process. Also use him or her as a conduit to that body.

- Most companies have access to an attorney or legal representative. This helps when developing and formulating policy that will work for the company. Each firm's needs and plant design will dictate much of how this policy is laid out, but we caution that there needs to be a strong monitoring segment or audit program integrated into the policy to make sure it is functioning properly. These should also be in place to tweak or improve the policy.*

Along the lines of employee advocates, some states such as Oregon have implemented legislation that stops employers from discriminating against victims of stalking and certain other crimes (sexual assault and domestic violence). This allows them "reasonable safety accommodations."[92] We think this type of legislation is needed in all states and countries. We should also mention that in states such as New York, laws have been passed not allowing employers to refuse to hire or employ crime victims. In New York employers cannot discriminate against victims in terms of compensation, condition of privileges, or employment (A 755, effective July 07, 2009).

---

* On October 20, 2011, The American National Standards Institute ANSIS, and The Society of Human Resource Management SHRM, developed what is being considered a standard for developing a workplace violence protocol. It can be found by going on the net and typing in ASIS/SHRM WVP.1-2011, Workplace Violence Prevention and Intervention.

The goals of this team are to generate a workable, sound workplace violence policy and to work with employees in the administration and adherence to this policy. Most states and many countries have online resources and examples to assist individuals in the throes of developing such policy.

Having these procedures in place not only helps thwart potential lawsuits, but it tends to increase confidence and reporting within an organization. Those businesses that neglect these problems can experience issues such as poor work performance, drop in general morale, worker attendance issues, worker conflicts (that can and do lead to violence), and increases in a worker's compensation costs. These factors can lead to employee complaints, which may fuel a perceived (or real) mistrust that tarnishes company image.

On occasion we are contacted on our website by people who claim to have been "mobbed" (a reported form of group harassment or bullying in the workplace where peers or management continually harass the victim in an attempt to severely demean or have that individual leave their employment). The people that contact us liken it to a form of workplace stalking, complaining that neither supervisors nor HR representatives addressed the complaints, or they didn't believe the actions transpired at all. Apparently there is enough research on this topic to start bringing it to the attention of legislators. The reason we bring this up is—a word to the wise. If you are an employer, either you and/or your HR personnel should make sure your policies are such that you do listen to your employees concerning all topics. Think about addressing them in such a fashion that will stand up in a court of law or a merit commission hearing. We will say again, in our field, we know many good litigators that thrive off indifference.*

---

* During our annual (2012) Association of Threat Assessment Professionals ATAP, conference we had the pleasure of once again listening to one Glen Kraemer, Partner, Curiale Hischfeld Kraemer LLP. Glen is one of the most articulate and informative individuals I have had the pleasure of listening to concerning workplace violence, workplace violence management, and workplace violence law. If you ever get the opportunity to attend a function where he is speaking, do it. You will not be disappointed.

Now, as to stalking in the workplace, it basically appears in two forms. The first is the stalker that follows his or her target into the workplace from the outside environment. The second is the stalking that is generated in the workplace itself. Either way, the problem has to be addressed.

We will discuss the two different types of stalkers as well as some of the security procedures we feel should be in place to protect both the stalker's target and his or her coworkers. We will refer to the stalker who comes from offsite as just that, the *offsite workplace stalker,* and the onsite stalker as the *onsite workplace stalker.* We know. Sometimes we are just amazed at how we come up with this stuff.

The offsite workplace stalker is usually involved in some type of intimate partner relationship, oftentimes with domestic violence overtones. However, you can experience an offsite workplace stalker who is predatory or seeking revenge on a target. In these situations, he or occasionally she is usually stalking in order to damage people or property at the workplace. (In some scenarios the stalker may be attempting to continue his or her relationship with the victim, whether real or not. The stalker's goal is to stalk that individual and not to cause injury or damage to things or coworkers, at least not initially.) In the case of the intimate partner stalking, the target and coworkers may start receiving incessant telephone calls, e-mails, texts, and faxes, completely clogging up and disrupting office systems. If they can get access to the company servers and know what they are doing, they can create pure havoc by installing spyware or other disruptive devices. It is not unheard of for these individuals to generate numerous annoying calls on a daily basis.

They may also attempt to contact both in-person and in a variety of other ways the target's coworkers for information on that target. The perpetrator may also try to make statements designed to get the target in trouble or fired. For example, we had one female stalker who was harassing a previous same-sex lover. She would damage her vehicle in the employee parking lot or take things from the victim's car she had given her as gifts during happier times. By taking only these specific items, she alerted the victim to the fact that she was the one doing all the damage, thus causing more fear. Then the offsite workplace stalker would contact the victim's employees either in-person or via the phone and try to "out" (tell the employees, who did not know or perhaps even care, about her sexual orientation). She would also tell the female employees to watch themselves around the victim because she (the victim) was always on the prowl for other women, which, of course, was not the case and very awkward for the victim because she was that particular business's office manager.

If the offsite stalker has been a previous employee, that person will oftentimes leave clues about how he or she will perpetrate the stalking campaigns prior to leaving that employment. These guys rarely operate in a vacuum. Coworkers, when queried, usually express what this individual talked about or obsessed about. (We want to emphasize that it is crucial to maintain a work environment where employees feel they can discuss issues such as these with management without fear of reprisal. If that is not the case, don't expect a free/honest exchange of information.)

It is not unusual for the stalker to vandalize the target's property, including vehicles or anything else that is available. The stalker may send packages with disturbing or threatening contents through normal mail. However, if that person sends packages that may contain explosives or other damaging devices, it has been our experience that these will be hand-delivered by an unknowing third party, the stalker, or someone who is willing to work in concert with that stalker. (Of course, this type of behavior is not cast in stone.) Most of the time, they don't want to take the chance that the devices will be discovered by a postal or UPS worker before it does what it is intended to do. During the times when these stalkers are interviewed about sending devices designed to harm, they will often tell law enforcement they didn't want to hurt anyone else other than their targets, for whatever that is worth. They also advised they wanted to make sure the package got to where they wanted it. We have had these devices delivered to an address clearly marked to a specific person, but someone else opens it out of curiosity. On at least one occasion, we then found that curious individual splattered all over the ceiling and walls of the location. Don't let curiosity get the best of you.

The offsite workplace stalker may come armed to your workplace and maim, severely injure, or kill not only the specific target(s) but others. Of course, a workplace shooter does not always follow some type of stalking behavior, but they have and can. Obviously, an onsite workplace stalker can also arm him or herself when coming to work.

For those of you in the public eye (politicians, other public figures, or celebrities), you and your organizational staff need to be very aware of these types of stalkers. These stalkers will oftentimes show up at any venue where their targets are to gather information and/or get a glimpse of the targets. Any contact should be logged and noted. Anyone assigned to security or protection detail should be given a photo or, at the very least, information concerning this particular individual. This way they can keep what we in law enforcement refer to as an "eyeball" on anytime that individual makes his or her presence known. We know some of our readers may be saying to themselves, "Isn't this section about workplace stalkers?" They would be right, but consider that people in the public domain, when working, are oftentimes outside of a structure amongst their constituents or, in the case of the celebrity, amongst the fans. An excellent example of that would be the terrible incident with Congresswoman Giffords.

The following are some security measures for these types of workplace stalkers.

We strongly recommend the following steps in regard to an offsite workplace violence stalking. We also recommend that if you have any concerns about implementing any of these suggestions/policies, you contact your legal counsel. Never do anything you can't live with. Again, we are not the end all to be all on these topics, and don't claim to be.

- The victim should notify local law enforcement and get them up to speed about what is transpiring between the target and the target's stalker.

- Next, the victim/target needs to notify the immediate supervisor and make sure he or she documents this contact with some type of report. As we have indicated, hopefully there is a workplace violence policy in place so that the procedures can be initiated. If the company has a human resource (HR) coordinator, that person should be brought into the mix. Depending on the medical plan and the company's policy, that coordinator might want to offer the victim some type of counseling, even though the stalking is coming to the workplace from offsite. We often get questions concerning the target's privacy. The workplace violence policy should address that issue by stating that the targeted employee should be required to give enough information as to assist in a safe workplace environment for both the employee and the fellow coworkers. Obviously, this would include the name and description of his or her potential assailant along with the fact that he may be armed or violent, and any information concerning civil or criminal issues pending. This would also include whether the stalker has a restraining order with a valid service. It is up to the target whether he or she wants to go into any of the gory details of the relationship. If related, that information should be kept among a few that are advised not to divulge it. If so deemed, management should have the option of being able to obtain a workplace or corporate restraining order against the perceived threat, which in this case is a stalker.

- If there is security available, they should be given the description of the stalker (a photo, if available) and the cars he or she may drive. Security should also provide for the target a well-lit parking space, preferably near a guard station. If possible, the target should be afforded an escort to and from that parking space.

- If the company has a threat analysis team, they need to be brought into the mix. (Some companies go outside for this type of service, but if it is done in-house, the team members need to have specific training about these types of issues. We strongly suggest the team members get some type of exposure to regular threat assessment information and/or training.) Security or a member of the threat assessment team needs to act as a liaison with local law enforcement and get them up to speed about what is going on in the workplace. This is critical because if the police are summoned, it would greatly assist the responding officers prior to rolling into a potentially dangerous situation. (This type of liaison is crucial in all types of stalking.) It is also important when dealing with a workplace violence employee that has been removed from that workplace.

- It is the responsibility of the target to keep a copy of his or her restraining order(s) if they exist so responding law enforcement can have access to them upon arrival. It's also the target's responsibility to keep supervisors abreast of any changes in the stalking condition. In other words, has the stalker gotten more persistent? Has the stalker threatened to come onsite? On the other hand, the targeted employee's supervisor needs to be held accountable for making the proper reports and keeping the necessary people aware of what is transpiring. (Again, this is true in both types of workplace violence stalking scenarios.) *Note: When we deliver seminars to companies concerning workplace violence of any type; what we suggest is that the workplace violence team (WVT) meets on a regular basis. If there is nothing urgent transpiring, great, but they can at least go over any topics that may pop up or one of the team has questions about.*

- Reception should be made aware that he or she needs to monitor any type of packages sent to the potential target. Was the target expecting this package? Were they mailed or delivered by courier or hand-delivered by the stalker or someone who does not fit the mold of a delivery person? Does the packaging appear strange such as having a greasy or oily residue or smell? Does the package have a company mailing label or is it hand-written? Any package that seems out of the ordinary should be submitted to security as a precaution. One of the things we might suggest as out of the ordinary is a package that has way too much postage, or has the person who is supposed to receive same name on several places on the package. Does the package have an authentic return or no return address?

Management also has the responsibility for training employees about workplace violence and other issues involving safety on a regular basis. Just like most companies have sexual harassment policies in place and conduct some type of annual review, the same should hold true for workplace violence training. Again, employees should be encouraged to report any problems they encounter about these issues. As previously indicated, it is very important the employee knows he or she will not be ostracized or diminished for making the proper report. (An example of why it is important for employees to report came up while we were conducting workplace violence training at a company that wanted to initiate training, and who coincidentally had recently had a problem with a long-term employee. The long-term employee had begun acting very erratically and had to finally be let go. Not too long after he was released, he was observed hiding by a vehicle next to an employee entrance wearing all camouflage clothing. The employees that saw him <u>initially</u> went on about their business, deciding not to report that incident to anyone because they felt it was not their place. The owners of the company did well to request the training so all their employees could get up to speed on the issues of workplace violence, and the value of reporting this and other incidents to their newly developed, workplace violence team (WVT) members.

Special note: The WVT members should advise all their fellow employees to consider conducting interviews outside of their workplace cubicles; especially if they keep personal photos or other personal items in said cubicles. Why? For the same reason we advise members of law enforcement. When a potential stalker walks into your personal space he or she will be looking for pertinent information on you. The same applies to people you encounter in a workplace scenario. Do you really know who this new client is, or what makes them tick? Keep in mind it is better not to give out unneeded personal or background information; especially until you feel comfortable with the individual you are dealing with.

The second group of workplace violence stalkers is those that become an issue within the workplace. We are referring to them as onsite workplace stalkers. These types of stalking begin in the workplace because a dating or intimate partner scenario that starts in the workplace becomes estranged and perhaps even violent, or it's due to an acquaintance type scenario where no sexual or dating relationship has transpired. An example of this would be a coworker becomes infatuated with another worker who only sees that specific person as another employee and nothing else. As we have discussed under the section entitled acquaintance stalker, these coworkers may have had coffee together or shared a work product, but their relationship has not progressed any further, at least not in the mind of the targeted victim.

As we have indicated, an effect of this type of stalking would be reduction in general work output, which could be accompanied by a complaint of a hostile work environment. Additional factors could be disruption in the office setting and even possible sabotage of the company's work product and equipment.

The security measures for this type of stalking scenario vary slightly from the ones we have discussed. First of all, once a supervisor is made aware of the problem, he or she needs to evaluate the problem. Obviously, if the investigation reveals a hostile work environment, the offending employee should be warned both verbally and in writing. If the individual continues, and all of management's efforts towards rehabilitation have failed he or she should be, at least in our opinion, terminated.* The employee, when hired, should be made aware of all company policies and sign a form stating he or she understands these policies. This form should clearly indicate that if the workplace violence policy is violated, termination can be one of the directions the company takes. We strongly suggest all workplace violence policies have a zero tolerance caveat. We know of scenarios where the company is so large they can transfer employees in conflict. It is always up to the individual company, but it has been our experience that mere movement from one physical plant to the next does not always take care of the problem. Therefore that company should be prepared to terminate, even if the employee is an integral part of the company. (Of course, that is easy for us to say, but may be extremely painful for management to wrap their arms around.) Remember, even if the onsite workplace stalker is moved, he or she may reoffend not only with his or her current target but another one not remotely involved with the first. As always, whether or not recidivism becomes an issue depends on many things such as stressors and personality traits exhibited by the transgressor just to name a few.

---

* Note: There are a variety of strategies that management can use when removing an employee that we and others that work in this field can and do recommend to staff that can soften that individual's removal. However, those techniques are better discussed in a more closed environment than this text.

Managers should keep in mind we have seen very successful law-suits where the company failed to protect the rights and <u>safety</u> of an employee because the instigator was upper management and deemed by the corporation to be someone they did not want to eliminate from the workforce. We can only suggest those in control make a decision. We hope it will be the right one. Unfortunately we have had reported cases where the victim was removed because the stalker was an employee the company felt they could not lose. We are not lawyers, however in our opinion if the business decides to take that route, it may be opening itself up to eventual litigation.

If you are going to remove any employee, especially one you feel is a problem, there are a few steps one should take.

- On the day of termination, have security collect any name badges, key cards, or company-issued cell phones or laptops.

- Change all the employee's passwords to the company com-puters. Database into the server a caution to notify the com-pany's IT personnel of any attempts to enter the server once the employee is fired.

- Have he or she clear out the desk and take any and all autho-rized items so the employee has no reason to come back to the workplace.

- Make sure the final check is handed to him/her and signed for. Also give the former employee a form that explains he or she is not allowed to come back onto the work grounds for any reason. If he or she requires something, he or she is to call first to get permission to come to the workplace. If that permission is granted, then an escort should be arranged for a specific date and time. He or she should be notified in writing, that if they enter or attempt to enter back onto the workplace without permission, they will be subject to the issuance of a workplace restraining order and potential arrest. When the employee is allowed to return, he or she shall park in a designated parking space that can be monitored by security or, at the very least, a security camera. Why? Because security should be able to watch the employee to ensure he/she is not getting something out of a vehicle such as a weapon. This parking space should be placed in a position where, if the employee's vehicle were to detonate, the blast would cause minimal damage. We are not paranoid, but in this day and age, a little caution definitely goes a long way.

Along the lines of employees and weapons, we recently had an interesting conversation with an executive of a company that has a worldwide operation. The executive, who completely supports safe ownership of guns, suggested that company managers make themselves aware of any existing laws in their state concerning employees being allowed to have a legally owned weapon in their vehicles when they come to work. They have found that in some states they cannot tell a worker that they can't have a weapon in their personal vehicle while on the work premises. If that is the case in your state, I would strongly suggest that security have cameras that cover the entire areas of parking. An internet search will advise you which states allow this option. It looks as though as many as fourteen states currently allow this.

- If the company you work for has the funds earmarked for security, we suggest a metal detector be placed where this employee is allowed to reenter the business. If that device is not feasible, a pat-down is not a bad idea. The ex-employee can always refuse. If he or she doesn't want to cooperate, you can also opt not to allow that individual back into your business. We think this sends a pretty significant message to the troubled ex-employee that he or she is not going to do whatever he or she wants.

- Just as a point of information, many companies now place in their employment agreements, which are signed by new hires, that if the employee wants to stay employed and an investigation concerning theft or wrongdoing is initiated, that person must submit to a polygraph test. We would suggest you extend the use of that test to any employee that may present a threat to coworkers' safety. It is just a thought. By the way, many businesses now require random drug testing as part of their requirements for employment. This could come in handy during a potential disciplinary action or termination scenario.

- Of course, when the employee is removed from the company's employ, all the security recommendations we discussed with the offsite workplace stalker apply.

The following are some sites for definitions of workplace violence and examples of policies that can be used to develop a workplace violence program within the company you own, operate, or work for. Ontario, Canada, has passed a mandatory workplace violence law. Bill 168 was passed in December of 2009, and it amended their Occupational Health and Safety Act. The bill actually took effect on June 15, 2010.[93] New York initiated The New York State Public Employee Workplace Violence Prevention Law, which went into effect in April of 2009.[94] This requires any public employers with twenty or more employees to implement a written program to prevent violence in the workplace.

Other sites to review are The National Institute for the Prevention of Workplace Violence at http://www.workplaceviolence911.com. Other organizations to review are the National Institute for Occupational Safety and Health (NIOSH) and Occupational Violence at http://www.cdc.gov/niosh/topics/violence. By going on the OVC website (http://www.ovc.gov/needinfo/index.html) and clicking on "Workplace Violence" then "Resource Links," you will find several sites such as the Department of Homeland Security and Occupational Safety and Health Administration (OSHA) that discuss workplace violence.

Chapter Three Summary

- A stalker's first contact can be letters, notes, gifts, or more.
- Stalkers are experts at vandalism.
- Many stalkers make threats, but some never do.
- A stalker's behavior can escalate to physical damage, sexual assault, or even the death of the victim.
- Stalkers can Injure pets for effect, or they can ransom them to generate contact with the victim.
- Stalkers are very adept at surveillance, which can include following, use of a global positioning system (GPS), cell phone spying, spy cameras, caller ID spoofing, use of family and friends, use of children to gather additional information on the victim, etc.
- Many will enter into the victim's residence to gather information or collect trophies.
- Disruption of household and other services is one of the tricks stalkers utilize.
- By placing ads in newspapers and online, stalkers can cause everyday citizens to assist in the harassment of the victim.
- Stalkers may file frivolous lawsuits or other civil acts to harass the victim.
- Identity theft is another destabilizing tool employed by stalkers.
- Cyberstalking is growing in frequency, especially among tech-savvy stalkers. They utilize spyware, phishing devices, IP sniffers, and keystroke or keylogging devices. Stalking by proxy is on the rise. All these create a great deal of havoc for the victim.
- Cyberbullying is on the rise and is just another tool in the cyberstalker's arsenal. This is especially prevalent among many of our younger stalkers.
- Workplace Stalking is a growing concern and should be addressed by all businesses large and small.

Chapter 4
I Am Being Stalked.
What Do I Do?

Before getting into what to do if you have a stalker on your tail, we should discuss how to stay away from these guys (or gals). No matter what you do, it is possible to still end up with a stalker through no fault of your own. That is why we wrote the book to both educate and assist. We will discuss security measures to not only forestall a stalking scenario but to stay safer in general. However, for now we just want to talk about a few ways to hopefully reduce your chances of becoming a notch on a stalker's belt.

Sixth Sense. That's right. Use your good old gut intuition. I have two daughters, and of course, I have sat down with them and talked about guys, safety plans, how to defend themselves, and escape routes. Both of them know how to shoot, and are getting better and better every time they hit the range to blast off a hundred or so rounds. Their mother probably shoots better than I do. (Seeing as I shoot on a regular basis, this is somewhat disconcerting.) The thing I have stressed the most is not to blow off first impressions. Unfortunately, in this day and age, women are taught not to injure the very fragile male ego. Many people tell women to let the guy down easy or mask her true feelings. Our response to that is that is truly a load of crap. We don't mean you have to be rude to people, at least not initially. It does mean let your intuition work for you.

Like it or not, we are animals, and that is a good thing. A good part of my lineage is American Indian. Indians are taught to feel their environment. Let the world you walk through tell you things, watch the birds, smell the odors the wind brings you, watch the sky, and hear what Mother Nature is whispering (and sometimes screaming) at you. Actually see what is going on in front of you rather than what someone wants you to see. I have taught my kids that first encounters can usually reveal a lot about the people you meet. If you are about to step into something in life, make sure it is not something that smells and will stick to the bottoms of your feet. In other words, if you meet someone, and the hairs on the back of your neck stand up, don't rationalize your feelings. Don't tell yourself there is probably nothing wrong with this guy or this gal. Your body's radar has executed a warning signal, so do not kiss it off. You don't know how many times my partner and I have talked to both men and women that have told us after being victimized, "You know, Detective, I had a feeling there was something wrong, but I gave this person the benefit of the doubt."

Saying No. Ladies, learn how to say no and really mean NO! If a guy approaches you and wants to date, and you feel this is definitely not Mr. Right, then tell him in no uncertain terms you are not available and will not ever be available for him. Don't say things like, "Well, I am in a relationship right now." That tells the guy you're in a thing now, but maybe tomorrow (or in the next few minutes) you won't be, so it's OK to approach you again.

Along the lines of dating, if you do decide to see someone, at least for the first couple dates, agree to meet someplace neutral. That means you have a way to get out of Dodge if necessary.

Don't Advertise. We know that we all have our personality quirks. My nickname is the Duck. It's something that has stuck with me from my years as a cop. Some people love specific animals such as wolves, cats, greyhounds, etc. That is all well and good, but try not to advertise these things. How many times have you seen a young girl driving a pickup truck with stickers on the back of her window talking about being a cowgirl, gymnast, swimmer, or some other thing she is into? Then you look on her license plate holder, and it may say something like "Sally loves horses" or "Dawn loves to ride." Other times you see a car with all those stick figures of children, pets, and/or family members pasted on the back window. Some cars advertise the kids' school, the sports team or high school they attend, and/or the city the person resides in. A potential stalker is going to connect the dots. In regard to the cowgirls, he now knows the female driving this pickup is probably named Dawn. She believes she is a cowgirl and loves to ride horses. That is a lot of information for this guy to start building on. Say Dawn works as an animal veterinary assistant. She just picked up a uniform from the cleaner, and it is hanging in the back of her vehicle. The uniform has a patch with the veterinary hospital where she works. She then pulls into her apartment complex, parks, and walks into the building. Our stalker contacts the apartment manager and tells him he works with Dawn at whatever her hospital is. He says he is having a hard time finding her apartment. The helpful manager gives him Dawn's apartment number and a map of the complex to find it easier. You think we are kidding, but this happens all the time.

While we are in this section, we will discuss another issue we have with those celebrities and prominent people we attempt to assist. Those who work with them concerning threat assessment would probably not like to see the celebs put their family members, especially their children, out there for the paparazzi and others to photograph, document, etc. Most are fairly mindful of this. Of course, there are times when photos are taken without permission, but there are other times such as commercials or other documentary scenarios where they appear fairly prominently. In these instances, a celebrity will have themselves and their family members photographed or videotaped at length, and they will give away huge amounts of information. Unwittingly they may also conduct these interviews in their homes. Sometimes these home viewing shows have no family members shown, but stalkers are extremely thorough in developing their research. Let us give you an example. We watched a program where a well-known celebrity did a walk-through of the home with a camera crew. The premise of the program was to show the architectural aspects of the home. As the crew entered the celebrity's little child's room, they did a panoramic shot. This shot showed some photos of the child, toys, where his or her bed was placed in the room, etc. As a stalker, I now know what colors the kid likes, the types of toys he or she plays with, and the layout of the room. That is a huge amount of information the stalker never had before and probably would have had a tough time getting. All that stalker has to do is tape-record that particular show or worse yet, pay for a copy. However the production is obtained the stalker now has plenty of time to sit and review the program over and over again, dissecting every frame for information that may assist in developing a plan of attack. This also applies to magazines such as the ones that show a celebrity's home in great detail. Stalkers will cut and paste every scrap of information on a target whether it is a celebrity, politician, or everyday person. Again, being in the public eye is like walking a tight-rope, but for those of us who work in the field of threat assessment, less information and exposure is better than more.

Don't Tell Everybody Your Life Story. How many times have you run across someone you are meeting for the first time, and before you can escape, that person has told you where he or she lives, what kind of food he or she likes, where he or she works, and on and on? Don't be one of those people. Most folks you encounter really don't care, and you may run across that one individual who you don't want to have any information about you.

An excellent example about giving up too much information was something we see all too often in the media. We were recently visiting another state when a news bulletin flashed on the tube. It said a young girl had been found raped and murdered in her condo by an unknown assailant. The news interviewed one of the neighbors, and this was what she told the on-scene broadcaster. Standing out in front of the condo complex, she told the reporter she was a single mom. She said she was very afraid for her twelve-year-old daughter, who was a latchkey kid and went into an empty condo every day by herself. I am not sure what this woman was thinking. If this was a serial predator, she might as well have drawn him a map to her very vulnerable child.

Along these same lines, and in this time of multiple military conflicts, do not advise unfamiliar people that your spouse is deployed. If you are married or have a significant other, you want people to believe he or she comes home every day.

As we were ordering our favorite drink at our local Starbucks, another thought came to mind. Every time you order, what does the barista ask you? Name? The place is usually loud, so we scream out, and she or he scribbles it on the side of your drink. Ever wonder how many people now know your first name? So what do I do? I use a nickname or just an initial. Obviously it has to be something you will remember. This applies to your local coffee bar, reservations at a restaurant, etc. If you think we might be getting a little picky, that is ok. Our goal is to make you think. Maybe even stop you from being someone's target.

Let's get back to what to do now you are being stalked.

Don't panic. Take a deep breath and begin reading through the rest of this chapter. I realize it is easy for me to say "don't panic." I am trained, and throughout most of the United States, I can carry a concealed weapon, which a great deal of stalkers are aware of. (By the way, we in law enforcement who confront and investigate stalkers do get stalked from time to time. As previously discussed; this also holds true for the parole and probation officers that end up with these yahoos. For us in law enforcement that is pronounced "yeah-whoos." It's not like the search engine.)

When I conduct seminars for parole and probation, I tell them, if they conduct interviews with their clients, don't have photos of their families, dogs, or hobbies in their offices or cubicles. Why? Because as we discussed in our section on the workplace violence stalker; the stalker will make mental notes of those items or worse yet photos with their trusty little camera phones if you step out of the office. Along those lines we also advise them not to leave these individuals alone in their offices because the stalker will take this opportunity to gather as much information on them or any other cases they are currently working. This same precaution should be thought about by those of you that have clients come into your offices. Do you really want strangers knowing personal information about you; especially information about your family?

By the way, this should not apply just to those in law enforcement or probation. I also instruct those being stalked, those who have to counsel stalkers, or those that may well be potential stalking victims not to leave out pertinent pieces of their personal lives for these guys to view. To a stalker, knowledge, especially personal information, is his or her lifeblood.

As indicated, we have had stalkers attempt to stalk us but in a very limited fashion. Usually they are trying to gather as much information about us as possible. They do this because we have become the bane of the stalker's existence. In other words, we are a complete pain in their ass, and they don't like it. It really bothers them because they can't exert any control over us. We still get cards, letters, and other communiqués from them. One example we gave in our last book and use from time to time in our lectures seems to illustrate the obsession with those like us who are actually placed in the law enforcement role of stalking the stalker. Therefore we think we should share, especially for those who have not availed themselves of our first text.

I had a stalker that was beating and harassing his ex-wife. He was a large, sleeved (tattoos covering both arms down to the top of his hands), bearded biker who worked as a bouncer for a local bar that dealt methamphetamine along with beer. He carried a blackjack (a type of club) most of the time and when he felt like it, a sawed-off shotgun. He had some strange proclivities such as stealing his ex's panty hose, eating the crotches out of them, putting them on, and then masturbating. He also forced another female to drive him to a motel where he raped her repeatedly along with other deviant acts. She allowed him to do this because he threatened to kill her daughter, which is was quite capable of doing. After I hooked him up for burglary and stalking, he was sent to prison for two years. While in prison my partner and I visited him so we could talk to him about a murder he was involved in. He had assisted another biker and major cocaine dealer in shooting to death a female associate.

After our interview, the head correctional officer (CO) pulled me aside and asked if I was Detective Proctor. When he had verified my identity, he explained that the dirt bag we had just interviewed kept a scrapbook in his cell. The binder contained news interviews I had conducted and clippings from newspaper articles that had been written about some of the robbery and homicide cases my partner and I had been involved in. The scrapbook also had a photo of me when I was interviewed by the Orange County Register concerning the children's books I write (under a different name). In that article there had been some personal information about how I was into science fiction among other things. We were in the paper and on the tube a lot due to the amount of crime that we were experiencing at that time. My partner and I had thought it a little strange when the stalker/murder suspect had said to me as he was leaving the interview room something about being a "Trekie" (a fan of Star Trek). After finding out about the scrapbook, that made sense.

The CO went on to say they had rolled on a fight call in the cell and found that this particular inmate's road dog (cellmate) had found the scrapbook and was in the process of tearing it up when the fight took place. Apparently our stalker's cellmate was a crook we had recently put away for a cold case murder that had taken place thirteen years earlier. Dummy had stabbed a fellow doper to death and dumped his body with his pants down near a local ATM. So needless to say, he was not too happy with my partner and me at the time. (What are the chances that, in a state prison with a large population, those two inmates who committed crimes in the same city and were investigated by the same two homicide detectives would be cellies?) Just as a point of information, that biker died.

My partner and the homicide detail are in the process of getting the actual trigger-man, whom we have identified, brought to justice.

Get Law Enforcement on Board

The first thing you want to do if you believe you are being stalked is contact your local law enforcement entity. Have the responding uniform patrol officer at least take some type of documentation about your dilemma. If they don't, calmly get his badge number, thank him or her for coming, and then go to your police department. Ask to see the watch commander. Explain that you strongly believe you are being stalked and why. Get the name and telephone number of the detective normally assigned stalking cases or, at the very least, domestic violence cases. (Most domestic violence detectives are trained or should be trained in how to investigate stalking.) Call that detective and explain what you believe is transpiring. Keep a log of all contacts. If you do not get any satisfaction, and unfortunately sometimes one does not, then continue your quest up the proverbial chain of command: the detective lieutenant, detective commander, chief's office, and then above. Hopefully this does not transpire, but we have seen it happen, thankfully, not very often, but it does.

Of course, there is always a caveat to a suggestion like this. We know some police department officials may get upset with us for suggesting a potential stalking victim keep plugging away but for only one reason. We have had cops contact us and tell us they want victims to get the attention they need, but some of the ones that contact them that believe they are being stalked are in fact delusional and a real problem for them. We understand, and we apologize for the stress we may have caused these detectives. On the other hand, there will be that victim that through what we are sure was an initial misunderstanding gets the help he or she needs by following our advice and climbing the chain of command. As to the delusional people, like anything else, one has to sort the bad out from the good. It goes with the job. Remember, we have found that some delusional people we have encountered are being harassed. In our opinion that needs to be addressed as well.

Before I go further, again, let me also talk to those with have family and friends who claim to be stalked but are in truth not completely there. Unfortunately I do have mentally ill people who read my books, see me on television, and go on my website. As previously indicated, some have delusional issues that are exacerbated by reading books like mine. I had one woman call me and say that her brother, who was mentally ill, told her continually she did not know what she was talking about because Detective Proctor said it was true in his book. She told me she had tried to burn my book on several occasions. She succeeded once, but to her dismay, her brother purchased another copy. What can I say? It is good to have fans, but at times, it can create issues.

Don't be like the kid in the fairy tales who cried wolf when you are dealing with law enforcement. Although it might seem like your stalker is lurking behind every corner, he or she is not. What I am saying is, if your stalker drives a blue minivan, not all blue minivans contain your stalker. Make sure it is the blue mini with the dent in the right front quarter panel with the correct license plate number before you call the cops to make a report. You don't want the desk officer or police dispatcher rolling his or her eyes and saying, "Here we go again." You have to be the best judge of your own situation. We want you to contact the police if you need help. Just take a breath and have a pretty good idea what you are dealing with is your stalker and not some phantom.

Each police department will have its way of investigating any type of crime, including stalking. Once you get them on board, we strongly suggest you begin a diary of sorts and log everything that takes place concerning your stalker. In the section on how we investigate the stalker, we will discuss the stalking logs we have victims fill out. (There are copies of those logs in the appendix section of the book.) The agency you will be dealing with may not have such a log, or it may have a better one.

Document, Document, Document

Documentation is crucial when involved in a stalking scenario. Whatever the stalker sends to you must be collected and logged. Here are some suggestions on how to collect and preserve what the stalker sends your way.

- *Notes, cards, letters, or gifts* should be collected and packaged in a plastic bag. We also like the plastic page sleeves you can obtain at a stationary store to house any letters or cards a stalker may send you. This way the investigator can look at them and make copies without contaminating any prints or possible DNA from the stalker. If the item is small enough to be placed in a zip lock type bag, then use it. Otherwise place it into a small kitchen trash bag. Take a black permanent marker and write the date, time, and location where you found or obtained the item. (Yes, we will make good CSIs out of you yet.) We want to preserve these items so they can be processed for any latent fingerprints or DNA. Unfortunately with the advent of television crime dramas such as *CSI* and *Law and Order*, our criminal element has become better trained on how not to leave trace and other evidence behind.

- *All e-mails* sent by your stalker need to be saved on a digital storage device (such as a thumb drive that can later be retrieved by law enforcement) or, at the very least, printed out. The same holds true for any faxes that are sent.

- *Text messages* can be stored on your phone and then later copied by displaying each text and machine copying them. You can do this or have the detective you are working with do this. If the detective obtains the stalker's phone records via a subpoena or a search warrant, the text messages may be displayed on the released records. Your phone records may show dates and times when a text came in. The reason we say "may" in this section is because, depending on the cell phone company your wireless device is with, how they display this information may be a factor. Unless it has changed, wireless providers really don't like getting stuck having to comply with all the subpoenas and search warrants that are served, which make them produce these records. Some of these providers have a set amount of time they will keep these records prior to getting rid of them. Many of them now charge law enforcement a fee to produce the records.

- *Instant messages* that one gets on his or her computer can be copied and then printed out. One needs to ascertain exactly how this is done depending on whether you are using an Apple or a PC system. Each system is different concerning this issue.

- *All telephone calls* generated by your stalker should at least be logged for date, time, and what was said. This includes cell phone calls. Get with the police who are handling your case, and see if they want you to tape-record the phone calls. Many states allow this type of action. It is a tremendous tool when the prosecutor has these available to him or her, but check first. Victims who are receiving rude, annoying, or threatening phone calls can usually have the phone company place what is called a "trap" on their phone line(s). This allows the phone company to document when a certain grouping of calls come into the victim's phone. The victim should coordinate with law enforcement prior to getting a trap set up.

We are told on a regular basis by victims that a patrol officer has told him/her to change phone numbers to help stop the stalker from making contact. The investigator in charge may end up having the victim change his or her phone number, but he or she will have to take into consideration that stopping the stalker from calling might create issues. It might cause the stalker to escalate and try to contact the victim by showing up to his or her house or place of work.

Talk to Your Kids

If you have children, depending on their ages, you need to sit down with them and explain what is going on. It is always tricky in a separation or divorce because of custody and other legal matters. That is why we strongly suggest that if you have made a decision to get divorced, you follow through with your paperwork as soon as possible. One of the things one needs to do quickly is have your attorney explain to the magistrate involved in your case that you are being stalked. That law enforcement is involved, and you would like a restraining order (or, at the very least, get the magistrate to make an order) advising the father or in some cases the mother that they not utilize the children as conduits to gather information on the person being stalked. If the relationship involves children and an estranged boyfriend, then the children's school should be notified of the problem and staff advised that the stalker should have no contact or pick up rights for the children. (This may also apply to the father, but the court will have to make a ruling concerning that issue.) Along those same lines, it's crucial to make a clear list of who you want to pick up the children, especially in the case of an emergency. If you recall, we talked about how we catalogue both the victim and her children. This is also discussed in the section of the book talking about our stalking protocol. Hopefully, the law enforcement agency you are dealing with will do this also, but if not, you must take it upon yourself to take good, clear photos of your kids, and if at all possible, get them fingerprinted.

Get Family and Friends Up to Speed

Family and close friends need to be notified. No one wants to be blindsided by an incident that may cause them or you disaster. Those closest to you need to know what is going on. This way they can help you and assist in protecting themselves. It is up to you about how much you want to tell them about you and your stalker. Like we have said, the stalker often will contact your friends and family to gather information. Some will harass this group to get to you. Victims complain that their stalkers have slashed their father or boyfriend's tires or left threatening letters or gifts with them because they could not establish the contact they craved. Some stalkers have told us they continually damaged their targets' relatives' property in the hopes of having the target acquiesce or comply with his or her wishes.

Your Workplace Should Be Notified

Like we have previously indicated, if you work, your workplace may be at risk, so you need to make your supervisor aware of your problem. Remember our discussion of workplace violence/stalking? Again, how much you tell your supervisor, security, or human resources contact is up to you, but you need to make them aware so they can assist you and develop a safety plan.

Stop All Voluntary Contact with Your Stalker

You must stop any contact with your stalker. Many readers may be asking, "Why is he even making this rule? It should be obvious that should happen." Well, folks, too often it does not take place. Both the cops and the prosecuting attorney are going to require a visible stoppage where they can point to a date and even a time when all contact was severed. If they cannot, it is doubtful a successful stalking prosecution can take place. We have victims that for a variety of reasons go back to the stalker (out of guilt, feeling sorry for the perpetrator, or because of an issue with the kids are just a few). This just cannot happen. Of course, you need to follow the detective's who is in charge of your case's recommendations. We are almost sure this will be one of his or her requirements.

Investigate utilizing your local Neighborhood Watch Program

If you have a watch program, you might want to think about getting them involved. Most communities in the United States have some type of neighborhood watch program run by their local police departments. Some stalking victims are hesitant about letting people know they are being stalked. So if you don't feel comfortable talking to your neighbors, then don't. We have found that some programs have been very helpful in gathering information on a stalker working their turf.

If you decide to make the watch aware of your situation, we suggest you have someone in your local police department that coordinates the watch get in contact with the block captain and explain things in as general terms as possible. No one needs to know specifics of the crime. They just need to know you are having issues and to be on the lookout for a specific person, vehicle, etc. Keep local law enforcement abreast of what the watch program members encounter as it pertains to the stalker.

Of course, the downside to many neighborhoods is that many people who live in them in certain locals don't really know their neighbors. However, in other more tight-knit communities, most know all their neighbors. Some might even know more about their neighbors than they would like.

Look into Obtaining a Restraining or an Order of Protection

Should you obtain a restraining order? We need to review a few things concerning this important topic. I have often been asked what my feelings are about restraining orders. It is my opinion that, on the whole, if the restraining or protective order is not backed by a strong law enforcement presence, they are pretty much not worth the paper they are printed on. (We are also aware in some jurisdictions if a restraining order is in place at the time of the stalking, the stalking can be charged as a felony. That is great, but it still doesn't change our opinion on having a strong law enforcement presence in place to back up the order at the time of its issuance.)

That being said, let's talk. First we should explain there are a variety of restraining orders, including the civil harassment restraining order, a domestic violence restraining order, a stalking protective or restraining order, a workplace violence restraining order, and in some jurisdictions even an elder abuse restraining order. There are also criminal stay away orders (sometimes referred to as orders of protection) issued by a judge or magistrate at the time of trial or at pre-trial hearings. For our purposes, we will only discuss a few types of orders. These orders may not be referred to as restraining orders or protection orders in all countries or even all jurisdictions in the United States. For example, in New South Wales, Australia, they have apprehended violence orders. In Victoria, Australia, they have intervention orders, and in the United Kingdom, some are referred to anti-molestation or non-molestation orders. In the state of Maryland, they can be referred to as peace orders.

TROs (temporary restraining orders): For our purposes, we will define a temporary restraining order as an order of protection that is initially obtained by a person to restrain another (a stalker) from pursuing, following, or harassing that individual. The victim obtains the order by going before a magistrate (each jurisdiction varies as to which court handles these types of orders). It may even be the superior court, municipal court, or justice court when applying for the TRO to be issued. Usually the requestor of the order is required to fill out information, which is referred to as the "standards of proof" section on the form. This is the part of the form that lists all the facts pertaining to what the stalker has done to cause the victim to seek the protection order.

This is just another of the reasons we suggest our victims keep logs or diaries concerning all stalking events. It is much easier to document all that has happened in a clear and concise fashion if one has this data organized in a chronological fashion.

Once you have submitted the paperwork to the court, they usually request you notify or at least show some type of valid attempt that you have notified the person who you want restrained about the issuance of the order. This way, he or she has a chance to appear in court and fight the order if he or she wishes. If the victim has made a "good faith" effort to locate and serve the stalker with the TRO and cannot complete the service, he or she may request the judge issue the order "ex parte." That means the order is issued without the other party being made aware of the court order. The TRO is usually only valid for a short period of time. Time varies from jurisdiction to jurisdiction, but it usually lasts from about fourteen to twenty days. During that time period, the victim is still supposed to try to serve the stalker. However, in many cases, the stalker is continuing to stalk and may end up being served by law enforcement.

We strongly suggest that either the detectives handling your case or a member of the court tasked to serve TROs (such as a sheriff or a marshal) handle the service. This way there is no cloud on the service once completed, and it is inherently safer (fewer challenges in court) than having a private citizen over the age of eighteen make the service. We also suggest you keep at least one or two certified copies of any TRO with you. This way, in case you need to present it to the police, you can. The National Stalker and Domestic Violence Reduction Act mandates all states in the United States to place civil restraining orders along with abuse prevention orders into the National Crime Information Center (NCIC) database.

Permanent restraining orders: Once the stalker (who can bring an attorney to present his or her case) has had his or her day in court, and the magistrate has found in your favor, a "permanent" restraining order is issued. The caveats and durations of these orders vary depending on the state or country one lives in, so we suggest you either contact your court information officer or go on the Internet to find out how long the orders can be issued for. Many states in the United States have permanent restraining orders lasting only three years. However, in the state of New Jersey, once a permanent or "final" restraining order is issued, and no expiration date is indicated, it can be in force forever or until one or both parties request another judicial evaluation of the order that results in the order being dismissed or modified. Many permanent restraining orders can be reinstated after the time period indicated if one can show just cause. California has a stalking restraining order that lasts ten years. Other states and other countries have begun to follow suit in regard to stalking orders of protection. (At present thirty-eight states in the United States have stalking protection orders in place.) Some states such as New Jersey may couch the stalking in a domestic violence order of protection. However, in that same state, if you are convicted of the crime of stalking, a permanent restraining order may be obtained as part and parcel of New Jersey's stalking penal code. To find out more about the restraining orders in your state, go to www.womenslaw. org. Another good place to review restraining order information in the United States is Civil Protection Orders, A guide to Improving Practice, www.ncjfcj.org/.../**civil-protection-orders-guide-improving-practice**

If you do decide to get a restraining order, we suggest you check with your court's victim/witness group to ascertain if you are able to obtain the order free of charge. Many states allow victims of domestic violence to obtain the order at no cost. The same scenario may apply to all orders of protection, but check first.

Emergency protective order (EPO): An EPO is designed to assist not only the victims but the cops dealing with them in the field. For the most part, here is how an EPO works. Say an officer responds to a domestic violence call. When he or she arrives and finds there is a reason to have one of the individuals restrained from the other, he or she then fills out an order of protection, calls it into the on-duty judge or magistrate, advises the judge of the circumstances, and the judge (finding just cause) issues the order for the victim while the officer is still in the field. If service can be made on the person to be restrained, that is great. If not, the order is issued in ex parte. The EPO is good for a short period of time (oftentimes seventy-two hours). This allows the victim to obtain a TRO against the person who needs to be restrained. Some jurisdictions also have emergency stalking protective orders that are issued in place of EPOs involving domestic violence. In other words, if the stalker is not a family member, spouse, or significant other, the stalking EPO can be issued, depending on the requirements of the jurisdiction handling the issuance of the order. For example, in Orange County, California, the EPO is good for a five-day period, and the officer obtaining the order does not have to list any kind of a relationship with the victim if it involves a stalking scenario. However, if it is domestic violence, child abuse, or elder abuse, the issuer has to explain how the victim is related to the subject being restrained. Some EPOs such as those in Orange County California can also have the issuing judge order child custody on the EPO, which places the child for the period of the order with a relative or non-restrained party for the safety of the child.

We were just contacted by a friend and colleague, Jane Shade. Shade is currently an Orange County Superior Court Commissioner in her spare time and a professor of law. Shade started out as a deputy district attorney and rose quickly through the ranks to where she is now. She is a long-time advocate for women involved in domestic violence and especially stalking. She has taught at various venues throughout the United States and elsewhere about the prosecution of domestic violence cases and stalking. She just advised me she was involved in a DVD training video on EPOs, which was produced by the Orange County Sheriff's Video Unit and OC Family Violence Council. She sent me a copy for review. I found the DVD extremely well-done, and it is an excellent short-burst training tool. (We realize this DVD is designed specifically for Orange County law enforcement. However, it is this type of training we would encourage all police agencies to develop for roll call or other in-house training. You don't have to have a large production crew to create these types of training.) By the way, Shade did a previous video on stalking that we utilize in our presentations. We thank people such as Jane who continue to assist victims of crime.

The laws of both EPOs and general restraining and stalking orders of protection are still evolving. For example, Massachusetts just passed a bill that allows people other than spouses, family members, or significant others to have a restraining order issued against them. We are familiar with this law because it stemmed from a case in Everett, Massachusetts where a young waitress was stalked continuously by a onetime patron. Her stalker was relentless and would not take no for an answer. Due to the laws in the state concerning stalking, the suspect was only arrested on minor offenses. One day the thirty-two-year-old waitress (Sandy) opened her front door to find a package that had been left there with her name on it. She took the package inside, entered her kitchen, and as she began to unwrap the box, met her demise by the bomb her stalker had left for her.

The waitress's sister, Cheryl Darisse, whom we have discussed previously, then began a one-woman attack on the legal system to have the stalking and restraining orders laws changed. She was able to get the stalking law changed in her state with a bill issued in her sister's name entitled Sandy's Law (Commonwealth of Massachusetts Section 43A, approved in August of 2000). She was also instrumental in getting this restraining order law affirmed. It only took ten years of hard work.

In the United States, under the mandates of the Full Faith and Credit provisions of the Violence Against Women Act, 18 U.S.C., 2265, all states, including tribal jurisdictions, must enforce "valid" protection orders issued by other states and Indian tribes, as if they were issued within their own jurisdictions. To make this simpler, let me give you an example. Say Mildred has a domestic violence restraining order in the state of Georgia, and she travels to California and is accosted by the person being restrained by that valid order. Then that subject can be arrested in California under the language of the Georgia order. The laws in the state in which the incident took place can apply to the penalty available to the judge reviewing the incident, even if those penalties are not the same as those in the initiating state. [95]

To better explain that, say state (A) where the order was issued only has the penalty for violation of the order as a misdemeanor, but the stalker is arrested in state (B) that makes it a felony for violating in their state. The stalker can then be prosecuted under the felony section. The same holds true if state (A) has a violation of the order as a civil penalty, and state (B) has it as a misdemeanor. Then the stalker or "respondent" (person the order was issued to) is prosecuted for a criminal offense. As to the respondent's release information being given to the holder of the restraining order, if the enforcing/arresting state has a policy that they will notify the victim when the respondent is about to be released from jail/prison, and the issuing state of the order does not, the enforcing state's release notification will be utilized. (We know these things can and do get complicated. That is why we try to break them down for you as much as we can.) If you would like more on this detailed law, please go to www.state.de.us/midatlanticffc/orders.htm and the OVC Bulletin #4, Enforcement of Protective Orders, United States Department of Justice.

The Full Faith and Credit Act covers not only the fifty states in the United States but the commonwealth of Puerto Rico, the US Virgin Islands, American Samoa, the Northern Mariana Islands, and Guam, which are all protectorates of the United States.

Violations of restraining orders varies from state to state. If you do have a valid restraining order from another state and are planning on travelling even for a visit to another state, it is always wise to carry a certified copy of that order with you in case you have to show it to law enforcement in the other state. Also, if you are planning on staying for a prolonged period of time in another state or are moving to that state, you should check if you have to file a formal affidavit with that particular jurisdiction about your restraining or protective order. Never assume anything. Always check with the state laws where you reside. Keep in mind that many states have developed their own laws pertaining to the Full Faith and Credit provisions set down by the 1994 Violence Against Women Act.

For those readers interested in gathering more information on procedures and violations of restraining and non-molestation orders in the United Kingdom, go to www.sentencingcouncil.org.uk. Search for their sentencing guidelines on protection and/or non-molestation orders. The site www.womansaid.org.uk will also assist you in finding out about these same orders of protection. Speaking of non-molestation orders, according to a statement put out by Women's Aid in the United Kingdom, as of 02-07-2007 in the United Kingdom, under the provisions of Section 1 of the Domestic Violence, Crime and Victims Act of 2004, it is a criminal offense to breach a non-molestation order.[96] According to the information of this new provision, a victim of a non-molestation order can opt to immediately call local law enforcement. They will deal with the violation as a criminal act or go back to civil court and handle it as a contempt of court issue. In January of 2010, the Guardian.co.uk reported that Spain began a campaign to obtain domestic violence/battered women protection in the European Union by recognizing their restraining orders across all member borders. They also discussed developing specialized police units to handle crimes involving battered women. Hopefully this type of legislation will allow the member states of the EU to do pretty much what the United States is currently doing in regard to state to state protection orders. We would love to see other countries' orders of protection accepted in the United States. We continually get requests from those persons who live outside U.S. borders wanting to know if there is a way their protective orders can be of use to them when they travel to the States.

Suing Your Stalker

More and more states are recognizing the victim's right to sue his or her stalker. California had the first such law under California Civil Code Section 1708.7. We assisted in writing a portion of a brief utilized by the attorneys of a victim who was being stalked while on the job for a major corporate entity. This first usage of the law took place in March of 1996, and the victim was successful in the litigation. Several other states such as Michigan (Mich. Comp.Laws Ann. 600.2954), Nebraska (28-113), Oregon (Or.Rev. Stat. 30.866), Rhode Island (R.I. Gen. Laws, 9-1-2.1), South Dakota (S.D. Codified Laws 22-19B-1), Texas

(Texas Civil. Prac. & Rem. Code Ann. 85-001), Virginia (Va. Code, 8.01-42.3), Washington State (WA.Rev.code Ann. 9A-36.083: this can be a civil remedy as a result of a conviction of RCW 9A. 36.080, Malicious Harassment), and Wyoming (Wyo. Stat. 1-1-126) have followed suit (forgive the pun). (More information concerning these state civil statutes can be found by going onto the National Center for Victims of Crime website and clicking on the Stalking Resource Center at http://www.ncvc.org/src/main. aspx?dbID=DB_CivilStalkingLaws188.)

Countries such as the United Kingdom and Scotland also appear to have similar civil remedies under their harassment laws.

One warning we should mention in this section, and this is not designed to dissuade, but to advise. Be prepared, if your case goes to trial you may have your stalker's attorney grill you on the stand concerning a variety of things many of which you may feel are personal, some very. This allows your stalker to once again gather information, have some control; especially when his or her attorney is attempting to rake you over the coals, and in some form or fashion have access to you via the courtroom. Of course, these suits can be settled without a formal trial, but we just wanted to let you know you may run into this scenario.

Develop a Security Plan

Once you realize you are being stalked, you need to formulate a security plan. This is not difficult and should not require taking a class in strategy or logistical analysis. Common sense is the key to this package. We suggest the following things in regard to the security plan. (We will discuss other security measures for your home further on in the book. What we are suggesting is not designed to make your fearful or paranoid. We just hope it will keep you safer.) The first thing that will help is the fact that you are actually sitting down and even thinking about a plan. Having a plan is *way* better than not having anything on your drawing board. Many of these tips can and should be used in everyday situations whether or not you are currently being stalked. We do not want you or your loved ones to ever end up in a compromising situation.

- *Make sure your vehicle is in good shape* and all service has been completed. Keep a small bag with some duct tape in your car. This way if you need to wrap a water hose, you can. (We realize duct tape is also one of the primary tools for an abductor's tool kit, but it also can be a necessary tool for you. Again, many tools have dual purposes.) Also think about buying a can of compressed air and goo, which can seal and re-inflate a tire. (Always read up on any product you are looking at buying to ascertain if there are any issues or precautions you need to take before deploying devices like these.) If you find yourself with a low or flat tire, drive to a well-lit service station, convenience store, or some other venue where there are both people and good visibility. This way anyone that might be following or stalking you can be seen. Get used to doing a security check on your car. What we mean is instead of just walking out to your car, opening your door, plopping your butt in the seat, turning the ignition, and hopefully taking off, do the following: as you begin walking towards your car, look around. See if there is anything out of the ordinary such as another occupied car you are not familiar with parked near your car. Look underneath the car to see if you are leaking any fluids or those nuts, bolts, or screws are not lying on the ground. See if there are any wires dangling down. Also check to see if you have anything like a package or pipe that should not be there. Of course, if you see a foreign package or pipe type device under your car, do not try to pull it out. Immediately get a safe distance from your car, and notify police. Walk around your car to make sure your trunk is shut. Check that no one is hiding inside your car before you actually get into the car. Look at your tires, listen for leaks, and see if one tire is lower than the others.

One of the oldest tricks in the book is for a suspect (not just a stalker) to damage a valve stem or otherwise cause a slow leak in the target's vehicle. When that individual realizes he or she has a flat tire and stops to check, the stalker assaults him/her. I have provided all my family members with tiny, high-powered flashlights that attach to key chains. This way they can conduct all these searches prior to getting into their vehicles. We also tell our stalking victims to take clear wrapping tape and place it on a small, unnoticeable place on the hood of the car where the hood aligns with the top portion of the vehicle's quarter panel (in other words, over the crease). You can also do this along the trunk where it opens. When you come out, see if that tape has been damaged by the trunk or hood being opened. If you place the tape where chrome meets chrome, you don't have to worry about damaging your paint job.

Obtain a key chain that allows you to keep your car keys separate from all other keys. When you leave your car for service or give it to a valet, only give that person your car keys, and you keep the rest. This prevents anyone from having duplicates made of your house or other keys. Also get in the habit of not leaving your keys in your car when you are filling it with gas or doing a quick run into a stop and shop. Lock your car every time you leave it unattended.

Because we are talking about those that drive, we also need to talk to those of you that take public transportation. We recently experienced a situation in our community where a seventeen-year-old cheerleader began taking the municipal bus to and from school because her parents could not afford to purchase her a vehicle. Over the course of a few weeks, she began having a forty-year-old male start moving closer to her seat by seat. Eventually he began sitting next to her and striking up conversations, which moved onto bringing her gifts and trying to gather more and more personal information. People, what kind of a pattern are we starting to see here? The teenager began getting spooked and did the right thing by telling her parents. At first they didn't believe it was a problem, but when this individual started showing up at the cheerleader's school campus and was seen at other venues she had attended, the police were called in. Fortunately the OC Sheriff put an undercover on the bus. The undercover sat in listening distance from the stalker and overhead several inappropriate comments and lines of questioning. The stalker was arrested. The moral of the story is first, listen to your kids and second, teach them to be aware like this young lady was. This applies to all who take public transit. Check your surroundings. Be aware of those individuals that seem out of place or are taking way too much time trying to be your buddy and gather personal information. If a nimrod is making you feel uncomfortable, try to change up your transportation schedule. We know if you take the bus, this can sometimes be tough. If it gets worse, notify the driver, security, or the cops.

- *Pack a bag with at least one day's worth of clothes.* If you need certain medications, put some in a pill container. Keep some extra cash with you or at least a good credit card. This is recommended just in case you have to stay at a friend's house or a motel room for a night due to an issue that your stalker has generated. If you have children, don't forget to do the same for them. Along these same lines, if you have pets, we suggest you make prior arrangements for someone such as a relative to take care of the pet(s) for a short period of time.

- *If you are going to travel,* even for a weekend, give a friend or family member a trip itinerary. This way, if you do not show up when you are supposed to, the proper authorities can be notified. Speaking of travelling, think about your hotel room keys. Some motels/hotels have been known to imprint those plastic keys with a lot of information, including your credit card information. If you leave the card behind in your room, some unscrupulous staff might be able to scan the card and gather your information. Because this was shown to be a problem, many chains have stopped putting personal information on the cards. Before you leave the cards in the room at check-out, ask the front desk if they put that data on the card. It is probably best just to turn the cards back into the check-in desk prior to leaving. Some have suggested that you keep a small strong magnet with you when you travel, or utilize the magnets that some hotels give you to attach to the outside door jams of your room to let staff know not to disturb or it is ok to clean. Once the hotel stay is done, you run the magnet over the entry card, thus removing the information. It is unknown how well this procedure works. Others have just taken the room keys and destroyed them later. Obviously, we cannot recommend that particular solution.

- *Don't be a creature of habit.* If you are like us, we know this is a tough one. The older you get, the more it seems you become that way (unless early onset senior moments have set in, and then you have no clue where you might end up or at what time). What we are saying is don't always take the same way to wherever you normally travel, primarily home or work. Get used to cruising your neighborhood before pulling into your driveway or garage. See if your stalker is set up on a surveillance outing waiting for you to come into your track, apartment, or condo complex.

- *Call or text someone you trust when you arrive at a location you are travelling to such as work, shopping center, etc.* You readers with kids, even young adult children, especially if they live with you, try to do this on a regular basis. My wife and I do. Every time our kids are going to be away from the house for any length of time, my cell phone is always close, and they know to call. They continually keep in touch either by text, e-mail, or calling, even when we are abroad or travelling in the United States. Trust me, it is not a leash. They appreciate that we really do care and are there to help if they need it. Remember, you now have a stalker. Reach out and touch someone.

- *Always have a working flashlight in your vehicle.* You never know when you need one. We know we told you that we have supplied our peeps with those little high-intensity lights that attach to your key chains and come in handy for a variety of reason, but we want you to also have a more powerful one. This flashlight or torch, for our U.K. readers should last a reasonable period of time and have a good beam for seeing a good distance around you, along with signaling for help.

- *Keep your cell phone charged.* Get a cell phone charger for your car so you can keep it charged even if you cannot immediately get back to the location where your normal charger is. If you have a smartphone, put a security code into it. If you lose or have your phone stolen, it should stop or slow down whoever ends up with it from gathering all your contact and other pertinent information. We are told there are some programs that allow one to hook up a smartphone to a desktop or laptop in order to break down the security code on the phone. Once again, this is just another tool some genius has developed that can help or hinder.

- *Cops are trained that whenever they enter any structure to scan for entrances and exits when they enter.* They are told to look for anything that looks suspicious or out of the ordinary before they conduct whatever business they are about to do. If they sit, they sit with their backs to a wall. Facing in a way that gives them a panoramic view of whoever is coming and going and whatever else is taking place in the space in front of them. Sitting in this position also stops them from having to worry about anyone sneaking up on them from behind. Too many gunslingers in the Old West got blown away from someone coming up on what we refer to as their six. So guess what? You are now going to do exactly what cops and military operators do. Start checking out your environment and sitting in such a way as to be able to see just about everything that is going on around you. It is not fool-proof, but it is at least a plan.

- *Field training officers (FTO's) are taught to make sure their new patrol cops (rookies) went home at the end of watch (EOW).* So when we work with our victims we kind of think of them as one of our new recruits. (*Oh, by the way think of an FTO as a mother hen with an attitude. None of us were ever considered warm and cuddly.*) One of the tasks we had our rookies do was always be aware of where they were. While driving down a darkened street, once we had gotten to where there were no street signs, we would tell the recruit to stop the patrol car and tell us exactly where he or she was. If they couldn't tell us both the street address and what the name of the street was, we had them get out of the car and walk to the nearest street sign to get their bearings. If they screwed up more than once, we would make them go to the nearest house, knock on the door (no matter what time it was), and ask what the name of the street was. I guarantee you, the first time they woke up both an angry and confused citizen at O dark thirty (cop slang for too damn early in the morning) that new boot would not ever forget where he or she was, at least not on my watch. The point is always know where you are going and where you are. If you are being stalked, you don't want to be lost as well.

We would also train our cops to try to get a visual of the location they were being dispatched to. Did it have an alley off the back? Were there schools nearby? If you are going to someplace you have never been, look it up on a map, or go on the Internet and use some type of download that gives you exact directions. Google Earth and other computer-generated programs can not only show you a fairly accurate visual of an area but oftentimes what the houses or commercial buildings in that sector look like. GPS is getting cheaper and cheaper to purchase. If possible, get one and use it, but remember to take a map along because sometimes GPS can surprise you about how it takes you from point A to point B. If you don't already know where the police and fire stations are in your locale, find out just in case you need to pay them a visit when out for a drive.

- *When you park your vehicle, do it in a well-lit place. Also make sure it's a place where it is easy for you to get to. You don't want to be walking a country mile away from people.* Don't sit in your vehicle doing tasks such as makeup, texting, tweeting, balancing your checkbook, etc. It gives an attacker an edge to move in on you while you are occupied. When you come out to your car to leave, and a van or enclosed vehicle has parked next to you, take a quick look inside the van. If someone is sitting in the back, at least think about moving away from the van and watching it from the interior of the store you just exited until you feel safe, it moves off, or someone walks out with you. (Again, we are not trying to instill paranoia. These are just thoughts to make you more aware.) The same holds true for a male sitting alone in his vehicle next to yours. Pay attention to how he observes you. If you can, get a license plate and/or other descriptors of vehicles you feel are suspicious. This especially wise if you are dealing with a stranger stalker. (Again, not every individual that looks over at you is a threat. Use some common sense.) By the way when you park your car in your driveway at home, be sure and lock the car. This tends to frustrate those that would open your car and activate your garage door via your remote.

- *If you are in a public building, don't take isolated stairways or corridors.* The more you are in view of people and lighted areas, the better.

- *The use of pepper spray and/or stun guns is a personal choice.* We will say that we have encouraged members of our family to use both. We have supplied them with stun guns that are flashlights as well. This allows them to check out their cars prior to getting in. One should always check with their local law enforcement or consult their state laws concerning the use and possession of these defensive weapons. If you do decide to utilize these items, get comfortable with them. Don't wait until you are in a stressful situation. You might end up pepper spraying yourself. (We will discuss firearms in the home safety measure section.) Personally, we do not like pepper spray because it always got all over us and the subject we were dealing with, especially when another cop ended up spraying both of us at the same time. That being said, it can be an effective tool. They now have some sprays that have a colored dye that is extremely difficult for the perpetrator to remove once he or she has been sprayed.

- *Beware of the broken wing technique.* This is a ruse that has been used by rapist, stalkers, and even serial killers. For example, Ted Bundy (well-known serial killer) used to wear a bandage or sling on his arm, feigning that he had broken it. Then he'd pretend to have trouble gathering his books or some other item into his VW. When the target came to give aid, Bundy bludgeoned the victim into submission. Remember, stalkers for the most part are a fairly intelligent group and are very capable of ruses.

   Another thing we have encountered is the male who comes up to you and says he is desperately looking for his small child and asks for your help to find the youngster. We know this really has a tendency to play on our heart strings, but you might get a quick description of the child and say you will call the police so they can respond to help. Don't traipse off with the guy who is directing you to a vehicle or the bushes. If he takes off when you suggest calling the police, then you know there is a problem. If he doesn't, and the police respond, you can work with them to assist in finding the child.

- *If for some reason (hopefully this never happens) you end up thrown into the trunk of your car or that of an abductor, and you are able, call for assistance on your cell if possible. At the very least, power it up.* Look to see if there is a trunk release mechanism in the car, pull it, and roll out as soon as the vehicle slows to a "reasonable" speed. (Obviously, reasonable to one person is not to another. Perhaps we should say what you feel is a survivable speed.) If you can force out a taillight and begin waving either your hand or something else to draw attention, it might help. One would only hope that a person sticking his or her hands or fingers out of the broken taillight compartment of a moving vehicle would tend to get some type of response.

- *Watch where and how you walk.* I don't know how many times I have seen lone women walkers or joggers walking or running with the flow of traffic along a road. This is dangerous on two accounts. First, if you are running against traffic (say along a sidewalk), you can see if an oncoming vehicle is out of control and going to fly off the road. Second, by running against traffic, you can see who is coming toward you and how they are eying you. For the occupants of the vehicle to stop, get out, and come after you, they either have to stop somewhere behind you and give chase or try to stop as close to you as they can and jump out. Either way you will not be surprised, thus having those extra needed moments for escape. If you are running with traffic, your attacker(s) can easily move in behind you and catch you off guard.

  Don't walk or run with your head down. Glance down from time to time for a visual on the surface you are traversing, but keep a wide range of vision with your head up in a position of confidence. You need to know what is in the bushes and what may be coming up on your peripheries. Studies have shown that a women that exudes confidence, has her head up, and a direct gaze is less likely to be confronted than one that acts timid and does not appear to be aware of her surroundings.

  While on the subject of walking, we should take this time to talk about proper footwear. We know that three- to four-inch stilettos may really enhance that mini, but how well can you run in them if you have to make a quick exit? If you are out with a male companion that you trust, you are usually good to go. However, if you know you are being stalked or are out and about by yourself, think about what you are walking in because a simple walk could always turn into a sprint. There are a lot of shoes out there that look good, are comfortable, and one can move in. *I know this because I see them advertised. As indicated, I mostly wear Converse combat boots, so no one asks me about style.*

- *If your stalker does somehow end up in your vehicle and forces you to drive, attempt to get others' attention, especially if you see a patrol car.* Obviously, legally we cannot tell you to run a stop sign or a red light or do something more radical. We can only tell you that there have been recorded instances where people who have been placed in these types of situations have been able to get to safety by reacting in unusual ways. It is always up to you how you want to proceed.

- *Develop a security word or phrase.* Sit down with your family members and make up an alert word or short phrase. This word is to be used if you or they are in danger, and you need to make them aware of a dangerous situation. It does not have to be a stalker. Say, for example, the stalker is in your home. You are able to phone or a family member does. When you talk to the family member try to slip in the word or simple phrase. This alerts them to notify law enforcement or, at the very least, not place themselves in harm's way.

- *Be aware of date rape drugs.* Drugs such as Gamma-Hydroxy-butyric acid (GHB), Ketamine, and Rohypnol are all drugs referred to date rape drugs. These drugs affect each individual differently, but they are designed to disable and disorient their intended targets. There is a drug known as burundanga that usually is found in South American countries (according to all we could discern, primarily in Columbia), and it has been used for similar purposes. The drug has been getting a lot of attention lately due to an Internet urban legend scenario about males giving it to women via a soaked business card. We don't know much about the business card ploy, but burundanga does have a factual basis as being placed in the drinks of tourists and others, allowing the perpetrator(s) to accost their victims, sexually assaulting, and/or robbing them.

These drugs do exist, so you need to watch your drinks (or for that matter whatever you consume) when out as much as you can. Obviously, if you are being stalked, you are already going to be on alert, but even if you are not, in this day and age, one needs to be aware in any kind of a social situation where drinks are flowing and distractions abound. There is a great deal of information on the Net concerning these drugs and the symptoms they cause. We suggest you take the time to familiarize yourself with that information.

Our generation had heard of only one such drug when we were growing up. It was referred to as a Mickey Finn. The drug that was placed in the victim's drink was chloral hydrate, which was probably developed around 1832 to assist with sleep. We have not heard of its usage in a long time, even though it could still be used. By the way, don't get confused. We were not around in the 1800s.

Safety Measures for Your Home

Now that we have discussed developing a general safety plan, we need to talk about security measures for your home. We realize you may not be able to do all the things we talk about, but at least you will be aware of them. Many of these measures should be followed by anyone wanting to better secure their residences whether they are being stalked or not.

We also want to advise you that, for the most part, nothing is impenetrable (at least with what the average person can afford). Given enough time in conjunction with the right tools, someone who is determined to gain entry into a dwelling can. However, the items we are about to discuss are designed to both slow down and alert the potential victim about what is going on. Thus giving said victim either a chance to escape or a longer time to allow help to get to them. Many times the mere fact the assailant is slowed down in his or her approach and knows the intended target is alerted will cause that person to stop the attack and flee.

Another position we had at one time during our tenure within the police department was that of being in charge of neighborhood watch and coordinating the citizen's academy. We bring this up because it helps to know where we are coming from on these recommmendations.

Exterior Security

- *Simply keeping vegetation clear from windows and doors can dissuade the use of same as concealment for a prowler or other predator.* Remove items such as ladders or tools that can be used by stalkers to force entry.

- *Lighting is one of the best ways to dissuade unwanted guests.* Decorative is less obtrusive than strobe or giant flood lights but still illuminates well enough. We also like motion activated lights. Many solar types are now available. This way, the light can be placed in areas that are normally hard to wire. Also if power is cut or somehow disrupted, these lights will still function. One of the security light systems we use and like to recommend is the kind that can be turned on while inside the house. We had our electrician wire up a small panel that allows us to turn on a few high-powered exterior floods that cover key areas at home, primarily the backyard. Obviously, these only go on when we feel the need to illuminate the property with a lot of instantaneous light.

- *We usually suggest obtaining a monitored burglar alarm.* Most alarm companies make their money on their monthly monitoring fees not on their initial installation charges. A basic system is pretty affordable. This usually includes sensors on entry points and motion detectors in the major zones of the dwelling. Usually alarm companies put their alarm controllers in the area where you come into the house and the master bedroom. Each of these control pads has a panic button that, when pressed, tells the monitoring company to call the police now. At an additional cost, the system can be set up with a radio sending unit that will still function if the telephone wires in the house are cut. There are all kinds of systems. Again we suggest getting the basic program if you are on a budget. Other systems have sophisticated listening devices that can monitor the suspects in the residence or send messages about intruders to the victim's cell phone or laptop. These systems have two-way microphones, and therefore, you can listen as well as communicate with the suspects while they are in your home. Hopefully this freaks them out, and they flee.

- *We also like the installation of security cameras.* More and more closed circuit camera systems are coming onto the market each year. Several are at discounted pricing. These cameras can be monitored via the Internet or by your local security provider. We are currently working a case where the victim's cameras are on a direct feed to the police department handling her case. They are able to view the victim's cameras just by going on the Internet with the proper security code supplied by that victim.

Many people who have these cameras can monitor their property from afar by just going to a website on their laptops or Internet-enabled smartphones. Some cameras have microphones so that any sound that a suspect (or for that matter a victim) makes can also be recorded onto a website or to a DVR recorder. These cameras can be hardwired or wireless. Some are even solar powered. Of course, they are more expensive. My associates and I just recently wired up twenty cameras on our church. As you can imagine, it was a daunting task. It took us about nine weeks because we had to make sure all the installations were clean. Only the camera faces could be seen by anyone looking for them. All wires were concealed or run in such a fashion that the public could not see anything. The cameras were set to record continuously for ninety days. After the ninety day run, the DVR reset for another ninety days. Trust us, if we can set up these types of cameras, anyone with basic construction skills can as well. As to getting them online and recording properly, that may take someone with computer skills (that would not be me) to get that part of the operation going.

- *As with your vehicle*, you can monitor someone entering your home by placing a piece of clear plastic tape at a point on your door or window. This can also be done to an interior door or drawer. We have had some cases in which the suspect was making entry without force, and the victim had no way of telling law enforcement where the entry was taking place until she utilized this technique.

- *Doors.* Again, we realize that doing any of these safety items depends on your individual budget. That being said, all of your entry doors should be solid core doors and not hollow core. Solid core doors are made from solid wood, metal, or fiberglass construction. This makes them more resistant to forced entry. A hollow core door, which is usually used for inside doors to closets and bathrooms, can easily be defeated by someone kicking a hole in them due to their construction of light wood veneers applied to a thin frame. You may also want to investigate purchasing what we call a heavy-clad steel door. These doors are usually special order and found on some high-end homes or safe rooms, which we will discuss in the interior security section. As the salesman told us, "They ain't cheap." You can reinforce your solid core wood doors by applying metal on one side of the door. When we have applied these outer metal skins, we affix them with a construction adhesive and carriage bolts. The shafts of these bolts should travel through the entire door, be counter-synced, and a nut attached to the interior portion of the door. All exterior doors, including the one that goes into your garage, should have some type of case hardened dead bolt with at least a one-inch throw on the bolt. In other words, the bolt that is activated by your key and goes into the casing around the door should be at least an inch in length. The dead bolt itself should have a roller bar inside the dead bolt shaft. This is a cut-resistant round bar that is inserted in the deadbolt. It spins if an intruder tries to cut through the bolt. There are single locking dead bolts that have a twist opener on the inside portion of the lock and a keyway on the outside. Then there is the double locking dead bolt that requires a key to open the lock on either side of it.

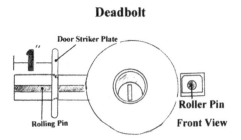

Deadbolt

Door Striker Plate

Rolling Pin

Roller Pin

Front View

Drawn by author.

Another thing we suggest to add strength to your door lock is to put three-inch wood screws in the striker plate where the deadbolt actually goes into the door frame. (Many home or hardware stores now carry oversized striker plates with elongated screws in a kit. They also carry metal brackets that fit around the entire lock and the area of the striker plate. These add more strength in case of an attempted forced entry.) Gates and any entry doors that have an insert panel of lighter wood, glass, or plastic should probably have a double locking dead bolt. This is so the predator cannot reach through the door and unlock it from the outside. However, so that one can escape in the case of fire or other emergencies, there should be a key within easy access to those in the home but far enough away from the door so the intruder cannot reach in and grab it. We suggest that when purchasing a dead bolt lock, look for one that has a casing that surrounds the outside of the key entry and that spins. This manufacture is designed to defeat an intruder using pliers or a gripping tool from twisting the key entry off the door.

Over the years, we have dealt with Hill's Brothers Lock and Safe Company. Hill's Brothers is a well-respected lock and safe company located in Orange County that services both the Los Angeles and Orange County metro area. I sat down with Paul Linder, who is an expert on residential and commercial locking devices. He also used to work for one of the largest lock manufactures in the world for numerous years. Linder advised the following about residential locking devices:

- Most over the counter residential door locks can be defeated with a portable drill or a lock bumping device. (Key bumping will be discussed further into this section.)

- He recommended first going on the Internet and reviewing the information on UL # 437, which are basically the requirements for high-security locks. The locks given this rating are resistant to attacks by drilling, picking, prying, etc.

- Paul recommended purchasing a higher end door lock made by Medeco (made in the United States) or Assa (made in Sweden). He advised these locks have propriety keyways with case hardened inserts that are highly resistant to drilling and cannot be opened with a bumping device.

- Paul said that many of the locks purchased at your home builder type stores are susceptible to key bumping. The locks that are entirely manufactured by Medeco, Assa, or have had their guts replaced by these two name brands cannot be bumped. Concerning door locks, we found that one of the newest types of entry door locks on the market today is the one that can actually be manipulated by ones smartphones. Once installed the owner merely accesses a program through a secured router. This allows the owner to lock or unlock the door remotely.

- *Sliding glass doors.* Obviously a sliding glass door can be breached by merely breaking through the glass, even if it is tempered as most are. However, most suspects don't usually want to draw that much attention to themselves. (Keep in mind that security processes are always being developed. Companies now sell and install a variety of films that can be placed on the glass that slows breakage and other damage from high winds.) This is another reason we like having a simple alarm system installed. Even if an intruder does break through the slider, a door or motion sensor should active and cause the proper response. There are a variety of devices that can be used on sliders. Some secure the door by having a rounded push pin placed into the door frame and door sliding bracket. Others are metal pole affairs that can be snapped into the frame and expanded. This way the door is much harder to be jimmied open. One can easily find these items online or by going to your favorite home center or hardware store.

- *Screen doors.* Your average flimsy, aluminum screen door is nice for ventilation but will not defeat any type of entry. Most good sized elementary school boys could rip one off its hinges by pulling and/or hanging on them (or better yet, running through one). We suggest one install heavy gauge metal security screens that have steel mesh ventilation panels welded to the screen door frame. The doors should have a single locking case hardened dead bolt. This way, one can have the entry door completely open and have the breezes come in without the concern of someone forcing entry into the home, at least not without alerting its occupants. This door allows the homeowner to both see and communicate with anyone at the door without worrying about that person pushing in the door. It also affords another layer of protection against a potential intruder. Remember, the standard solid core entry door can be closed behind the security screen door.

- *Windows.* All your windows should have some type of locking device either built into their construction or that can be attached. There are a myriad of devices available online or at your local hardware store. Some clip onto the window track. Others are piston type devices that need holes drilled into the window track. The device is then screwed down on one side of the track, allowing a piston or rod to be pushed into the window frame and locked with a key. This stops the window from being forced open. If nothing else, a stick in the window frame slide is better than nothing. Most of these devices are designed to allow the window to be opened at various lengths for ventilation. There are also battery-operated window sensor alarms that, when attached and activated, will send out a piercing alarm note when someone tries to force entry.

Another easy fix to stop someone from pushing your sliding glass window up and then out is to drill some small holes in the top portion of the window slider and screw in some number eight sheet metal screws along the interior portion of the window slide. This allows just enough clearance for the window to slide. This will help eliminate that problem.

- *Electrical and utility boxes.* Most exterior electrical panels have a place where a padlock can be installed. Put a padlock on so a potential intruder has a problem trying to shut down your main power. Speaking of padlocks, think about what you are buying. If you are going to buy some wimpy padlock that can be easily broken or simply twisted off, you might as well not bother. Remember, this is not something you would use on Aunt Mary's antique jewelry box, so man up (sorry, ladies, just a figure of speech) and get something that a potential predator would have to work up a sweat on. There is a new Internet video in cyberspace that shows some pubescent kid giving a seminar on how to use an aluminum beverage can to open padlocks similar to the ones you used on your high school locker.

When looking for a padlock, look for ones that have at least a 9/32-inch shackle. Many times stainless steel case hardened shackles (to slow down a cutting assault) usually work pretty well. The shackle (the curved piece that goes through the hole of the hasp or thing you are trying to secure) should lock into the base at both the heel and toe of the lock. Another thing we suggest when purchasing a good quality padlock is to buy one that has what is called a "shrouded shackle," or purchase one of these devices to go over the lock. This allows only a small portion of the shackle to be exposed to someone attempting to cut it. Master has one that has a "boron carbide" shackle. We are not sure if that is something that is new, but it looks pretty sturdy. (A *Popular Mechanics* article from July of 2010 rated padlocks by conducting a variety of assaults. They found the Master Magnum M93XKADLH and the OnGuard 5101 were both good, reasonably priced padlocks.) The better ones have a pick resistant tumbler system with at least five pins. Combination padlocks obviously don't require you to carry around a bunch of keys. If you install a keyed padlock, we suggest having it keyed to another lock (say to a storage shed). That way the owner can access his locks without walking around like a jailer. (It is probably not a good idea to have it also operate your front door.) These padlocks usually also have a key retention feature. This stops one from removing the padlock key until the shackle is confirmed in the locking position, thus allowing the key to be removed.

- *Placement of telephone lines.* We strongly suggest that when you have your phone lines attached to your home, you have the phone box placed at the top of a roof eave. This helps prevent your stalker from cutting your phone lines. We have not heard of any problems with the phone company not wanting to install in that location. We are pretty sure they would understand your request for such a placement.

- *Other types of available locks.* How many times have you watched a television program, especially a comedy, where you see the character answer his or her front door by unlocking all kinds of door locks? Chances are one of those locks is a "rim lock." A rim lock comes in what is called a standard or jimmy-proof design. These locks have two separate parts. One attaches to the door itself, and the other attaches to the surrounding door frame. This lock kind of works like

Door Jam

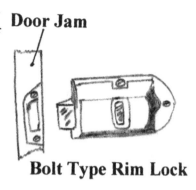

Bolt Type Rim Lock

Drawn by author.

your hands coming together and clasping. When you shut the door and activate the lock's vertical dead bolt, it drops through at least two rings, which securely fastens the door. These locks can have keyed locks on them or just twist handle to work the mechanism. The locks have to be aligned to work properly, so they may have to be adjusted from time to time depending on any movement or settling of your structure.

Door Jam

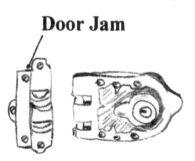

Pin Rim Lock

Drawn by author.

Cane bolts are used to secure a double door in which one door is designed to be stationary until the locks are released. This allows the door to be opened at times such as when moving furniture in and out of the structure. Obviously installing the cane bolt assembly with just simple screws does not work anywhere near as well as having the bolt assembly actually penetrate the floor and upper portion of the door frame. Some of these types of bolts are set directly into the side of the solid wood core door, which adds additional strength to the entire door.

Special note: Another Internet scam is the purchasing of what is called "bump keys." These are door keys that can be slipped into a standard front door lock by any would-be thief. The thief then strikes the back of the key, which forces the key into the tumbler mechanism. Once forced, a sharp twist opens most standard locks. The way to protect against this is by purchasing high-end tumbler door locking mechanisms, which can be pricy. These keys are outlawed in states such as California unless you are a licensed locksmith, but they can be easily purchased on the Internet for not a lot of money.

So if you come home and find that someone (including a stalker) has been in your residence, and you cannot locate a P.O.E. (point of entry, then you might want to consider that a bump key was used to gain entry.

Interior Security

- Check out what is in your home. What do I mean by this? Now you have a stalker, you need to make at least a mental inventory of your home about where things are. Remember, a stalker may enter your residence to trophy collect, gather information, or just mess with your mind. So if you have a pretty good idea of where things are, then when they are not there anymore, you will get up to speed faster. That being said we would suggest you develop a list of your valuables, which includes description of property, serial number (if applicable), and value. If you have something like jewelry or doll collections that cannot easily be described or serialized, we suggest taking photos or documenting them via videotaping. This will also help you when you have to give your insurance company an itemized list in case of theft, fire, or any other reason. For example, people who have gun collections are oftentimes required by their insurance companies to provide a description and serial number of all of their guns so they can be placed on a special writer on their policy.

Note: One of the things we now tell law enforcement when we train them to think about doing is if their threat assessment indicates a potential for immediate violence, rape, sexual ideations (thoughts of or intentions thereof), or any kind of abduction concerns, they should get permission to photograph the inside of the home and draw a general floor plan sketch of the interior of the dwelling. This is done so that in the case of an entry team breaching your home (SWAT or other responding officers) know what they are going to see inside your home, giving them a better chance of a smooth prosecution at time of entry. Obviously if your local law enforcement hasn't read this book or been trained by us, they may not use this tactic. When we worked in the crime prevention section of the police department, we used to photograph and diagram all the liquor stores and banks in the city. This way our metro and SWAT personnel would have a better chance of devising entry strategies into these locations. It was a good program. Doing the same for a stalking victim is also beneficial.

- *Safe rooms.* If you remember the film *Panic Room* with Jodi Foster, you will better understand what a safe room is. Of course, most people cannot afford the more sophisticated panic or safe rooms commercially built by licensed security contractors. Some of these rooms can have the look and feel of a hotel room designed with the latest video cameras and other high-end electronics and air filtration systems. What we are describing is the build of a simple safe room to be utilized if, for some reason, you and family members cannot immediately get out of your home when confronted by an intruder (not just a stalker).

When we advise people about developing a safe room in their home, we suggest the following:

  - Try to pick a room that has a phone, computer or both. For this reason, it often becomes an office space. To make it safe or, in our case, safer, install a solid core door or metal cased door with a high-end security dead bolt. If one wants to install more locks, that's fine. Reinforce the jams around the door by rebuilding the jam with stacked lumber on both sides bolted into primary studs all around the jam.

- Put three-quarter-inch plywood on at least the portions of the room on either side of the door. If you can, put this plywood on all the interior walls of the safe room. What this does is slows down any attack your intruder might attempt through plaster or drywall to get to you and your loved ones. Of course, you would then drywall over the plywood and paint as normal. (What you are trying to do is give yourself as much time as possible before the cavalry arrives.) This room may also assist you in case of a violent storm if you have no other safe room.

- Inside the room we suggest you have the following supplies: a flashlight, batteries, first aid kit, bottled water, some type of portable toilet, and a CB radio (if all your phone lines are cut and you can't get out with your cell phone, you'll need some way of summoning the police). There are more sophisticated radios that can be purchased for this use, but if cost is a factor, a CB may be your best bet.

If you have wireless Internet, you might also want to think about using one of the online Webcam programs such as Skype to communicate with a loved one or someone else who can summon help. If your intruder shuts down your power, having a battery back-up is a good idea.

- Think about getting a fire extinguisher. There are all kinds of extinguishers such as carbon dioxide, Halotron 1 or Halotron, dry powder, etc. Carbon dioxide (CO_2) (Class BC) and Halotron 1 can be used on electrical fires in electronic devices as well as some normal fires You should, however, read up on its chemical properties and hazards, as there are some. The extinguisher has to be used correctly as so not to cause injury to the user. Some types of extinguishers may not be allowed in your jurisdiction. Dry powder or A, B, C fire extinguishers can be used on many types of fires but will definitely mess up your electrical gear and blow dust everywhere. We suggest you research the extinguisher you would like to have in your room, if any. Your dry powder type of extinguisher is also the cheapest to purchase.

- As to the use of weapons, that is definitely up to you. You could have pepper spray, a stun gun, or other weapons described as "less than lethal" on hand. If your state allows, you could have a Taser (a weapon that, when deployed, shoots darts attached to electrodes). Once the darts strike the target, the shooter can push a trigger, which sends a charge down the attached lines into the assailant. This short circuits his or her nerve bundle, decommissioning him/her. We have always liked the Taser because it neutralizes the intruder/stalker without in most cases doing permanent damage. (Once again, you should always check with your local police department and/or state as to regulations on ownership and usage.) Keeping and using a gun for protection will be discussed next. The safe room is designed to be used as a last resort. We always would prefer you getting out of any place where danger threatens including your home if necessary. But we also want you to survive so keep that in mind when you deliberate about designating one of your rooms as a safe room. A website to search when looking at safe or panic rooms is the International Association of Certified Home Inspectors at (http://www.nachi.org/safe-rooms.htm). Of course, contacting a reputable security company is another option.

- *Firearms.* I am a life member of the National Rifle Association (NRA). My family and I are avid target shooters. Therefore, they are all trained in the *SAFE* use of firearms, and they are skilled and proficient in the deployment of many different types of weapons. Obtaining and using a handgun or rifle is a personal choice that depends on a variety of issues, state and federal laws, your specific need for ownership (personal protection, recreational shooting, or hunting), etc. If you decide to purchase a gun for protection, always remember that when you fire that weapon and send that round down range, it can never come back. Unless it is somehow deflected, it is going to go where you directed it. In our opinion, you must be able to resign yourself to the taking of another human life before you really consider using a gun for protection. We do have friends, who are also former and current stalking victims, that are CCW'd, meaning they have gone through training and have been issued a permit to carry a concealed weapon. Believe me, they do carry or, as we in the business, say they pack. They all practice, and none of them look at their weapon as toys or something to play with. You shouldn't either.

When I train my kids and others to shoot, safety is number one. Practice, practice, practice is number two. You had better be extremely proficient and comfortable with your weapon. There should be no surprises, operational or otherwise, when you go hot with live rounds. When you fire a weapon in a stress situation, a couple of things happen. First, you get what is referred to as tunnel vision. Your body goes into what feels like slow motion mode. Your field of vision is drawn to your target, whatever that might be. You lose most of your peripheral vision. Second, your training takes over. In other words, muscle memory becomes king. You shoot like you have trained. You may feel the gun recoil and hear the muffled sound of the round(s) leaving the barrel but not much else. So brother or sister, if you have not trained and trained, you could be in a real bad place. Because my partner and I worked homicide, we were the team assigned to any officer involved in a shooting. Every cop we ever debriefed told us the same thing. Once they had identified a deadly threat, they remembered deploying their weapons and firing. They went into automatic mode, and they all thanked God for all the training they did. Everyone of them said their intention was to eliminate the threat. Whether or not they killed the suspect didn't enter into their actions at the time they were pulling the trigger.

We are not sure everyone takes the time to really sit down and consider this issue. I know when you become a cop or go into the military that is one thing you have to do. For you, your family, and your fellow coppers, each of us had to make a clear and honest decision if a situation presented itself where we had to use deadly force, we would. If you don't make that conscious decision prior to it ever happening, it is our opinion that you will be hard-pressed to do what is necessary when the time comes that you have to. I did fire my weapon on duty, and I meant to stop the person I was shooting at, knowing full well that before I ever got into the situation that my actions could result in the taking of another human life.

If you own a gun and are willing to use it to protect yourself and/or family members, that's fine. Just understand that once you shoot someone, that person may well die. Be prepared. You should also understand that if you commit a violation of law while deploying your weapon, you will also suffer the consequences for doing so. It is our stand that you need to be able to protect yourself, but for God's sake, please make sure you identify your target before you shoot. No one, especially us, wants to hear about a stalking victim (or anyone else for that matter) who blew away a relative or a neighbor that strayed. Yes, we are well aware that neighbors can and are continually identified as being stalkers. We think you know exactly what we mean; those people that would harm an innocent party. Hopefully we have made our point. That being said, we cannot overemphasize that you should always become familiar with your weapon and practice with it on a regular basis. (We strongly suggest you and whoever else is going to have access to the weapon be trained by a certified range master on how to deploy, fire, and care for your gun(s).)

Always keep your weapons secured from those you do not want to share the gun with. This especially applies to children. We strongly suggest you obtain a gun safe. There are many types out there. Some can be quickly opened with a push button, mechanical, or digital code. Others take keys or mechanical combination locks. We prefer semiautomatic handguns because you can keep the unloaded gun and loaded magazine separate until the time comes you have to load the magazine into the weapon, rack a round into the chamber, and go hot. This is our preference; you may have your own.

- *Safes.* While we are discussing interior security, we should briefly mention the use of safes. Especially in this day and age, the data safe is increasingly common. According to VaultandSafe.com, anything over 150 degrees will destroy your data, including CDs, DVDs, thumb drives, tape-recordings, etc. They recommend you look into obtaining special fire-resistant safes that can keep the interior below that temperature for a minimum of one hour and preferably two. Underwriters Laboratories (UL) rates safes, and not all safes are the same. For example the data safes come under the UL classification of UL-72. Other safes are rated as burglary and fire protection (BF Series). We are told there are other ratings for specific types of commercial safes, which we don't need to get into. Some safes are designed to prevent theft or withstand fire. Some have both capabilities. Safes come in all sizes, weights, and configurations. They are designed to be freestanding, placed in the floor, or in the wall of a structure. The UL assigns letters for different classifications of safes. According to the SafesSanFrancisco.info website, the letters TL help the purchaser to understand what types of tools the safe will sustain when assaulted. TL-15 tells you that this safe has a combination lock that will withstand a variety of tools being used to open same such as hand tools, picking tools, portable electric tools, grinding points, carbide drills, and pressure applying devices for a period of fifteen minutes. TL-30 means it will withstand the same assault for thirty minutes. The higher the number, the more time it will usually hold up. The TRTL rating adds the use of oxy-fuel and gas-cutting torches. TXTL rating adds torches, hand tools, and explosives. So if you are going to pick a safe, go to reputable locksmith or safe dealer, and get all the facts before you lay down your hard-earned money.

Along the same lines of safes for data storage, one might want to think about using Internet data storage. There are a number of them out there. You can set them up so that when you are using your computer, you can save all your files to that storage location. Many are designed to automatically store that information. This would include photos and other personal data. We have never used such a storage medium but are seriously looking at giving it a try. (Remember, this storage medium may also be at risk, depending on the newest hacker running amuck out in cyber-land.)

A good article to review concerning a variety of issues from credit card theft to door locks with certain cyber intrusions is the June 2011 *Consumer Reports* issue entitled "Your Security: 25 Things Cops and Crooks Say You're Doing Wrong.

Chapter Four Summary

- Develop your sixth sense. Become more aware of your surroundings.
- Learn how to really say *NO*.
- Don't advertise.
- Have a plan. Don't panic.
- Get law enforcement involved.
- Talk to your kids, family, and those at your workplace.
- Document everything concerning your stalker.
- Look into whether you should obtain a restraining or protective order.
- See if your state or particular country jurisdiction allows you to sue your stalker.
- Develop a security plan for your car, the place you live, and where you work.
- If you are going to have a weapon, check all federal, state, and local laws concerning ownership and use.
- If you are going to have a gun, everything discussed about ownership of the other weapons applies. Become proficient in its use. Secure it safely from children and others. Always know what your target is at all times. Understand that gun ownership is a huge responsibility.

Chapter 5
Our Approach to
Investigating Stalkers

L aw enforcement officers should find this chapter very helpful. However, if you are a stalking victim, victim advocate,
educator, student, or just someone who is curious about how
a stalking investigation can and (we believe) should transpire, you
will also find this chapter helpful and hopefully very informative,
especially with the types of examples we utilize in this part of the
text. In other words, if you're not a cop, don't worry. This chapter
will include data that will help you understand why we suggest this
is how a stalking case should be managed both as it applies to the
stalker and their victims.

By the way, when I lecture about how we investigate stalkers, I
preface my statements with: Just because I was a cop in California
where the stalking law was born, and we have been doing this for a
long time, doesn't mean we are the know all to be all. All we ask is
you approach the things we present with an open mind. If it works
for you, then great, if it doesn't by all means don't use what we have
laid out.

 Before we explain our specific protocol and why we
think it works pretty well, we need to talk briefly about
the general overall law enforcement response to stalking.
Through our extensive contacts with stalking victims both in the

United States and abroad, we have heard both wonderful and not so brilliant stories about how victims have been treated by their local law enforcement entities.* For the most part, those inadequacies in law enforcement contacts stemmed from a lack of training. It was not that those in uniform did not care or did not want to help. Even in our police department, when we first began working stalkers, we had an incident that comes to mind. We discussed this particular incident in the last book, but it portrays a victim's frustration with a police contact in such a descriptive fashion that it bears being told again. This particular incident was given as an example for a Japanese television news program shortly after the female stalker was arrested. Of course, there was a lot more to the story than what we are expressing in this example.

At the time of this incident, there was a male stalking victim that would continually call about his ex-girlfriend. She followed, harassed, and hounded him continually. She damaged his property and confronted any other female he came in contact with. On one occasion the victim called a swing shift dispatcher and complained that the female was again at his residence harassing him. It just so happened that the beat cops in his area were all very large, virile, experienced coppers. When the three uniformed officers arrived, on scene, they found this extremely attractive, well-endowed, raven-haired, skimpily clad female still pounding on our "poor" victim's front door and demanding entry. When the officers inquired what the problem was, the distraught male told them she continually came to his house and tried to get him to let her in. He said she had disrobed on several occasions and demanded sex from him. The victim later told me (I was the detective assigned to his case) that the lead officer shook his head in disbelief, put his arm around him, looked back at this voluptuous female, walked him over to the corner of his living room, and said in a subdued

---

* For those that are not aware, the word "cops" was derived from early England when Sir Robert Peel developed the first police force, and the officers were referred to as bobbies or peelers. Others later referred to these officers as "cops" or constables on patrol.

tone something to the effect of, "Dude, what the hell is your problem? Let her in, take care of her needs, and then kick her out the door."

Needless to say, this guy, who had been terrorized for a prolonged period of time, didn't think this advice was what he needed. Once I talked to all the officers involved, and we did a department-wide training, they quickly came to realize that this guy really had been subjugated by this female. From that point on, whenever a call came out of that patrol area, it was handled in a completely different manner. The stalker was eventually removed from this particular victim's life, and I am proud to say the officers of my almamater are still doing an excellent job on the stalking front.

Those organizations that continually train their officers on stalking and have administrators that support a no-nonsense approach toward domestic violence, stalking, and the like tend to offer victims the help they need and deserve. It is when that training is lacking, or there is no clear direction from the department's administration, that victims (stalking and otherwise) fall through the cracks. In this chapter and the book's appendix, we have included a few of the groups who have proven their medal as shining examples of how the crime of stalking can and should be addressed.

This training must also extend to the judges or magistrates that are going to hear these types of cases. Yes, we want our jurist to be impartial, but they also need to continually make their decisions based on educated positions couched with the facts of the case. Can judges not be aware and make assumptions based on lack of information? Oh, you betcha. One example of that was a case in which a stalker continually hounded his ex-wife to get back with him. He repeatedly wrote her letters about how good she looked and how he missed fondling a certain part of her anatomy. He grilled his kids about their mother's coming and goings. It got to the point that complete strangers wrote letters to the victim about how badly the stalker was berating her children. The stalker forced the kids to leave doors open on the victim's house. That way he could gain entry when she was not home and conduct searches for information on her comings and goings. He would repeatedly follow his ex from town to town, oftentimes tailgating her. He parked his vehicle exactly one thousand yards from her residence to surveil her. (The restraining order said he had to stay at least a thousand yards from his wife.) When he came to pick up his children for a visitation, they would run to the neighbor's home. They would cry and crawl under the neighbor's beds to hide. The stalker did many other things throughout the course of the stalking that caused both the victim and their children extreme mental anguish.

We had the lead on the case, and when we appeared in front of the preliminary hearing judge, I testified as both the detective in charge and as a stalking expert. The preliminary hearing judge bound the stalker for trial. This judge even commented there was no doubt in his mind that the victim's ex-husband was a stalker. The case went to trial in the superior court before another judge. (We should say that this rarely happened. Most stalkers pled out prior to trial, most to multiple felonies.) Halfway through the trial—we had not been called in to testify during this portion of the trial—this judge stopped the proceedings and said he had no idea why this case ever got to his court. It was not a criminal problem and should be heard in family court. This particular judge was blind to the facts and, at the very least, completely unaware of the basic caveats of the California stalking law. (We are being diplomatic about what we really thought about this judge's behavior.) The stalker was convicted on minor charges. The victim sold her home, left our jurisdiction, and from what I am told as a result of this trial, has pretty much become a shut-in.

What has helped our cause was the recent addition of domestic violence judges hearing DV cases, including stalking. They are all superior court judges and commissioners. This means they can hear both preliminary hearings and preside over jury trials.

Thankfully most (if not all) have some degree of training in what transpires in a stalking scenarios.

What Can Happen When There Is Not a Stalking Protocol in Place?

We are about to tell you a true story, but of course most of the names and some of the places have been changed to protect those involved. Not too many years ago, a female social worker who worked with children ("Beth") was in an estranged relationship with her husband ("Sam") who she was attempting to divorce. For the past few weeks the husband worked as an armed security guard, and he also had a restraining order filed against him by an Orange County court. Sam knew about the order but was fleeing from service of that order. Many attempts for service had been made. For the past several weeks, Sam had also been actively stalking Beth. He began a campaign of making threatening phone calls, harassing her at work, and demeaning her as much as possible. He was pushing for them to reconcile, and Beth was done.

At the time of this incident, Sam had been trying to convince Beth to allow him to pick up their four-year-old son and his older sister. (She was from a previous relationship prior to marrying Sam.) Beth had refused and placed a no pick-up order at the girl's school because of previous issues with Sam when they resided in Orange County.

Beth had recently placed her four-year-old son in day care near where she worked in a Los Angeles County city. One day, when she went to pick up her young son, the day care workers told her Sam had picked up their child. He told the staff he was taking him to a doctor's appointment. There were two problems with this. One, Beth had never given Sam permission to pick up their child, and two, her son did not have a doctor's appointment. Sam's actions raised a red flag. Beth, a very intuitive woman, had been feeling something strange was up with Sam and his recent behavior.

Beth immediately called the large metropolitan police department near the day care center. When Beth got the police dispatcher, she told her of her plight. The dispatcher asked her if she had copies of the restraining order and child custody papers with her. Beth said she didn't, and the dispatcher said they normally did not send officers out on a domestic call like this unless the caller had the proper paperwork. The dispatcher said she would check with her supervisor and call her back. According to Beth, the dispatcher never called her back. Beth who had another cell phone received a call from Sam on that phone. He told her he still had their son, but due to car problems, Sam wanted Beth to drive to a location on a major street near the day care so he could drop off her son. Beth was still very concerned and made a mental note that Sam had called earlier in the day saying he wanted to pick up her older daughter from school as well.

Beth drove to a large arterial street located not too far from the day care. When she arrived her concerns worsened. Sam was stopped along the street curb, and she could not see her son. She parked her car so it was heading in towards the front end of Sam's vehicle. Sam got out of his car and brought their son to her car. He placed the boy into the car seat, which was in the back of Beth's SUV. He did not strap in the sleeping child, which was not like him at all. Beth also noticed Sam was carry-ing a small canvas bag with him.

When Beth went back to strap her boy into his

seat, she saw Sam open the SUV's right front passenger side door. He slid into the seat and reached into the bag. Beth said this was totally out of character for Sam because he hated her car. He told her this all the time and would never get into it. As Beth looked at Sam, he leaned over the front seat and pulled out a loaded semiautomatic handgun, which he began to fire at her.

Beth immediately ran to the back of her car away from her child, around the driver's side of her car, and down the road. Because she was concerned about where Sam had parked, she had called 911 to alert the police. (This was prior to actually contacting Sam

Sam shooting at Beth.

on the street.) Caption Sam shooting at Beth. According to Beth, when she got the California Highway Patrol dispatcher, to try and summon assistance the dispatcher placed her on **HOLD**. (In California, when you dial the emergency 911 number on your cell phone connects you to the California Highway Patrol who then directs your call.) Beth said when she was running down the street, Sam had taken up a position on the right rear quarter panel of her SUV. He fired numerous rounds at her as she ran down the street and waited for the Highway Patrol dispatcher to get back on the line.

Beth fell to the ground in the middle of the street and then got back up to keep running. Beth saw a late model BMW coming toward her. The driver stopped to see if she needed assistance. The female driver of the BMW was in fact an off duty Orange County supervising probation officer coming home from work. The supervisor did not carry a gun. When the supervisor pulled up next to Beth, who was yelling for help through the supervisor's open passenger window, Beth didn't notice Sam was busy coming up behind her and reloading his weapon as he ran towards them. Just as the BMW's driver was about to gather some information from Beth, Sam opened up on Beth and the supervisor. He sent rounds through the back windshield and other portions of the BMW. All of a sudden Beth jumped into the supervisor's car through the open passenger door window as she was shot twice in her lower extremities.

The supervisor stepped on the gas and sped away from the shooting scene. As they drove away, Beth pled for her to go back so she could check on her child. Finally the dispatcher came on Beth's cell phone. Beth handed the phone to the supervisor who summoned the police. Paramedics treated Beth and transported her to the hospital for her injuries.

When the first responding uniformed officer arrived at the shooting scene, Sam's car was gone. The officer quickly checked the SUV and found no one inside. He began to secure the crime scene and look for witnesses, which he is supposed to do. When the second officer arrived, he checked with the first officer and then went back to Beth's SUV to look for evidence. What he found was terrifying. He looked into the backseat of the SUV and could see the lifeless hand of a small child poking out from underneath the rear seat of the SUV. The boy was covered with Sam's jacket. His small body had been stuffed under the seat, covered by his cowardly father, who had shot him more than once at point-blank range.

Sam, who had fled the scene, apparently was staying at a Christian halfway house located on the west end of Westminster. He came into the house and, amazingly, went to his room to sleep.

When the late news came on, people in the halfway home put two and two together and contacted the Westminster Police with their suspicions. Three uniformed patrol officers were dispatched. One of which was my former partner, Cliff Williams, who had worked with me in the Family Protection Unit (FPU). Cliff had recently left the FPU when he was promoted from detective to patrol sergeant. The officers did not have much information to go on. They were waiting for an update from the dispatcher's contact with the agency where the initial crime had reportedly taken place hours earlier.

When the officers first arrived at the middle-class residential neighborhood, they got out of their cars and walked up the street toward the two-story, split-level halfway house. As they approached from the west, they had no idea that Sam had been alerted. It's unknown exactly how, but Sam was now standing along the west wall of the halfway house waiting for the officers. As Sergeant Williams was in the process of contacting the neighbor directly west of the halfway house, Sam reached over the top of the fence and opened up (began firing) on the two officers standing in the neighbor's driveway. All officers pulled back to the street corner. Williams radioed for immediate assistance, an air unit, and a special weapons and tactics (SWAT) team.

The on-scene officers' main job then was to establish a perimeter so that Sam could not escape and await SWAT. (Orange County now uses regional SWAT teams made up of SWAT officers from cities throughout the county, so it takes them very little time to respond. Westminster and other cities

SWAT gear carried by on duty SWAT patrol officers. Courtesy of Westminster P.D.

have their on duty patrol officers who are also SWAT officers take their SWAT gear on patrol. There is also a group of specially trained patrol officers called police rifle officers (PRO) that carry modified M4 .223 caliber assault rifles.) The air unit conducted a run throughout the neigh-

Large juniper, Sam was hiding in.

borhood using their forward looking infrared (FLIR) equipment, which can find suspects by the heat signature they emit while concealed or running. They declared the back and side yards had no inferred contacts. Sergeant Williams and a patrol/SWAT officer, Don Webb (now Sergeant Webb), decided to check down the street to ascertain if the suspect had moved or if citizens were in harm's way. They used the wall of the last house on the block as cover.

Williams had his duty semi-auto handgun and SWAT officer Webb was armed with a fully automatic 40 caliber MP5 machine gun, turned the corner. Sam, who had secreted himself in a large juniper bush along the west side of the corner house, opened up on them. Sergeant Williams was shot in the back from about twelve feet away. The impact of the round struck a nerve bundle through his vest, so he could not immediately

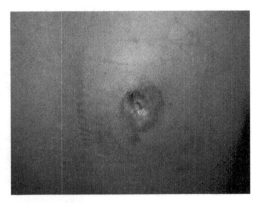

Gunshot wound to Sgt. William's back. Courtesy of Sgt. Williams.

return fire. The SWAT officer, still taking rounds, turned, fired, and cut Sam down. Sergeant Williams, to his credit, was still barking out orders as he was drug from the scene, placed into a marked police unit, and whisked off to the hospital. Both Sergeant Williams and SWAT officer Webb were awarded medals for their valor and courage under fire, which is apropos. This incident resulted in the horrible death of an innocent four-year-old child, the wounding of his mother, and the shooting of a police sergeant. That's not even mentioning the endangerment of an entire residential neighborhood. All participants paid a very high price.

Forensic Threat Assessment

After this incident, I received a call from my ex-partner, Detective Terry Selinske, with whom I worked robbery/homicide for over fourteen years. Selinske still worked for the department and let me know about the incident. I was in the Midwest conducting a two-day seminar. During the second day, I was in the process of telling a classroom full of cops about the incident while being videotaped by a local news team when it hit me. Tears welled up in my eyes, and I had to take a break. The thought of that little boy being executed by his father finally hit me like a ton of bricks. Then there was my former partner, with a wife and three kids, who got dumped by this hemorrhoid. Homicide detectives are an unusual breed of people, and not too much bothers them except for kids being hurt or killed.

I later contacted Sergeant Williams and asked if he knew what had caused all this to happen. He said he didn't and asked if I would be willing to find out. Cops want to know what makes guys like Sam tick. That way they can hopefully stop something like that from happening again. Williams and I worked several stalking cases together, and we followed my protocol to conduct our investigations. I was very curious about the hows and whys of this case, so I was happy to investigate.

Even though I had recently retired, the department was gracious enough to allow me to use their interview room to conduct an in-depth forensic threat assessment of the incident. I had already done some field interviews prior to talking to Beth at the police department. The resulting assessment generated some very interesting information. For a variety of reasons, we are not going to discuss all the data, but we do want to offer some idea about Sam's background and what led to him becoming a stalker/murderer. Here are some of the findings:

- Sam was well-educated, and while attending college, he worked for another large metropolitan city's district attorney's office as an intern. At the time of his death, he worked for a large security agency as an armed agent. He was very athletic and seemed to be a health nut, but according to Beth, he would sneak junk food and drink more than he should have. He did not appear to require much sleep. Beth also described Sam as being very secretive.

- Sam had difficulty keeping a job. He would complain about being singled out or discriminated against. (We were unable to verify these complaints due to some confidentiality agreements where he had been employed.)

- At the time of Sam's death, he was a member of a local church and had been befriended by that church's pastor. That was how he came to rent a room in the halfway house in Westminster.

- According to Beth, Sam had been both mentally and physically abused by his father. His mother was diagnosed in her twenties with a schizophrenic disorder. It's unknown what type of schizophrenia she suffered from. She was heavily medicated and hospitalized from time to time. (We ask our victims questions about the stalker's background, including any previous abuse.)

- Sam was diagnosed with bipolar disorder while Beth and he were living in another state. (According to the *DSM-IV-TR*, bipolar disorder can be misdiagnosed as schizophrenia and vice versa. Furthermore information on schizophrenia indicates it is often a hereditary disorder.) Sam quit seeing his therapist and was not taking his prescribed medication for his condition. It is not known whether Sam was diagnosed with bipolar I or II disorder, but from Beth's descriptions, Sam's behavior was depressed for long periods of time accompanied by what clinicians have described as "hypomania."[97] (Please note, this is pretty much how we lay out our threat assessments for the crime report. Obviously we are not qualified to testify about Sam's mental health condition, and we can't identify or diagnose his ailments. As trained observers, however, we can comment on what we and others have seen concerning his behaviors.) Beth described one incident where Sam was euphoric when he purchased her a brand new Land Rover, and about three weeks later, he became very angry over buying her the car.

- During the interview, Beth described several other behaviors exhibited by Sam that we had seen in other stalkers. These people were later diagnosed with passive-aggressive personality disorder.[98] (Corsini's *Dictionary of Psychology* describes this behavior as "the actions of a hostile person demonstrating aggression in a passive way.")[99] These incidents with Sam included the following:

  1. Shortly after Beth and Sam were married, they moved to another state so Sam could become a correctional officer for that particular state. Beth and Sam had talked about having children, and according to Beth, there didn't appear to be any issues. The moment Sam found out she was pregnant with their son, though, Sam's entire personality changed. Sam basically abandoned Beth, and he said he no longer wanted a child. Sam left newspaper clippings out so Beth could

easily see them. The ads that Sam circled were for one-bedroom apartments. Sam began telling Beth to abort the child. Sam did not attend the birth of their son.

2. Sam would tell Beth that while he was in the marines, he would go out on trainings or other missions, and guys in his unit would not come back from these missions. Beth said she got the distinct impression Sam told her this to frighten her, and if she didn't cooperate with his wishes, she would end up missing as well. Beth discovered that Sam never finished basic training in the United States Marine Corp, even though he told her he had a successful career there. (We were never able to verify this.)

3. Beth indicated that Sam had a thing for hurting animals. While living in their first apartment, a neighbor's cat would wander into their residence. Beth liked the cat and showed it some attention. Shortly after the cat disappeared. Sam made a point of telling Beth he had killed the kitten. Beth also said when they lived in the city where Sam shot her and killed their son, they purchased a Labrador puppy. When Sam would come home from work, Beth would be awakened by the cries and whimpers of the dog, which Sam appeared to be abusing. Beth said the dog's cries were very disturbing. After Beth left Sam, she came over to his residence to check on the dog, which she could not take with her. When she walked into the living room, she saw Sam sitting on a chair with a bottle of booze and a pair of bloody scissors atop a table. When she heard the dog whimpering in the garage, she went into the garage and found that Sam had cut the dog's tail off with the scissors. Beth went to her car and called the police to report the incident. She was told to call animal control because cops did not handle that type of call. When she called animal control, they responded, but they told her they could not find the dog. Sam told them it had run away.

4. Just before Beth left Sam, after an argument, Sam walked into their garage, got into the family car, turned it on, and sat in the car as the garage filled with exhaust fumes. Finally Beth went out and confronted Sam. He told her, "If you don't do what I want, I will kill myself." (Remember, this is a technique some stalkers use to generate sympathy or employ as a control mechanism.)

- Sam used alcohol to self-medicate. Beth was told he used other drugs, but she did not know what they were.

- Beth said she moved back to California with her older daughter and her one-year-old son. She could no longer stand Sam's bizarre behavior. Not too long after she moved back to California, Sam, who was having problems at his job, quit and moved back to California. He got a job with a well-known youth organization. When Beth first moved back to California, she lived with her mother in Orange County. During that time, Sam sent her support checks, but he filled them out in her mother's name. He also attached notes telling Beth's mother that he really appreciated the way she (not Beth) took care of his kids. Not long after being in the employ of the youth organization, Sam was fired because he could not work well with others, would not cooperate, and intimidated his coworkers. Beth said this was a continual pattern with Sam in the workplace. He always put himself above others and felt he knew more than them. (According to the *DSM-IV-TR*, these all could be signs of passive-aggressive personality disorder.) While living with her mother, Beth filed a domestic violence case against Sam, which caused a lot of concern for Beth's daughter.

- Sam worked and left a series of security jobs. He purchased a handgun, which he always had concealed on him. He also began working for himself, but he had to quit because he neglected to fulfill his customer contracts. (Do you see the emerging pattern?) He finally ended up at the security company he was with when he killed his son and shot Beth.

- After Sam's continual pleading and promising, Beth moved herself and the kids back in with him in the city where the shooting occurred. Over a period of time at that residence, law enforcement responded to domestic violence calls. Unfortunately, according to Beth, they never took any kind of crime or information report. (I was also unable to locate any report prior to the shooting. There may have been radio log entries, but none were brought to my attention.) According to Beth, on one occasion, Sam even called the police to file a (false) crime report against her. One of the responding officers obtained her phone number and advised her not to go home because they felt Sam was a danger to her. (Please note, it is crucial for law enforcement to document all calls concerning domestic violence or stalking.) It is unknown what this particular police agency's policy was concerning the documentation of domestic violence oriented calls. Westminster police policy is to document any call for service concerning a domestic violence type scenario.

- Beth found it unusual that ever since their son turned three (going on four), Sam wanted to spend time with him.

- Shortly after the incident with the dog, Sam began stalking her. He would come to her place of work and attempt to cause problems. He would vandalize her car, leaving pieces of paper with his handwriting on them so she knew it was him. He began trying to embarrass her at work again. He would call her repeatedly to tell her how she had messed up his life. She tape-recorded several of the calls, notified police, and the person she talked to told her there was nothing to be done because Sam had not made a "direct threat." (This is why we tell victims to contact a detective that handles stalking or, at the very least, domestic violence cases.) Sam would call coworkers pretending he was talking to Beth and make lascivious remarks. One day he dropped all the kids' toys and clothes on the front doorstep of her job with a note saying he no longer wanted to be the kids' father. All this harassment forced Beth to quit her job out of embarrassment and grief he had caused her and her coworkers.

- Beth was able to obtain a restraining order from the Orange County Superior Court. She had paid for it to be served by the sheriff, but Sam, who understood he would have to give up all firearms and could not purchase any more as long as the restraining order was in place, kept evading service.

- During all of this, Sam filed for divorce, which forced Beth to go before a judge in Los Angeles County for the child support and visitation hearing. According to Beth, at the hearing, Sam told the court he did not want visitation. The judge told him he could not do that. When Beth told the judge about the stalking, harassment, and Sam's anger issues, the judge said that he had a tendency to believe her, but he also told her, "Quite frankly, Beth, I think you are exaggerating." Because she had no police reports to back up her claims, the judge was not willing to send Sam to an anger management class. The judge was also made aware of the restraining order issued in Orange County, but he told Beth that was an Orange County issue. He was not going to have Sam served in his court. (The judge could have had Sam served with the order in his courtroom, even if it was issued in another jurisdiction.) After hearing what the judge had to say, Beth "felt completely helpless." (Again, we have no reason to disbelieve Beth's information, but we were not able to verify what transpired in that courtroom. As a non-law enforcement entity at that time, we did not have access to the court log.)

- Beth said that once Sam found out she was in a committed relationship and realized they were not going to reconcile, he called her (prior to the shooting) and left this message on her phone: "I gave you enough chances. You promised me that we would be together forever and ever. I am going to take what's mine. If you don't reconcile with me by...then life as we all know it will change." Beth again called the police department, and she was told again that was not enough for them to act on.

The rest you know. To prevent these types of events from transpiring, we have developed a stalking protocol. This protocol has been in existence since 1992. Of course, it has been amended over the years. It appears the agency Beth dealt with had no such protocol.

Background on the Stalking Protocol

The protocol we have developed is about twenty-five pages long, so we are not going to include it all in this book. Instead we will give an overview of what we instruct law enforcement on concerning the investigation and handling of a stalking case. For those involved in law enforcement that wish for a complete copy of the protocol on CD, please feel free to go to my website, www.DetectiveMikeProctor.com, and use my e-mail to contact me. We will send you a copy along with some other information. This includes a copy of the last article I wrote for the 2007 edition of *Journal of California Law Enforcement*, "Stalking Investigations, What We've Learned Since 1991."

We have learned over the years of working stalkers (as has many of the threat management teams also involved in this process) that stalking cases take a multidisciplinary approach. This model has been developed to not only successfully prosecute a stalker but also to assist the victim(s) throughout the process as much as possible. At least that

Retired Chief Andrew Hall, developer of the FPU. Author's personal file.

was the case with my unit, the Family Protection Unit (FPU) of the

Westminster Police Department. This was the brainchild of now-retired Chief of Police Andrew Hall. He developed the FPU when he was a lieutenant in charge of administrative services in the late 90s.

When we first began working stalking cases, it was early 1991. The Los Angeles Police Department dealt with the first stalking case of stalking ever filed. Ours was the first in Orange County and the second case filed in the nation. The case took my partner and me

Service With Integrity

about three months before we finally got someone in the Special Prosecutions Unit of the Orange County District Attorney's Office to file the case. This was because no one had ever prosecuted a stalking case before. Therefore nobody had any experience in the prosecution, and nobody seemed to want to be the first.

It was probably a good thing the case came to the homicide unit of our police department. Homicide dicks are used to putting in long hours and generating multipage, all-inclusive cases. Our first stalking case involved a businesswoman who had been stalked for about nine years prior to contacting us. The case came to homicide because an insurance investigator called us to say he believed he had uncovered a murder-for-hire plot. After our initial investigation, we found the stalker had been causing all the problems.

While investigating the case, we found stalking cases were not difficult to work, but they did require a specific fashion of investigation. Thus came the development of our first protocol, which is still continually tweaked as new information surfaces.

We believe the following training should be required for anyone assigned the task of investigating stalkers. (Of course, these are all suggestions. We realize training budgets are very tight these days.)

- *Get some training in profiling.* Both my partner and I found attending profiling schools put on by the Behavioral Science Unit of the FBI and others helped working homicide cases. The same training assisted us when working stalking cases as well. However, my partner and I were fortunate to be trained by one of the best in the field, who at the time was an FBI profiler in their behavioral science unit, Mary Ellen O'toole, PhD.

- *Take at least one class in abnormal psychology.* When you work stalkers, you must have at least some idea of what makes them tick. Is the suspect presenting any symptoms of psychological disorders? This information can be invaluable when conducting interviews or setting up what you will be looking for in a search warrant. If you don't want to apply to a college to get the credits for the class, talk to a professor who is teaching a section of the class. See if he or she will allow you to audit the class. We find most professors are pretty open to law enforcement officers sitting in.

- *Get some training in sexual assault.* Most states have excellent courses designed for the law enforcement professional concerning sex-generated criminal activity. Some stalkers are spurred on by their sexual desires. Our first book on stalkers was (and perhaps still is) recommended to sexual assault investigators that have attended some of these POST-related classes.

- *Get some training in domestic violence.* Most stalking detectives are cross-trained in handling domestic violence cases. Prior to me leaving law enforcement, POST was in the process of developing an expert-level police investigators domestic violence class. I had already taken the advanced domestic violence investigator training. More information is always better than none. Remember, the largest number of stalking cases stem from domestic violence/intimate partner scenarios.

- *If you get the time, a case management class would not hurt.* We will show you how to put a stalking case together, but if you already have skills developing casebooks, it will be a plus.

Line Training

If your line personnel (division commanders, lieutenants, sergeants, and everyone on down) are not trained in what stalking is and how it manifests, a stalking protocol will not work. We can easily teach for an eight-hour period or longer, but you can get the basics across in a half-day session. States like California mandates stalking training. It is usually included in the compulsory domestic violence training. Detectives tasked with actually conducting a stalking investigation, however, should have a lot more training than just a few hours of this assigned education. This is especially true if the instructor is not that well-versed in the investigation of stalking either.

If you can, get your district attorneys, judges, and court commissioners trained up as well. The more people with a better idea of what you need to successfully prosecute a case, the better off everyone (including the victims) will be. We made it a point to train our felony and as many misdemeanor DAs as possible. We supplied all judges hearing criminal cases with a copy of our book. Surprisingly most read it and commented they were better for it. Previous exposure to what entails stalking always helps a detective who enters a jurist's courtroom to obtain a search or arrest warrant for the crime of stalking.

Please note, this protocol has been and is being used (all or in part) by law enforcement throughout various jurisdictions. The protocol's value is that it can be plugged into existing department programs, or it can be used as a model to develop a completely new one. We have never told any requesting agency that this is the only game in town. We only ask that they look at it to determine if it will work for them like it has worked for the Westminster Police Department and others in the past.

The Family Protection Unit (FPU)

Before we get into our basic protocol, we should discuss the unit we worked in prior to leaving the Westminster Police Department. We will talk about other agencies but because this protocol was utilized by this unit and was enhanced during our tenure there, we should explain it a bit. As previously indicated, the Westminster Police Department's Family Protection

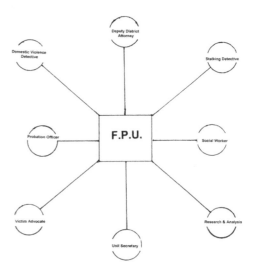

FPU organizational chart.

Unit was the brainchild of now-retired Chief Andrew Hall. As the administrative lieutenant directly under the chief of police, he saw a need to stop uniform patrol officers from continually responding to the same residence over and over again on domestic violence-related calls. (Stalking being one of the reasons for the department's callouts.) Therefore he came up with a model program entitled the FPU, which was started via a government grant. The multijurisdictional unit contained a detective sergeant, a stalking detective, a domestic violence detective, and a sexual assault detective. All were cross-trained in each other's disciplines. The unit also contained a secretary assigned to organizing cases, an Orange County domestic violence probation officer —whose sole task was to monitor the unit's DV, sexual assault, and stalking cases, a senior Orange County social worker, a victim advocate whom at the time came from the Women's Transitional Living Center, and the unit's own Orange County prosecuting district attorney to handle the cases generated by this unit. This allowed for all cases to be vertically prosecuted. In other words, once a detective was assigned a case, it was his or hers from the time of arrest to prosecution and sentencing. The district attorney handled the evaluation of all search and arrest warrants and followed the case from filing to prosecution to sentencing. This allowed the FPU to become very, very successful at putting away the bad guy, and it greatly reduced the continual calls for service from one location. At the writing of this book, the unit was still intact and doing well.) (The prosecuting attorney's position was removed from the team due to budgetary issues.) The FPU was profiled in an article we wrote in *Law and Order Magazine*, a well-known police professional publication.[100]

Cultural Considerations

Before we discuss the stalking protocol we teach and send to other agencies, we need to talk about something that is often discounted during not only the investigative process but the general discussion of stalking. That issue is culture. Over the years we have been exposed to many cultures, both on and off the job. Each has a different slant on life, which includes that culture's mores and teachings. Therefore it helps to know what you are walking into when you get a case that involves someone from a different world than you are used to dealing with.

I remember responding to a call where a father of Middle Eastern descent had chained his daughter to a drainpipe and was beating the living hell out of her because she had disobeyed his wishes concerning the dating of a certain boy. He, for the life of him, could not understand why I was so upset with what he was doing. He explained he was allowed to do this in his country. As we cuffed him and transported him to jail, we explained that he lived in our country now, and we didn't allow that type of behavior. There were other times when dealing with different cultures led to this type of outcome. *We should also note that not too far back in our very own culture (discussed in literature around the late 1800's) a man could beat his wife with a rod or stick that was no bigger around than his thumb. This was known as the "rule of thumb." In our own culture we have and are hopefully continuing to evolve in the way we treat not only our spouses, but other human beings as well.* (Some would argue that was where the term rule of thumb comes from, but for our purposes we will stick with it.)

There are places in the world where the females are still considered second-class citizens. They are subjected to regular and (way too often) condoned abuse. We get requests for assistance from a variety of countries, and we must advise these women that we would love to help them. However, until their countries' views of its women change, there was not a whole lot we could do. Here are some examples of what we are talking about.

A country that borders the United States, Mexico, has one of the worst human rights records, especially when it comes to women. Sexual assault, torture, and domestic violence not only transpire on a regular basis but oftentimes go unreported due to the lack of cooperation from law enforcement in that country. On the 2011 Human Rights Watch website, they stated that ninety percent of the women who experienced domestic violence issues and other abuse did not report it. (For more information, see http://www.hrw.org/en/world-report-2011/mexico.) We realize that currently just staying alive in many of the states in Mexico is a daily struggle.

While here, we need to give you some examples. While working homicide, my partner and I would develop a case, get an arrest warrant, and then hope the suspect didn't scurry back across the border like a cockroach. Unfortunately, most of the time the undocumented aliens we were dealing with did just that. Our police department and many others currently have Unlawful Flight to Avoid Prosecution (UFAP) warrants for several people who fled back across the border. One case that comes to mind is when an undocumented alien kidnapped a chef, tortured her, and raped her. He then drove her to a water tower, dumped her semi-conscious body out of his car, and backed over her torso. He then took a piece of broken asphalt and slammed it down on her head, crushing it. He was already wanted in Mexico for another killing, and as of today he is still on the run. Our investigation revealed that this suspect had no compassion for women, and for the most part treated them like dirt.

On another occasion, I was recently asked to come to the police department for a meeting with Detective Selinske concerning a cold case homicide that that transpired in 1988. Prior to our meeting, the sergeant mentioned they just received two separate domestic violence and attempted murder cases involving female Hispanic victims. Stalking had transpired in each case. One woman was almost beaten to death; the other was stabbed in the chest, back, and head but miraculously survived. Both male, undocumented Hispanic suspects were in the wind (ITW) and back across the border. The sergeant commented that in each case the victimized women were very surprised at the response they received from law enforcement. They expressed that because they were undocumented and had little status in the community that the police would even take their case and try to help them.

We also get requests for assistance from stalking victims in countries such as India, where domestic violence is a tremendous issue. Women are still burned, slapped, kicked, and brutalized on a regular basis. (Not every woman is being abused, but it is a significant number.) Stalking is a big issue there. Until recently it had not really been approached in a sincere, legislative fashion. According to an April 6th, 2011 article in *Daily News and Analysis*, a recent bill was presented under the Indian Penal Code Section 509(B) to address the crime of stalking. We hope it passes.[101]

We also receive complaints from women in Turkey. We have associates with friends and relatives in Turkey, and from time to time, they still go back to their country of origin. What they tell us is that the wealthier areas of Turkey exhibit less honor killings and cases of domestic violence toward women because they are better educated. They are aware, however, of domestic violence and stalking even in the more upscale portions of the country. (Of course, domestic violence can raise its ugly head anywhere.) They said that in the past eight years, a new regime has started taking over, and the country is leaning more towards the "strictest Muslim outlook." They feel this will cause more problems for the women in their country. For more on honor killings and domestic violence in Turkey; go to a fairly recent online article written in the Southeast European Times website. This reveals that honor killings and domestic violence are still a huge problem in that country.[102] Again, every place domestic violence transpires, even though it may not be initially referred to specifically as such so can the crime of stalking.

These types of killings and abuse of women are not just taking place in Middle Eastern countries. It occurs in the West as well. According to a September 26, 2011 article in *Newsweek* entitled "Mary or Else" by Michelle Goldberg, both the United States and the United Kingdom are experiencing a greater number of forced marriages and other honor based violence.[103] Outside of the United States, Canada, and portions of the E.U. however, it appears the laws and law enforcement's approach to intimate partner violence and stalking are weak to non-existent. This means we have difficulty assisting stalking victims requesting our help from a variety of countries abroad. (We also have a very difficult time understanding how a woman who has been brutalized and sexually assaulted is at fault for embarrassing her family and how that makes it OK for a family member to kill her in order to save face.)

One thing we also run into are some countries' problems with passing a stalking law due to their concerns about "pursuit." For example, in Swaziland there is a practice known as "kusoma." In this practice a male that wants to have an intimate relationship with a female follows her to her place of work or home and continually asks for her favor. The Swazi legislature has been discussing enacting a stalking law, but there are concerns it may conflict with this time honored practice.[104] It is fine to court, but again when that leads to continual pursuit, courtship no longer exists. In Switzerland they also seem concerned with the issue of pursuit. In 2007 and 2008 a portion of the legislature tried to pass an anti-stalking law. The measure failed over concerns that a strict law might inhibit or criminalize socially accepted behavior.* Some legislators feel civil laws are in place to help stalking victims. From reviewing several articles on the Internet, that outlook is apparently "not shared" by a growing number of people in that very civilized country.

When we first started working with the new Vietnamese immigrants arriving in the community where we involved in law enforcement, there were many things we had to learn about their culture in order to assist them. For example, some rubbed coins (cao gio) into their children's chest, back, and legs, oftentimes leaving marks. They believed it assisted in the child's recovery from illness. We had to explain that, in California, it was considered child abuse.

When it came to stalking (or pursuit), the behavior we were seeing was definitely considered stalking. In their culture, however, we were told by many family members that the male was "allowed" to pursue. According to some, it was a sign the male was very interested in the woman he was going after, so the woman should learn to put up with it. It was difficult to get the victims to report the crimes because their families urged them not to.

In 2008 we did an interview with a well-known Philippine newspaper on youth stalking. From what I could gather, it is a country that is trying to get a better handle on stalking within the ranks of its populace, but like they explained, they have a long way to go.**

---

* For more on the Swiss stalking situation, and a description of some of their civil laws that some legislators feel take care of the problem go to http://www.stalkingriskprofile.com/docs/Stalking%20and%20Swiss%20Law.pdf

** In regard to the Philippines, you might want to review the Republic Act No. 9262, The Anti-violence Against Women and their Children Act of 2004, http://www.familymatters.org.ph/Relevant%20Laws/RA%209262%20Anti-Violence%20Against%20Women.htm.

Not too long ago, I conducted a television interview with a South Korean news magazine. The filming was done in conjunction with William "Bill" Hodgman, the head deputy district attorney for the Los Angeles County District Attorney's Office Target Crimes Division. As previously indicated, this division handles many of the high-profile cases, including stalking cases. Hodgman regularly lectures law enforcement and other district attorneys here and abroad on how best to handle any kind of high-profile case, especially when a big media presence is involved.

Hodgman was filmed first, and he did an outstanding job of explaining the criminality of stalking. As I watched the crew and listened to some of their questions, I began to form some opinions as to what they thought about the issue of stalking. Prior to going on camera to discuss stalking examples and the behaviors stalkers tend to exhibit, I asked the interviewer, "You don't believe you have a stalking problem in your country, do you?" Hodgman smiled as the interviewer, who looked as though he wasn't expecting to be queried, hesitated and then said, "No, I don't think we do."

After another forty minutes or so of the interview, had transpired; both Hodgman and I had laid out a great deal of information about the crime of stalking in that short time frame. The interviewer thanked us for our time, and as we were getting up to leave, he commented that, after listening to us, he felt they did in fact have a stalking issue in their country, and he felt our interview would help people better understand the problem. In this case, our work was done, but both Hodgman and I will continue to try and educate those of other countries and cultures as to workings of the stalker.

Another group in the United States with their share of domestic violence, sexual assault, and stalking is the American Indian. (There are, of course, various tribes scattered throughout the country.) I am proud to say I am part Choctaw and Chickasaw, but that by no means makes me an expert on Indian tribal customs. I recently taught at a domestic violence conference in Coeur d' Alene Idaho. While talking to some of the participants, I found that several were involved in the counseling of the various tribes scattered throughout that state. They were very interested in the stalking phenomenon as it would pertain to assisting them in their counseling endeavors.

In 2012 I taught in Utah. Members of the Ute tribal prosecution team and victim advocate group drove over one hundred and fifty miles to the training. Hearing of their journey greatly impressed us indicating both their concern for their tribal members and zeal to obtain training. They advised that stalking was an issue in theirs and other tribes and they welcomed the training, and they would like to see more of it; especially if it were to involve tribal police as well as tribal elders with the hope of giving them both a better understanding of the dynamics of stalking.

A study conducted jointly by the stalking resource center of the National Center for Victims of Crime and the Native American Circle, Ltd. stated that about 17 percent of American Indian and Alaskan native women are stalked within their lifetime.[105] The study indicated that each of the many tribal communities have different and "complex relationships" spanning their various cultures.[106] They also have different policing factions within their jurisdictional boundaries, which can differ from tribe to tribe. Even though the basic elements of stalking are the same, how they are perceived and handled can differ. So the better those investigating and assisting the stalking victims know the tribal culture, the better they can handle that particular stalking scenario. (The Stalking Resource Center has a section describing many of the Indian tribes located within United States borders stalking laws go to: http://www.victimsofcrime.org/our-programs/stalking-resource-center/stalking-laws/tribal-codes.)

These are just a few examples of how cultures can impact an investigation. There are many cultures, and each has its own specific traits. It is not our intent to cast the spotlight on any one particular culture. However it is extremely important to try to get up to speed on a victim's cultural proclivities before you decide to get involved as law enforcement, a victim advocate, or a mental health counselor in their stalking scenario.

 Before we get into the basic protocol, we need to explain why victims like this protocol so well. Just about every victim we have talked to or consulted for (in the United States or abroad) has indicated to us what he or she would like to see from law enforcement in response to his or her plight. These victims want to be treated with respect. They want the case officer to really try to understand what they are going through. They only want to deal with one (or, at the outside, two) detectives. They don't want to be passed around. They want the detective in charge to communicate with them on a regular basis and keep them in the loop. If they are required to fill out paperwork, such as obtaining a protective or restraining order, they would like some help. If and when they have to show up in court, they would like someone to walk them through what to expect both in and outside of the courtroom. They all requested counseling, if possible, for not only them but family members affected by the ordeal.

Trust us, we only learned these things through trial and error as we developed and later honed this protocol. Those assigned the task of dealing with stalking victims need to keep these things in mind.

The other thing we want to emphasize concerning the readers in the law enforcement community that are reviewing this protocol, that if your agency is not large enough to support this type of team effort please think about this. One, as will be discussed, reach out to your local community, or two, think regionalization. More and more small departments that either surround a larger metropolitan based agency or in many situations a centralized prosecution division are regionalizing their assets, whether it be special weapons and tactics teams, bomb squads, computer and other forensic groups, vice/narcotics, auto theft and even threat management teams which you all desperately need. We firmly believe that the best way to conduct a successful stalking investigation is via a multi-disciplinary or team effort.

The Basic Protocol

The primary responding officer's first duty is always to identify what type of crime he or she is dealing with and then take the appropriate steps. In the case of stalking, if this is the department's first contact with the victim, no other crime reports are in place, and/or a detective has not already been assigned the case, the officer is advised not to take a stalking crime report, unless there are extenuating circumstances. This does not mean the officers should gloss over the crime. They should be trained how to identify stalking, and

Digital belt recorder on officers Sam Brown.

they should know what questions to ask the victim, but they should not try and take a full-blown stalking crime report. If the victim experienced rude and annoying phone calls, vandalism, or cyberharassment, officers are trained to look further than just the initial crime. They do this by asking a series of questions that delve further into the incident. Please note, all officers who respond to a stalking call should also tape-record their interviews with their belt-held tape recorders. (All Westminster Police Department patrol officers are assigned digital tape recorders. These are affixed to their utility belts.) These recorders can be easily activated when conducting an interview. Officers are required to utilize this device when performing a stalking or any type of domestic violence investigation. (They also come in handy when officers are involved in other criminal investigations. It can even be used during a traffic stop when the officer believes it would be beneficial to have the contact recorded.) The following are examples of the types of questions to ask a victim: how long has this activity been going on? Have you filed any other crime reports? Are there any restraining orders currently on file? Have there been any (restraining orders) in the past? The officer should take either a simple crime report, say for vandalism, or an incident report. That incident report should include all the information gathered. He or she should then indicate on the crime report that a stalking scenario might be taking place. *Obviously, if a crime of violence or other arrest able felony crime has taken place, the assigned officer will take appropriate action.*

We have found the best uniform cops are those trained by their field training officers (FTOs) to realize that just because they are the first responders and not detectives, it doesn't mean they are drones. They are not just there to keep the peace and take a simple police report. Whenever they encounter a crime, they are all investigators. Therefore, it is their job to ask intuitive questions and complete the best possible initial investigation in the time available. As a lead detective, those officers were the guys we searched out when we wanted a task completed. They were also the officers considered first when the time came for promotions to detective.

If officers feel the need to file an emergency protective order (EPO), then they are encouraged to do so. Once the order is filed, they should attempt to serve the suspect in question if at all possible. Obviously, if the stalker can be arrested at the scene on other charges or for any outstanding warrants, then the officer should make the arrest. If an arrest is made, the officer should attempt to file a bail enhancement on the suspect. In that case, provide all the pertinent information about any suspected stalking or other violence directed toward the victim.

The primary reason that if no other stalking cases or stalking warrants are outstanding that we do not have the primary officer generate a crime report for stalking or arrest the suspect on suspicion of stalking is that the average stalking crime report is between two hundred fifty and as much as seven hundred pages long. These reports contain the initial threat assessment interviews, threat assessment evaluation forms, victim catalog sheet, and stalking chronology, search warrant and search warrant return along with the actual crime report. To get

Author reviewing a stalking file.

Patrol officer going over the department's stalking log.

the proper filing, the handling detective must do a lot of work on the case prior to its submission to the prosecuting attorney. Of course, in any type of criminal investigation, if the officer feels the only applicable felony charge he can arrest the stalker for is that of stalking, and he or she feels the victim is in imminent danger, that officer is obliged to make the arrest and charge the person for stalking. Whether the case can stand on its own and be filed immediately will depend on how quickly the detective in charge of the case can get up to speed as well as the district attorney reviewing the case. Along these same lines, if the officer feels the suspect cannot be eliminated from the situation, or he or she cannot be located, thus placing the victim at risk, the officer can request the watch commander to call out a FPU detective. (In another city, this may be a domestic violence detective.) This detective can then make arrangements (via the unit's victim advocate) to have the family placed in an emergency shelter if they are unable to stay with friends or relatives. The responding officer can also give the victim information on stalking as well as a stalking log, which the officer has available. If the stalker is the victim's spouse, the officer will serve him or her with the EPO (emergency protective order), thus eliminating that person from the victim's home.

Once the initial crime report is filed, it will go to the detective unit's sergeant, who is cross-trained in stalking and will be able to send it off after review to the FPU.

It is the task of the FPU detective assigned to the case to do the following:

Contact the victim. The unit detective will call the victim and ask him or her to bring in every piece of evidence. This includes phone messages, e-mails, notes, cards, gifts, other police department's crime reports (if any), photographs, or anything else the victim feels might be germane to the case.

Conduct a threat assessment interview. We recommend all threat assessment interviews with the victim be videotaped. This is done for a variety of reasons. One, the handling detective can easily go back over his or her interview(s) while writing the report. Two, the demeanor and emotions of the victim can be recorded. Three, both the defense and the prosecution have no doubt about what actually transpired during the course of the interview. (Some investigators have also opted to simultaneously tape-record and videotape. It is oftentimes easier to listen to an interview and take notes than watch it on videotape. Whatever works is fine with us.)

The threat assessment interview is designed to establish what exactly is going on between the stalker and the victim. It helps determine if a stalking is really transpiring. The detective in charge can also ascertain the stalker's lethality toward the victim. If a stalking is taking place, the detective needs to know what kind of stalker he or she is dealing with. The detective also needs to know how much time there is for investigation. For example, if the lethality levels are low, the detective has more time than if the lethality levels are high, and immediate action needs to take place. This action could include pushing restraining orders, securing the victim and family members, and/or attempting to make a quick arrest without all the necessary investigation prior to taking the stalker into custody.

During the first portion of the interview, the victim should be encouraged to establish his or her entire relationship with the potential stalker in a chronological fashion. The interviewer can then go back over each area the victim covered in a more in-depth fashion.

There are a series of questions we train detectives to use when dealing with specific types of stalkers. For example, if you are dealing with a stalker who had a sexual relationship with the victim, the investigator should ask specific questions about the normalcy (or lack of normalcy) in their relationship. This gives the investigator a clearer picture about the stalker's behavioral patterns and how he or she may be expected to react in other situations. Because this book is designed for the general public, we are not going to provide the exact questions. Remember, stalkers do read our books. If anyone in law enforcement would like a copy of our overall protocol, we are glad to furnish a copy as long as the requestor can provide us with details as to their authenticity as to being a law enforcement professional. Also the appendix section includes a copy of what we suggest investigators fill out when conducting a threat assessment form. This form, that is just a few pages filled out by the lead detective, provides any detective involved with the case an overview of the stalker's threat potential. We have also included a form utilized by law enforcement in Great Britain for their threat assessment interviews, as a way to compare as well as glean more information.

We will say that one question we ask of those individuals who were intimate with their stalkers is whether the stalker ever discussed being abused or molested. The reason we ask this question is, if the victim has children, those kids could be at risk for sexual or other abuse from this particular stalker.

If the victim is being stalked by a stranger, we would get into an in-depth discussion about what the victim does, where he or she goes, where he or she works, etc. The victim's habits are the only clues available to attempt to find the stalker. Please note, if we are dealing with a stranger stalker, the lead detective may decide to deploy a surveillance team from our metro division in an attempt to pick up the stalker as he or she continues to stalk. This team may also be deployed if there is an immediate lethality issue and the stalker is known. Obviously, if your agency does not have a metro team, other detectives or officers will have to come into play. The primary concern, however, should always be victim safety.

One thing we look for when conducting these interviews is evidence of other unreported crimes such as burglary, assault, vandalism, etc. If the detective in charge can prove up these crimes and add them to his case, all the better. Another big question we teach investigators to ask is about any other stalking victims. Remember, many stalkers are serial in nature. In other words, they will stalk more than one individual in the course of their lifetime. Detectives need to ask the victim about other victims because stalkers will talk about other people they have stalked. They will not come out and say, "You know, I stalked Mary Jo," but they will talk about

Mary Jo. The stalker will say how she did him wrong or that he hounded her. In California and certain other states, evidence of prior bad acts can come into trial if the judge allows them. Also the statute of limitations may not have run out on the previous stalking, and the detective may be able to add that crime to his or her charging sheet.

For example, we worked a stalker that eventually ended up killing his spouse. Even though he had not stalked her prior to murdering her in her sleep, our investigation revealed another woman he had briefly been married to that he had stalked. He had followed her to various states over a period of years. This same investigation revealed he had kicked this woman in the stomach with hobnailed boots, telling her he was going to perform his own abortion on their unborn child. Even though this suspect had an extensive criminal history and did joint time (time in state prison), none of the crime reports ever talked about this woman. We found her by digging and digging and digging into this clown's background. Unfortunately that particular crime did not fit the murder statute when committed, but the woman's testimony at his current murder trial was heartrending and weighed heavily when it came to showing the true character of this individual.

As previously discussed, of all the stalking cases we investigated that led to formal prosecution (which were a lot), we only had one go to trial. The rest pled guilty to felony stalking and/or numerous other felonies prior to trial because we had built such a huge case against the stalker. My partner used to tell me the suspects would die of paper cuts from reading through their cases before they could walk from any of the charges. The only stalker that went to trial received twice the time the judge had offered him for a guilty plea. Remember, don't just make the stalking charge, but look for multiple felonies the stalker committed during the act of stalking, and file those charges along with that stalking charge.

The following is an excellent example of what happens when law enforcement officers are trained in both stalking and threat assessment. Late this year I received an extensive e-mail from a detective ("Brett"). Brett had obtained a copy of my first book and attended a training I conducted in his home state in the New England area. He related an incident where our training coupled with his good instincts saved a life. (You can train until you are blue in the face, but unless the cop has his or her stuff together, it doesn't do a great deal of good.)

Brett and his wife had been friends with his neighbor ("Denise") since 1995. Denise has two sons, ages thirteen and fifteen. The thirteen-year-old was Brett and his wife's "God son." During the time they lived across the street from each other, Denise obtained a divorce and later began dating again. After a period of time post-divorce, she began dating a male whom we will refer to as Tommy. Tommy and Denise dated for several months. The detective met and talked to Tommy on three or four occasions and found him to be personable. In the summer Denise and Tommy were talking about moving in with each other.

That all drastically changed in the last part of that month. Brett's wife got a call from Denise. Denise said she had broken up with Tommy. As their separation progressed, Tommy began showing up at Denise's home unannounced. According to Denise he began acting very strangely. Tommy was following, continually calling, and conducting other "pursuing" behaviors. He also took himself off the psychiatric medications he had been taking. Tommy began talking about possibly harming himself. Brett also found out that Tommy owned guns. (These are obviously red flags.) Denise confided in the detective that she was becoming very fearful of Tommy.

Brett told Denise that Tommy was a stalker. He said Denise needed to obtain a protective order and get their local police department involved. He also advised her that, in his experience and training, Tommy's stalking behavior was escalating. Denise told the detective she did not want a restraining order because it "would set him off." Brett advised his neighbor that was the very reason she needed to get the police involved.

Brett and his family had been vigilantly watching and checking on Denise. On July 3, Denise sent her children to visit relatives, and she was shopping at a local Walmart on the morning of the fourth. Brett got up (he was on light duty due to back surgery), and he received a call from his mother-in-law wanting the family get-together at their house earlier than planned. Brett decided not to follow his mother-in-law's request, and thank God he was the typical son-in-law. As he went to check something in his trunk, he saw Tommy's car pull up to Denise's house.

Tommy exited his car carrying two bags. Both appeared to be heavy. Tommy went around to the back of Denise's house and was not seen from again. Brett moved as fast as possible back into the house to notify the local PD. He feared the worst was about to take place.

While Brett was doing that, the detective's wife saw Denise was driving down the street toward her home. She immediately ran outside, stopped her, and told her to stay away from her home.

Brett also notified the police department where Tommy lived and asked to send units to his house to check on the welfare of his children from a previous marriage. Brett feared Tommy murdered them prior to coming to Denise's residence to commit a murder/suicide. (This is not an uncommon occurrence in these types of scenarios.)

In the meantime the locals had surrounded Denise's home and were attempting to establish a dialogue with Tommy. All of a sudden he began yelling out the front window that he only wanted to talk to the detective across the street. Brett immediately went outside to assist with his wife yelling something at him about putting on his bulletproof (or, in this day and age, bullet-resistant) vest. (This is the typical wife of a cop. She worries about his safety, but where was her vest when she ran into the middle of the street to stop a friend from going into the line of fire?)

SWAT arrived as the detective took a position where he could talk to Tommy. The detective said the nice and personable Tommy had dramatically changed to an angry, possessed individual. He told Brett, "You are going to take my last will and testament." When Tommy indicated he had several thousand dollars in the house for his son, Brett was relieved. At least Tommy had not killed his kid. Tommy then began a campaign of demanding Denise be brought to him. When the detective told him that wasn't going to happen, Tommy became more and more frustrated and enraged. Out of the blue, he asked Brett how his back was and if he had the surgery he was planning. Obviously this was a clear indication Tommy was truly having some mental issues.

Tommy told Brett that if anyone entered Denise's residence, he was going to "blow them away." (This was a good indication he was armed.) Throughout the approximate fifty-five-minute stand-off, a SWAT negotiator stood next to Brett and provided him with questions to ask, which was a great help. During the standoff other SWAT personnel evacuated his family and others from their residences. Brett remembers his kids giggling as they were pulled over fences by the adept SWAT cops because they had made a game of the evacuation process. (Leave it to cops to make it fun getting out of harm's way.) One of the SWAT supervisors later told the detective that his wife initially wouldn't leave without the macaroni salad she had just prepared. Obviously the salad stayed, and she left.

Throughout Brett and Tommy's conversations, Tommy never whimpered or cried. About three minutes before the end of the situation, Tommy began talking about shooting himself. Brett pleaded with Tommy not to pull the trigger, but a few seconds after Tommy disconnected the phone, Brett and SWAT heard the loud report of what they suspected and later verified was a self-inflicted, fatal gunshot wound to the head. When SWAT entered Denise's home, they found Tommy atop Denise's bed, dead with two loaded handguns next to him. Brett indicated that the stalking escalated to this fatal point in only six days.

Like we have said, stalking does not have to be a prolonged scenario. That is why law enforcement needs to identify it, classify it, and jump on it as soon as possible.

Folks, if Brett and his family had not recognized the telltale signs of stalking and reacted as they did, Denise would not be at home enjoying her two kids like she is today. In our minds, both Brett and his wife are heroes.

 Throughout many portions of this text we have used the words threat assessment. Threat assessing is becoming such an important tool in a variety of law enforcement pursuits and that is why its use needs to be drastically increased within the confines of not only ours but the nations of the world oftentimes volatile society. With horrific crimes like Virginia Tech, Columbine, the Colorado theater massacre, and most recently Newtown, many legislators immediately jump on the ban the gun or specific type gun band wagon. They tend to demonize the gun seller as well as the gun manufacturer as the cause of these senseless incidents. We can at times well understand their frustration; they feel they have to do something. In truth, it is the gun that is the *tool* that is used by the addled shooter, not the other way around. We have investigated and seen many multiple homicides that are accomplished via the use of knives, swords, bats, chemicals, explosives as well as a variety of other devices. We do agree that the gun is the weapon of choice in most of these terrible atrocities, but while the gun debate continues; there is another *tool* that needs to be discussed.

Whenever most of these criminal events are reviewed the ones tasked with finding the answers will oftentimes find that these perpetrators did not operate in a vacuum. One or more individuals either saw what the subject was doing to prepare for his or her strike, or at the very least had some knowledge about what the individual was about to do via conversations, letters, the Internet or some other form of communication. Yet, most of these persons made no attempt to contact law enforcement with their concerns. When interviewed they indicated they didn't want to get the subject in trouble, or they didn't think the cops would do anything, or they didn't want to be looked at a rat or as some type of tattletale. Also keep in mind some of these or the actors (perpetrators) to come may have not of had any formal contact with a mental health professional, or if they did it was not in a format that allowed that mental health provider an avenue to report such contact.

<u>In our opinion this type of outlook has to stop</u>. The public must be encouraged to come forward when they see Johnny making bombs in his bathroom, or collecting a weapons cache legal or otherwise, or declaring his fervor in eliminating a specific target. The other side of this equation is that law enforcement needs to be open to getting concerned citizens coming forward, and not castigate the messenger whether or not the information proves to be valid or flawed. Once advised of a specific situation, law enforcement needs to seriously evaluate the issue before coming to a rational conclusion. They must then become a more *proactive*, not just a reactive force. Even if no criminal act is yet to take place, they may have tools at their disposal to short circuit this troubled individual's plan of attack. At the very least placing these people on their radar is essential. We would continually do this concerning stalkers or others that had been brought to our attention. Therefore, openness and better training when it comes to <u>threat assessing</u> is crucial in this day and age, if we, both the public and the police, are to start identifying and eliminating these societal threats before they go postal. Remember, this openness is what we stress in our workplace violence training. Well, folks, I am here to tell you that it does

and will work if everybody takes on the challenge. So don't ignore, but explore (obviously keeping yourself out of harm's way) when it comes to a possible encountered threat, and then report it to the proper authorities.

One might ask can you be more specific. We will try. Example: A citizen comes to the police department. He or she says Tim is acting kind of suspicious; he seems obsessed with this or that. Instead of the desk officer telling the person reporting this behavior that it doesn't sound like Tim has a committed a crime and he can't do anything until that happens; the officer takes an information report that documents the contact. That report is then directed back to the area of the police department no matter how small that has someone trained in threat assessment. That individual puts Tim into a specific file, or perhaps this initial contact raises some questions the officer/detective might have which causes him to start gathering more information on Tim. Maybe Tim's name never comes up again, great. However, if another citizen contacts the police about Tim or a police officer runs across Tim and a contact report is filed it once again goes into Tim's file. Then say information comes to the officer or team tasked with threat assessment that good old Timmy is now acting even stranger, buying guns, or maybe materials that could make an explosive device, fertilizer, gun powder, or is reportedly continually going to specific websites that might cause concern, it is probably time to visit with Tim a bit, and see what is going on; thus hopefully eliminating a threat. So if no one ever comes forward, and the police never develop information, Tim and people like him are free to create havoc. *Yes, I will get off my soapbox now and move on.*

Examples of Threat Assessment Evaluations

Here are two examples of threat assessment evaluations from cases submitted to me from this by a police department we will refer to as the "Wonderland Police Department." Even though we retired from the ranks of the

Westminster Police Department, we still evaluate cases they submit to us. We also evaluate cases from other police departments, such as the disguised "Wonderland PD." Having these cases submitted to us works out for the department because they get the case profiled, and we still enjoy conducting evaluations. We chose the following examples because we felt they were interesting. Of course, the names, dates, and locations have been changed to protect those involved.

This first case involves a stalker who we believe has a mental condition referred to as an Erotomanic type delusional disorder. This disorder involves the person believing the individual he or she is pursuing is in love with him/her. Dr. Michael Zona coined this type of stalker as an Erotomanic stalker. In this case, the stalker has never dated the female victim. He met her through contact with her brothers and was arrested on several occasions for his continual stalking behaviors.

Stalking chronology concerning one Jimmy Vu, 00-00-00. (We developed the chronology by obtaining the officer's reports.)

Target (victim): Tina Jon, 00-00-00

1. On 08-21 at approx. 2146 hrs., Jimmy is contacted by Wonderland Police Department Officer J. Lee. Lee is called by Tina to her residence because Jimmy will not take no for an answer. When Vu advises tells Jimmy that Tina does not want anything to do with him, Officer Lee walks him up to the front door of the residence so Tina can tell him the same thing. He says he now understands and leaves. (Please note, at the time of this incident, Jimmy has been friends with Tina's twin brothers, Larry and Mark Jon, for several years. That is how Jimmy encountered Tina. Since the second incident with Jimmy, the brothers severed the relationship with Jimmy.) An incident report, Dr# 08-0000, was taken.

2. On 08-26 at approx. 2323 hrs., WPD Officer J. Lee is patrolling the area of Tina's residence in a marked unit and in uniform. Lee sees a subject lurking around the garage area of Tina's residence. He is wearing a gray hoodie sweatshirt with the hood over his head, Levi's, and tennis shoes. When Officer Lee confronts the subject, he identifies him as Jimmy, who later admits to being there to see Tina. Jimmy had been drinking (HBD) at the time of contact. Lee contacts Tina and learns the following stalking behavior. On Sunday 08-24- at about 1100 hrs., Jimmy shows up at Tina's church, the Vietnamese church near Saratoga and Jefferson Streets in "How Are You City" and attempts to contact Tina, who again tells Jimmy she does not want to see him and drives away. On Monday 08-25- at approx. 0845 hrs., Tina leaves her home to go to work, at which time she is again confronted by Jimmy. He was parked in front of her residence waiting for her. He pleads, "Hear me out!" Tina ignores him and drives to work. On Tuesday 08-26 at approx. 1015 hrs., Tina is at school near the math building of "Many Thanks College" when she is once again confronted by Jimmy. Mia yells at him to stay away, causing attention to be drawn to Jimmy. Jimmy is later contacted by campus police and told to stay off campus. Obviously Jimmy is not enrolled there. Officer Lee advises Tina to change her home number because of Jimmy's continual calling. She tells the officer she did so early Tuesday 08-26, and she felt that was why Jimmy had showed up to the house.* Tina also tells Officer Lee that Jimmy's continuing harassment is causing her to become very fearful. (This is the first statement of fear and emotional distress.) Officer Lee requests Tina place Jimmy under citizen's arrest for 647 (H) CPC, which they did. Jimmy is arrested and

---

* Remember what we said about having the victim change her phone number prior to the detective in charge getting the case? The fact the stalker had no way of contacting the victim caused him to change his approach. We are not criticizing the officer. We are just pointing out what can happen.

Mirandized. He admits to contacting Tina on the above listed dates and times. **He also said, due to his arrest, he felt Tina would not want anything to do with him, and he would cease and desist**. WPD DR# 08-0000.

3. On 08-30 at approx. 2245 hrs., Tina arrives home from the movies with her boyfriend, one Josh Doe, age twenty-nine. As Tina approaches her front door, she sees Jimmy there. He is pacing back and forth and ringing the doorbell. Tina immediately runs back to Josh's car and gets in. As soon as she gets into his car, Jeremy calls the police and then begins yelling at Jimmy out of his window. Jimmy runs over to Josh's car and begins banging on the window. (It is unknown if he bangs on the passenger side window where Tina is.) While in Josh's car, Tina calls her father, who tells her Jimmy has been outside their residence for the past thirty minutes, walking around and ringing their doorbell at least six times. Tina tells WPD Officer J. Bent of her previous trouble with Jimmy and says she wants him arrested. She is fearful and tells Bent that, due to Jimmy's continuing harassment, she has started carrying Mace, has chained and padlocked the front gate of her residence, and is going to remove the doorbell. Tina also tells the officer she started a journal of everything Jimmy has done to her. This is the second expression of increasing fear and emotional distress by Tina to law enforcement. Jimmy is arrested and transported. He refused to make a statement. Refer to DR#08-0000. I could not tell from the police report what clothing Jimmy was wearing at the time of his arrest.

4. On 09-03 at approx. 1559 hrs., Jimmy once again came to Tina's residence in an attempt to contact her. He rang the doorbell near their gate and was observed by Tina's mother, who told Jimmy Tina was not there and to go away. (At that time Tina was upstairs calling the police.) Jimmy refused

to leave, stating he didn't believe Tina's mother and was going to jump the fence into their backyard to see Tina. When the police arrived, Jimmy said he believed Tina was in love with him. He could not articulate how he came to this conclusion. He just knew it. Jimmy indicated he just needed some time with Tina to convince her of her feelings. He also felt he should be exempt from arrest because of his feelings for Tina. (Jimmy is what we refer to as an erotomanic stalker. Jimmy believes Tina is in love with him. Dr. Michael Zona, forensic psychiatrist, first coined this stalker typology. Zona says this kind of stalker delusionally believes the victim is in love with his or her stalker.) WPD Officer W. Surfer also saw Tina's diary, which logged Jimmy's stalking behavior. Officer Surfer also noted in his report the other WPD contacts, which included his previous arrests for trespassing/prowling. Officer Surfer also indicated that when he talked to Tina, she was visibly upset and stressed by Jimmy being there. She was crying. (This is the third statement and expression of fear and emotional distress.) Jimmy was taken into custody for misdemeanor stalking, 646.9(A) PC, and transported to WPD. He made no statement after being Mirandized. He was served with an EPO and indicated to Officer Surfer that he would not abide by the restrictions outlined by the EPO. Concerned, Officer Surfer requested a bail enhancement. Refer to WPD DR# 08-0000.

5. On 03-18 at approx. 2248 hrs., both Tina and her brother, Larry, (whose bedrooms are on the second story of their residence) hear what sounds like footsteps directly under Tina's bedroom window. Initially when they look out they do not see anything, but when Larry moves to another location, he is able to see Jimmy, standing on the ledge of the residence's outer wall. Larry calls to Jimmy, who acknowledges him. He tells Jimmy to leave before he calls the police. Larry then exists his house to find Jimmy's unoccupied

vehicle parked close-by. WPD Officer P. Proof responds and takes DR# 09-0000 for violation of a restraining order, PC 166 (a) (4). (It is unknown why a DR. for felony stalking was not filed.)

6. On 03-19 at approx. 1539 hrs., Jimmy again showed up at Tina's (now being referred to as Jane Doe). She ran back into her house and called police while Jeremy, one of her brothers, confronted Jimmy in front of their residence. When Officer A. Tonner (handling officer) and Senior Patrol Officer M. Ingersol arrived, they contacted Jimmy, and his statements were recorded via Officer Tonner's belt tape recorder. Jimmy told Tonner he knew he wasn't supposed to be there. Jimmy admitted he had an active restraining order against him. The officer found Tina was again very upset and had been crying. Tonner arrested Jimmy initially for violation of the restraining order and transported him to WPD. Under Miranda, he confessed to being at Tina's residence the night before and throwing rocks at her bedroom window to get her attention. When he heard Jeremy's voice, he became afraid and fled. Jimmy indicated Jeremy didn't understand the concept of flirting, and Jimmy felt it was OK to continue pursuing Tina. He also admitted pleading guilty to misdemeanor stalking and having a restraining order in place. With that information, Tonner added the charges of felony stalking and booked him into OCJ (Orange County Jail). Refer to DR#09-0000.

7. On 04-11 at approx. 00:00 hrs., Wonderland Police again were called to Tina's residence. She was in her bedroom alone when she heard someone (she believed Jimmy) whispering her first name through her bedroom window. When she looked at the window, the shade was still down, but the window was open about two inches. She did not remember it being that way. She was also concerned because Jimmy had climbed onto her roof before and attempted to get her

attention via the window. At the time of the incident, prior to or after, no one saw Jimmy. WPD Officer N. Levi was the handling officer. When he contacted Tina, she was visibly upset. She told Officer Levi when she heard the voice calling from her window, she was "freaked out," and her heart was "pounding." Tina also told him she hoped she wouldn't "end up dead." Officer Levi had recently been in trial on another case, which happened to be in the same courtroom where Jimmy was being sentenced for his last stalking conviction. The judge sentenced him to wear a GPS ankle bracelet and was served with a ten-year stalking restraining order. Levi drove to Jimmy's home in a neighboring city, talked to him briefly, and then arrested him for violation of a restraining order and stalking with a prior conviction. Officer Levi interviewed Jimmy after he was Mirandized. Jimmy told Levi he thought he was bipolar. None of the facts presented to us indicate Jimmy has been diagnosed with that type of condition. Jimmy then said he was trying to forget about Mia, and one of the ways he was doing that was by going clubbing and trying to date other women. He advised Officer Levi he had never dated Tina, and she never indicated interest in him. From the police report, we could not tell if Jimmy was supposed to be or had been issued a GPS ankle bracelet at the time of this incident. Refer to DR#09-0000 by reviewing WPD Officer A. Tonner's DR #09-0000. Tonner's report answered our question about Jimmy's ankle GPS device. According to Jimmy he did not have an appointment to get one until 05-07-.

8. On 05-01 at approx. 0712 hrs., WPD Officers A. Tonner and O. Ayers responded to Tina's residence on a call of Jimmy again being there. When they arrived, they saw Jimmy standing in the back side patio area of the Tina's residence. He had been looking for Tina, who, according to the family, was so traumatized she had to move out of their residence. Officer Tonner confronted Jimmy, who freely admitted he

was not supposed to be there. He wanted to be forgiven and given a second chance. The family member said Jimmy had also sent Tina an e-mail, which had been turned over to a victim/witness counselor. He then told officers he would not come over to the house any more once his GPS device was installed. It would cause him to remember what his terms of probation were. Jimmy was once again arrested. He waived his Miranda rights and told Tonner he had no idea why he was once again at Tina's residence. He didn't have a clue why he kept violating all the orders he had been served with. Shortly before Jimmy was transported to OCJ, Tonner received a phone call from Larry, Tina's brother. Larry told him a dozen roses had been sent to Tina on 05-01. The flowers had been sent by Jimmy. Jimmy was confronted about the flowers and said he didn't know anything about "roses" being sent. Tonner hadn't told Jimmy the flowers were roses. Officer Tonner then found a receipt in Jimmy's property indicating he had sent Tina flowers on 04-11, the same day he reportedly was outside her window. A probation hold was placed on Jimmy, and he was transported to jail. Officer Tonner told probation of the flower incident, which was also a violation of the restraining order and probation.

Before we get into our threat assessment of this case, notice that even though the suspect was contacted by a different patrol officer just about every time, those officers were up to speed on stalking and what this particular suspect had been up to. Why? They had all been trained in how to deal with stalkers, and they communicated with each other. We would like to see all law enforcement groups be able to do this. Victims are so much better served when those two things take place. To the members of this agency (including the newbies who will contact me with questions on a case or for additional training), we are pretty proud of what you do. (That would be to members of the Westminster Police Department and members of "Wonderland PD.")

GENERAL THREAT ASSESSMENT AND SUGGESTIONS

On 11-07 we were contacted by Wonderland Police Department Detective Terry Starko. He requested we review several crime reports concerning one Jimmy Vu, whom the police department had arrested for a series of stalking incidents. He was concerned for the victim's safety and wanted our opinion concerning these incidents. We agreed to look over the cases and give a brief opinion concerning these issues. See attached résumé for our expertise. (Because this is an example used in the book, our résumé is not given. However, whenever we submit a threat assessment for a particular police agency, our résumé is attached as a matter of course. This way whoever reviews the assessment can see our expertise.)

Opinion

It is my opinion that Jimmy Vu, for whatever reason, believes the victim, Tina (currently listed in DR#09-0000, 09-0000, and 09-0000, which for the purposes of this book are not actual crime report numbers), is truly in love or infatuated with him. Even though he has been incarcerated numerous times due to this belief, he still does not feel the orders of protection apply to him because of this belief system. He will more than likely feel the same way about being placed on formal probation. Even though Jimmy knows what he is doing is a violation of the law, he doesn't really seem to care. He claims he wants to forget the victim and date other females, but in all actuality, he cannot. It is my opinion he will continue with his stalking behavior. I have not interviewed the victim, so I do not know exactly what initiated his pursuit of the victim. He has been friends with her brothers for some time, and he had access to the victim's residence and, if Tina resided there, the victim herself. From reviewing the crime reports, they do not indicate previous problems or dating inquiries being made upon the victim by Jimmy until the last year or so.

Lethality Issues

The victim is obviously very traumatized. It even reached the point she left her residence, whether temporary or not. She indicated she was afraid of being killed by Jimmy. Tina has definitely exhibited fear and emotional trauma on several occasions. From what I have read, there does not seem to be any direct threat of violence directed toward Tina or her family members at this time. I must always caution, however, not all stalkers exhibit violent behavior. Also not all stalkers make, utter, or project a direct threat. That is why stalking is considered a course of conduct crime where only a credible threat is necessary. Any type of repeated and unwanted harassment can turn violent if the right set of circumstances are in place. I have been advised that Jimmy may use drugs. It's unknown what type, but depending on the quantity and type of drug (methamphetamine, etc.), this can be a catalyst for acts of violence.

Jimmy talked about being bipolar. The reports show no indication he has been diagnosed with this type of disorder. From what I have seen in those diagnosed with the disorder, it causes various stages of depression followed by some type of manic episodes.

The type of stalking behavior exhibited by Jimmy is that of an Erotomanic stalker. This is a typology developed by Dr. Michael A. Zona, a forensic psychiatrist. In *The Psychology of Stalking: Clinical and Forensic Perspectives*, Zona describes this type of stalker as one who believes he or she is loved by the victim. (Jimmy tells law enforcement Tina is in love with him. He can't explain why, but she is.) **My concern is suicide.** We have seen these types of stalkers kill themselves or commit murder/suicide, taking their targets with them. I do not have enough information about Jimmy to judge his proclivity in this area.

Oftentimes these types of stalkers tell us they just need enough time with the victim to show them that they are in love with them (the stalker) (thus the continual pursuit). From the statements the Wonderland officers gathered, Jimmy expressed these sentiments as well.

Suggestions

I would suggest, especially with the recent e-mail or e-mails being sent, that a probation search be conducted (depending on whether search and seizure (S&S) is attached) on Jimmy's computer and any other digital devices able to transmit e-mails. I would also strongly request a search be conducted of Jimmy's car and residence. The searcher should look for any photos of the victim, her residence, vehicle, siblings, or significant others or recordings, digital or written, that contain information concerning the victim. It has been my experience that oftentimes stalkers will log about their targets (victims). They will also collect other data or personal items belonging to the victims. (Please note, if items are found during the search that can be shown to have been removed from Tina's residence without her or any of her brother's permission, an additional felony charge of 496 CPC, possession of stolen property, can be charged. At the very least, residential burglary, 459 CPC, can be charged as well.)

I would talk to Jimmy's parents and siblings to ascertain if he has ever attempted suicide, talked about it, and/or discussed taking the victim with him if he cannot get what he wants from her.

I would have the department's mental health coordinator check to see if Jimmy has sought any mental health care. If so, see what information can be gleaned concerning these contacts.

I would suggest following the stalking protocol and fingerprinting and photographing the victim and the vehicle(s) she drives. This is on the remote chance Jimmy decides to develop an abduction strategy.

I would notify her place of business and supply them with a photo of both him and the vehicle he drives. If they see the individual, they can notify law enforcement.

After we wrote this evaluation and submitted it to the detective in charge, we contacted the department's mental health coordinator, who informed us Jimmy had been seeking mental health assistance for quite some time. After his contact with Jimmy and reviewing my evaluation, he was also quite concerned about the possibility of suicidal ideations.

Concerning this case, we were recently contacted by a producer, who we have worked with, on another stalking special for national television. (We were a consultant for the first special.) She said that one of the people we had suggested she contact for her latest project, Tina, had called her. The victim was extremely upset because the suspect ("Jimmy") had been writing her letters from prison, and he was slated to get out of custody soon.

We notified the detective in charge of Tina's case, who said they were already on it. Due to the diligent work of the detectives, good old Jimmy was again arrested as he was released from prison. He was charged with another felony stalking charge and placed back into custody for, we hope, a few more years. In California and many other states, you can be prosecuted for conducting a campaign of stalking while sitting behind bars. (Check the stalking resource center to ascertain if your state also has that legislation in place. If not we suggest contacting your legislators to get that added to your state's stalking section.)

We were also asked to conduct a threat assessment evaluation on this second stalking suspect. He was a domestic violence stalker who had been stalking and harassing his estranged wife for a long time. (Due to the violent nature of this case, we have purposely disguised the true names and the police agency that handled it.) This was one of those exacerbated cases that unfortunately involved children. We had been made aware of this particular stalker's behaviors for a long time by detectives involved in the case, and we felt an attachment for this poor victim and her children. It should be noted that as we have discussed in other chapters of this book sStalkers will oftentimes go to great lengths to pursue their victims. In this case, the stalker travelled to London to track her down. Once my evaluation was submitted to the case detective and added to his charging package, both to my disbelief and his, the suspect was not initially filed on by the district attorney. We both felt this was due to budgetary cuts and, in my estimation, lack of training. The case was submitted to a district attorney, who was charged with filing and taking care of six large cities' domestic violence/stalking cases in the western portion of Orange County. One prosecutor assigned to evaluate all those cases would be a daunting task in the best of conditions. The situation did not bode well for our victim or other victims, who could fall through the cracks of such an understaffed system.

Threat Assessment of Jane Doe
Wonderland PD Case # 00-00000

Information reviewed for this assessment: The information I had concerning this stalking and domestic violence case was a seventeen-page crime report, #1-----0, written by Wonderland Police Officer S. Tooth, and a follow-up report written by Detective Kevin Investigator, who at the time was assigned to the domestic violence unit of this department. He is currently working robbery/homicide. His investigative report included transcribed phone messages left on Jane Doe's answering machine over a period of days. The suspect in this case was one Loser, Big Bad. Officer Tooth's report also contained copies of Jane Doe's handwritten diary. I was told Loser had a violent criminal history, which included state prison time. He was possibly a three-strike candidate. I was also told Detective Investigator had recently arrested Loser on a warrant stemming from misdemeanor spousal abuse. This took place in front of Loser's young children (two boys and a girl) in a neighboring city on 06-21. At the time of this evaluation, Loser was still in custody in Orange County Jail and was serving time on that charge. I would have preferred to have interviewed Jane Doe prior to writing this assessment, but I was told she had already suffered a great deal of mental trauma from the long-term abuse by her estranged husband, Loser. Her counselors felt that reviewing these events could precipitate another mental breakdown. Not wanting to cause Jane Doe any further anguish, I conducted the evaluation with the information I had.

If I had interviewed Jane Doe, I would have asked the following questions:

- When Loser went to London in pursuit of her, how did he get there? Were her parents available for interview? Was there any witness that could corroborate her statements about the death threat(s) Loser left on her phone while in London?

- In regard to the numerous assaults, who could detectives contact to verify these incidents? Did she ever seek medical attention for these injuries? If so, where could detectives obtain copies of the attending physician's medical reports, which could contain Polaroid's, digital photos, X-rays, MRI disc, etc.?

- Who were the people who took care of her children in day care? Could they be interviewed about how the children acted when contact with their father (Loser) was imminent (i.e., cowering under tables and desks, not wanting to see Loser, etc.)?

- Could she supply the names of individuals, primarily women, that Loser was known to frequent with? Could she also supply the names of Loser's mother and father? Could detectives interview them for background and details about his behavior? Did she know if Loser was the victim of abuse while growing up?

- Did Loser use or keep pornographic material in the house? If so, what kind was it (heterosexual, bondage, rape, etc.)?

If he went on porn-oriented websites, does she know which ones?

- Could she supply any names of her coworkers that could attest to Loser's incessant calling, comments he made, and/or any comments she made right after she received a call from him?

- Once she received sole custody of her children and got a new apartment in her name (only in July of 20--), did she have knowledge of Loser ever entering the apartment without her consent? (The primary reason for this question is that Loser is and was stalking Jane Doe. If he entered the apartment for the purpose of stalking, it can be charged as residential burglary.)

- Finally were there any individuals in the apartment complex who were friendly with Loser that could have information about his behavior or his access to the weapons described by his children (especially the semiautomatic handgun that he allegedly placed against their heads and dry fired)?

Note: I was contacted by seasoned Wonderland detectives and those involved with the current care of Jane Doe and her children about this case. They felt there were definite lethality issues attached to the case, and they wanted my assistance with a threat assessment. Because I am not only a criminal consultant (I am also a victim advocate), I have conducted this assessment at no cost to any involved parties. For more information on my background and expertise, go to www.DetectiveMikeProctor.com, or see my attached résumé.

Special Note: This evaluation is written under the assumption that Jane Doe is telling the truth.

(This is something we regularly put in our evaluations, especially when we haven't personally interviewed the victim in question.)

Conclusion:

The following are my opinions on this case:

- Loser is a danger to his wife, Jane Doe, and their three young children. The two male children, the oldest being nine years, are especially at risk.

- I believe that, given the opportunity, Loser will most definitely cause additional physical and mental trauma to Jane Doe and her children. He is quite capable of killing them and has indicated by his statements that he may be willing to commit murder/suicide. He has also indicated that he believes the police are out to get him. Having talked about and expressed suicidal ideations increases his lethality factor for the victim and any law enforcement entity he comes in contact with. Police officers that are not familiar with him are particularly at risk. His continued substance abuse will act as a catalyst to greater violence. Not able to hold down a job, he appears to be living on the streets (at least from time to time). He is probably using drugs (his drug of choice is reported as methamphetamine), and he presents a diminished appearance, which indicates lack of continual hygiene. All these are signs that his overall mental and physical conditions are deteriorating. This makes him potentially more unstable.

- Loser will continue to stalk Jane Doe.

- His behavior and the telephone messages Detective Investigator transcribed indicate that, as a child, he regularly observed his father abuse his mother. This tends to leave a very negative imprint on a child. Loser appears to be acting out just as his father did. It also appears that his mother was very protective of him and may still be enabling Loser. (Without conducting further interviews, I cannot verify this information.)

- Another problem that seems to be present is the fact that even though Loser is an abuser, he has grown accustom to Jane

Doe taking care of him and his needs. Loser also appears to view Jane Doe as his property.

These are just some of the reasons he will continue to pursue/stalk Jane Doe.

Facts in support of my conclusions:

Officer Tooth's report contains a great deal of information and is event-chronicled. Therefore, I am not going through a step-by-step stalking chronology. Rather, I will discuss certain events that key into my conclusion.

- Jane Doe and Loser began dating in January of 19__. (Officer Tooth's report does not express under what circumstances they met. This might be helpful.) Their oldest boy was born in July of 19__. (According to Officer Tooth's crime report, Loser and Jane Doe were married in May of 19__.) As of 19__, they began living together in an apartment in the Valley, and that was when the abuse started. The abuse began verbally and then led to Loser striking Jane Doe in the head. He hit her hard enough to flatten her head against whatever objects she was standing next to in the apartment. At one point he threw Jane Doe to the floor of the apartment and placed the heel of his boot on her throat. He pushed down with so much force he began choking her. (This type of behavior is very common in domestic violence abuse cases, and it can easily lead to the death of the victim. This and similar actions are often viewed as "control tactics.") During this time and throughout most of Loser's continual reign of abuse, Jane Doe was passive because that was the way she was trained. (Jane Doe indicated in her diary entries that she was a good Muslim woman. As such, she was supposed to do what her husband told her to do and not question him. In an abuse situation, this is obviously not a positive quality, and in her case, it seemed to prolong her agony.) During the course of this early abuse, Loser was away from home for days at a time without communicating with Jane Doe. He left no support (no money or food) for her and their infant.

- During their early years together, Loser, Jane Doe, and their child moved to West Orange County. There they had another boy.

- Loser had a violent criminal history, which included state prison time. If that is the case, there is a good likelihood his forcible rape and sodomy of Jane Doe on 01-18-2___ was another show of power and control. We have found that rape, especially sodomy, is all about employing power and control. This is true if the abuser is a stalker or not. It is also used to degrade and debase the victim. Jane Doe said that while Loser was sodomizing her, he told her, "You are nothing to me but a blow-up doll." (This adds to his outlook of her as his property and only there to satisfy him.) As a note to the reader, whenever Loser was sexually assaulting his battered wife, he would make terrible, demeaning comments about her looks and what she was there to do for him. Even though those comments were listed in the actual submitted threat assessment, we see no reason to present them here. Loser may have either been the victim or perpetrator of sodomy during his time in prison. At the very least, he may have seen it used to control and degrade other inmates. Up to that time, Jane Doe complained that Loser just seemed to use her as a tool for his sexual gratification with no concern for hers. She also indicated he was probably out with other women, whom he said satisfied him more than she did.

- When the abuse and abandonment got worse, Jane Doe and her children moved to London in January of 20__ to be with her parents. She told Loser she no longer wanted anything to do with him. Loser, who supposedly did not know the parent's address, pursued Jane Doe to London. In the summer of 20__, she received a phone call from Loser. The caller ID indicated the call was coming from a London phone. Loser said something to the effect of if he finds her, he will kill her and take the children. In June of 20__, there is "reconciliation," and she moves

Stateside with Loser to the city of Wonderland. (We would like to have asked Jane Doe more about this supposed reconciliation. It has been our experience that threats, at least implied ones, are part and parcel of these agreements. (Due to the lack of both law enforcement and domestic violence intervention and counseling, it seemed Jane Doe could not be directed away from her apparent lingering attachment issues to Loser. Without any kind of intervention, this is a common occurrence.)

- While in Wonderland they had their third child together. This time it was a girl. Jane Doe said that from November of 20__ until August of 20__, Loser continued to degrade, abuse, and assault her. (Adding a female child into this abusive mix is a potential red flag to us, as there is the ever-present threat of sexual abuse from Loser.) Many of these attacks took place in front of their children. On more than one occasion, the older boy attempted to come to her aid but would be kicked and punched by Loser. On another occasion the younger boy reported that Loser put both his hands around his neck and began choking him. The youth told Jane Doe that Loser had hurt him, and he thought he was going to die. (Once again, Loser exhibited choking behavior. It is unknown if this learned behavior is from watching his father do this to his mother, or if it happened to him at a young age.) Loser also allegedly pointed a gun (described as a semiautomatic) at both boys' heads and pulled the trigger, terrifying the boys. (Officer Tooth interviewed the boys separately and on tape. A senior social worker also interviewed them separately at a different location. In each instance the boys did not appear to deviate from their stories or their implicit fear of their father. Both indicated that they felt their mother could no longer protect them from him.)

- Jane Doe indicated that sometime between November of 20__ and January of 20__, Loser went into a rage and once again began banging her head into the wall. She was passive in the hopes he would cool down. About thirty minutes went past, and he again confronted her in the kitchen of the apartment. He had a heavy electric clothing iron, and he was about seven feet from her when he threw it at her head. She moved, and it missed her. (This constitutes assault with a deadly weapon under 245 (a) (1) CPC.) He then ran after her with a pair of steel machine hair clippers. Once he caught her, he began to strike her with the clippers on the left temple of her head for about five times, which caused slight bleeding and swelling on the left side of her head. She logged the incident in her journal. (This act could fall under the statute for torture, 206 CPC, because Loser's intent seemed to be to cause cruel or extreme pain.)

- After being assaulted in a neighboring city in front of her place of work on 06-__, Jane Doe finally severed her relationship with Loser and moved into an apartment located in Wonderland. Once that took place, Jane Doe reported that Loser started following her and telling her he had been observing her and the children. He called her numerous times to harass her and threaten to kill her. (It is unknown if any of those particular calls were tape-recorded.) Loser also told her he was a two-strike felon and to stop contacting the police. He said if she called the police when he came around, he would kill her and the kids before the police ever got to the apartment. It was during this time period he told Jane Doe about wanting to commit suicide. *"I cannot go to jail again,"* Loser said on *a phone message. "I will just kill myself."* He also said he had nothing to lose. He said if the police tried to contact him, he couldn't predict the outcome of that encounter.

- In support of my belief that Loser's father abused his mother, Loser left this phone message, "I had to tell my dad the other day that I hate him for living his life. And all the things I saw him do, maybe I took it maybe I took it as that is what women are supposed to put with because my mama put up with for so many years." Maybe I thought it was love that kept a woman around after a man hit her. I never meant to put no hands on you." Loser also admitted to striking Jane Doe in other messages he left.

Suggestions:

- Conduct further interviews of potential witnesses to corroborate Jane Doe's story in the hopes of filing stalking, assault with a deadly weapon, and perhaps torture charges.

- Approach the district attorney for a child abuse filing on Loser. List his children, especially the two boys, as victims. Have the children run through Child Abuse Services Team (CAST) to see if statements can be verified and charges filed.

- Conduct a victim profile. Obtain photos and prints of Jane Doe and all her children. This includes full vertical photos. Photograph the car she drives. Include the license plate in the photo. Document any marks, scars, or tattoos. Find out who has the latest dental records on her and her children. (Contact the detective's secretary so he or she can direct whichever detective is still involved in this case to the location of the stalking victim sheet in the Wonderland police computer.) This profile should be kept on file in the event something happens to Jane Doe or one of her family members. If abduction does take place, Wonderland detectives can then put out a detailed bulletin to those involved in the search.

- At the very least, (we would request prison time and additional felony charges) but if not push for formal probation with search and seizure. I strongly suggest Loser be placed with the Orange County probation officers assigned to high-risk domestic violence offenders. (I have personally trained many of these officers.) Loser should have a GPS ankle device attached.

- If Loser violates again, which he probably will, felony stalking charges should be sought. This will constitute his third strike.

Note: Two years after this evaluation was generated, we received word that Loser had committed rape and felony assault on another woman and was being prosecuted. The new prosecutor assigned to the case reviewed all the police department's crime reports, including our evaluation. The prosecutor decided to charge Loser with all additional charges as well. Hopefully upon conviction, Loser will go to the joint for three strikes, which is twenty-five to life. Like they say, the wheels of justice turn slowly but grind exceedingly fine. One can only hope Loser gets a very caring roommate.

The Basic Protocol (Continued)

Develop a victim data sheet. Once the lead detective on the case feels a stalking is taking place, and he or she has conducted a threat assessment interview, the detective should then process the victim. The first step is photographing the victim. (These photos should be of the

Identification technician obtaining both the victim and her child's digital fingerprints.

face and any marks, scars, or tattoos the victim may have. There should also be full up and down photos, or full torso shots.) Fingerprint the victim, and document in writing any marks, scars, or tattoos. If the victim has children, they will also be photographed and fingerprinted. The victim data sheet the detective will fill out has driver's license information, vehicle description(s), and license number(s). These descriptions will contain things like dents or any kind of customization. Those cars will also be photographed. We do this to have a current and accurate record of the victim in case anyone turns up missing. If this does occur, the police can put out an exact photo of the victim and the car he or she normally drives. This way, it's not an aged or old photo, and it's not just a photo of a car that looks similar to the victim's. We have never had a victim complain about this procedure, and in many cases, victims have thanked the detective(s) for taking the time to do it. (For an example of a victim catalogue sheet, go to the appendix section of this book.) With the advent of DNA testing, we have been suggesting that departments also obtain DNA samples. (How this sample is stored and in what database should be checked into prior.)

As we have indicated prior, another thing we have just started advising law enforcement to do in cases with a high degree of lethality is have a CSI team go out to the victim's residence and complete a diagram of the inside. If they feel photographing the inside would be beneficial, then so be it. Why do we do this? Because if SWAT, a metro team, or any other law enforcement entity needs to do a breech into the victim's residence during a hostage situation (which takes place more than we would like), then they have a much better idea of what to expect when they gain entry into the victim's residence.

Get a victim advocate involved. Once we determine that a stalking is taking place, the next step is to assign one of the department's victim advocates to the victim. The victim advocate is tasked with gathering the necessary paperwork for the victim to obtain a restraining order (if the lead detective feels this is the right move).

Victim advocate and a metro detective T. Richards, now Sgt. processing the victim's paperwork.

If an arrest is imminent, we might wait on the restraining order until the suspect is arraigned. In that case, the district attorney would have the judge issue a criminal stay away order against the stalker. If the detective gave the OK for a restraining order to be issued, the victim advocate would help the victim do his or her paperwork and go with the victim to the issuing court. The advocate walks the victim through the entire process. At no time is a victim merely told to go get a restraining order. That is a huge undertaking for a victim who is already under a great deal of pressure. If a restraining order is obtained, either the handling detective or the department's metro team should serve the order to the stalker. This is done so the stalker knows the police are actively involved in the investigation.

If required, the victim advocate can also get housing or other things for the victim and family. The advocate then follows the victim throughout all court appearances, sitting with and comforting him/her. The advocate can even take the victim to the appearances if necessary. (As an aside, my wife, an avid quilter, used to make blankets for those children coming into the department with abuse or stalking issues. This type of caring gesture tends to comfort the child, but it also helps the detective or social worker tasked with conducting a first interview with that child.)

Secure a social worker. The detective can contact the Orange County social worker assigned to the unit if he or she feels the victim needs assistance. The detective can also request, in the case of children, that the social worker conduct a separate and impartial interview with the victim and her children. This ascertains if abuse or other potential criminal charges can be pursued against the stalker.

Keep in touch with your victim. Some threat management units have specific times they must contact their victims. For example, the detective in charge is advised to contact the victim at least once every seven days. It has been our experience, however, that once you start pursuing a case against the victim's stalker, the victims will keep in touch with you at least once a day or even more. We used to get pages from victims two to three years after their cases were adjudicated because the stalker had made contact again, or they believed he or she was once again attempting contact.

Obtain a review by the department's mental health coordinator. If the police department has a mental health coordinator like the FPU or the LAPD's Threat Management Unit (TMU) does, run the threat assessment by the coordinator to see what insight he or she can provide. We strongly suggest to those we train that they make sure the coordinator has some training in stalking prior to utilizing them. In an article we wrote for the *Journal of California Law Enforcement*,[107] we discussed the multidisciplinary approach, and we explained that even if the department is small with limited resources, it can always reach out to the community. We have found there are many mental health and other professionals willing to give their time, albeit on a limited basis, to be helpful and to "get into the fray."

Conduct a civil background check. Once you have researched your stalker's criminal history, get on the computer, and run a complete civil background on your stalker. Remember, many of these stalkers do this to their victims. They go onto various "people check" websites, pay their few pieces of silver, and find out everything they want to know about their victims. Do the very same thing to them. Civil checks will offer information such as previous residences, neighbors' addresses and phone numbers, any property they may have or currently own, any civil court cases, some access to cell phones or other phone numbers, civil restraining orders, and in some cases, places they have worked. This gives the investigator more places to look for information on their stalkers.

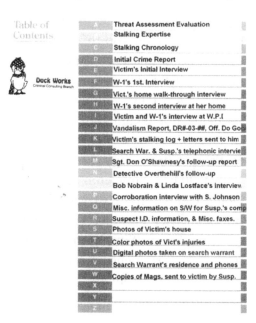

A	Threat Assessment Evaluation
B	Stalking Expertise
C	Stalking Chronology
D	Initial Crime Report
E	Victim's Initial Interview
F	W-1's 1st. Interview
G	Vict.'s home walk-through interview
H	W-1's second interview at her home
I	Victim and W-1's interview at W.P.I
J	Vandalism Report, DR#-03-##, Off. Do Go
K	Victim's stalking log + letters sent to him
L	Search War. & Susp.'s telephonic intervie
M	Sgt. Don O'Shawnesy's follow-up report
N	Detective Overthehill's follow-up
O	Bob Nobrain & Linda Lostface's interview
P	Corroboration interview with S. Johnson
Q	Misc. information on S/W for Susp.'s comp
R	Suspect I.D. information, & Misc. faxes.
S	Photos of Victim's house
T	Color photos of Vict's injuries
U	Digital photos taken on search warrant
V	Search Warrant's residence and phones
W	Copies of Mags. sent to victim by Susp.
X	
Y	
Z	

Duck Works
Criminal Consulting Branch

Table of Contents

Develop a stalking chronology. We advise detectives to develop a stalking chronology prior to writing their actual stalking crime report. This chronology is simple. Each time the stalker makes contact, whether criminal or not, the detective notes it in chronological order. Once the detective has done this, it makes it extremely easy to write an overall report because the stalking chronology acts as a sort of bibliography.

The stalking chronology assists district attorneys who are conducting an initial case review, and it also helps the judge or magistrate who is going to review the case for a search or arrest warrant. We even instruct investigators to use the chronology in their search warrant affidavits in order to better inform judges about a case's merits.

Example of a Stalking Chronology

Note: We have taken this chronology off the supplemental police report and changed all the names, dates, and locations to protect the victim/witnesses in this case. The facts are true.

Stalking Chronology #1: On 12-10, Rudolf Kerry was assaulted both inside and outside his residence by one Derrick Richard Simpleton. Simpleton also threatened to kill Kerry during the course of the assault and entry into his house. (Charges for this offense include 646.9 CPC—felony Stalking, 459 CPC—felony residential burglary, 422 CPC—felony criminal threats, and 240/242 CPC—misdemeanor assault and battery.) (DR# 00-0000)

Stalking Chronology #2: On Saturday December 14, between 1700-1730 hrs., Simpleton observed Kerry washing his white 2007 Dodge Charger in his driveway. Simpleton bragged to Sharon Fox, his ex-girlfriend and Kerry's current girlfriend, that he had been watching Kerry. (Simpleton lives in a town twenty-five miles away from Kerry's residence. Kerry lives on a cul-de-sac street, which is a good distance from any major arterial streets in the city of Fantasyland. Simpleton had no reason to be in Fantasyland other than to surveil and harass Kerry. (Charges for this offense are continuation of the crime of stalking.)

Stalking Chronology #3: On Friday December 19, Simpleton called Kerry and verbally abused and threatened him for over ten minutes. He told Kerry, "I am willing to do whatever it takes, even go to prison, to stop you from seeing her [Fox]!" (This was quite prophetic as Simpleton later pled guilty to multiple felony counts and ended up doing two and a half years in the joint.) "I will use all my time and go to any effort and put all my being into stopping you from seeing Sharon!" Kerry took these comments as a direct threat to his safety. (Charges included another count of 422 CPC—felony criminal threats and the continuation of the crime of stalking.)

Stalking Chronology #4: On Monday December 23, at about 1635 hrs., Sharon Fox left a message on Kerry's answering machine telling him not to make contact with her. The message was made under duress, and you could hear Simpleton's voice in the background coaching Fox what to say on the tape. Fox was later contacted and said Simpleton had come over to her house and forced her to make the call. (The tape was collected, and continuation of stalking was added to the list of offenses.)

Stalking Chronology #5: Someone took a $2000 paycheck from Kerry's home mailbox on or about December 23 or 24. (We recovered the envelope in which the check had been mailed during a search of Simpleton's residence.) (Charges included continuation of stalking, federal theft of mail, and 496 CPC—felony possession of stolen property.)

Stalking Chronology #6: Sometime around January, Simpleton drove to Kerry's workplace, which was located in a town about forty miles from Simpleton's residence. He entered Kerry's parking structure looking for Kerry's car. The company's security personnel stopped him from attaining his goal. (Please note, Kerry's place of business is a secure government contractor. We located notes and maps detailing Simpleton's travels to that location when we conducted a search of his house.) (Charges included the continuation of stalking. The situation was a possible threat management problem for Kerry and his employer. Both were notified and briefed along with the law enforcement agency that had jurisdiction where Kerry worked.)

This stalking chronology has over twenty entries. It should give the reader a fairly good idea of how we develop a chronology. It is designed to be an easy read for a prosecutor, judge, or another detective who reviews the case. This particular stalker had multiple felony charges filed against him, pled guilty, and was sentenced to state prison. He was wealthy, had three separate attorneys represent him, and had no other criminal history prior to this prosecution. Remember, many of the stalkers we have investigated have never been arrested before. That is why, in many cases, even though the stalkers are convicted on felony charges (sometimes even multiple felony charges), the judges tend to give them formal probation with no search and seizure rights. This means their person, place of residence, and/or vehicle can be searched day or night by his or her probation officer or other law enforcement officer. It has been our experience that many of these characters reoffend, and then they are sent to state prison not on other charges but as a result of violating formal probation. Either way, it eliminates the stalker from the picture for a while, giving peace to the victim and those around him or her.

Please note, this next chronology was written by the secretary of the victim, a prominent surgeon. This was done after finding out we were consulting on the case and obtaining a copy of our book. However, we find many victims already have written extensive chronologies prior to us getting involved. The names of the suspects, witnesses, and victim(s) have been changed to protect anonymity. You will notice this chronology fits one of the female stalking examples we gave in the book.

Date	Event
May 0000	Dr. James meets Rose at a tailor shop near James's place of work. Dr. James gives Rose his business card with his telephone number.
May 15, 0000	Rose calls the office and leaves a message for Dr. James to call her.
May 20, 0000	Dr. James and Rose have a dinner date.
June 08, 0000	Dr. James discusses some of his business programs with Rose for his surgery center, which is located in a beach community. Rose researches this business opportunity for Dr. James after Dr. James supplies Rose with additional information.
June 10, 0000	Rose appears at the surgery center office unannounced and uninvited. She questions all staff regarding their positions and responsibilities. Dr. James's office staff is upset by Rose's presence and actions. They voice their concerns to Dr. James. Dr. James informs Rose that his staff was upset by her unauthorized visit.
July 19, 0000	Dr. James invites Rose to a friend's house for a get-together. As Dr. James showers before the party, Rose retrieves his cell phone and proceeds to call Veronica, Dr. James's former girlfriend. Rose tells Veronica not to call Dr. James or the staff ever again or visit the office. Rose tells Veronica that Dr. James said he didn't want her to ever call again. Rose says she will be running the office, which is completely false. She tells Veronica to stay away and not to send any referrals to the office. Then

she hangs up on Veronica. Rose later erases all of Dr. James's female contacts from his phone.

July 21, 0000   At 3 p.m. office staffer Mary answered a phone call from Rose, who stated, "You tell Linda and Jean (other staffers) to watch their backs!"

The stalking chronology goes on for several pages and documents threat after threat from Rose. She even came into the doctor's office and told them she was in charge and would be running everything for the doctor, which he knew nothing about. The chronology also details all the vandalism, following, and harassment Rose perpetrated during her reign of terror. We think you get the picture that the average citizen can assist law enforcement by documenting and developing a stalking chronology.

Obtain search warrants. We strongly suggest during the course of the stalking investigation a search warrant be issued to search the stalker's residence(s), outbuilding(s), vehicle(s), storage facilities (if any), and all computer and digital storage devices. In our protocol that we supply to law enforcement, we have a dedicated section that details how to write that specific portion of the warrant. It has to include

Westminster Police Detective Mark Lauderback holding an Uzi assault weapon taken in stalking search warrant. Courtesy of the Westminster Police Department.

many things for the forensic technician to later conduct a search of all the media obtained. We also have a copy of a search warrant (with names modified) to give to law enforcement as an example. This can be obtained by going on our website and requesting a copy, but we can only provide this if you are active law enforcement.

Search warrants are an extremely helpful tool in gathering not only evidence but information about the stalker. Most of the warrants we have initiated have also been useful in filing other charges, many of which were felonies against the stalker. For example, with just one search warrant, we found that a stalker had several unregistered assault weapons, a complete, upscale marijuana cultivation lab, cocaine and other drugs, books on how to get revenge, and stolen mail and other personal items

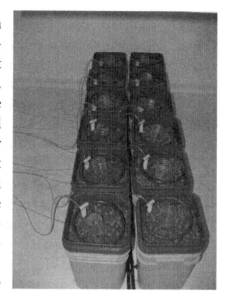

Custom marijuana growing pots found in a stalking search warrant.

belonging to the victim. A forensic search of the stalker's computer also revealed the sites he had used to gather information on both the primary stalking victim and another secondary victim.

We suggest the search warrant be served as close to the stalker being arrested as possible. This is done so that any information gathered via the search warrant can be used at the time of interview and eventual charging. Prior to the arrest and search warrant, the lead detective should do several other things. However, we will only divulge those things to fellow coppers.

Conduct a tape-recorded primary interview. Once the stalker is taken into custody, be prepared before you talk to him or her. Nothing is worse than going on a fishing expedition when conducting an arrest interview. My partner and I had interviewed so many suspects together we pretty much knew what the other was going to do. When I slowed down, he would jump in and vice versa. He may have been the bad cop, or I might have, but it was not because we planned it. One, or even both of us, would get pissed off at the suspect, and sometimes it was at the same time. Most of the time, I would act stupid, which according to my partner, was not a huge reach for me. That seemed to get more information about the incident. There were times when it seemed the suspect actually took pity on my ignorance and was forced to enlighten me. My partner, an excellent interviewer, was always able to quote chapter and verse when it came to the incidents of the crime.

Even though you have a theme or a direction when you go in for an interview, the detective should be prepared for the unexpected. This could include a quick cop out (confession) to one or multiple crimes. There are many stalkers who, once you get them going, want to tell their side of the story. We tell detectives to play up that fact. We have found many stalkers truly feel they have been victimized.

If at all possible, try to have your case "vertically prosecuted." What do we mean? This means having only one prosecutor handle your case from filing, through trial, and into sentencing. This way the case is not passed off from district attorney to district attorney. The criminal prosecution maintains consistency, and this elicits a much better outcome. Trust us, there have been times when a prosecutor gets the case the day before trial (if you are lucky). Sometimes it is the morning of trial. This situation is fraught with problems. We are not blaming the district attorney. We are merely blaming the system.

A little information about a stalking trial. Each state is different when it comes to prosecuting any crime. This includes stalking. Some states require a grand jury be impaneled. The prosecutor then brings in officers and other witnesses in front of the grand jury to explain the facts of the case and hopefully have the grand jury hand down a complaint. During these proceedings the defense is not allowed to present any kind of evidence or statements in support of his client. (In some situations the defense may have the client show up to answer questions, but that is a very rare event.)

Once a grand jury indictment is handed down, then the case goes to a normal trial.

In other states, a grand jury can be empanelled and the case submitted to them for a complaint, or a preliminary hearing process can take place. In a preliminary hearing both the defense and the prosecuting attorney go before the judge and present portions of their case. The prosecuting attorney will usually present as much of his or her case as they feel necessary to get the suspect bound over on charges. A detective or investigator in many states (such as California) can testify at a preliminary hearing on a victim's or a witness's behalf. Once the defendant is bound over for trial, the defense will oftentimes plea-bargain or merely plead out to the original charge(s). If the case went to trial, and a victim or a witness became unavailable to testify for a valid reason, the judge could decide whether statements that would normally fall under the hearsay rule could be admissible in trial. Those statements could be admitted even if the defendant or the attorney was not able to examine (ask questions of) the person who could not be at trial. With the advent of the 2004 supreme court decision entitled the Crawford Decision, or Crawford v. Washington, that all changed. Crawford was about a defendant's Sixth Amendment right to confront his or her accuser(s).

With the Crawford decision, if the witness or victim becomes unavailable, then the defendant has no way of cross-examining that person. Therefore, according to the ruling, it is a violation of one's Sixth Amendment rights. This decision has slowed down sexual assault and other prosecutions. It has also greatly slowed down the trial process because the district attorney must call all witnesses to testify, in some cases, both in the preliminary and full trial. This is a costly and lengthy process.

Truth be known, we as detectives testified for almost every primary involved individual in the proceeding (victim, witnesses, etc.). For the majority of cases, once the defendant was bound over, he or she either pled out to the exact charges or strikes a plea bargain. Thus very few cases actually go to trial. However, many major cases were also adjudicated after the preliminary hearing. Homicides and a few other major cases made it to trial (at least at the level we were working). Misdemeanor cases also regularly go to trial, but there are no preliminary hearings for misdemeanor offenses.

In regard to stalking, as indicated, most of the cases I worked as the lead detective never went to trial. I retired before the Crawford decision was in place. According to detectives I have talked to about Crawford, defense attorneys appear less likely to plead their clients out without going to trial first. They apparently feel there is always the chance the victim will be too traumatized to appear in court or get frustrated with the whole judicial process, which in our estimation, is still not always victim-oriented.

The Stalking Trial

If you are going to be involved in a stalking trial, the detective in charge should do the following things. (The detective in charge needs to remember that he or she has gotten the victim this far. The task at hand needs to be completed with a positive outcome.) Please note, if for some reason the detective does not tell you these things, then you should be aware of them anyway. By all means, if you have questions ask the handling detective.

- If possible, assign a victim advocate to be with and assist your victim going to and coming from court. If he or she needs someone to watch his or her children, see if that cannot be arranged by the advocate. Plan on having the advocate in court with your victim.

- Advise your victim to dress in comfortable, discreet clothing. Encourage him/her to be as professional as possible.

- Obviously, testifying is not an easy task for victims. Advise the victim to listen to the questions asked by the district attorney, defense, and magistrate. Explain to the victim that if he or she does not understand any part of the question, he or she should ask for clarification. The victim should then take a moment and answer the question to the best of his or her ability. Tell the victim looking directly at the person asking the question helps one better understand the question. Also advise the victim that he or she does not have to look at the defendant unless asked to identify that person in court. After all, the defendant will often attempt to intimidate the victim with facial and/or body movements while in trial. Also explain that, if there is a jury, it is fine for the victim to direct his or her testimony to the jury when answering a question.

- Advise the victim that he or she may be contacted by the district attorney prior to the trial to go over certain facts of the case. This is a fairly common practice.

- Tell the victim not to talk to anyone but the investigator on the case, the district attorney, or his or her victim advocate before, during, or after the trial while in the courthouse. A victim (or witness) should never talk directly to a juror during the trial. This same caveat would hold true for any potential witness in the case.

Most detectives also explain to their victims that they don't have to talk to a defense investigator if they do not wish. Explain that if they are contacted by anyone, they should demand to see their credentials. If they are not convinced by the person, don't talk. Get a phone number, and verify who that individual is. We have had defense investigators contact a witness/victim and tell the victim he or she is with the PD or PD's office. The victim talked to that person and then found out the individual was from the public defender's office, not the police department. Of course, when questioned, the public defender's investigator said there was no intent on their part to confuse or mislead the victim.

Chapter Five Summary

- It has been our experience that one of the best ways to handle a stalking case is to take a multidisciplinary approach.
- The detective assigned the case should conduct a threat assessment evaluation to ascertain if a stalking is taking place and the seriousness or lethality of the stalking.
- The stalker should be evaluated with both a criminal and civil search. Other victims, if any, should be located and interviewed.
- The victim should be processed along with any siblings or significant others that could be at risk. The victim should be kept in the loop as much as possible during the course of the investigation.
- The detective in charge should develop or, at the very least, obtain and follow a set protocol when handling a case.
- The use of restraining or protection orders should be evaluated prior to issue. If used, the victim should be walked through the process of obtaining one.
- Search warrants should be obtained, and if an arrest is to be made, the search warrant and arrest warrant should be served as close to the same time as possible.
- If the case goes to trial, the lead detective should sit down with the victim prior to trial and go over the courtroom procedure, including the dos and don'ts he or she must follow.
- Stress the use of vertical prosecution in stalking cases.

Appendix A

Examples of Victim & Threat Assessment Logs, along with The Orange County Superior Court's KKS (Keeping Kids Safe) program protocol.

REPORT #_____

Victim's Stalking/Harassment Log

<u>INTIAL DATE OF INCIDE</u>NT: _____
DETECTIVE OR OFFICER ASSIGNED: _____
Suspect: _____

GENERAL INFORMATION CONCERNING HOW THIS LOG IS TO BE FILLED OUT: Be as concise as possible about the information you log. Document the incident' as to date, time, and location. If there are any witnesses, include their names and contact information. If the person you believe is stalking/harassing you left anything behind (letter, note, gift, photo, etc.), do not destroy it. Store it in a safe location so you can retrieve the item and give it to law enforcement. Again, make sure to log the location you found the item and the date and time you found it.

If the subject contacts you via the Internet, save and/or print all e-mails. If the Internet contact is an instant message (IM) or something that cannot be saved but is readable on the screen, attempt to take a photo of the contact, or highlight the contact and push control C. In a Paint program, push control V, and then print what was on your screen. (This is only valid for a PC with Windows.) Make sure you date and time the photo. With cell phone voice message, save until law enforcement can tape record that message. If it is an e-mail send it to a printer. If it is a text message, make a copy of the message off your phone. In other words, all communications are important. Consult with the detective in charge of your case to see if he or she wants you to record any incoming calls. The time, date, and content of all phone calls should be logged. (Please note, technology is always changing. If you are having trouble preserving your stalker contacts, ask an information technology (IT) person for help.)

LOG ENTRIES:

Date: _____   Time: _____
Location of Occurrence: _____

_____
Witness(es): Yes [ ] or No [ ] If yes, information on witness(es):

_____
Describe Incident: _____

_____
Item(s) left or sent by subject: _____

_____
Date: _____   Time: _____
Location of Occurrence: _____

_____
Witness(es): Yes [ ] or No [ ] If yes, information on witness(es):

_____
Describe incident: _____

_____

Item(s) left or sent by subject: _____
_____

Date: _____   Time: _____
Location of Occurrence: _____
Witness(es): Yes [ ] or No [ ] If yes, information on witness(es):
_____

Describe incident: _____
_____

Item(s) left or sent by subject: _____
_____

Date: _____   Time: _____
Location of Occurrence: _____
_____

LOG ENTRIES CONTINUED

Date: _____   Time: _____
Location of Occurrence: _____
_____

Witness(es): Yes [ ] or No [ ] If yes, information on witness(es):
_____

Describe Incident: _____
_____

Items left or sent by subject: _____
_____

Date: _____   Time: _____
Location of Occurrence: _____
_____

Witness(es): Yes [ ] or No [ ] If yes, information on witness(es):
_____

Describe Incident: _____
_____

Items left or sent by subject: _____
_____

Date: _____ Time: _____
Location of Occurrence: _____

_____

Describe incident: _____

_____

Items left or sent by subject: _____

_____

_____

Date: _____ Time: _____
Location of Occurrence: _____

_____

Witness(es): Yes [ ] or No [ ] If yes, information on witness(es):

_____

Describe Incident:_____

_____

Items left or sent by subject: _____

_____

Date: _____ Time: _____
Location of Occurrence: _____

_____

Witness(es): Yes [ ] or No [ ] If yes, information on witness(es):

_____

Describe Incident: _____

_____

Items left or sent by subject: _____

_____

Date: _____ Time: _____
Location of Occurrence: _____

_____

WESTMINSTER POLICE DEPARTMENT
VICTIM STALKING LOG

Detective assigned to case: _____   DR # _____

Victim's Name: _____

Suspect:s Name: _____

This stalking log is designed to allow you to record and track your stalker. This log is to be filled out as accurately as possible.
Please use a No. 2 pencil or black ink when filling out and listing times of occurrence. If you need additional logs, contact Westminster
Police Department.

Please use A.M. or P.M. when listing times.

Date of incident	Time	Type of Contact; i.e. phone, personal, etc.	What was said; occurred	Evidence Collected

Threat Assessment Forms

Stalker Threat Assessment Information

Case No.:_____Detective in Charge: _____

Suspect (Last, First, Middle): _____

AKAs: _____

D.O.B.(s): _____ Social Security No.(s): _____

F.B.I. Index No. : _____ CII Rap No.(s): _____

Military service: _____

Driver's License No.(s): _____

Marks, Scars, and/or Tattoos: _____

Last Known Address: _____

Landline No.(s): _____ Cell Phone No.(s): _____

Does suspect have a computer? If so, where and what kind?
(Laptop, Notebook, Desktop): _____

E-mail: _____

Social Network Account(s): _____ Blog(s): _____

Vehicle(s): Description and License No(s): _____

_____

Workplace: _____

****

Record(s) of restraining or protective orders issued (City and State): _____

_____

Previous arrests for stalking, violence, domestic violence, or threats? : Yes [ ] No [ ] if yes, where and what were the disposition of the case(s): _____

_____

Copies of case(s) attached: Yes [ ] No [ ]
History of drug or alcohol abuse? : Yes [ ] No [ ] If yes, what type of abuse and duration of usage? : _____

_____

History of weapons possession and/or use? Yes [ ] No [ ] If yes, what type of weapon, and how was it used? : _____

_____

History of mental illness? : Yes[ ] No[ ] If yes, what was suspect's diagnosis, and can we access the suspect's records? : _____

_____

History of any changes in suspect's personality after he or she sustained any kind of injury or trauma?
Yes [ ] No [ ] If yes, what kind of trauma and what kind of personality changes? : _____

_____

Was suspect molested or abused at a younger age? : Yes [ ] No [ ] Unknown [ ] If yes, describe incident: _____

_____

Does the suspect utilize pornography? : Yes [ ] No [ ] Unknown [ ]
If yes, what type and to what extent is his or her usage? : _____

_____

_____

Does the suspect keep logs, ledgers, or diaries? : Yes [ ] No [ ] If yes, obtain these items for review.

Does suspect maintain a job, get along with coworkers, etc.?:

_____

_____

_____

Was a civil records history run on suspect? : Yes [ ] No [ ] If no, record check must be run and report attached.

Military history? Yes [] No [], If yes, can you obtain records?

Will the suspect's parents agree to interview(s)? : Yes [ ] No [ ]

Names and contact information of anyone who might have intimate information on the suspect's background: _____

_____

_____

_____

S-DASH (2009) Risk Identification Checklist For Use in Stalking and Harassment Cases

Risk identification is not a predictive process and there is no existing accurate procedure to calculate or foresee which cases will result in homicide or further assault and harm.

The S-DASH (2009) Risk Checklist was created by Drs Lorraine Sheridan and Karl Roberts in conjunction with Laura Richards, BSc, MSc, FRSA and on behalf of ACPO and in partnership with CAADA.

PLEASE DO NOT CHANGE THIS RISK IDENTIFICATION CHECKLIST
If you do have comments or suggestions please send them to:
Laura Richards, BSc, MSc, FRSA
Criminal Behavioural Psychologist
(E): laura@laurarichards.co.uk
(W): www.laurarichards.co.uk
(W): www.dashriskchecklist.co.uk

Risk Identification for 'Domestic' Stalking and Harassment Cases

This risk identification can be used in ALL cases of stalking and harassment. It should be completed by professionals if there are two or more incidents of stalking and harassment (reported or unreported) and/or if the victim is extremely frightened. These questions direct you to specific areas that will give you an indication of the victim(s) risk of future violence/harm. Most the behaviours will be about coercive control. Do not think it is any less serious if there has been no physical violence. The more 'yes' answers you have, the higher the risk that the suspect could physically attack the victim at any time.

Please ensure that you write the additional notes about the context of what is going on and link the risk identification responses to a risk management/safety plan.

THE CONTEXT AND DETAIL OF WHAT IS HAPPENING IS VERY IMPORTANT. THESE ARE ALL RISK FACTORS OF SERIOUS HARM. TICK THE RELEVANT BOX AND ADD COMMENT WHERE NECESSARY TO EXPAND ☑		
Name of Victim: Date form completed:		
Name of Abuser: Date of Birth:		
Name of Professional:	Yes ☑	No ☑
Reference number:		
1. Is the victim very frightened?	☐	☐
2. Has (Insert name of abuser(s) ......) engaged in harassment on previous occasions(s)? (this victim and/or other victims)	☐	☐
3. Has (Insert name of abuser(s).....) ever destroyed or vandalised the victim's property?	☐	☐
4. Does (name of abuser(s).....) visit the victim at work, home, etc., more than three times per week?	☐	☐
5. Has (........) loitered around the victim's home, workplace etc?	☐	☐
6. Has (........) made any threats of physical or sexual violence in the current harassment incident?	☐	☐
7. Has (........) harassed any third party since the harassment began? (e.g. friends, family, children, colleagues, partners or neighbours of the victim)	☐	☐
8. Has (........) acted out violently towards people within the current stalking incident?	☐	☐
9. Has (........) persuaded other people to help him/her? (wittingly or unwittingly)	☐	☐
10. Is (........) known to be abusing drugs and/or alcohol?	☐	☐
11. Is (........) known to have been violent in the past? (This could be physical or psychological. Intelligence or reported)	☐	☐
Other relevant information/additional observations made by Practitioner (e.g. level of fear in victim, details of threats and violence, duration of harassment, various harassing behaviours engaged in by abuser, victim's beliefs concerning abuser's motives, weapons owned by abuser, nature of unwanted 'gifts'/items left for victim, attitude/demeanour of abuser including mental health issues and whether victim has responded in any way to the abuser)		

The S-Dash Risk Identification Checklist was authorized for publication in this book by Laura Richards, BSc, Msc, FRSA et al. She, Dr. Lorraine Sheridan and their group are also tireless victim advocates for the rights of victims in the United Kingdom and Canada. The reader can find a great deal more information on S-DASH risk assessments involving stalking and topics such as domestic abuse, harassment, and honour-based violence by going on the Internet and entering "S-DASH risk assessment."

The following is a copy of the Keeping Kids Safe (KKS) proto-col. (It has been printed in this book with the permission of Cathy Harmon, director of the KKS program for the Orange County, California Superior Courts.)

KEEPING KIDS SAFE (KKS) PROGRAM

PREPARING YOUR CHILD FOR THE VISIT

It will help your child if visits are as pleasant as possible. The following is a list of suggestions to help your child prepare for visits:

• Use words your child understands.

• Do not tell your child too far in advance of the first visit.

• Tell your child you will return when the visit is over.

• Describe the environment (for example, playroom, toys, and games)

• Tell your child that he/she will be with Mommy or Daddy during the entire visit.

• Tell your child that there will be grown-ups present to make sure he/she is okay and safe.

• Tell your child he/she will not be forced to say or do anything he/she doesn't want to during the visit.

• Regardless of your concerns, fears, or anger present, the visit is a good experience. Since the visit is court-ordered, try to make it pleasant for your child.

WHAT HAPPENS AFTER A VISIT? TIPS TO PARENTS

• Be aware that your child's behavior may be different as they transition from one parent to another

• Refrain from questioning after visits

• Give the child time to talk if he/she wants to

• Plan a comfortable transition after visitation such as a park, mall, popcorn, bubble baths, etc.

WHY VISITS ARE IMPORTANT

• Child is able to maintain a safe relationship with both parents.

• Child can see that the parent is all right.

• Child can see that the parent cares about him/her and wants to see him/her.

• Visits maintain connection between parent and child that helps the child develop and maintain a sense of self.

• Visits help the child see parent realistically. Children have a relationship with the other parent in their minds, thus, contact allows for realistic relationship rather than idealized or devalued ideas.

KEEPING KIDS SAFE (KKS) PROGRAM

F.A.C.E.S., Inc.
Tel.: **(714) 879-9616**
505 E. Commonwealth Avenue, Ste 200
Fullerton, CA 92832 ❖

La Familia
Tel.: **(714) 479-0120**
1905 North College Street
Santa Ana, CA 92706 ❖

SAFE EXCHANGES
AGREEMENT FOR SERVICE

IT IS AGREED THAT EACH PARENT AND THE STAFF WILL MAKE EVERY EFFORT TO ENSURE CHILDREN HAVE A SAFE AND ENJOYABLE TRANSITION FROM ONE PARENT TO THE OTHER. TO DO SO THE FOLLOWING PROCEDURES MUST BE FOLLOWED.

I AGREE TO THE FOLLOWING TERMS AND CONDITIONS:

1. **SCHEDULING**

   a. The times of exchange will be:

Day		Time of Exchange		Time of Arrival	
Day	_____	Time of Exchange	_____	Time of Arrival	_____
Day	_____	Time of Exchange	_____	Time of Arrival	_____
Day	_____	Time of Exchange	_____	Time of Arrival	_____
Day	_____	Time of Exchange	_____	Time of Arrival	_____

   b. The times and frequencies of exchanges are subject to the court order and availability of the KKS program.

   c. All exchanges must be approved and scheduled by the Program Coordinator or designate.

   d. I will arrive at and depart from the KKS Center at the prearranged times. Repeated lateness or not leaving immediately will result in service being discontinued.

2. **FEES FOR SERVICE**

   a. I agree to pay a _____ registration/intake fee. I agree to pay _____ for each exchange (an exchange is a drop off or pick up). (costs are determined by the agency)

   b. The fee is payable at the time of the exchange and a receipt will be issued. I will pay this fee unless otherwise discussed with the Program Coordinator.

   c. If I, or my attorney, have subpoenaed a KKS Program staff member and that person is required to make an appearance, that **subpoena must be accompanied with a non-refundable $250 deposit in certified funds for witness fee. If the subpoenaed party is required to make an appearance, I will pay an additional $100 an hour after 2 hours. Travel time is included when calculating the amount I must pay. Subpoenas must be legally served; subpoenas sent by mail or fax will not be accepted.**

   d. If I am late for the exchange, I will be charged $1.00 for each minute after the first 5 minutes. If I am more than 15 minutes late, the exchange will be cancelled.

   e. In addition, I will pay a $10 fee for late cancellation or if I do not show up for an appointment and have not called.

   f. Summary reports will be completed and given to all parties prior to a court date or upon request at no charge. If reports, other than summary reports are requested, I will be charged $30 an hour for the preparation of these reports.

3. **SAFETY RULES**
   a. I will arrive and depart at the times specified. The arrival and departure times of the other parent will be staggered by at least 15 minutes.
   b. If there is a protective order, the restrained party will always arrive first and leave last. For my safety, I can call the KKS Program staff from a cell phone or nearby telephone to make sure the other parent has arrived and is inside the building, before coming on the premises.
   c. I will park at _____ (to be filled out by agency).
   d. I will enter through _____ to be filled out by agency).
   e. Only I am allowed to exit the vehicle to drop off and pick up my child unless, for my safety, other arrangements have been made. No additional persons will be on the premises.
   f. After arriving, I may be required to wait in a designated area until notified by staff. When I am told it is safe to leave, I will leave immediately.
   g. Either I or the other parent will be with the child, except for the actual exchange.
   h. I will not be under the influence of either illicit drugs or alcohol when I drop off or pick up my child. If it appears that I am, my child will not be released to me and the court will be notified. If I am the sole custodial parent and my emergency contact person cannot be reached, then the police or Child Protective Services will be called.
   i. I will have proper child restraint devices (car seats, seat belts) when transporting my children to and from the visit. An exchange will not be accommodated and Child Protective Services or the police may be called if these legal requirements are not met.
   j. I will not be verbally (e.g. shouting, profanity, abusive language, etc.), or physically aggressive nor attempt to intimidate anyone at the visitation site.
   k. Surveillance cameras may be on during the exchanges.
   l. Weapons or any articles that that could be used as weapons are not permitted on the premises.
   m. The use of verbal aggression (e.g. shouting, profanity, abusive language, etc.), physical aggression, or acts of intimidation towards anyone are prohibited.
   n. Any suspected child abuse will be reported to the Child Abuse Registry.

4. **RELAY OF INFORMATION BETWEEN PARENTS**
   a. Program staff will relay written information between parents only if it concerns the immediate care of my child. I understand that program staff has the right to copy this written communication.
   b. I know that it is prohibited to use the visitation or surrounding areas to have court documents served on the other parent.

5. **PICK-UP AND DROP-OFF OF CHILDREN BY CUSTODIAL PARENT**
   a. At the time of intake, the custodial parent will provide the names of two emergency contact people who may be designated to provide transportation, if necessary. These individuals will be required to show photo identification.
   b. I will say a brief, positive goodbye when I drop off my child.
   c. Should the custodial parent fail to pick up the children at the scheduled time, the emergency contact person will be notified. If KKS program staff is unable to reach the designated persons, Child Protective Services will be contacted.
   d. In cases where there is joint custody and a parent fails to pick up the child, the child will leave with the parent who is present, and the other parent must call the KKS Program to arrange another time that is convenient for all parties.

6. **WRITTEN REPORTS AND INFORMATION**
   a. I understand that program staff will not take sides, will remain neutral and will not make conclusions or recommendations regarding custody and visitation. Observation notes will be kept by program staff during each exchange. Program staff will also keep a record of all phone calls and other interactions.
   b. I will notify the monitor one week prior to a court date and a summary report will be provided to the court and to all parties at no cost.
   c. If requested or ordered by the court, or requested by any party or their attorneys or the attorney for the child, a report will be provided at no cost. I will receive a copy of this report as will all parties. If reports, other than summary reports, are requested, I will be charged $30 an hour for the preparation of these reports.
   d. If an exchange is not allowed by program staff for the safety of the child or if program services are terminated, all parties and the court will receive written notice which will state the reason for the termination.

7. **ADDITIONAL INFORMATION**
   a. I will not smoke on the premises.
   b. I will provide the program with any additional court orders regarding visitation, exchanges, restraining orders, etc., I receive while in this program.

8. **CANCELLATIONS**
   a. If a cancellation of a visit/exchange is necessary, I will notify the Program Coordinator or designate as soon as possible. If the cancellation is less than 24 hours before the visit, I will be charged a cancellation fee of $10 unless I can provide proof of emergency.
   b. When an exchange falls on a holiday, I must cancel one week prior to the visit or the cancellation fee will be charged.
   c. If I am more than 15 minutes late and have not made other arrangements, the exchange will be cancelled and I will be charged the cancellation fee.
   d. If I do not show up for 3 scheduled exchanges, have not called and not shown proof of emergency, a report will be sent to the court, stating non-compliance on my part and my continued participation in the program will be evaluated by program staff.
   e. If an exchange is cancelled and needs to be rescheduled, I will make arrangements with program staff.

9. **TERMINATING SERVICE**
   a. The KKS Program reserves the right to refuse access, cancel or terminate a visit or all services if I violate the Agreement for Service or if the Program Coordinator feels it is not in the best interest of my children and/or others involved to accept or to keep my case.
   b. If I challenge the authority of program staff, services can be terminated.
   c. I will receive a written notice of the specific reasons the termination or non-acceptance, and a copy of this notice will also be sent to the court, the other parent and any attorneys.

10. **COMPLAINT PROCEDURE**:
    a. If I have problems or concerns regarding KKS Program services I will discuss it with the respective staff member and/or the Program Coordinator. If unresolved, I will request a "Client Complaint Form" and fill it out as thoroughly as possible.
    b. It is the program's responsibility to ensure a safe visit to all participants. KKS Programs strive to provide services in a sensitive and thoughtful manner reflective of their concern for the well-being of children and families. Should I have a question or concerns regarding the service I receive at any time, I have been encouraged to contact the Program Coordinator and/or _____ (service provider executive director/manager and phone number here).

11. CONFIDENTIALITY

a.   No privilege of confidentiality exists between me and the provider. This includes any communication, whether written, observed or heard between program staff and myself, myself and child, staff and child, or myself and the other parent.

b.   The psychotherapist-patient privilege does not apply during therapeutic visitation.

c.   This information will be shared when: requested or ordered by the court or subpoenaed to produce and/or testify; requested by a court mediator, court investigator, or evaluator in conjunction with a court-ordered mediation, investigation or evaluation; required by Child Protective Services; requested by a law enforcement agency; when a report is requested by either party or their attorneys, it will be provided to all parties; and to another KKS program if my case is transferred.

d.   In addition, my case file may be reviewed during an evaluation of the KKS Program.

e.   KKS Program will keep any identifying information, such as address, place of work, phone number etc., confidential. This information will not be included in any reports except when ordered by the court, reporting child abuse or to police agencies in the event of abduction.

f.   During visiting hours or program activities, I may observe or have contact with other families in this program. I will respect their privacy and keep this information confidential.

12. GUIDELINES TO HELP MY CHILD

a.   I will respect my child's relationship with the other parent.

b.   I will reassure my child that I want them to have a good relationship with the other parent.

c.   I will not ask my child to relay information to the other parent.

d.   I will not speak ill of the other parent in front of my child.

e.   I will avoid quizzing my child about the other parent's activities and relationships.

f.   I will not quiz my child for details about the visit.

This **AGREEMENT FOR SERVICE** has been explained to me and I agree to and understand the terms and conditions listed above. I have been given a copy of this agreement. I understand failure to comply may result in immediate withdrawal of the service being offered.

_____   _____
Parent's Signature   Date

_____
Print Parent's Name

_____   _____
Staff Signature   Date

_____
Print Staff Name

KEEPING KIDS SAFE (KKS) PROGRAM

F.A.C.E.S., Inc.
Tel.: **(714) 879-9616**
505 E. Commonwealth Avenue, Ste 200
Fullerton, CA 92832✥
1651 East 4th Street, Suite 128
Santa Ana, CA 92701✥

La Familia
Tel.: **(714) 479-0120**
1905 North College Street
Santa Ana, CA 92706✥

VISITING/NON-CUSTODIAL PARENTS
AGREEMENT FOR SERVICE

IT IS AGREED THAT EACH PARENT AND THE STAFF WILL MAKE EVERY EFFORT TO ENSURE CHILDREN HAVE A SAFE AND ENJOYABLE VISIT. TO DO SO, THE FOLLOWING PROCEDURES MUST BE FOLLOWED.

I AGREE TO THE FOLLOWING TERMS AND CONDITIONS:

By initialling the sections below, I agree that the terms and conditions have been adequately explained to me and I understand them.

_____**1.** **SCHEDULING**

   a.   The hours of visitation will be: Day_____ Time of arrival _____
               Length of visit _____

   b.   The frequency and duration of visits will be subject to the court order and availability of the KKS program. All visits must be approved and scheduled by the Program Coordinator or designate.
   c.   I will arrive at and depart from the KKS Center precisely at the prearranged times. Repeated lateness will result in service being discontinued.

_____**2.** **FEES FOR SERVICE**

   a.   I agree to pay a _____ registration/intake fee.
   b.   I agree to pay _____for each hour of supervised visitation. **There is a minimum charge of 1 hour**.
   c.   The fee is payable immediately prior to each visit and a receipt will be issued. **If I do not pay, the visit will not occur**. I will pay this agreed upon fee unless otherwise discussed with the Program Manager or designee.
   d.   If I, or my attorney, have subpoenaed a KKS Program staff member, **that subpoena must be accompanied with a non-refundable $250 deposit in certified funds for witness fee. If the subpoenaed party is required to make an appearance, I will pay an additional $100 an hour after 2 hours. Travel time is included when calculating the amount I must pay. Subpoenas must be legally served; subpoenas sent by mail or fax will not be accepted.**
   e.   If I am late in arriving for my visit, I will be charged $1.00 for each minute after the first 5 minutes. If I am more than 15 minutes late, the visit will be canceled.
   f.   In addition, I will pay a $15 fee for late cancellation or if I do not show up for an appointment.

g. Summary reports will be completed and given to all parties prior to a court date at no charge. If reports other than summary reports are requested, I must pay $30 in advance, for the preparation of these reports.

____3. **SAFETY RULES**
a. I understand that my child, if age appropriate, will be interviewed prior to the first visit.
b. I will arrive and depart at the times specified. The arrival and departure times of the other parent will be staggered by at least 15 minutes.
c. I will park at _____ (to be filled out by agency).
d. I will enter through _____ (to be filled out by agency).
e. When I arrive for my visits, I will come alone. No additional persons will be waiting on the premises or surrounding areas.
f. After arriving, I will visit or wait in a designated area until notified by staff. After the visit is over, I will not leave until told by program staff. I will then leave immediately.
g. I will not be under the influence of either illicit drugs or alcohol at the time of the visit. If it **appears** I may be under the influence, my visit will be terminated or will not occur.
h. All parcels and bags will be checked as they come into the visitation area; any items for the children must be unwrapped.
i. Program staff will be present at all times during the visit.
j. Surveillance cameras may be on during the visits.
k. I will not bring any weapons or any articles that could be used as weapons on the premises.
l. I will not be verbally aggressive (e.g. shouting, profanity, abusive language, etc.), physically aggressive, or attempt to intimidate anyone.
m. In the event of a medical emergency, the custodial parent will be notified. If it is necessary for my child to receive emergency treatment, my child will be removed only when accompanied by program staff.
n. Any suspected child abuse will be reported to the Child Abuse Registry.

____4. **VISITATION RULES**
I agree to the following:
a. I will focus the visit on the present so that my child experiences a calm and pleasurable visit. References to past events and future plans will be avoided in discussions my child. (Past events may have caused stress/trauma and the child is uncertain about the future.)
b. I can invite, but not demand or coerce, physical contact with my child.
c. The monitor must be able to hear all contact and conversations between me and my child. I will not whisper, write notes or talk in a language that the monitor cannot understand.
d. I will not discuss the court case, possible outcomes, the reason for supervised visitation, future living arrangements, visitation modifications, etc.
e. I will not speak ill of the other parent, his or her relatives, friends or loved ones.
f. I will not ask the child for information about the other parent's household, friends, income or activities or ask my child to pass on information to the other parent
g. I will not ask my child for information about where he or she goes to school, where he or she lives or any other identifying information.
h. I am responsible for my child during the visit.
i. If my child misbehaves, I will not spank, hit or threaten, but will use other age-appropriate techniques.
j. I am responsible for the clean-up of toys, food and beverages at the end of the visit.
k. I understand there is to be no permanent alteration of my child during visitation without prior approval of the custodial parent including, but not limited to, change of clothes, haircuts, tattoos, body-piercing.

l.   Cameras for still-photography are permissible unless the court order states otherwise or there have been allegations of sexual abuse. I will use the camera according to KKS Program rules. I will not use or bring to the visit a cell phone, pager, and other recording equipment (e.g. video cameras, tape recorders).

m.   I might bring toys, videos, clothes, etc. for my child to take home with him/her. These will be age-appropriate and I will bring no violent toys, games or videos. If I want to bring a large item such as a bike or skateboard ramp, I will discuss this with the monitor, who may contact the other parent, prior to me giving it to my child. I recognize that the other parent may refuse to take an item home.

n.   Gifts of animals of any kind will not be allowed.

o.   I may bring craft projects, games, toys, videos, etc., to use during the visit. I will bring age-appropriate and non-violent items.

p.   If my child needs assistance using the restroom, either the monitor will provide this assistance or the monitor will be present when I assist my child.

q.   When the visit is over, I will say a brief positive goodbye

r.   If I do not adhere to any of the terms and conditions of this agreement, or if the provider, for whatever reason, determines the visit is to be terminated, I will say goodbye and leave immediately. I will receive a written notice specifying the reason the visit was terminated.

____5.   **SPECIAL CONDITIONS IF THERE HAVE BEEN ALLEGATIONS OF SEXUAL ABUSE**

a.   I will not give my child gifts, money or cards.

b.   I will not photograph, audio-tape or videotape my child.

c.   I will not have physical contact with my child such as lap-sitting, hair-combing, stroking, hand-holding, horseplay, changing diapers, etc.

d.   I will not use hand signals or body signals.

____6.   **VISITORS**

a.   Except in unusual circumstances, and if agreed upon by the other parent and the Program Coordinator, I must first obtain prior approval from the court before bringing any additional visitors. Attendance of other visitors are subject to space availability, therefore I must contact the Program Coordinator in advance. Visitors who do not comply with the rules will not be allowed at the site.

____7.   **RELAY OF INFORMATION BETWEEN CUSTODIAL AND NON- CUSTODIAL PARENTS**

a.   During on-site visits, program staff will relay written information between parents only if it concerns the immediate care of my child. Staff will read this correspondence and reserve the right to photocopy it.

b.   I will not attempt to correspond (e.g. regarding child support, declarations of love, threats, etc.) or give messages to the other parent by means of my child or program staff. This includes hidden notes that may be placed on the child or in their belongings.

c.   I know that it is prohibited to use the visitation or surrounding areas to have court documents served on the other party

____8.   **MEDICATION**

a.   If medication is needed during visits, written consent from the custodial parent is required, giving me permission to administer the medication. Only prescription medication will be accepted in a pre-measured dose. Arrangements are to be made with the Program Coordinator or designate prior to the visit; otherwise, the custodial parent is to remain on site (in a separate area) and be available to administer the medication. The KKS program staff will not be responsible for the supervision /administration of any medication.

9.   WRITTEN REPORTS AND INFORMATION
a.   I understand that program staff will not take sides, will remain neutral and will not make conclusions or recommendations regarding custody and visitation. Observation notes will be kept by program staff during each visit. Program staff will also keep a record of all phone calls and other interactions.
b.   I will notify my monitor one week prior to a court date and a summary report will be provided to the court and to all parties.
c.   If requested or ordered by the court, or requested by any party or their attorneys or the attorney for the child, a summary report will be provided. I will receive a copy of this report as will all parties. There is no charge for this report.
d.   If my visit is terminated or if program services are terminated, all parties and the court will receive written notice which will state the reason for the termination.

10. ADDITIONAL INFORMATION
a.   I will not smoke on the premises.
b.   I will provide the program with any additional court orders regarding visitation, exchanges, restraining orders, etc. I receive while in this program.

11. CANCELLATIONS
a.   If a cancellation of a visit/exchange is necessary, I will notify the Program Coordinator or designate as soon as possible. If the cancellation is less than 24 hours before the visit, I will be charged a cancellation fee of $15, unless I can provide proof of emergency.
b.   When a visit falls on a holiday, I must cancel one week prior to the visit or the cancellation fee will be charged.
c.   If I am more than 15 minutes late and have not made other arrangements, the visit will be cancelled and I will be charged the cancellation fee.
d.   If I do not show up for 3 scheduled appointments, have not called and not shown proof of emergency, a report will be sent to the court, stating non-compliance on my part and my continued participation in the program will be evaluated by program staff.

12. TERMINATING SERVICE
a.   The KKS Program reserves the right to refuse access, cancel or terminate a visit or all services if I violate the Agreement for Service or if the Program Coordinator feels it is not in the best interest of my children and/or others involved to accept or to keep my case.
b.   If I challenge the authority of program staff, services can be terminated.
c.   I will receive a written notice of the specific reasons the termination or non-acceptance, and a copy of this notice will also be sent to the court, the other parent and any attorneys.

13. COMPLAINT PROCEDURE
a.   If I have problems or concerns regarding KKS Program services, I will discuss it with the respective staff member and/or the Program Coordinator. If unresolved, I will request a "Client Complaint Form" and fill it out as thoroughly as possible.
b.   It is the program's responsibility to ensure a safe visit to all participants. KKS Programs strive to provide services in a sensitive and thoughtful manner reflective of their concern for the well-being of children and families. Should I have questions or concerns regarding the service I receive at any time, I have been encouraged to contact the Program Coordinator and/or _____ (service provider executive director/manager and phone number here).

_____ **14.   CONFIDENTIALITY**

a.   No privilege of confidentiality exists between me and the provider. This includes any communication, whether written, observed or heard between program staff and myself, myself and child, staff and child, or myself and the other parent.

b.   The psychotherapist-patient privilege does not apply during therapeutic visitation.

c.   This information will be shared when: requested or ordered by the court or subpoenaed to produce and/or testify; requested by a court mediator, court investigator, or evaluator in conjunction with a court-ordered mediation, investigation or evaluation; required by Child Protective Services; requested by a law enforcement agency; when a report is requested by either party or their attorneys, it will be provided to all parties; and to another KKS program if my case is transferred.

d.   In addition, my case file may be reviewed during an evaluation of the KKS Program.

e.   KKS Program will keep any identifying information such as address, place of work, phone number, etc., confidential. This information will not be included in any reports except when ordered by the court, reporting child abuse or to police agencies in the event of abduction.

f.   During visiting hours or program activities, I may observe or have contact with other families in this program. I will respect their privacy and keep this information confidential.

This **AGREEMENT FOR SERVICE** has been explained to me and I agree to and understand the terms and conditions listed above. I have been given a copy of this agreement. I understand failure to comply may result in immediate withdrawal of the service being offered.

_____   _____
Parent's Signature   Date

_____
Print Visiting Parent's Name

_____   _____
Staff Signature   Date

_____
Print Staff Name

KEEPING KIDS SAFE (KKS) PROGRAM

F.A.C.E.S., Inc.
Tel.: (714) 879-9616
505 E. Commonwealth Avenue,Ste 200
Fullerton, CA 92832❖
1651 East 4ᵗʰ Street, Suite 128
Santa Ana, CA 92701❖
30111 Niguel Road, Suite D
Laguna Niguel, CA 92677❖

La Familia
Tel.: (714) 479-0120
1905 North College Street
Santa Ana, CA 92706❖

CUSTODIAL PARENTS
AGREEMENT FOR SERVICE

IT IS AGREED THAT EACH PARENT AND THE STAFF WILL MAKE EVERY EFFORT TO ENSURE CHILDREN HAVE A SAFE AND ENJOYABLE VISIT WITH THE OTHER PARENT. TO DO SO, THE FOLLOWING PROCEDURES MUST BE FOLLOWED.

I AGREE TO THE FOLLOWING TERMS AND CONDITIONS:

1. **SCHEDULING**
   a. The hours of visitation will be: Day_____ Time of arrival for visit _____
   Time of arrival for pick-up _____
   b. The frequency and duration of visits will be subject to the court order and availability of the KKS program.
   c. All visits must be approved and scheduled by the Program Coordinator or designate.
   d. I will arrive at and depart from the KKS Center precisely at the prearranged times. Repeated lateness will result in service being discontinued.

2. **FEES FOR SERVICE**
   a. I agree to pay a _____ registration/intake fee.
   b. I agree to pay _____for each hour of supervised visitation.
   c. If I, or my attorney, have subpoenaed a KKS Program staff member and that person is required to make an appearance, **that subpoena must be accompanied with a non-refundable $250 deposit in certified funds for witness fee. If the subpoenaed party is required to make an appearance, I will pay an additional $100 an hour after 2 hours. Travel time is included when calculating the amount I must pay. Subpoenas must be legally served; subpoenas sent by mail or fax will not be accepted.**
   d. If I am late for the visit, I will be charged $1.00 for each minute after the first 5 minutes. If I am more than 15 minutes late, the visit will be canceled.
   e. In addition, I will pay a $15 fee for late cancellation or if I do not show up for an appointment and have not called.
   f. Summary reports will be completed and given to all parties prior to a court date or upon request at no charge. If reports, other than summary reports, are requested, I will be charged $30 an hour for the preparation of these reports.

3. **SAFETY RULES**
   a. I understand that my child, if age appropriate, will be interviewed prior to the first visit
   b. I will be I will arrive and depart at the times specified. The arrival and departure times of the other parent will be staggered by at least 15 minutes.

c. If there is a protective order, the restrained party will always arrive first and leave last. For my safety, I can call the KKS Program staff from a cell phone or nearby telephone to make sure the visiting parent has arrived and is inside their building, before coming on the premises.

d. I will park at _____ *(to be filled out by agency).*
e. I will enter through _____ *(to be filled out by agency).*
f. Only I am allowed to exit the vehicle to drop off and pick up my child unless, for my safety, other arrangements have been made. No additional persons will be on the premises or surrounding areas.
g. After arriving, I may be required to wait in a designated area until notified by staff. When I am told it is safe to leave, I will leave immediately.
h. I will not be under the influence of either illicit drugs or alcohol when I drop off or pick up my child. If it appears that I am, my child will not be released to me and the court will be notified. If my emergency contact people cannot be reached to provide transportation, the police will be called.
i. I know that all parcels and bags my child will keep with them during the visit are subject to be checked as they come into the visitation area.
j. I will have proper child restraint devices (car seats, seat belts) when transporting my children to and from the visit. Child Protective Services or the police may be called if these legal requirements are not met.
k. I will not be verbally (e.g. shouting, profanity, abusive language, etc.) or physically aggressive nor attempt to intimidate anyone at the visitation site.
l. In the event of a medical emergency, I will be notified and program staff will assist me in coordinating proper care. If it is necessary for my child to receive emergency treatment, my child will be removed only when accompanied by program staff.
m. Any suspected child abuse will be reported to the Child Abuse Registry.

4. VISITATION RULES

a. I understand that I can request a completed list of the rules for visitation but the basic rules are:
   i. Program staff will be present at all times during the visit.
   ii. The monitor must be able to hear all conversations between the child and the visiting parent.
   iii. Discussions of the court case, possible outcomes, future living arrangements, etc. are to be avoided by the visiting parent.
   iv. The visiting parent is not to speak ill of the custodial parent, their relatives, friends or loved ones.
   v. The visiting parent is not to gather information about the other parent, their household, friends, income, and activities nor ask the child to pass information to the other parent.
   vi. The visiting parent is not to ask the child where they live, what school they go to or other identifying information
   vii. Surveillance cameras may be on during the visits.
   viii. Weapons or any articles that that could be used as weapons are not permitted on the premises.

b. If these rules are violated, or the child becomes upset for any reason, the visit may be terminated and all parties will be notified.

5. GUIDELINES FOR THE CUSTODIAL PARENT FOR A SUCCESSFUL VISIT

a. I may provide a well-loved stuffed toy, blanket or game for my child's emotional comfort during the visit.

b. I will respect my child's relationship with the visiting parent.
c. When I drop off my child for a visit, I will say a brief and positive goodbye.
d. I will not ask my child to gather information from the visiting parent or pass notes to the visiting parent.
e. I will not speak ill of the visiting parent in front of my child.
f. I will not share detailed court information with my child.
g. I understand that my child may receive toys, clothes, games, etc. from the visiting parent or may bring home craft projects made during the visit. These will be age-appropriate and non-violent. Any large items (i.e. bikes, skateboard ramps, etc.) may be cleared through me via program staff prior to my child receiving them.
h. I will not quiz my child for details of the visits.

6. **VISITORS**
   a. Except in unusual circumstances, and if agreed upon by the custodial parent and the Program Coordinator, any additional visitor must obtain prior approval from the court.

7. **RELAY OF INFORMATION BETWEEN CUSTODIAL AND NON- CUSTODIAL PARENTS**
   a. During visits, program staff will relay written information between parents only if it concerns the immediate care of my child. Staff will read this correspondence and reserve the right to photocopy it.
   b. I will not attempt to correspond or give messages to the visiting parent by means of my child or program staff. This includes hidden notes that may be placed on my child or in his/her belongings.
   c. I know that it is prohibited to use the visitation or surrounding areas to have court documents served on the other party.

8. **MEDICATION**
   a. If medication is needed during visits, I must provide written consent giving the visiting parent permission to administer the medication. Only prescription medication will be accepted in a pre-measured dose. Arrangements are to be made with the Program Coordinator or designate prior to the visit; otherwise, I must remain on site (in a separate area) and be available to administer the medication. The KKS program staff will not be responsible for the supervision/administration of any medication.

9. **PICK-UP AND DROP-OFF OF CHILDREN BY CUSTODIAL PARENT**
   a. I am responsible for the drop-off/pick-up of my child, unless otherwise specified by the court order.
   b. I must provide the names of two emergency contact people who are designated to provide transportation, if necessary. These individuals will be required to show photo identification.
   c. I will inform KKS staff of my whereabouts during the visit and, if possible, provide a phone number where I can be reached.
   d. If I fail to pick up the children at the scheduled time, the emergency contact person will be notified. If KKS program staff is unable to reach the designated persons, Child Protective Services will be contacted.

10. **WRITTEN REPORTS AND INFORMATION**
    a. I understand that program staff will not take sides, will remain neutral and will not make conclusions or recommendations regarding custody and visitation. Observation notes will be kept by program staff during each visit. Program staff will also keep a record of all phone calls and other interactions.
    b. I will notify the monitor one week prior to a court date and a summary report will be provided to the court and to all parties.

    c.   If requested or ordered by the court, or requested by any party or their attorneys or the attorney for the child, a summary report will be provided. I will receive a copy of this report as will all parties. If reports, other than summary reports, are requested, I will be charged $30 an hour for the preparation of these reports.

    d.   If a visit is terminated or if program services are terminated, all parties and the court will receive written notice which will state the reason for the termination.

11.   ADDITIONAL INFORMATION
    a.   I will not smoke on the premises.
    b.   I will provide the program with any additional court orders regarding visitation, exchanges, restraining orders, etc., I receive while in this program.

12.   CANCELLATIONS
    a.   If a cancellation of a visit/exchange is necessary, I will notify the Program Coordinator or designate as soon as possible. If the cancellation is less than 24 hours before the visit, I will be charged a cancellation fee of $15, unless I can provide proof of emergency. When a visit falls on a holiday, I must cancel one week prior to the visit or the cancellation fee will be charged.
    b.   If I am more than 15 minutes late and have not made other arrangements, the visit will be cancelled and I will be charged the cancellation fee.
    c.   If I do not show up for 3 scheduled appointments, have not called and not shown proof of emergency, a report will be sent to the court, stating non-compliance on my part.

13.   TERMINATING SERVICE
    a.   The KKS Program reserves the right to refuse access, cancel or terminate a visit or all services if I or the visiting parent violates the Agreement for Service or if the Program Coordinator feels it is not in the best interest of my child and/or others involved to accept or to keep my case.
    b.   I will receive a written notice of the specific reasons for the termination or non-acceptance, and a copy of this notice will also be sent to the court, the other parent and any attorneys.

14.   COMPLAINT PROCEDURE
    a.   If I have a problems or concerns regarding KKS Program services, I will discuss it with the respective staff member and/or the Program Coordinator. If unresolved, I will request a "Client Complaint Form" and fill it out as thoroughly as possible.
    b.   It is the program's responsibility to ensure a safe visit to all participants. KKS Programs strive to provide services in a sensitive and thoughtful manner reflective of their concern for the well-being of children and families. Should I have questions or concerns regarding the service I receive at any time, I have been encouraged to contact the Program Coordinator and/or _____ (service provider executive director/manager and phone number here).

15.   CONFIDENTIALITY
    a.   No privilege of confidentiality exists between me and the provider. This includes any communication, whether written, observed or heard between program staff and myself, myself and child, staff and child, or myself and the other parent.
    b.   The psychotherapist-patient privilege does not apply during therapeutic visitation.
    c.   This information will be shared when: requested or ordered by the court or subpoenaed to produce and/or testify; requested by a court mediator, court investigator, or evaluator in

conjunction with a court-ordered mediation, investigation or evaluation; required by Child Protective Services; requested by a law enforcement agency; when a report is requested by either party or their attorneys, it will be provided to all parties; and to another KKS program if my case is transferred.

d. In addition, my case file may be reviewed during an evaluation of the KKS Program.
e. KKS Program will keep any identifying information, such as address, place of work, phone number, etc., confidential. This information will not be included in any reports except when ordered by the court, reporting child abuse or to police agencies in the event of abduction.
f. During visiting hours or program activities, I may observe or have contact with other families in this program. I will respect their privacy and keep this information confidential.

This **AGREEMENT FOR SERVICE** has been explained to me and I agree to and understand the terms and conditions listed above. I have been given a copy of this agreement. I understand that failure to comply may result in immediate withdrawal of the service being offered.

_____   _____
Custodial Parent's Signature   Date

_____
Print Custodial Parent's Name

_____   _____
Staff Signature   Date

_____
Print Staff Name

Custodial Parent's Agreement for Service
Revised 7/30/2008

KEEPING KIDS SAFE (KKS) PROGRAM
INTAKE COVER SHEET

F.A.C.E.S., Inc.
Tel.: (714) 879-9616
Contact:
Antonieta Fraga ext. 33
505 E. Commonwealth Avenue,
Suite 200
Fullerton, CA 92832❖
1651 East 4th Street, Suite 128
Santa Ana, CA 92701❖

La Familia
Tel.: (714) 479-0120
Contact: Zamara John
1905 North College Street
Santa Ana, CA 92706❖

☐ CUSTODIAL PARENT   ☐ NON-CUSTODIAL PARENT

Prior to beginning visits or exchanges, **both** parents must attend an intake interview.
If your intake interview was conducted at the courthouse, you must call the agency within twenty-four (24) hours and advise them that you have completed these forms. You may or may not be required to bring in the items listed below prior to your first monitored visit or safe exchange. If the Court has scheduled the appointment for you, you must call the agency within **twenty-four (24) hours** to confirm.

AGENCY_____

DATE_____   TIME_____

Please bring the following to the intake interview.

☐ Copy of the most recent court order for supervised visitation

☐ Copy of any court orders pertaining to custody, restraining orders, protective orders

☐ This completed intake application form

☐ Recent photograph(s) of child(ren) (for custodial parent only)

Note: Fees for supervised visitation services are based upon a sliding scale.

KEEPING KIDS SAFE (KKS) PROGRAM
INITIAL INTAKE

F.A.C.E.S., Inc. **Tel.: (714) 879-9616** 505 E. Commonwealth Ave, Suite 200 Fullerton, CA 92832❖ 1651 East 4th Street, Suite 128 Santa Ana, CA 92701❖	**La Familia** **Tel.: (714) 479-0120** 1905 North College Street Santa Ana, CA 92706❖

PERSONAL INFORMATION:

Case Number:	Grant Code (for program staff only)		Date:	
First Name:	Middle Name:	Last Name:		AKA/Maiden Name:
Date of Birth:	Age:	Driver License Number:		
Home Address:				
Home phone number: Cell number:				
Occupation: Work Phone Number:				
Employer Name: Employer Address:				
Work hours:				
Make of Car, Color, and Year: License plate number:				
Marital status with child's other parent (upon entry into program): □ Married (Living in the same household) □ Separated (Still legally married to each other but living in separate households)" □ Divorced (People who have received a legal divorce from each other □ Unmarried (Never married to each other) □ Do not know				
Cohabitating relationship with child(ren)'s other parent: □ Never lived together □ Lived together in the past □ live together at this time □ Do not know				
Primary Reason for Supervised Visitation or Monitored Exchange :				
Relationship To Children: □ Custodial Mom □ Non-custodial dad □ Non-custodial Mom □ Grandparent □ Custodial Dad □ Legal Guardian				

2

434

Do You pay or receive child support?	Are you ordered to pay or receive child support?
□ Yes, I Pay child support □ Yes, I receive child support □ No, I do not pay nor receive child support □ Do not know	□ Yes, I am ordered to pay child support □ Yes, I am ordered to receive child support □ No, I am not ordered to pay nor ordered to receive child support □ Do not know

Individual Annual Income Before Taxes (include all sources of income:
- □ No income
- □ Less than $10,000
- □ $20,000 - $29,999
- □ $10,000 - $19,999
- □ $30,000 - $39,999
- □ $40,000 or above
- □ Do not know

Identifying body marks (including tattoos, birthmarks, and scars):

Emergency Contact person:
   Name: Phone Number:

DEMOGRAPHIC INFORMATION (THIS INFORMATION IS COLLECTED FOR DATA PURPOSES ONLY. THESE VISITATION AND MONITORING SERVICES MAY BE PARTIALLY FUNDED BY A GRANT FROM THE FEDERAL GOVERNMENT. ALTHOUGH WE ARE REQUIRED TO REPORT THE FOLLOWING, NO PERSONAL INFORMATION IS RELEASED WHEN REPORTING.)

	Yes	No
Do you have any special accommodations?	□	□
Is your English limited?	□	□
Are you an immigrant/refugee or asylum seeker?	□	□

Ethnic Background (check each that applies):
- □ Asian
- □ Native Hawaiian or other Pacific Islander
- □ White (non-Hispanic
- □ Black/African American
- □ Hispanic/Latino
- □ American Indian
- □ Other

Are you able to receive services in English? □ Yes   □ No

What language are you most comfortable speaking :

- □ English
- □ Cambodian
- □ Japanese
- □ Tagalog
- □ Spanish
- □ Armenian
- □ Korean
- □ Other _____
- □ Vietnamese
- □ Cantonese
- □ Mandarin
- □ Americansign
- □ Samoan

3

435

LEGAL INFORMATION

Have you been ordered by the court to attend any other program? ☐ Yes ☐ No

If you answered "**yes**," through which court? ☐ Criminal Court ☐ Family Court

If "**yes**" what programs?

Is there an attorney representing the child(ren)? ☐ Yes ☐ No
If you answered "**yes**," please indicate the attorney's name and telephone number below:
Attorney's name:
Attorney's phone number:

Are you represented by an attorney? ☐ Yes ☐ No
If you answered "**yes**," please indicate the attorney's name and telephone number below:
Attorney's name:
Attorney's phone number:

Estimate how many times you have been to court concerning visitation disagreements:

Is there a Restraining Order preventing you and the other party from having contact with each other?
☐ Yes ☐ No

Who referred you to Supervised visitation Services?

☐ Court Order (judicial officer or Family court mediator or judicial council form)
☐ Juvenile Court Order
☐ Criminal court order
☐ Non-profit agency
☐ Other civil court order
☐ Social Services agency
☐ Child protective services
☐ Attorney
☐ Self referral
☐ Title IV (d) (Child support case) Family Law facilitator
☐ Other

What is the **Primary** Reason for Referral?

☐ Sexual Assault
☐ Domestic Violence
☐ Stalking
☐ Child Abuse
☐ Parenting concerns
☐ Abduction risk
☐ Lack of access to children
☐ Reintroduction/lack of contact

☐ Substance abuse:
   (if yes, please specify)
  ☐ Alcohol
  ☐ Psychoactive drugs
  ☐ Prescription drugs
☐ Do not know (court order doesn't specify)
☐ Other _____

Have Criminal Charges Been Filed Regarding This Primary Reason?
☐ Yes ☐ No

Is there any Restraining Order in effect now that prevents one parent from coming near or having any contact with the other? ☐ Yes ☐ No

4

FAMILY ISSUES: IN ORDER TO PROVIDE THE MOST APPROPRIATE SERVICES, PLEASE ANSWER THE FOLLOWING QUESTIONS REGARDING OTHER FAMILY ISSUES YOU MAY HAVE:	

1. Has the other parent ever **sexually abused or assaulted** you or any member of your family?
☐ Yes ☐ No

2. Has the other parent ever **stalked** you? (Stalking includes following you, appearing at your home or place of employment, making harassing phone calls, sending excessive emails, leaving unwelcomed messages or objects, vandalizing your property, etc.)
☐ Yes ☐ No

3. Have there been any instances of **Domestic Violence**?
☐ Yes ☐ No
☐ Against you ☐ Against the other Party ☐ Against both Parties

4. How many times have the police been called regarding a domestic violence incident?

5. If there is a Restraining or Protective Order:
How many times have the police been contacted to enforce the Restraining Order? _____
When was the last time Police were contacted to enforce the Restraining Order? _____
Have criminal charges been filed for Domestic Violence? ☐ Against Me ☐ Against the
other Parent

6. Do you or the other Parent own any **weapons**?
You: ☐ Yes ☐ No
Other Parent ☐ Yes ☐ No

If you answered "Yes," please describe the type of weapon:

7. Has the other party **used or threaten to use these weapons** against you, your children or another family member
in a domestic violence dispute? ☐ Yes ☐ No
If you answered "**yes**," please explain:

8. If there was any type of Domestic Violence (including either Physical, Stalking Emotional or Psychological Abuse) did your **child(ren) ever witness** this abuse? ☐ Yes ☐ No

If your child(ren) did not witness it, did he/she **live in the same household** where this took place? ☐ Yes ☐ No

9. Has/Have your child(ren) ever been;
Sexually Abused ☐ Yes ☐ No
Physically Abused ☐ Yes ☐ No
Emotionally Abused ☐ Yes ☐ No
If you answered "**yes**," please explain.

10. Have you ever been involved with **Children Protective Services**? ☐ Yes ☐ No
If you answered "**yes**," please explain.

11. Do you have concerns about the other party's **parenting skills**? ☐ Yes ☐ No
If you answered "**yes**," please explain.

5

437

12. Has the other party **threatened to take the child(ren)**? ☐ Yes ☐ No If you answered **"yes,"** please explain.	

13. Has the other party ever been **accused of child abduction**? ☐ Yes ☐ No If you answered **"yes,"** please explain.	

14. **Substance Abuse allegations or History**:
Is there a history of or current abuse of alcoholic beverages:
☐ You ☐ Other party ☐ None

Is there a history of or current Use of illegal drugs:
☐ You ☐ Other party ☐ None
If any, please state substance of choice: _____
How often are these substances used? _____

Is there a history of or current abuse of prescription drugs:
☐ You ☐ Other party ☐ None
If any, please state substance of choice: _____
How often are these substances used? _____

Do you believe that there is a current problem with drugs or alcohol?
☐ You ☐ Other party ☐ None

Length of sobriety:

15. Have there been instances where:
☐ You have **violated court orders** ☐ The other party has **violated court orders** ☐
None
If **"yes"** please explain:

16. If you are the non-custodial parent, do you feel you have **lack of access** to your children?
☐ Yes ☐ No

17. Are there any **other family issues** that we should be aware of in order to provide safe visitation
services to you and you(r) child(ren)? ☐ Yes ☐ No
If you answered **"yes,"** please explain.

18. Does coming to this program cause you any **concern for your safety or the safety of your children**?
☐ Yes ☐ No

CUSTODY AND VISITATION ARRANGEMENTS

1. If there are different custody arrangements for each child, please explain:

6

2. What visitation arrangements existed before your current order? Please explain:

3. Have you and the other party ever used the services of another supervised visitation agency?
   ☐ Yes ☐ No
   If you answered "yes," please provide the name of the
   agency:_____
   Please provide the tel. number of the agency: _____

4. What was the last date of contact between the other parent and the child(ren)?

5. If your child(ren) does/do not presently live with you, when was your last contact with the them? Please explain.

6. Does/do your child(ren) have any special needs? ☐ Yes ☐ No
   If you answered "yes," please explain.

MEDICAL INFORMATION

1. Do you have any medical problems that the agency staff should be aware of? ☐ Yes ☐ No
   If you answered "yes," please explain.
   Diagnosis/Disability:
   Medication(s):

7

AUTHORIZATION OF EMERGENCY MEDICAL TREATMENT
(FOR CUSTODIAL PARENT ONLY)

I, _____, do hereby authorize the _____ (agency name) staff of the Keeping Kids Safe program to obtain emergency medical treatment for the child(ren), if necessary.

CHILD(REN)'S NAME(S):	EXISTING MEDICAL CONDITIONS OR ALLERGIES

Physician's Name: _____   Phone Number: _____

Parent's Signature: _____

AUTHORIZATION FOR EMERGENCY CONTACT
(FOR CUSTODIAL PARENT ONLY)

I, _____, do hereby authorize my emergency contact to be called if the visitation supervisor considers it necessary to pick up and drop off or other emergency. I release the KKS program, the agency, its employees and volunteers from all claims, and I assume all risk claims which may arise as a result of acts or omissions by the following emergency contact person.

Who should be called if you are not available and an emergency happens?

Emergency Contact 1	Emergency Contact 2
Name:	Name:
Address:	Address:
Work phone #:	Work phone #:
Cell phone #:	Cell phone #:
Relationship to Custodial Parent:	Relationship to Custodial Parent:

PLEASE ATTACH COPY OF CALIFORNIA DRIVER LICENSE OR OTHER PHOTO ID.

Emergency Contact persons are expected to be familiar with rules and procedures, and agencies reserve the right to refuse to work with anyone who is disruptive to the program.

_____   _____
Signature of Custodial Parent   Date

8

440

KEEPING KIDS SAFE (KKS) PROGRAM
(FOR CUSTODIAL PARENT ONLY)

Please provide us with a description of each child that will be receiving services.

NAME	BIRTH DATE	AGE	HEIGHT	WEIGHT	HAIR COLOR	EYE COLOR	MARKS	SCHOOL	GRADE	MEDICAL ISSUES

9

For agency use only:

If this family is not able to be fully served, were they:

A. PARTIALLY SERVED (Received some service(s), but not all of the services they needed, if those services were provided under your Safe Haven's grant.)

B. NOT SERVED (Sought services and did not receive service(s) they needed, if those services were provided under your Safe Haven's grant.

Reason this family is not served or partially served. (Check all that apply.)

- Program reached capacity
- Hours of operation
- Program rules not acceptable to party(ies)
- Services not appropriate for party(ies)
- Transportation problems
- Services inappropriate or inadequate for people with substance abuse problems
- Services inappropriate or inadequate for people with mental health problems
- Insufficient/lack of culturally appropriate services
- Insufficient/lack of services for people with disabilities
- Insufficient/lack of adequate language capacity (including sign language)
- Geographic or other isolation of party(ies)
- Party(ies) not accepted into program
- Other (specify): _____

If this family was not accepted into the program, indicate the reason:

- There was a danger
- Conflict of interest
- Client unwilling to agree with program rules
- Other (specify):

We included the entire Keeping Kids Safe protocol because we strongly feel that all countries, states, and municipalities around the planet with court-ordered visitation should avail themselves of a program similar to this one. It has proven its worth over and over again. We hope this information acts as a guide for victim advocates worldwide. For more information on this program or to contact those individuals that implemented it, please go to: www.occourts.org/directory/family-court.../kks/index.html.

Appendix B
Stalking Victim Advocates

The individuals presented in this section are just some of the fine people slogging through the trenches day after day to assist those in need. We thought we would just highlight a few.

Kathleen Baty

KATHLEEN BATY-SPEAKING BIO

Kathleen Baty is CEO of Safety Chick Enterprises. She is also the author of *College Safety 101* (Chronicle Books 2011) and *A Girl's Gotta Do What a Girl's Gotta Do* (Rodale 2003). Baty was the victim of an obsessive stalker for over fifteen years, culminating in a kidnap attempt at gunpoint. Teaming with US Congressman Ed Royce in 1990, Baty played a key role in the passage of our nation's first anti-stalking law. In the years since, Baty's reputation has grown as a dedicated and articulate victims' rights advocate and personal safety/threat assessment consultant. She is known to millions through her appearances on TV programs such as *The Today Show* and *America's Most Wanted*. She also helped create the country's first Peace Officer Standards and Training stalking telecourse for law enforcement. Baty provides personalized training and motivational presentations for agencies and groups all over the country.

Hamish Brown, MBE

Hamish Brown is a retired detective inspector from Scotland Yard's Specialist Crime Directorate. He retired in 2004 after over thirty years of service with the Metropolitan Police in London. Even though Brown has substantial experience in the investigation of rape, murder, and other serious crimes, he developed an expertise in investigating the crime of stalking. He has become one of the United Kingdom's leading authorities on stalking. Brown regularly lectures to diverse audiences in the United Kingdom and elsewhere in the world. He also actively consults for those in need in a variety of countries. He is the author of the UK Home Office's highly successful publication *Stalking and Other Forms of Harassment, An Investigator's Guide.* Brown was awarded a Member of the British Empire (MBE) in Her Majesty the Queen's Birthday Honours List for his work on stalking. This was presented to him by His Royal Highness Prince Charles at an investiture ceremony held at Buckingham Palace. Brown's website is www.HamishBrownMBE.com.

Judie Dilday

Judie Dilday, a former stalking victim, is the president and founder of End Stalking in America, Inc. Dilday is a specialist instructor on victimization, victimology, and stalking for the Arizona Peace Officer Standards and Training Board (AZPOST) and is actively involved in training law enforcement. She authored "Stalking 'The New Epidemic of the New Millennium'" and coauthored "Strategies for Effective Law Enforcement Response: Model Lesson Plan on Stalking for Law Enforcement Training" and "Threat Management Policy for the Workplace," which has been implemented in major corporations throughout the United States. She has also been featured on local and national television stations. Dilday has served on the Arizona Board of Directors for the Association of Threat Assessment Professionals, the Arizona governor's task force, and numerous violence against women advisory boards. She is also an instructor for the Arizona Victim Assistance Academy. She presented at the National Organization for Victim Assistance (NOVA) on several occasions. In addition, Dilday is a past recipient of the Woman of the Year Award presented by the National Association of Female Executives. In 2005 she was presented with Arizona's first stalking proclamation from Governor Janet Napolitano. (She was first in the nation to declare January as Stalking Awareness Month.) Dilday has been honored by countless community organizations and the Maricopa County Attorney's Office for her dedication and assistance to stalking victims. Dilday has testified before the House of Representatives and the Senate on stalking issues and bills. Although she spends a great deal of time educating the public and law enforcement, her number one priority is providing direct, immediate, one-on-one assistance to potential or current stalking victims.

John Lane

John Lane: Vice President of Crisis and Resilience Consulting

John Lane serves as vice president of Crisis and Resilience Consulting for Control Risks North America, which is based in Los Angeles. Lane focuses on issues of workplace violence within the corporate environment, specializing in threat assessment, case management, the creation of prevention and response programs, and response. He has worked with numerous clients across North America, including some of the most well-known Fortune 500 companies. Lane also specializes in providing assessments/management to clients who are inappropriately pursued (i.e., stalked).

Clients include entertainment celebrities, professional athletes, and other public figures.

In this capacity John has most recently:

- Conducted the internal corporate investigation of a multiple homicide, which occurred within the workplace of an international manufacturing company. As follow-up, Lane delivered training to approximately nine hundred supervisors/managers at twenty-five locations within North America;

- Conducted the gap analysis and assisted in the development of a workplace violence prevention program for a well-known entertainment studio;

- Provided threat assessment and case management for several academic institutions faced with potentially life-threatening situations; and

- Developed for a Fortune 500 company the template language for a workplace violence policy and procedures to be utilized on an international level (non-North American-centric).

Lane's knowledge base and case experience have been developed over the last twenty years in both the private and public sectors. Before joining Control Risks, Lane was a partner in a threat assessment company based in Los Angeles. During his ten years in the private sector, Lane consulted with a variety of corporations. He provided risk assessment, case management, and training relative to the issues of workplace violence. He also provided consultations to a variety of public figures who found themselves the objects of inappropriate pursuits. Prior to this Lane was a member of the Los Angeles Police Department (LAPD). He served for twenty-five years before retiring as a lieutenant in 1997. During his last seven years with the LAPD, he developed its Threat Management Unit, which gained international recognition for its management of aggravated workplace violence cases involving city employees. He participated in the resource group that developed the workplace violence policy for the city of Los Angeles.

Lane founded the Association of Threat Assessment Professionals (ATAP) and has served as the president of the Los Angeles chapter and on their National Board of Directors. Created in 1992, ATAP has united both public and private sector professionals dedicated to the enhancement of knowledge and service rendered to targets of threat and/or harassment.

Lane is also known for having created the National Threat Management Conference in 1990. This four-day event, which draws between five hundred and six hundred attendees, is considered the most prominent conference of its kind in the world. Lane has not only planned and coordinated the majority of the conferences, but he has made presentations at twelve of them.

Lane holds a Master of Arts degree from the University of Southern California in public administration.

Wayne Maxey

Wayne Maxey, CPP

Commander (Retired)

San Diego County District Attorney's Office

E-mail: waynemaxey@gmail.com

Wayne Maxey retired from the San Diego County District Attorney's Office in April 2010 after twenty-six years of law enforcement service. His last assignment was as the commander of the Special Operations Division, where he managed the investigations and threat assessments to the district attorney and district attorney employees. He also dealt with cases involving political corruption, attorney misconduct, police misconduct, officer-involved shootings, internal affairs, and background investigations. In 1996 he was the first investigator assigned to the DA's newly formed stalking unit. He has evaluated, investigated, and managed hundreds of cases involving stalking, threats, and workplace violence. He has been involved in the development of numerous training curricula for law enforcement and other professionals tasked with the assessment and management of stalking and threat cases.

In the past Maxey served as the president of the San Diego chapter of the Association of Threat Assessment Professionals (ATAP) and served on the ATAP National Board of Directors.

Maxey authored a chapter entitled "Stalking the Stalker: Law Enforcement Investigation and Intervention" in the book *Stalking Crimes and Victim Protection* (CRC Press, 2001). He has authored two peer-reviewed journal articles on stalking, threat assessments, and workplace violence.

Maxey is a licensed private investigator and a certified protection professional. He is currently working in the private sector as a consultant. As such he is assisting organizations in the development of workplace violence policies, training assessment teams, and managing cases.

Ann Moulds

Action Scotland Against Stalking:
www.ScotlandAgainstStalking.com

Action Scotland's Motto:
"The safety of the people shall be the highest law." Cicero

In March 2009, Ann Moulds from Scotland spoke out publicly about her terrible experience of being the victim of a long and horrendous stalking scenario perpetrated at the hands of a sadistic sexual stalker. When her stalker received a lenient sentence and walked free from court, Moulds had no choice but to relocate over eighty miles away. In doing so she lost her home of thirty years and her business. She also left behind her friends and family. Her case was classed as one of the worst recorded in Scotland.

In Scotland and across the UK stalking was not a recognized crime. Moulds was determined that stalking should become a recognized criminal offense. (At the time of her stalking, it was still handled as a civil problem.) She was determined to get something done.

Her national campaign, "Action Scotland Against Stalking," was instrumental in introducing new stalking legislation into Scotland. Her tireless work and campaigning were designed to improve the response to stalking victims, and it paved the way for England and Wales to recast their existing anti-stalking legislation in favour of a specific offense for stalking.

Moulds continues to work feverishly to introduce anti-stalking policies into the National Health Service (NHS), universities, schools, and colleges. She continues to raise stalking awareness by speaking at conferences and seminars and delivering workshops to criminal justice officials, the NHS, local authorities, human resources personnel, along with victim support agencies throughout Scotland.

In June of 2011, Moulds launched the Scottish National Stalking Group. It is the first of its kind in the UK. Members comprise key representatives from government organizations and agencies across Scotland. This powerful and innovative group will be the main driver for change when it comes to addressing stalking.

With a background in adult mental health, Moulds is an accredited psychotherapist and lecturer with many years of experience working within the NHS, the voluntary sector, and private practice. Moulds has been instrumental in the development of the Scottish government's proposed Victims and Witnesses Bill. The launch of the ""The Ripple Effect" DVD and training tool kit in January of 2012 sponsored by the South West Scotland Criminal Justice Authority. The training will help raise awareness and assist in the crime impact on victims. This training, along with her input, has paved the way for many new and innovative approaches to addressing the crime of stalking.

In June of 2010, Moulds received the SCVO Campaign of the Year Award. In November of 2010, she also was honored at the Scottish Politicians of the Year Awards with Public Campaigner of the Year. In October of 2011, she was bestowed with the Emma Humphries Memorial Prize for outstanding individual achievement towards helping to stop violence against women. Under Ann's watch, she has seen: The year 2010, also saw the launch of the first UK 'National Stalking Helpline' sponsored by the Suzy Lamplugh Trust. New legal guidelines issued by the Crown Office Prosecution Services in England and Wales, as well as a 'Cyber Stalking Research Study' done by Dr. Carston Maples and Dr. Emma Short of the University of Bedfordshire. The first 'National Stalking Clinic" launched in 2011 by Dr. Frank Farnham designed to offer rehabilitation programs for stalking offenders. 'Regional Road Shows' in various home counties, and the launch of new 'National Cyber Stalking Guidelines' in 2012, by cyber stalking expert Jennifer Perry. In November of 2011, The Home Office (London) issued a Stalking Consultation Review of the 1997 Harassment Act following the launch of an Independent Parliamentary Inquiry into Stalking Law Reform by Harry Fletcher of Napo and Laura Richards. In March of 2012, Prime Minister, David Cameron formally announced the Governments intention to criminalize stalking.

Ann is very proud of the fact that three years after she began her arduous trek to bring the crime of stalking to the forefront on April 18 three nations, Scotland, England & Wales got together to celebrate the UK's first National Stalking Awareness Day at the Scottish Parliament and Westminster London.

Rhonda Saunders

RHONDA B. SAUNDERS, JD
Gould School of Law, USC 1982
Member of SAG and AEA
320 W. Temple Street, Suite 540
Los Angeles, CA 90012
www.StalkingAlert.com

For the past twenty-six years, Ms. Saunders has been a criminal prosecutor. Prior to her career as a lawyer, she worked extensively in New York City and Los Angeles in theater, opera, and film.

Ms. Saunders established Stalking and Threat Assessment Team (STAT) for the Los Angeles District Attorney's Office and the LA stalking task force. She had many successful stalking and threat prosecutions. She convicted Robert Hoskins of stalking and making terrorist threats against the entertainer Madonna, Fernando Rodarte of making threats against Los Angeles Supervisor Gloria Molina, Jonathan Norman of stalking producer/director Steven Spielberg, Dante Soiu of stalking actress Gwyneth Paltrow, Marlon Pagtakhan of cyberstalking *Star Trek*'s producer Brannon Bragga and actress Jeri Ryan, and Mark Hatten for threatening Anna Nicole Smith and assaulting her elderly neighbor when he came to her defense. Ms. Saunders obtained her Juris Doctor from the University of Southern California Law School in 1982.

Ms. Saunders is an internationally recognized expert in the areas of stalking, workplace violence, and criminal threats. In 2005 she was invited by the German government to lecture at that country's first stalking symposium, which was held in Kassel, Germany on November 11, 2005. She has lectured to prosecutors, law enforcement, and victim advocacy groups in Alaska, California, New Mexico, Louisiana, New York, Washington, DC, Canada, and Great Britain. From 1998 through 2004 she was on the faculty of the United States Secret Service Threat Assessment Center (NTAC) in their training division. In 1994 she revised California's Stalking Law Penal Code Section 646.9 so law enforcement and the courts could effectively protect victims from stalking. In 1997 she wrote Penal Code Section 646.92, which allowed law enforcement to issue emergency restraining orders in stalking and workplace violence cases. In 2000 she increased the penalties for aggravated stalking. Ms. Saunders is a past president of the Los Angeles chapter of the Association of Threat Assessment Professionals (ATAP). In August 2000 ATAP awarded her the National Achievement Award. In 2001 Soroptimist International awarded her the Woman of Distinction Award in recognition of her contributions to combating stalking and workplace violence. In 2004 she received recognition from Mothers Against Drunk Driving (MADD) for her efforts in supporting victims of this crime.

Recent media appearances include *Good Morning America, Anderson Cooper 360, The Joy Behar Show, The Insider, The Today Show, Dr. Phil, Issues with Jane Velez-Mitchell, Nancy Grace, Hollywood 411, Extra, Inside Edition, CBS News Special Report, CBS Evening News* with Katie Couric, *The Catherine Cryer Show, Court TV, Hollywood Heat, Entertainment Tonight, Soap Talk, Access Hollywood, The Making of the Fan, The Stalking and Killing of Rebecca Schaeffer, E-Entertainment International,* a twelve-part documentary on stalking by Eclipse Productions, and MSNBC; and BBC's "*Stalking the Stalker.* She is also specially featured in the DVD reissue of *Misery.* She starred in Court TV's production of *Reasonable Fear,* which was based on three of Ms. Saunders's stalking prosecutions. The following year she also appeared in Court TV's three-part documentary *The Investigators–Hollywood Stalkers,* which was based on eight more of Ms. Saunders's stalking cases. Her website, www.StalkingAlert.com, has reached close to forty thousand people.

Ms. Saunders has published articles on stalking and workplace violence in the entertainment edition of *Los Angeles Lawyer* and the Los Angeles Sheriff's Department monthly magazine, *Star News.* Her chapter, "Stalking from a Legal Perspective," appears in the book *The Psychology of Stalking.* Edited by Dr. J. Reid Meloy, this was published by Academic Press in May 1998. In July 2008 her chapter, "Psychological Issues Involved in the Prosecution of Celebrity Stalking Cases," was published in *Stalking, Threatening, and Attacking Public Figures.* Edited by J. R. Meloy, L. Sheridan, and J. Hoffman, the book was published by the Oxford Press. Her most recent book, *Whisper of Fear: The True Story of the Prosecutor Who Stalks the Stalkers,* Berkley Press, was released in November 2008 and in paperback in October 2009. Lifetime Cable Network is producing a two-hour movie of the week in 2012 based upon this book.

Appendix C

Websites of those researchers in the field of stalking that we would recommend reviewing. Of course, you may find others that are well worth looking at, but we are familiar with these hard working academics.

J. Reid Meloy, PhD

http://drreidmeloy.wordpress.com/

Kris Mohandie, PhD

http://www.specializedtraining.com/Presenter.aspx?ID=23

Professor Paul Mullen,

https://www.stalkingriskprofile.com/about/paul

Mary Ellen O'Toole, PhD

Mary Ellen is an FBI profiler and threat assessment expert.

www.Dangerous Instincts.com

Dr. Michele Pathe, MBBS, MD, FRANZCP

http://www.stalkingriskprofile.com/about/michele

Rosemary Purcell, PhD

http://newsroom.melbourne.edu/expert/dr-rosemary-purcell

Lorraine Sheridan, PhD http://www.vawpreventionscotland.
org.uk/node/1086

Appendix D
Websites for Additional
Stalking Information

United States

Bureau of Justice Statistics, Special Report, Crime Victimization Survey, "Stalking Victimization in the United States," 2009: http://www.ovw.usdoj.gov/AboutStalking.htm

End Stalking in America: http://www.esia.net/

National Stalking Resource Center: www.victimsofcrime.org/our-programs/stalking-resource-center

Office on Violence Against Women, United States Department of Justice: http://www.ovw.usdoj.gov/AboutStalking.htm

Working to Halt Online Abuse (WHOA): http://www.HaltA-buse.org/

Wired Safety, www.wiredsafety.org.

European Union (E.U.)

Network for Surviving Stalking: http://www.nss.org.uk/

Stalking and Harassment Legal Guidance, Crown Prosecution: http://www.cps.gov.uk/legal/s_to_u/stalking_and_harassment/

The National Stalking Training Academy: http://www.cspacademy.ac.uk/NationalStalkingTrainingAcademy.htm

Action Against Stalking: www.ScotlandAgainstStalking.com

Protecting Women from the New Crime of Stalking: A Comparison of Legislative Approaches Within the European Union: http://stalking.medlegmo.unimo.it/RAPPORTO_versione_finale_011007.pdf

Stalking Risk Profile, initiated by researchers from Australia, the United Kingdom, and Canada: http://www.StalkingRisk-Profile.com/

Pathways To Survive Stalking for Women Victims, Project Europa,

http://ec.europa.eu/justice_home/daphnetoolkit/html/projects/dpt_2004_1_091_w_en.html

Appendix E

This is the newest amendment to the Protection from Harassment Act of 1997 on stalking.

111 Offences in relation to stalking(1)After section 2 of the Protection from Harassment Act 1997 (offence of harassment) insert—

"2AOffence of stalking(1)A person is guilty of an offence if—

(a)the person pursues a course of conduct in breach of section 1(1), and

(b)the course of conduct amounts to stalking.

(2)For the purposes of subsection (1)(b) (and section 4A(1)(a)) a person's course of conduct amounts to stalking of another person if—

(a)it amounts to harassment of that person,

(b)the acts or omissions involved are ones associated with stalking, and

(c)the person whose course of conduct it is knows or ought to know that the course of conduct amounts to harassment of the other person.

(3)The following are examples of acts or omissions which, in particular circumstances, are ones associated with stalking—

(a)following a person,

(b)contacting, or attempting to contact, a person by any means,

(c)publishing any statement or other material—

(i)relating or purporting to relate to a person, or

(ii)purporting to originate from a person,

(d)monitoring the use by a person of the internet, email or any other form of electronic communication,

(e)loitering in any place (whether public or private),

(f)interfering with any property in the possession of a person,

(g)watching or spying on a person.

(4)A person guilty of an offence under this section is liable on summary conviction to imprisonment for a term not exceeding 51 weeks, or a fine not exceeding level 5 on the standard scale, or both.

(5)In relation to an offence committed before the commencement of section 281(5) of the Criminal Justice Act 2003, the reference in subsection (4) to 51 weeks is to be read as a reference to six months.

(6)This section is without prejudice to the generality of section 2."

(2)After section 4 of that Act (putting people in fear of violence) insert—

"4AStalking involving fear of violence or serious alarm or distress(1)A person ("A") whose course of conduct—

(a)amounts to stalking, and

(b)either—

(i)causes another ("B") to fear, on at least two occasions, that violence will be used against B, or

(ii)causes B serious alarm or distress which has a substantial adverse effect on B's usual day-to-day activities,

is guilty of an offence if A knows or ought to know that A's course of conduct will cause B so to fear on each of those occasions or (as the case may be) will cause such alarm or distress.

(2)For the purposes of this section A ought to know that A's course of conduct will cause B to fear that violence will be used against B on any occasion if a reasonable person in possession of the same information would think the course of conduct would cause B so to fear on that occasion.

(3)For the purposes of this section A ought to know that A's course of conduct will cause B serious alarm or distress which has a substantial adverse effect on B's usual day-to-day activities if a reasonable person in possession of the same information would think the course of conduct would cause B such alarm or distress.

(4)It is a defence for A to show that—

(a)A's course of conduct was pursued for the purpose of preventing or detecting crime, (b)A's course of conduct was pursued under any enactment or rule of law or to comply with any condition or requirement imposed by any person under any enactment, or

(c)the pursuit of A's course of conduct was reasonable for the protection of A or another or for the protection of A's or another's property.

(5)A person guilty of an offence under this section is liable—

(a)on conviction on indictment, to imprisonment for a term not exceeding five years, or a fine, or both, or

(b)on summary conviction, to imprisonment for a term not exceeding twelve months, or a fine not exceeding the statutory maximum, or both.

(6)In relation to an offence committed before the commencement of section 154(1) of the Criminal Justice Act 2003, the reference in subsection (5)(b) to twelve months is to be read as a reference to six months.

(7)If on the trial on indictment of a person charged with an offence under this section the jury find the person not guilty of the offence charged, they may find the person guilty of an offence under section 2 or 2A.

(8)The Crown Court has the same powers and duties in relation to a person who is by virtue of subsection (7) convicted before it of an offence under section 2 or 2A as a magistrates' court would have on convicting the person of the offence.

(9)This section is without prejudice to the generality of section 4."

Index

Chapter Notes

Chapter 1: Stalking History and Stalking Definitions

1   http://www.accessreports.com/statutes/DPPA1.htm

2   http://www.victimsofcrime.org/our-programs/stalking-resource-center/stalking-laws/criminal-stalking-laws-by-state/california

3   http://www.victimsofcrime.org/our-programs/stalking-resource-center/stalking-laws/criminal-stalking-laws-by-state/oklahoma

4   http://www.victimsofcrime.org/our-programs/stalking-resource-center/stalking-laws/criminal-stalking-laws-by-state/delaware

5   http://www.legislation.gov.uk/asp/2010/13/contents/enacted

6   http://www.victimsofcrime.org/our-programs/stalking-resource-center/stalking-laws/criminal-stalking-laws-by-state/california

7   http://www.victimsofcrime.org/our-programs/stalking-resource-center/stalking-laws/criminal-stalking-laws-by-state/missouri

8   http://www.victimsofcrime.org/our-programs/stalking-resource-center/stalking-laws/criminal-stalking-laws-by-state/montana

9   http://www.victimsofcrime.org/our-programs/stalking-resource-center/stalking-laws/criminal-stalking-laws-by-state/tennessee

10 http://www.victimsofcrime.org/our-programs/stalking-resource-center/stalking-laws/criminal-stalking-laws-by-state/texas

11 http://www.victimsofcrime.org/our-programs/stalking-resource-center/stalking-laws/criminal-stalking-laws-by-state/alaska

12 http://www.victimsofcrime.org/our-programs/stalking-resource-center/stalking-laws/criminal-stalking-laws-by-state/vermont

13 http://www.victimsofcrime.org/our-programs/stalking-resource-center/stalking-laws/civil-stalking-laws-by-state

14 http://www.victimsofcrime.org/docs/src/model-code-2007.pdf?sfvrsn=0

15 http://www.victimsofcrime.org/our-programs/stalking-resource-center/stalking-laws/federal-stalking-laws

16 For additional federal sections that might assist you with a federal stalking case, go to the Stalking Resource Center under the section on federal stalking laws:

17 Katrina Baum, Shannan Catalano, Michael Rand, and Kristina Rose, "Stalking Victimization in the United States: Findings from the National Crime Victimization Survey." Washington,

DC: US Department of Justice, Office of Justice Programs, Bureau of Justice Statistics, January 2009.

18 Ibid,p.1

19 For an extensive report on stalking in the European Union, please go to Protecting Women from the New Crime of Stalking: A Comparison of Legislative Approaches Within the European Union: http://stalking.medlegmo.unimo.it/RAP-PORTO_versione_finale_011007.pdf

20 For further information, refer to: http://www.bailii.org/ie/legis/num_act/1997/0026.html#zza26y1997s10

21 http://laws-lois.justice.gc.ca/eng/acts/C-46/page-175.html

22 For more information go to the Home Office Study: http://www.lancs.ac.uk/fass/sociology/papers/walby-hors.pdf

23 http://www.homeoffice.gov.uk/crime/violence-against-women-girls/

24 http://www.homeoffice.gov.uk/publications/crime/call-end-violence-women-girls/vawg-eia?view=Binary

25 http://www.harassment-law.co.uk/law/act.htm

26 Ibid.

27 For more on the Non-Fatal Offences Against the Person Act, 1997, go to http://www.irishstatutebook.ie/1997/en/act/pub/0026/index.html.

28 http://www.hsph.harvard.edu/population/womenrights/uk.women.97.pdf.

29 http://www.atapworldwide.org

30 For more information on this study, go to http://bjp.rcpsych. org/cgi/content/full/187/2/168.

31 http://www.gesetze-im-internet.de/englisch_stgb/englisch_ stgb.html#StGBengl_000P238

32 Federal Republic of Germany's 2008 crime statistics, produced by Bundeskriminalamt (Federal Criminal Police Office), Section KI 12, Wiesbaden, Germany

33 http://www.bka.de/nn_194552/EN/Publications/Poli-ceCrimeStatistics/policeCrimeStatistics__node.html?__nnn=true

34 http://www.bka.de/nn_194552/EN/Publications/Poli-ceCrimeStatistics/policeCrimeStatistics__node.html?__nnn=true

35 http://www.unisi.it/dipec/palomar/italy007_2009.html

36 http://webapps01.un.org/vawdatabase/searchDetail. action?measureId=8662

37 Ibid

38 http://www.austria.gv.at/site/cob__37006/6845/default.aspx

39 http://www.antiviolenzadonna.it/menu_servizio/documenti/ studi/id204.pdf p. 43(Protecting Women from the New Crime of Stalking: A comparison of Legislative Approaches within the European Union.)

40 Ibid., p. 46

41 Ibid., p. 58

42 http://www.abs.gov.au/ausstats/abs@.nsf/mediareleasesbytitle/
    F9E5031D932C2908CA2571C500784266?OpenDocument

43 http://www.austlii.edu.au/au/legis/act/consol_act/ca190082/
    s35.html

44 Rosemary Purcell, Michelle Pathe, and Paul E. Mullen, "The
    Prevalence and Nature of Stalking in the Australian Commu-
    nity," *Australian and New Zealand Journal of Psychiatry* 36, no.
    1 (2002): 114–120.

45 http://www.austlii.edu.au/au/legis/act/consol_act/ca190082/
    s35.htm

46 http://www.japantimes.co.jp/text/nn20050127a2.html#.
    UAWqGPWo_bw

47 http://hourei.hounavi.jp/hourei/H12/H12HO081.php   (Japa-
    nese stalking law in Japanese that can be translated.)

48 See the section on women at http://www-rohan.sdsu.edu/fac-
    ulty/rwinslow/asia_pacific/japan.html. (Scroll down to bold
    caption-Women.)

Chapter 2: Types of Stalkers

49 www.**bpw-international.org/.../conference-4th-ybpwi-meet-
    ing-Youn**

50 **Barry Rosenfeld**, "Recidivism in Stalking and Obsessional
    Harassment," *Journal of Law and Human Behavior* 27, no. 3

(June 2003): 251–265, http://stage.web.fordham.edu/images/ Undergraduate/psychology/rosenfeld/recidivism.LHB.pdf.

51 Ibid.

52 Michael A. Zona, Russell E. Palerea, and John C. Lane Jr. "Psychiatric Diagnosis and the Offender—Victim Typology of Stalking," in *The Psychology of Stalking: Clinical and Forensic Perspectives*, ed. J. Reid Meloy (San Diego: Academic Press, 1998), 76.

53 Ibid., p. 77.

54 Ibid., p. 78.

55 Ibid., p. 79.

56 http://www.cdc.gov/violencePrevention/intimatepartnerviolence/definitions.html

57 http://www.cdc.gov/violenceprevention/pdf/ipv-FactSheet.pdf

58 Judith M. McFarlane et al., "Stalking and Intimate Partner Femicide," *Center for the Study and Prevention of Violence* 3, no. 4 (Nov. 1999)

59 http://www.victimsofcrime.org/our-programs/stalking-resource-center/stalking-laws/stalking-legislative-updates, the National Center for Victims of Crime, Stalking Resource Center

60 http://blogs.sacbee.com/crime/archives/2012/06/sacramento-man-draws-7-year-sentence-for-stalking-neighbors.html#more

61 R. Purcell et al., "Stalking Among Juveniles," *British Journal of Psychiatry* 194, (2009) 451–455, http://bjp.rcpsych.org/cgi/content/abstract/194/5/451.

62 Bonnie S. Fisher, Francis T. Cullen, and Michael G. Turner, "Sexual Victimization of College Women," (Washington, DC: US Department of Justice, National Institute of Justice, 2000), http://www.ncjrs.gov/pdffiles1/nij/182369.pdf.

63 http://hiddenmarks.org.uk/2010/about/hidden-marks/

64 *Diagnostic and Statistical Manual of Mental Disorders (Text Revision)*, 4th ed. (Washington, DC: American Psychiatric Association, 2000), 126.

65 http://www.leginfo.ca.gov/cgi-bin/displaycode?section=ccp&group=00001-01000&file=525-534

66 Opinion and analysis from Scientific American's Board of Editors, "A Neglect of Mental Illness," *Scientific American* 306, no. 3 (March 2012): 8.

67 Debra A. Pinals, MD, *Stalking: Psychiatric Perspectives and Practical Approaches* (Oxford University Press, 2007), 165.

68 Raymond J. Corsini, *The Dictionary of Psychology* (Philadelphia: Brunner/Mazel, 1999), 658.

69 Ibid., p. 658.

70 Ibid., p. 626.

71 *Diagnostic and Statistical Manual of Mental Disorders (Text Revision)*, 4th ed. (Washington, DC: American Psychiatric Association, 2000), 701.

72 Ibid., p. 706

73 Ibid., p. 721.

74 *Diagnostic and Statistical Manual of Mental Disorders (Text Revision)*, 4th ed. (Washington, DC: American Psychiatric Association, 2000), 725.

75 Ibid., p. 690.

76 Ibid., p. 694

77 Ibid., p. 710.

78 Thomas R. Insel, "Faulty Circuits," *Scientific American* 302, no. 4 (April 2010): 44–49, http://www.scientificamerican.com/article.cfm?id=faulty-circuits

79 http://www.house.leg.state.mn.us/hrd/pubs/ss/sscivct.htm

80 Mike Proctor, Det., *How to Stop a Stalker*, (Amherst: Prometheus Books, 2003), 92–94. For further information go to "Female Stalkers and Their Victims" at http://www.jaapl.org/cgi/reprint/31/2/211.pdf. Google "Female Stalkers and Their Victims," and you will also come up with this information.

Chapter 3: A Stalker's Bag of Tricks

81 http://www.aroundthecapitol.com/code/getcode.html?file=./civ/01001-02000/1708-1725

82 Consumer Reports, "Social Insecurity," *Consumer Reports*, (June 2010): 24.

83 Consumer Reports, "Your Security: What Cops and Crooks Say You're Doing Wrong," *Consumer Reports* 76, no. 6 (June 2011): 25.

84 http://www.ncsl.org/IssuesResearch/Telecommunication-sInformationTechnology/CyberstalkingLaws/tabid/13495/Default.aspx

85 http://www.ftc.gov/ogc/coppa1.htm

86 http://www.legislation.qld.gov.au/LEGISLTN/ACTS/1999/99AC018.pdf

87 http://www.wiredsafety.org/gb/stalking

88 http://www.haltabuse.org/about/about.shtml

89 https://www.ncjrs.gov/internetsafety/cyber.html

90 http://www.anglia.ac.uk/ruskin/en/home/news/cyber-bullying.html

91 Jaana Juvonen and Elisheva F. Gross, "Extending the School Grounds?--Bullying Experiences in Cyberspace," *The Journal of School Health* 78, no. 9 (September 2008): 496–505.

92 http://www.leg.state.or.us/09reg/measpdf/sb0900.dir/sb0928.en.pdf

93 http://www.iapa.ca/main/articles/2009_workplace_violence.aspx#overview

94 http://www.labor.state.ny.us/workerprotection/safetyhealth/workplaceviolence.shtm

Chapter 4: I Am Being Stalked. What Do I Do?

95 http://www.ojp.usdoj.gov/ovc/pulications/bulletins/legal-series/bulletin4/welcome.html

96 http://sgdatabase.unwomen.org/uploads/United%20King-dom%20-%20Domestic%20Violence%20Crime%20and%20Victims%20Act%20%282004%29.pdf

Chapter 5: Our Approach to Investigating Stalkers

97 Hypomania is defined as the mildest degree of mania characterized by a sense of exhalation, euphoria, and optimism, also see tireless activity, loquacity, uninhibited behavior, and preoccupation with unrealistic schemes and solutions to problems. Usually disturbance is not sufficient to interfere with occupational functioning or require hospitalization, and delusions are not present. Raymond J. Corsini, *Dictionary of Psychology*, 462.

98 Passive-aaggressive personality disorder is the diagnosis of a chronic disturbance in the personality characterized by the use of various means to resist normal social and occupational behavior, such as procrastination, stubbornness, inefficiency, or misplacing important materials. Raymond J. Corsini, *Dictionary of Psychology*, 698.

99 Ibid., p. 698.

100 Michael Proctor, "The Family Protection Unit," *Law and Order* 53, no. 4 (April 2005): 94–97.

101 http://www.dnaindia.com/india/report_national-commission-for-women-for-making-stalking-a-crime_1528978

102 http://www.setimes.com/cocoon/setimes/xhtml/en_GB/features/setimes/articles/2011/04/11/reportage-01

103 http://www.thedailybeast.com/newsweek/2011/09/18/forced-marriage-and-honor-killings-happen-in-britain-u-s-too. html

104 http://www.stalkingriskprofile.com/what-is-stalking/stalking-legislation/international-legislation

105 http://www.victimsofcrime.org/docs/src/addressing-stalking-in-native-american-communities.pdf?sfvrsn=2

106 Ibid.

107 Michael Proctor, "Stalking Investigations, What We've Learned Since 1991," *Journal of California Law Enforcement* 41, no. 4 (2007): 15–19.

Detective Mike Proctor, Det. Retired's Bio

- Graduated with a B.A. in Geography, a minor in Safety Education, teachable minors in Physical Education & one in Business, from California State University at Long Beach in 1970. Also has a Lifetime Standard Teaching as well as Community College credential.

- Worked for thirty-three years for the Westminster Police Department, located in Orange County California. During his tenure at Westminster P.D., he worked uniformed patrol, as an S.R.O. (school resource officer) and chief's administrative aid. He worked Metro, and for the majority of his years on the department was a robbery/homicide and predator crimes detective. While at the Police Department, he received numerous awards and commendations, including The Defender of Justice Award given to him by members of the California State Legislature for his continued work on stalking.

- In 1991 he began investigating stalkers. He is considered one of the pioneers in the investigation of stalking, and stalking threat assessment. He was one of the commissioners assigned to P.O.S.T. (Peace Officers Standards and Training) to develop the first known training video and workbook on the topic of stalking in 1996.) He has developed a stalking protocol that is utilized by law enforcement entities both in the United States and Abroad.

- He is a consultant for OVC (Office for Victims of Crime) out of Washington DC., and in Jan. of 2013 was "Spotlighted" by OVC for his work on stalking and threat assessment. He is a member of NCVC (National Center for The Victims of Crime), who he also consults for. He was recently empaneled on the board of The National Stalking Academy in the United Kingdom.

- He is regularly quoted in the print media a 2012 issue of the Economist being the latest, as well as consults for television and radio both in the United States and abroad. He has appeared on America's Most Wanted, Case Closed, CNN, Fox, Japanese and Korean television to name a few.

- Proctor has written several articles for professional law enforcement journals along with two books designed to assist the victims of stalking, victim advocates, educators, and law enforcement. How to Stop a Stalker, Prometheus Books in 2003, and his latest Antidote For a Stalker, released in December of 2012 currently on Amazon.

He lectures both in the United States and elsewhere outside of the U.S. He assists states in amending their laws and countries in obtaining same. His most recent work was in Scotland and Norway. He can be reached via his website, www.detectivemikeproctor.com

CPSIA information can be obtained at www.ICGtesting.com
Printed in the USA
LVOW04s2243250914

405967LV00013B/321/P